Democratic theory and practice

Democratic theory and practice

Edited by
GRAEME DUNCAN

CAMBRIDGE UNIVERSITY PRESS

Cambridge
London   New York   New Rochelle
Melbourne   Sydney

Published by the Press Syndicate of the University of Cambridge
The Pitt Building, Trumpington Street, Cambridge CB2 1RP
32 East 57th Street, New York, NY 10022, USA
296 Beaconsfield Parade, Middle Park, Melbourne 3206, Australia

First published 1983

Printed in Great Britain at
the University Press, Cambridge

Library of Congress catalogue card number: 82-14653

British Library Cataloguing in Publication Data

Democratic theory and practice.
1. Democracy
I. Duncan, Graeme
321.8'01   JC423

ISBN 0 521 24209 6 hard covers
ISBN 0 521 28526 7 paperback

SE

Contents

List of contributors

ALAN CAWSON teaches politics at the University of Sussex. He has written on social policy and urban politics, and is the author of *Corporatism and Welfare*.

PAUL E. CORCORAN, Senior Lecturer in Politics at the University of Adelaide, teaches political philosophy and is the author of *Political Language and Rhetoric* and *Before Marx: Early French Socialism and Communism, 1830–1848*.

GRAEME DUNCAN taught in Australia and now teaches politics at the University of East Anglia. He is currently working on studies of Australian politics and of politics and human nature.

VINCENT GEOGHEGAN is a lecturer in political science at the Queen's University of Belfast and is the author of *Reason and Eros: The Social Theory of Herbert Marcuse*.

IAIN HAMPSHER-MONK is a lecturer in politics at the University of Exeter, editor of the journal *History of Political Thought* and author of articles on seventeenth- and eighteenth-century political theory.

DAVID HARRIS teaches in the political science department at the University of British Columbia.

HENRY S. KARIEL teaches at the University of Hawaii. He is currently at work on a book elucidating the character of play – that is, of action not orientated by pre-defined results.

RICHARD KROUSE teaches political theory at Williams College. He has published on liberalism and democratic theory and is currently at work on a study of left critiques of liberalism.

DR MICHAEL LEVIN is Principal Lecturer in Political Theory and Institutions at the University of London, Goldsmiths' College.

MICHAEL MARGOLIS, Associate Professor of Political Science at the University of Pittsburgh, is the author of *Viable Democracy*. His professional experience includes visiting lectureships in politics at the Universities of Strathclyde (1965–67) and Glasgow (1973–74).

DAVID MILLER is Official Fellow in Social and Political Theory at Nuffield College, Oxford. He is currently working on a short book on anarchism and a larger study of the theoretical basis of market socialism.

PAUL NURSEY-BRAY, Senior Lecturer, University of Adelaide. Has taught in Africa (University College of Rhodesia and Nyasaland, 1965–7; Makerere University, Kampala, 1967–71). Has published several articles on African political theory.

CAROLE PATEMAN is Reader in Government, The University of Sydney, and Fellow of the Academy of Social Sciences in Australia. Author of *Participation and Democratic Theory*; *The Problem of Political Obligation*; currently working on a collection of essays on problems in feminism and political theory.

ALAN RYAN teaches politics at New College, Oxford. He has written books on the social sciences and on Mill.

DENNIS THOMPSON, Professor of Politics at Princeton University, is the author of *The Democratic Citizen: Social Science and Democratic Theory in the Twentieth Century*, and *J. Stuart Mill and Representative Government*.

Backgrounds to the arguments

I

Introduction

GRAEME DUNCAN

Democratic practice throws a dark light on democractic theory. In present circumstances it might seem more fitting to come in black, ready to celebrate democracy's last rites, rather than to engage in old debates, offer reinterpretations of remote (long past and recent) thought, confront specific problems and offer alternative perspectives on liberal democracy. None of these essays deals directly with the so-called crisis of the liberal democratic state, being cast more in a traditional mould. But they were written in a full awareness that liberal democracies are under serious threat and in the hope that critical reflection on democratic theories and practices will help provoke open and far-reaching thought, which may touch matters which the more apocalyptic crisis theory marches singlemindedly across. The authors are all conscious of the deficiencies of liberal democratic and other ostensibly democratic states, and of the shortcomings of rightly honoured democratic thinkers. Democracy is a rare and desirable political form, vulnerable in theory and practice and always incomplete in certain respects.

The absence of substantial and successful democratic practice, whether in nation-states or in the lesser arenas seen by some as the appropriate locus for democracy, has led to a variety of responses, few of which threaten to dispel the prevailing gloom. The Marxist's bold and continuing insistence on the need for fundamental economic transformation before a truly popular will can emerge is normally dismissed as either absurd or as cynical, given 'socialist' experience. The bold and fanciful constructions of the surviving advocates of 'classical democracy' seem mere utopias, as relevant to the present as is ancient Athens. Empirical political scientists clutch their beloved reality with an air of slightly bewildered desperation, which might drive them back, not to the straightforward and undemanding democratic method defined by one of their mentors, Joseph Schumpeter, but to his anxiety at the prospects for the democratic process in the context of capitalist transformation and collapse. Many democratic politicians, who at least are positive, applaud the separation of politics from the people, which apparently tilts the

balance in the democratic system towards decisiveness rather than re-
sponsiveness. The growing insulation of bureaucratic and political strata
overcomes one alleged weakness of modern governments – an excess of
democracy. As democracy becomes a distant image, lacking substance, it is as
if Rousseau's critique of the political practice of large states has returned with
a vengeance.

While new accounts and critiques of liberal democratic practice appear,
familiar complaints persist. They come from a variety of perspectives. From
the Left the complaints concern especially the distribution of power, with
democratic governments seen as under the control, or undue influence of,
'power elites', 'the military–industrial complex', organized corporate
interests and so forth. Given the concentrated forces arrayed against them,
and the biased or elusive character of rules and frameworks, the people do not
– perhaps cannot – get into real politics. Conservatives, focusing upon the
malice and ignorance of democratic voters, are more worried at the danger of
mass politics and the indecisiveness of governments and are likely to regard a
detachment of rulers from people as a saving grace.

Throughout the spectrum, however, there has come a new urgency and
bite to political argument and especially to argument over state powers and
democratic involvement, because of current fears and uncertainties, often
expressed in the form of crisis theory. One form of such theory is that
democratic pressure manifests itself particularly in the form of electoral
demands, typically the demand for provision of various kinds, and that the
satisfaction of these demands helps attach people to the system, or helps
confer democratic legitimacy upon the democratic apparatus as a whole.
More concretely, governments must be able to finance welfare systems to
meet established expectations, normally in the form of electoral demands.
But there is a central problem. How can the state – particularly during
recession – simultaneously pay for its multifarious activities and stimulate the
growth necessary to finance them? It is subject to contradictory imperatives:
the pursuit of one weakens its ability to meet the other. The imposition of
high taxes will frustrate business and lead to a loss of legitimacy, as will the
failure to provide adequate welfare support. Its inability to satisfy the
conflicting demands upon it constitutes the so-called legitimation and fiscal
crises of the state.[1] The excess of political demands over resources leads to
indecisiveness and muddle. According to the theories of overload and
ungovernability, government becomes a kind of arthritic octopus. Although
there is some overlap between conservative and socialist depictions of current
difficulties, responses differ markedly. The conservative is likely to demand a
sharp reduction in the role of the state and to challenge rights to welfare state
provisions regarded by socialists as vital to political democracy and to one's
human status. The conservative will more likely see autonomy, even

humanity, undermined by excessive state provision. The socialist seeks new strategies to provide for valued welfare programmes, seeks to return the state to people's affections and perhaps takes the opportunity to widen and revitalize the democratic life necessary to sustain a people's polity.

The apparent loss of faith in governmental power and the lack of trust in democratic representation is seen frequently as corrosive, undermining what remains of liberal and democratic optimism. Yet to connect a shortage of civic virtue with 'a widely held belief that the state does not, and perhaps cannot, speak effectively to the grievances of diverse constituencies',[2] need not lead to defeatism or to calls for a retreat from democracy or the castration of the state. Interpretive theory, incorporating the intersubjective context and the particular intentions and beliefs of the participants, may gain a radical or liberating potential because of beliefs in people's capacity as reflective and critical creatures who resent inconsistencies between beliefs and institutional practices. Hence, despite the parlous condition of the modern state, some optimism is preserved through a positive interpretation of various currents of disaffection.[3]

Given the manifest and often novel problems facing liberal democratic states, it may seem a luxury to discourse still on hallowed but long-dead thinkers, as if they might speak directly to us. Classical democratic theory is dead, goes the cry – if ever it was alive or, indeed, existed. But the various theories which, roughly grouped, make up that artificial composite, 'classical democratic theory', are a significant part of the body of ideas which have helped shape Western civilization, and people's conceptions of themselves. Only barbarians, rejecting history or continuity, would deny the importance of critical exploration of what remain, in some sense, dominant political ideals. Such exploration includes examinations of their compatibility with each other, and of what form, if any, they might take in the actual world. Of course there is a great deal of dispute over the question of feasibility, because that is answered in terms of one's own epistemology and views on human nature, social structure and economic resources. Rousseau, Madison, de Tocqueville and Mill are historically significant figures, though some were much more deeply involved than others in actual political practice. In any case, all of them attempted to influence events and were seized and used by others with less theoretical expertise and concern. But what they actually meant – and none of the present authors have quite the old-fashioned nerve to say that they are presenting what their thinker(s) really meant! – is not always transparently clear. Fierce disputes over interpretation naturally persist.

Mill's democratic theory might seem clear and straightforward as compared with that of Rousseau, but Alan Ryan brings out the shortcomings of those common interpretations which present Mill's democracy as based on utility and Rousseau's on rights. He also stresses that for each of them a significant political role was played by a small number, with a considerable degree of political passivity amongst the masses of the people, so that each recommended system inclines toward elective aristocracy. Neither was a participatory democrat, though participatory themes, arguments and visions can be drawn from the writings of both.

The examinations of classical democratic theorists in the following pages confirm a point which might have seemed obvious – that classical democratic theory, so embracingly defended and so comprehensively dismissed, is not single and static. It is diverse and discontinuous and there has never been a common agreed version.[4] The study of Madison and de Tocqueville, both of whom followed arguments and models of Montesquieu, reveals the existence of distinct rival theories. That of Madison was more elitist and instrumental and wary of the people. Democracy is given a protective function. That of de Tocqueville was developmental, participatory and educative, reconstructing Montesquieu's aristocratic intermediary bodies in a democratic way, to draw people into public life, filling the 'vacuum of the public spirit', which Leviathan might otherwise occupy. These are convincing forerunners of recent divisions and indicate that there is no neat historical division between classical (normative, developmental) and modern (empirical, protective) democratic theory. In the established literature straw men – classical, empirical, radical, liberal democratic theory – have multiplied and while these are useful polemically, and allow differences to be heightened, they must be recognized for what they are. Sartori is right to condemn 'polemical artifacts', though wrong to hold anti-elitists responsible, and his own presentation of anti-elitism is just such a 'polemical artifact'.[5]

Not only are there very different examples of classical democratic theory and conflicting interpretations of particular classical democrats, but there are sharp divisions within specific traditions of democratic thought, e.g. within liberal democratic thought over the respective roles of leaders and masses, the appropriate degree and forms of participation, and the character and function of the market. But beyond this, there are quite varying accounts of democracy, of which the most historically significant and academically fertile has been Marxism, with its powerful critique of liberal democracy and its radically different image of a good society – itself sometimes presented as the realization of democracy. Problems have emerged from that unelaborated vision of the future, including the related ones of whether adequate provision had been made for political decision-making, and whether room was allowed for diverse values, beliefs, interests and particularities. Some recent Marxist theorists have come out explicitly against the deformity of socialist practice and especially Stalinist degeneration, drawing democracy and socialism close together. Democracy becomes an integral part of socialism, rather than simply a possible means towards it, in the sense of providing the proletariat with means of organization and self-expression. Mihaly Vajda, for example, values the enforcement of their interests by the most varied particularities. 'Bourgeois' freedoms, once dismissed in so cavalier a manner, are vital to this process. As he now sees it, the essence of democracy is

not merely the political-juridical equality of isolated individuals (the latter holds true even of 'plebiscitarian democracy' i.e. totalitarian dictatorship, as well), but the total complex of social decision-making as a whole which, through its organizational framework, enables every individual to articulate and assert his own interests . . . The articulation and assertion of interests can take place only in an organized form of common public confrontations between individuals who are in an equal situation from certain points of view – i.e. the particular groups of the society.[6]

The vision is not grand or redemptive, accepting both a continuing clash (and compromise) of interests, and the difficulty of acknowledging new social particularities which emerge during historical change. What is required is the creation of humanized and democratic forms to settle unavoidable clashes of interest. 'The real antagonist of democracy in the modern world is not the presence of particularities and their selfishness, but the denial of their justification.'[7] This Marxist theory accepts the conflict of interests which is so central in the liberal perspective, while insisting that all interests are adequately represented and that they are compromised through fair and democratic processes.

Marxist theory offers one challenge to the somewhat ethnocentric or provincial perspective of liberalism, according to which liberal democracy is the legitimate or universally appropriate form of democracy. It is argued instead that there are truer or equally true democracies, and that different structural foundations or social preconditions to those found in the liberal West produce, quite naturally, different but possibly democratic political systems. The African consensual one-party system, for example, is presented as properly democratic, challenging the destructive furies of self-interest which thrive in the factional and pluralistic politics of the West. Certainly Senghor, Nyerere and others confront us with a sharp option, unity or destructive disunity (as in faction and the aggregation of discrete in-dividuals), and they insist that material conditions are vitally relevant to the kind of democratic order that can be established. Their own is justified in terms of their special circumstances and is, at least by implication, morally preferable as well. This version of a consensual and communitarian society, resting upon an idealized version of traditional communal life, has its theoretical lineage traced back to both Rousseau and Marx. But whether we accept it in practice as democratic or as a form of governance which is appropriate to the particular circumstances in which people find themselves, is another matter. Similarly, Macpherson's account of the theory of third-world democracy needs to be confronted with the relevant practice, just as he confronts liberal theory with the actual life of liberal democratic societies. Only that can determine what we make of a 'democratic' invocation of 'the will of an undifferentiated people as the only legitimate source of political power'.[8] Do we accept either that consensus within a community allows a one-party system to work in a democratic manner, or that the political choices within a one-party state may be as wide as those in a pluralist state? This difficult set of questions is taken up in Paul Nursey-Bray's sympathetic but critical essay. We may still conclude, swallowing prejudice, that the contribution of Senghor and Nyerere is to African rather than to democratic thought, especially if the theoretical conditions are not met, and are not likely to be met, in practice.

All of these approaches are concerned with the expression or embodiment of democratic ideals within specific historical and geographical circumstances: they were meant to be implemented within actual societies. Each will have its own account of the facilitating or necessary structural conditions of democracy. Within Marxism, it may be conscious and collective human control of the economy, or within liberalism, the free market, which from a Marxist perspective inhibits or prevents democracy. The older classical democratic theories, most of which form part of 'the liberal tradition', and which, like it, are widely condemned for remoteness from the real world, had their realistic as well as their critical aspirations, but it would be absurd to hold that they have, as part of our background, an especially compelling claim upon us, or that they should not be confronted with 'the facts of modern life'. There are various ways in which they might be wrong or implausible or irrelevant – speaking to other circumstances, imputing ideal characteristics to citizens regardless of their actual conditions, or sheltering internal incoherences.

There is a well-established and much-discussed division between two kinds of democratic theory. On the one hand there is classical democratic theory and its contemporary offspring, participatory or anti-elitist theory. These are critical, normative and idealistic, if not unworldly. In the other corner there is descriptive or empirical or even scientific democratic theory. This consists in classifications, analysis and generalizations from actual political practice. Leaving aside for the moment the complex questions of whether or where the argument actually joins, certain general points about democratic practice can reasonably be made. It is clear, for example, that democracy in practice falls well short of the classical Greek standard of the 'lawful rule of the many in the true interest of the community'.[9] People fall short of that ideal, and perhaps philosophically questionable, standard, in terms of morality, rationality and knowledge and in terms of actual power. Again, those familiar harsh portrayals of democratic societies as atomized masses of isolated and private individuals, with public life a travesty of its classical model, appeal to more than the merely literary imagination. There is no need for another résumé of the sad findings of voting surveys at this point. But what there is a need for is the recognition that the existence of bad or imperfect democracies does not allow simple claims of the order that 'classical democratic theories have been invalidated by later experience'.[10] Theories have different purposes and levels, they categorize phenomena in different ways, and differences are rarely resolvable in any straightforward or immediate way. As Iain Hampsher-Monk has underlined, we are interested in linguistic appropriation and try to hold on to democracy because of its (continuing) commendatory overtones, which – given that we mean different things by democracy – involves inevitable slides or shifts of technical definition.[11]

An adequate theory of democracy must contain the following elements: an account of the values or principles which democratic institutions are to realize, e.g. rule of the people, or popular choice between candidates for government; a specification of the political model which best or most realistically achieves that end; and a justification of the preference for those principles and that institutional set as against others. The possible organization of these three elements is manifold. Democracy as a means of embodying or expressing or representing the popular will, or as rule by the people, has a variety of possible implementations or forms, e.g. it may be seen as that form of government resting upon universal franchise, civil liberties and the rule of law, or as requiring a connecting or interlocking system of direct democratic arrangements, or as a plebiscitary system. Those who see democracy as a representative system may disagree over how representative institutions need modifications in relation to other values, for example, efficiency. Justifications will vary also. Representative democracy can be supported in developmental or in protective terms, though there are likely to be systematic relationships between the underlying values and the recommended empirical models. And quite other conflicts will emerge between those with different goals, such as between those to whom democracy means a particular degree of activity and competence of the citizenry, and those to whom democracy means certain institutional features or arrangements which do not require – and may rule out – a vibrantly democratic people.

Hence there are clear differences of both goals and democratic specifications between 'participatory theory' and that modern empirical theory which, whether offering a group, party, or a leadership elite model,[12] perceives democracy as essentially procedure – procedure which is itself justified in terms of coherent, efficient and (loosely) representative government. The defenders of democratic participation and equality naturally dismiss such an empirical model in terms of biased frameworks or distributions of power, and the emptiness of the political life which is conceded to the masses. And yet, while these theories are very different, confrontation at all points is not inevitable. It is possible to use an idealized descriptive theory, for example one which has free competition between elites at its centre *and* to seek and to value a democratic society characterized by much fuller and more significant citizen participation. One could respect Schumpeter's 'realistic' understanding of democratic political activity in complex modern societies, acknowledging both that free and open competition between elites is better than the lack of such competition, other things being equal, and that the theory has its own idealistic and anachronistic aspects.[13] Corporatist tendencies may challenge open and free elite competition, leading the student of corporatism to ask whether elected governments make the important decisions and perhaps, in view of the unaccountability of corporate power, to emphasize the need to extend democratic politics into 'the hierarchical and inegalitarian structures of corporatism'.[14] Elite competition may be stressed at the macro-level, popular participation at the micro-level. But to the radical democratic theorist of a Marxist persuasion, such comfortable compromises fail, destroyed by tensions or contradictions in the real world, if not by the conflicting logics of expertise and participation.

In their accounts of liberal democracy, Marxist critics have been concerned, broadly, with the structural impediments to human emancipation within capitalism and, more specifically, with the relationship between representative institutions and capitalist society. Representative government, despite the openings which it provides for proletarian organization, remains the highest form of the capitalist state and a means to class ends. It is sometimes argued that liberal democratic theory contains elements which can be rescued or universalized in the interests of more critical and far-reaching conclusions. Carole Pateman suggests that the effort to universalize liberal principles to both sexes 'pushes beyond the confines of liberal democratic theory and practice'.[15] Macpherson attempts to rescue the humanist side or the ethical core of Mill's liberalism (man as exerter and developer of human capacities), presenting it anew as a critique of liberal democratic societies and states.[16] However, from a Marxist perspective Macpherson's attempt will seem ineradicably flawed, a form of left-wing liberalism or utopian socialism which is too much buried within the older order and its political evolution. A more common Western Marxist view is that liberal democratic capitalism has, as a matter of historical fact, reached a fatal cross-roads, with one way leading to the extension of capitalism, the other to the extension of democracy.[17] If mass support is mobilized successfully for liberal democratic institutions, the argument runs, it may well entail 'more than the transformation of the capitalist economy. It may also set in motion forces for the supersession of liberal democracy itself, in favour of a socialist democracy which integrates political equality and majority rule with popular sovereignty.'[18]

At a more static level, Marxists are generally critical of liberal democratic theory because of its isolation and separation of the political from 'real, economic life' and because of the possessive individualism which is seen as central to it,[19] and they are critical of liberal democracies in practice, where the deficiencies of the ideology which foreshadowed and reflected them reappear. They reject liberal consent theory on several connected grounds, which can be brought out in the complex question: Who is consenting, to what, and under what terms? The consenting agent of liberal theory is diminished through an examination of the processes of socialization, ideological manipulation, social control, false consciousness, and the inequality of power.[20] Along with feminism, Marxism draws attention to the limiting and damaging conditions under which supposedly free choices are made, though feminism, through its central assault on patriarchy and patriarchalism, pushes beyond Marxian as it does beyond liberal democratic theory and practice. Actual choices remain restricted, according to the Marxist critic, not only because of the character of the so-called agents, but because there is little separating the rival claimants for power, and because the system or framework itself is never in question, as an object of choice. The assault on liberal consent theory is likely to be underpinned by a series of broad – and potentially illiberal – distinctions, between the real and the expressed will, between representation and transformation, between a static and a dynamic popular will. Only in certain conditions – most notably, conditions of rapid social change, which amongst other things helps wash away the muck of ages – is a true and autonomous popular will likely to emerge. Vincent Geoghegan outlines Marcuse's hostility to the vast discrepancy between liberal democratic pretension and fact, and his concern at the absence of authentic political debate, with the masses becoming 'an oppressive aggregate of isolated units and not a genuine community', capable only of the extremes of passivity and sudden wildness. Marcuse restates, though with a very different political intent and set of moral values, the observations on modern democratic societies made by many conservative political scientists. But unlike them, he envisages a breakthrough. Moved partly by glimmerings of embryonic forms of cultural and political autonomy, the optimistic Marcuse depicted a socialist democracy combining communal feeling and autonomy, a qualitatively different way of life to be achieved through autonomous common action.

Such a grand vision may seem out of place now, when a reduction in democratic participation seems more likely than its increase. Indeed, that may be an understatement, as beleaguered governments begin to undermine the economic and social rights and powers which help guarantee such political autonomy as exists. These essays are not strongly idealistic, though Henry Kariel, rejecting our instrumental concerns, our pursuit of end-products, offers us the diverting prospect of an expressive politics, 'a process of appearances, expressions, performances, actions'.[21] Much of the analysis has a critical thrust, and rests on the assumption that theory can throw some light upon, and help transform, practice. Several of the essayists demand an extension of the notion of politics and of the sphere of application of democracy. Corporatism, for example, 'brings strategically important functional groups inside the state. In effect the political sphere is extended into civil society.'[22] Feminist theory, through its general critique of social relationships of sexual domination and subordination, both widens the scope of democratic theory to include personal and domestic life, and emphasizes the patriarchal character of what is (falsely) characterized as private life. It demands that democratic ideals 'be put into practice in the kitchen, the nursery, the bedroom'.[23] Tawney and Crosland are presented as advocates of the social democratic modification – or of the democratic repudiation – of capitalism, thereby returning the social to democracy.[24] An adequate democratic theory would also need to come to terms with the problem of bureaucracy, perhaps finding ways to democratize the administrative process that dominates the politics of the modern state.[25] Out of these broad and probing analyses of democratic politics, the ground might be prepared for a more hopeful picture of democratic futures than much of modern life seems to warrant.

The essays are arranged in sections which may suggest – wrongly – that there is more difference than connection between them. The section divisions are for rough guidance only. The first two essays deal particularly with the changing meanings and evaluations of democracy. 'Classical theories' includes – unusually – both Marxist and African one-party theories. 'Revisions and critiques' includes Marcuse, a prophet as well as a critic, and revisions of established theories in the light of corporatist tendencies. 'Possible futures' covers both contemporary criticisms of established theories and practices, and efforts to create a fuller, more far-reaching or more adequate democracy.

2

The limits of democratic theory

PAUL E. CORCORAN

From the perspective of twenty-five hundred years of Western political thinking, almost no one, until very recently, thought democracy to be a very good way of structuring political life. This opinion was not always due to inattention. Thucydides, Plato and Aristotle gave very close and critical scrutiny to democracy within Periclean Athens, and to that city's later more radical experience with democracy in the aftermath of the Peloponnesian wars. They found Athenian democracy, both in theory and in practice, to be vengeful, impolitic in war and peace, unstable and mean-spirited in its internal affairs. Democracy represented a new age for these thinkers. It was an age brought on by a new generation of ambitious men, the product of a city grown too large, the exigencies of war and the consequent decline of aristocratic influences. Conceptually, democracy – the rule of the masses (*demos*) – was a perversion of polity or timocracy, the lawful rule of the many in the true interests of the whole community, of which, in their view, Athens had had no real experience. Both Plato and Aristotle, in their most sympathetic treatments of the rule of the many, move quickly to detailed discussions of oligarchy, scarcely mentioning the polity and giving short shrift to democracy.

Roman thought followed the views, generally, of Plato and Aristotle on the relative merits of the rule of the many. Roman law and constitutionalism, exampled in the writings of Cicero, were nevertheless infused with Stoic conceptions of a universal natural law and a common divine birthright of human reason. These ideas provided Roman thought with the principles of 'essential' human equality and an individual access, through reason, to universal moral precepts. Such views were considerably richer in egalitarian spirit than the Aristotelian treatment of equality as a question of equity in distributive justice and merit for services rendered to the state.

For much of the Christian period, democracy was not an issue, although the Conciliar movement in the fifteenth century offered at least a diversion in the direction of popular participation and a broadly based idea of corporate authority. The idea of popular political sovereignty was simply incompatible with the theocentric concept of princely power and the increasingly rigid imperial structure of the Roman Church.

In fact, until Jean-Jacques Rousseau, in the eighteenth century, extended the conceptions of social contract and popular sovereignty as far as they could possibly go, very little was said on behalf of democracy. The ideas of social contract and popular sovereignty were primarily secularizing tendencies of the Reformation and Enlightenment, but in themselves were far from having necessary implications for political democracy, although such a potential was evident and even feared. But the Natural Law school and such liberal thinkers as John Locke were satisfied that the social contract must be either historically remote, or hypothetical, or a safely tacit entailment of the individual's obligation to political authority. Locke also expected that popular sovereignty could be adequately realized in the form of a monarchy or what amounted, in Parliament, to an oligarchy. In this liberal tradition, which encompasses Thomas Hobbes, popular sovereignty implies not much more than the idea that power implicitly *resides* – once upon a time, or occasionally, or simply notionally – in the people, but this is very far from holding that the people actively *rule*, either in whole or in some large part.

In consequence, Rousseau looms as the radical figure he understood himself to be when he formulated his social contract. There individuals do consciously enter into community. It is an intimate, obliging and morally redemptive community. A person's character as individual and citizen is indistinguishable. The people rule collectively, incessantly and absolutely. In Rousseau, then, we have a theoretical Rubicon. Beyond the urgent stream of complex civil association he envisioned (capable of passing laws, administering policies and establishing institutions of religion, education and censorship), lies the far shore of anarchism: not the rule of the people, but no rule at all. On the near shore, democracy lies compromised by the faint-hearted liberals, whose community is riven by faction, weakened by private interests and governed by remote rulers.

To alter the metaphor in part, it would appear that modern democratic theory moves in two major tributaries of political thought, one of a potentially radical sort flowing from Rousseau, and a second, perhaps less perilous one, fed by the more individualistic English liberal stream. This, of course, is a gross simplification, but there is little else one can do in a tradition so richly elaborated from common sources in the Enlightenment and the English and French revolutions.

Contemporary – let us say post-World War II – democratic theory has been concerned to show what is wrong with each of these two branches, or how one branch could surely profit from a closer adherence to the character of the other. This is a rather incestuous intellectual family. Yet one can see why the issues are important, morally and politically. Democracy is the world's new universal religion. When its dogmas of liberty, equality, self-determination and human rights are violated so often and so barbarously; and the faithful tend, as ever, to be fewer than the faithless, then it is not surprising that we have, and ought to have, generations of theologians trying to shape and clarify the democratic canon. It is my present endeavour to provide a contrast to this effort. One way to do this is to emphasize the perspective of the anti-democratic tradition, and simply restate how rare, and how recent, it is to find democratic political life valued. William Gladstone, the Liberal Prime Minister whose Reform Bill of 1884 opened up a semblance of democratic electoral participation in England, was said by a biographer to have suffered one of the most deeply offending cuts of his career when a political opponent once called him a 'democrat'.

It is a fact, now routinely ignored by the democratic faithful as a position beneath contempt, that the great preponderance of political thinkers for two-and-a-half millennia have insisted upon the perversity of democratic constitutions, the disorderliness of democratic politics and the moral depravity of the democratic character. It is perhaps a point of some irony that so many contemporary democratic thinkers want to insist that democracy does not really exist in the world as we know it, but that it ought to; while the classical Greek thinkers had no doubt at all that democracy in various practical tendencies did exist, but that it ought not. In taking a position suspended, however precariously, between democratic and anti-democratic theory, we shall attempt to examine the nature of this impasse. To heighten the contrast, the heretical view will have to be given particular emphasis. Thus my discussion of democracy will be largely on the negative side. The intention here is simply to point out the pitfalls and derailments which have spoiled many serious attempts to elaborate democratic theory. Because much of the material is familiar and reviewed in detail in other chapters, the present argument will be in the form of a very condensed commentary, in which allusions will often have to serve for the better coinage of a fully documented argument.

A point of departure for this inquiry might be stated in this hypothesis: 'What if the modern democratic tradition in political theory is fundamentally *wrong*, both in its presuppositions about social and political values and in its labours to purify democratic theory and apply it in social practice?' In effect, this question invites us to suspend our beliefs and turn the intellectual plane upside-down. This altered perspective would seem to imply the following consequences, which will be discussed in turn.

I.   Attempting to 'define' democracy as an ideal form of political constitution is fundamentally untenable as a theoretical effort.

II.   It is a fruitless effort to attempt to construct democratic 'models' for political society.

III. The association between democracy and utopian thought, rarely intended but often implied by democratic theorists, is an especially revealing solecism.

I

Democracy as an ideal. This assumption may be attacked on three grounds. The first two appear in the philosophical and moral critiques of democracy provided by Plato and Aristotle. The third challenge derives from the institutional and procedural critique marked out by modern critics of democracy, in particular Roberto Michels.

Plato and Aristotle both argued that democracy, far from being an 'ideal' political constitution, was not even a 'form' of constitution, *sui generis*, but was in fact a distortion or corruption of something else. The Classical critique of democracy is familiar ground, and need not be reviewed here in any great detail.[1] Now of course it is easy to be cynical and patronizing about the method of resolving constitutions into the just and unjust governments of the one, the few and the many. But we need to be reminded that the perennial effort, even when only implicit, to see democracy as a superior moral or organizational doctrine is strictly a survival of Platonic idealism, and this fact often lives unhappily with other features and claims of democratic theory. It might appear to be a particularly serious heresy to accept Plato's formalistic and idealist critique of democracy, since that would amount to the acceptance of moral idealism and the preclusion of any empirical and 'value free' theory. But the weaknesses of these positivist hopes are notorious, and the tendency of democratic theorists to establish ideals – whether moral ones, or ones supposedly postulated as objective analytical benchmarks – is well known. Accepting the Classical relegation of democracy to the status of a remote and inherently defective approximation of the just society may well be an extreme and unattractive option, but this would at least mitigate the logical contradictions of trying to 'define' democracy as an ideal in the face of empirical and theoretical embarrassments.[2] Later we must return to the question left unanswered here: 'If democracy is not an ideal, then what is it?'

If, in our present state of suspension, we *accept* that democracy – that is, the rule of the people, or rule in the interests of the greater number – is not an ideal, and is not even a properly constituted 'form' of government, then we are obliged to go on to consider Plato and Aristotle's moral critique of democratic politics. Here again, we are on familiar terrain concerning the claimed vices of democracy: the majority's ambivalence to a comprehensive social justice; political instability, often tending to war and tyranny; the lack of moral virtues, promoted by a politics of ambition, popular rhetoric, majoritarianism and general licentiousness; the entrenchment of a few in 'long possession of office';[3] the injustices occasioned by a superficial and selfish ethic of egalitarianism; the widespread pursuit of indolent pleasures; the absence of genuine social or moral aims. Now it should be quite frankly realized that Plato and Aristotle considered these to be not simply problems *in* democracy, but problems *of* democracy. The moral degradation in democratic politics was an active, reciprocal phenomenon. The sort of people who possessed these vices wanted democracy, and democracy in turn promoted and extended a democratic character amongst the populace. The Classical thinkers knew all about the 'socialization process'.[4]

On their own philosophical grounds, Plato and Aristotle's moral critique of democracy is unanswerable. They have only focused upon the mean and fractious spirit that even some democratic thinkers have discerned in liberal democracies. The major question is whether or not one is willing to meet them on their grounds, and of course most would not do so. This reluctance, however, solves no theoretical questions. Certainly the Classical critique of democracy cannot be disproved, empirically, without actually doing the work. Such a project, *pace* Karl Popper, could in fact be formulated in empirically falsifiable propositions concerning the presence or absence of the moral and structural criteria implied in the Platonic and Aristotelian critiques (such as stability, partisanship, cultural values, inclination to tyranny, *inter alia*). Just as the presence of vicious behaviour in a democracy does not on its own prove Plato's case, viciousness in an oligarchy or monarchy does not automatically prove the democrat's case. Few of us would want to make an empirical testing of Plato's propositions about the character of democratic man,[5] and despite our prejudices the studies which have tried to show positive correlations between liberal views and political efficacy in liberal democratic nations,[6] or between political participation and the moral enhancement of the individual,[7] are not convincing.

It is both worthwhile and somewhat amusing to remember that Marxist and other modern critiques of democracy typically repeat the Classical arguments in a new, but kindred, vocabulary. The tenor of Plato's censure is felt in Marx's views on the baseness of bourgeois life and the corruptions of its supportive institutions, or in his apparent revulsion at the democratic licentiousness conjured up in his vision of 'crude communism'.[8] But there is also the general inability of Marxist thought to take any concept of citizenship seriously, in so far as civic values must be the product of ideological control and mystification to cover the class division and general moral degradation characteristic of societies which claim to enjoy freedom and equality.[9] On the political right, such thinkers as José Ortega y Gasset and Nicolai Berdyaev complain in a not dissimilar way about the dangers and destructiveness and moral impoverishment of societies succumbing to democratic revolutions.

One might go still further and actually claim that modern democratic theory itself accepts the moral critique of democracy, even in the thought of such major exponents as Thomas Paine and James Madison. This is why the Madisonian 'science of politics' placed so much emphasis upon separated powers, checks and balances, divided electorates and limited terms of office. The whole constitutional structure was intended to mitigate the effects of the whims of the mass will, the innate ambitions of all politicians and the tyrannical tendencies of majorities.[10] A number of contemporary theorists have lamented this as a kind of early sell-out of true democracy: a capitulation to Montesquieu's Anglophilic republicanism in default of Rousseau's pure faith. But it is difficult to see what is being sold out, apart from Rousseau's singularly extreme ideas. Here it must be emphasized that Rousseau's civil compact was and could be radically democratic only because he was eagerly prepared to establish it on the basis of a miraculous transformation in man's moral character. Rousseau freely acknowledged that such a society required an obligatory adherence to a supreme being – the metaphysical counterpart to Plato's philosophical idealism.[11] Theorists who attempt to rescue Rousseau conveniently tend to forget this.

Now let us turn to the institutional and procedural critique of democracy. It seems to me that the critique mounted by Roberto Michels early in this century is sound and unanswerable. Based upon an extensive examination of modern European party systems and bureaucracies of all types, Michels' argument concluded that there was a natural, necessary and inevitable tendency within all social organizations toward oligarchical control.[12] This phenomenon seemed so clear and inexorable that he did not hesitate to claim for it the status of a natural law governing human experience. The moving and profound irony expressed by Michels is that the very means by which socialist and democratic parties endeavour to create a democratic society is the procedure through which it must necessarily be lost. There is a Pyrrhic victory when a popular party organizes itself successfully and forms a stable, effective leadership competent enough to master the complexities of policy formulation, electoral success and governmental administration. It is a victory, not for democracy, but for a battle-hardened, professional elite. Here one need not accept Platonic idealism, or even any aspect of the moral critique of democracy, to accept Michels' argument. Cases in point abound in political democracies of every stripe – Western, African and Asian – to support this thesis.

There is a sense in which post-World War II democratic theory – whether the 'revisionist' and pluralist notions of Dahl, Schumpeter, Schattschneider and other American writers, or the theoretical efforts devoted to expounding socialist and African forms of one-party democracy – is an attempt to come to terms with the critique of Michels. Against the theory of elites, contemporary democratic theory has striven for definitions of 'consensus' and 'legitimation' which are somehow more realistic or cynical, which have a closer fit with empirical facts of apathy, political alienation, power groups and ruling elites. But all of these exertions do not reverse Michels' views, even if they do sometimes represent advances in empirical research or, unhappily, appear to be implicit ideological rationales for quiescent patriotism and national brands of party politics. In fact, the attempts at revision uniformly confirm Michels' argument. The brute fact remains that democratic politics (albeit not alone) cannot prevent the creation of remote, stable and entrenched centres of power which tend to promote general apathy, cynicism and ignorance about politics among the masses of people. About forty years ago, a number of intellectuals thought television would change all of that, but we can readily see what has become of this hope. Over a century ago, John Stuart Mill thought public education would do it. Two centuries ago, Thomas Jefferson thought a free press would do it. But nothing has altered the chasm between oligarchs and public, and now mass communications and scientific technology, especially as they relate to our physical and material security, have actually caused the chasm to deepen and widen. It remains the challenge of democratic theory to provide a bridge.

II

Democratic models. If democracy is not tenable as an ideal, and is procedurally self-defeating, then there must be real doubts about constructing 'models', either for practical reform or for hypothetical–deductive investigations of justice and rights.[13] Nevertheless, the recurrent efforts to devise models of democracy betray the survival of formalism and idealism in modern democratic theory. It would seem to be another rescue effort: the fleshing out of an elaborate structural and moral model of social behaviour, so as to keep a hold on the essence of the thing, embodied in an abstract form, while at the same time making the model detailed enough to provide an explanation for quantities of empirical facts – such as poverty, sexism or declining voter turn-out – which apart from the model's 'dynamic' do not seem very democratic.

Although we often run across the term 'classical models of democracy', our previous examination illustrates the historical inaptness of such a reference. We see romantic references to Athenian democracy (often taking architectural form), and sometimes to Pericles, but the bulk of modern scholarship has shown that the Athenian democracy was so restrictive as to deprive it of any such legitimate identity, at least with respect to contemporary applications. Other chapters in this book raise questions about the very meaning of 'classical' democratic theory. Modern scholars have gone looking for classical models in James and John Stuart Mill, or in Paine or Jeremy Bentham. These figures may be 'classical' in the acknowledged tradition of democratic thought, but their views on democracy are extraordinarily indeterminate. One may safely conclude that modern attempts at constructing institutional models of party government or moral systems of liberal individualism reveal the impasse which must be reached in any effort to construct a model of democracy. This includes, *inter alia*, the models of Dahl, Cassinelli, Rawls, Nozick, Easton (at least by extension of his systems model) and Friedman's *laissez-faire* market model. Indeed, those who are still at pains to set forth a model are among the first to confess that none yet exists.[14] This impasse is most commonly illustrated by the care with which the model-builder isolates certain key values – property, 'social justice', absolute individual rights, 'system stability' – from the grasping hands and unreliable intentions of the democratic process. And it is illustrated yet again in the way rationales are provided for manifestly undemocratic social realities, such as political elites and legally privileged parties, economic and social influentials, pluralistic power, requirements for absolute majorities, and other sacred values or stubborn realities beyond the pale of democratic choice.

My general point under this heading is that the idea of a model rests upon the faulty assumption that the essence of democracy is contained in a formal structure, or in a determinate set of necessary relations. Its *nature* is presumed to reside in its formal properties alone, that is, in its *structure*. This is a type of idealism that not even Plato or Aristotle would countenance, since they were firm in holding that the nature of a thing could only be understood through an examination of its *telos*, its aim or purpose. In fact, this kind of analysis was used by them to point out that democracy, lacking justice as the comprehensive aim of the *polis*, really had no *telos*, and was therefore a perversion of nature.

III

Democracy and utopia. It is worth noting in the present context that utopian thought is rarely, if ever, expressed in the symbols and forms of political democracy. Another way to express this is to point out how seldom democratic ideas have appealed to the utopian imagination. This point bears more reflection than it can be given here. But it is noteworthy that most, if not all, of the utopian literature which springs to mind offers a form of political and social life that does not envisage a vigilant and regular participation of the whole community in matters of policy and power. Utopias, if such they be, of an anarchist stamp may be an exception to this point, but even here one must be doubtful whether the visions of William Godwin, Proudhon or Bakunin are either properly utopian or democratic, in so far as both of these terms are generally taken to imply a good deal of elaborate and binding social structure. Even the socialist utopias described in the early nineteenth century took for granted that special groups or special persons would be responsible for planning, administration and execution. Where everything else would be shared in harmony and association, in some cases equally, there was still no ordination that the exercise of power must be the jealous, daily concern of the whole community. The absence of democratic ideas, it would seem, is not just an accidental lacuna in the genre of utopian literature.

Utopian ideas of community sometimes play a powerful rhetorical role in radical and revolutionary movements, but one might well argue that utopian models, or indeed any other models, have had very little to do with historical democratic movements and the salient victories which have been won through popular political struggles against hierarchical oppression. The Athenian democracy, the English Civil War and the American Revolution were political struggles, grounded in broad cultural divisions, interests and power. They were not intellectual or utopian movements guided by philosophies or clear-cut utopian designs. This point accepts, in the main, C.B. Macpherson's historical analysis of the emergence of capitalist liberalism, but also reveals as pointless or anachronistic his apparent theoretical aspiration that it might somehow be otherwise.[15]

If democracy is not an ideal, what is it? It would appear to follow from what has so far been argued that democratic thought is not a proper vehicle for metaphysical or systematic social theory. Conversely, and what is more certain historically, such theory is not the vehicle for democratic thought. Many people have said that democracy is about means and not ends, and that is certainly one conclusion that may be drawn from this argument. But let us not dismiss the case prematurely by concluding that democracy is nothing more than a kind of politics of procedure in which interests are advanced according to some plan of war, or by a more or less orderly competition.

Real, historical democratic constitutions, such as they exist, are bold moral and theoretical compromises. The English, American, French and Russian revolutions, which eventually produced such constitutions, are all excellent cases in point. Indeed, these historical compromises have produced a genre of political and historical literature to defend or lament critical moments in the life of each revolution. One would certainly be hard pressed to discover a consistent adherence to even procedural means, much less moral ideals, in these revolutionary movements, even in their intellectual and propagandistic dimensions. They were set in real circumstances, with real lives and interests at stake. That, in fact, is the very point to be gleaned from Pericles' famous funeral oration, which is often erroneously assumed to be a classical portrayal of Athenian democracy in terms of moral ideals and laudable institutions of participation.[16] Acknowledging the compromising and contextual origins of democracy enables us to discover the meaning of the paradox, usually noted ruefully by some recent theorists, that the greatest democratic theorists have been democracy's most candid critics. The following examples come to mind of supposedly 'lapsed' democrats: Madison, Hamilton and Jefferson; John Stuart Mill; Michels; and more recently Schumpeter, Schattschneider and Dahl. One might even, upon closer inspection, make some surprising additions to this list. Aristotle, Locke, Rousseau and Marx each had a direct interest in gaining recognition of the rights and duties of the whole community, but each also had grave doubts about how this might be institutionalized without ruining these rights for the great majority of the people.

Democracy, then, whether as a revolutionary movement or a competitive struggle for the people's vote, is essentially a form of political action. It is a means of achieving aims of a utilitarian sort (at most) by attacking narrow interests with less narrow ones. The question must then arise whether democracy is the legitimate province of the theorist or philosopher. Perhaps this is the difficulty underlying the failure to discover a widely accepted 'classical' democratic theory, while the failure itself has evolved into several classical critiques of democracy. This volume, by its focus on the relationship between theory and practice, confronts the tensions on the frontier dividing the provinces of philosophical inquiry and utilitarian action. The inquiry is particularly frustrating, because the recognizable aims or ends of democracy are bound up in the process itself – for example, suffrage, parliamentarism, civil rights, equality – and are not theoretically extrinsic to it, either morally or metaphysically. Democratic thought, therefore, emerges in the struggle for social power, or to put it in perhaps a fresher way, a struggle (for money, status, interests, ideals, dreams: it makes no difference) between people who nevertheless find themselves by language, geography, culture and common circumstances to be members of the same community. Democratic thought, as if in defiance of philosophy, emerges in such a conflict, and is limited to debating *how* power may be won, whether by electoral contract or popular revolt, and how it may thereafter be retained or deprived, and in any case restrained. Indeed, these two aspects – popular struggle and constraint – are perfectly illustrated in the theoretical debates over the 'revolutionary' and 'reactionary' phases of the American Revolution (1776 and 1787) and the French Revolution (1789 and 1793). In other words, democratic theory, far from being cut off from practice, *is theory about practice*, and how that practice may be modified or transformed.

To say that democracy is incompatible with moral ideals and metaphysical systems – that democracy is condemned to an orderly but mundane debate over means and a studied ignorance of ends – is not a closure of theoretical inquiry. Means cannot exist in isolation. The question remains: 'What kind of means?' This question persists in an almost painful tension as theory, but only because theory operates as a dialogue with real political issues and actual practice. The inquiry is forced outwards, inevitably, to broader theoretical and normative issues. Are one-party African states democratic? Are democratic parties inherently oligarchical? Is political democracy a by-product of liberal capitalism, and therefore a likely excrescence in the post-capitalist or post-industrial economy? Must electoral politics either be corrupt in an old-fashioned way, or mindless in the sophisticated use of the mass media?

Democratic theory addresses these questions in a way that is reminiscent of the Socratic dialogue. Such theory constitutes a continuous dialogue with political problems, some old and some entirely new, in which the actuality of the discourse – the contact with real problems with a view to action – is possible only by virtue of being unable to bring ideals, aims and moral values into sharp focus as universally binding recommendations. There is no monopoly – indeed, there is a kind of embargo – on truth, and it is this feature which sustains the dialogue. At times democratic theory is indistinguishable from political rhetoric in pursuing power, bolstering ideological positions or attacking the legitimacy of regimes. At other times, especially in the Rousseauian tradition, it seeks to define a *mysterium* of communal life in which a sacred compact and a General Will create a moral freedom transcending the individual will. But in such cases as these, it would appear that the agreement to disagree has been broken.

The critics of democracy have been, in the past two centuries, largely silent interlocutors in the dialogue, in deference to an evolving consensus that democratic life is the pattern appropriate to the age. The character of democratic theory as frustrated, conscience-stricken and suspicious of its allies is therefore oddly paradoxical with the virtually unanimous belief that somehow life would be richer and democracy easier if we could but reach a truer, more realistic, more inclusive definition of democracy. But by its very nature, democracy is not susceptible of such idealization, and it is essential to the existence of the dialogue that it should not be treated so.

All of this is not to say that traditional democratic theory, in all of its varieties, has not had a moral content. But this moral content – human equality, legal justice, natural rights, circumscribed power, social justice – is not *inherent* in democratic ideas. The ethical values are not coincident with or derived from the theoretical premises of democracy, but are rather eclectically gathered from several bodies of theory – idealism, Roman law, Christianity – which are often seriously at odds with political democracy. Here we find the limits of democratic theory, a kind of identity crisis, not only as concerns the frustrations and contradictions and culs-de-sac which have already been mentioned with regard to theories about democracy's formal properties, but in the difficulty one faces in speculating theoretically as to the fundamental nature of democracy. For example, when inquiring as to the source of power, its origins, the reply of democratic theory – 'the people' – is trivial and romantic. In trying to examine the ends of power, democratic theory finds itself impoverished, begging for a loan. These misfortunes come at a price, which is the rejection of the radical critiques of democracy and the philosophical foundations on which they are built. Democratic theorists have generally been prepared to pay this price, but it is essential that they know what exacts it, and what its effect is on the stable identity and tangible contents of the object.

3

The historical study of 'democracy'

IAIN HAMPSHER-MONK

This chapter concerns the debate between 'empirical' and 'classical' theories of democracy.[1] In it I want to draw attention to a hitherto neglected aspect of that debate, namely the historical process by which a word like 'democracy' gains its commendatory overtones. To call a state a democracy was not always to praise it, and the argument here is that an understanding of how this came about can clarify some of the issues involved in considering whether or not states or theories are properly to be called democratic. Although the methods used derive from linguistic philosophy, my purpose is to direct attention towards the values and aspirations of historical agents using the term rather than to a purely conceptual analysis of it. It is nevertheless hoped that this will clear the way for more substantive discussion.

The major thrust of empirical theorists has been to demonstrate that the social and institutional characteristics of modern liberal-democratic states contravened the values and ideals of classical democratic theories. Berelson and others demonstrated in a series of voting studies that modern citizens were largely uninterested and uninvolved in politics, ill-informed on issues and irrational in their choices. It was further argued that where citizens were not apathetic, the existence of highly partisan attitudes threatened the stability of the whole democratic system. The observation that political power, far from being wielded by the people, was competed for between elites, further undermined one of the more literal characteristics imputed to supposedly democratic polities. But instead of concluding, as they might, that modern democracies needed to embark on a major campaign of political education, or alternatively that they were not, in some important sense, democracies at all, these investigators proceeded to redefine the term in accordance with the empirical evidence: '. . . what we call "democracy" . . . does seem to operate with a relatively low level of citizen participation. Hence it is inaccurate to say that one of the necessary conditions for "democracy" is extensive citizen participation.'[2] Empirical theorists incorporated the oligarchical structures of modern society, no less than the 'functional apathy' of the individual citizen into their revised theories of democracy. Since such features, no matter how incongruous, were found in actual democracies, it followed that such features must form part of the meaning of 'democracy'.

Defenders of the classical theories, on the other hand, argued that the presence of these incongruous features was precisely what prevented these states from being justifiably called democracies. The empiricists were 'abandoning a whole tradition of political thinking',[3] their argument was variously presented as misleading, false, or a deliberately ideological move calculated to defend, as democratic, otherwise clearly oligarchical political systems.

Quentin Skinner pushed the discussion further, and by an analysis of the 'speech acts' involved, claimed to expose the linguistic mechanics of the revisionist's argument.[4] To call a system democratic, he pointed out, is not only to denote certain minimal institutional characteristics, it is also, ineluctably, to praise it. I want to look at this analysis in detail shortly, but for the moment let us just note the broad strategy. There is no general agreement as to what the minimum or essential institutional characteristics are for a regime to be entitled to be called a democracy; and empiricists, it was claimed, had used this conceptual fuzziness to extend the denotation and include as praiseworthy those Western polities studied, or made the basis of models, by revisionists.

It is not clear that the analysis presented so far has established the impropriety of modern liberal-democratic states laying claim to the label, or of political scientists abstracting from such states models of, 'democracy'. After all, both make universal adult suffrage and freedom of political activity central. Each side bases its argument on an assumption about the proper content of the descriptive term 'democracy', but since it is precisely this which is at issue the argument makes little progress. Specifically, what is lacking is any demonstration that there *is* a limited and legitimate way of recognizing what is to count as 'rule by the people' which *has* been eroded. The problem seems not that the empirical theorists have illicitly distorted the criteria for deciding when the people are ruling, but that traditional theories and usages (whichever are meant by this) have not been shown to give us agreed and determinate criteria in the first place. Unfortunately, to expect classical theorists to have provided some trans-historical institutional criteria, applicable equally to their own and to modern societies is at the least unlikely, and according to some accounts of the nature of the history of ideas, impossible.[5] It seems, then, that any concentration on the purely empirical criteria which characterize democracies will be incapable of resolving the issue. For first there is no agreement on such criteria, and secondly such criteria as there are, must, *ex hypothesi*, relate to the specific historical conditions experienced by a past society, which may be quite foreign to ours.[6]

But there is another criterion we can invoke here, and it is to a consideration of this that the rest of the essay will be devoted. As already suggested, the use of the word 'democracy' not only indicates certain, evidently rather imprecise, institutional arrangements, but also commends the political system concerned. Up to now analysis has concentrated on the empirical characteristics denoted by the term. What we need to understand is the relationship between the descriptive and the commending 'speech acts' performed by using the word 'democracy'.

A wide range of words do not simply describe aspects of the world, but are themselves actions in the world.[7] Most notoriously, to say 'I promise' is not simply to describe a mental or verbal act, it is rather to perform the very act in question. Another range of words commit the user by endorsing the success of the activities so described. For example, if I say that Marx proved that capitalism would collapse, I am endorsing Marx's claim, and if I want to dissociate myself from it I had better say something like, 'Marx claimed to have shown that capitalism would collapse.' The question is: 'Just what are we committing ourselves to when we describe a polity as democratic?'

The particular speech acts we are concerned with are those descriptive words which possess evaluative overtones. They not only describe a state of affairs but also grade, rank, evaluate or otherwise judge them. Thus to call someone 'generous' not only describes his behaviour but also, irresistibly, commends him. Thus far the argument has come already. My point is that the relationship between description and praise is not contingent. Historically, words of praise or blame have their origin in words which are almost purely descriptive. Words gain their capacity to praise what they denote from qualities, values and social attitudes intimately connected with the behaviour, individuals, or institutions denoted. In his *Short History of Ethics* Alastair MacIntyre puts the general point succinctly:

> . . . it has often been held to be an essential feature of such moral predicates that any judgements in which one is ascribed to a subject cannot follow logically as a conclusion from premises which are merely factual. But in the Homeric poems, that a man has behaved in a certain way is sufficient to entitle him to be called 'agathos'. When this [social] hierarchy collapses, the question can be opened up in a more general way, of what the qualities are which we should wish to see in a man . . .[8]

There is clearly a point in the life of such words when the presumption that they refer to specific values rather than to generalized praise or blame is lost. As in the case of 'agathos' they can then be applied according to completely subjective criteria of evaluation. This is not a deliberate or even a self-conscious tactic; it is a shift which may occur unnoticed and unintended, but for all that it is as irrevocable as any other change in intellectual climate.[9]

The criteria for the application of moral terms do not, of course, always disintegrate to the extent that they have in the case of words such as 'agathos', which becomes equivalent to our 'good'. Although it is important that we indicate the qualities in virtue of which we praise something, it is also important in an open society that we be able to choose which judgements to make. Language commonly contains, for this purpose, pairs of words which enable us to evaluate differently actions which have a similar descriptive content.[10] Thus brave–foolhardy, generous–prodigal, obstinate–persevering are pairs which evaluate similar actions according, it might be argued, to a 'chivalric' or a 'protestant' ethic.

If we accept this account of the generation of moral terminology and of the relationship between their descriptive and evaluative potential, then the relationship between the two is clearly not contingent. By calling someone 'a gentleman' we do not simply praise him, and also indicate an arbitrarily connected style of behaviour; rather we indicate a determinate mode of life and praise him for just that, because we endorse the social approval of the kind of behaviour embodied in the illocutionary force of the word. We can do all this at once because such behaviour used to be characteristic of certain dominant and respected groups in society whose values are, or at least were, considered worthy of emulation even by those socially excluded from such groups. The nobility effected another contribution to our moral language in the period before the 'gentlefolk'. 'Noble' individuals no longer have to exhibit a pedigree to qualify as such, but they do have to exhibit behaviour regarded as typical of thoroughbreds.

The non-contingency of the two speech acts which such words perform can be demonstrated by considering the case of the male sympathizer with the women's movement who might decide not to pick up handkerchiefs, open doors or give up seats to women on the grounds that in doing so he would insidiously reinforce their social subjection. Such action might well be praiseworthy but could hardly be called gentlemanly: it involves a rejection of the whole set of assumptions and values on which being 'gentlemanly' rests. Of course it is highly unlikely that anyone practising such actions would want to employ that term to commend them. What *is* important to notice is that anyone who did so would be performing an identifiably ideological redefinition of the word 'gentleman' and its cognates. Such a move would be illegitimate at least to the linguistic (and social?) conservative, because it attempts to use the generally commendatory force of the word as the hinge on which to swing the meaning away from one identifiable set of acts and values towards a totally different set of acts and values. Both sets of actions arguably count as 'socially praiseworthy attitudes towards women', and this makes the move conceivable. However, because there is still considerable consensus over what counts as 'gentlemanly' behaviour (even on the part of those who disagree with the values implied by it), the revision is patently objectionable. If the relationship between the descriptive and evaluative functions of the word became so tenuous that the act of praising was unspecific as to the particular values approved of, then such objections would be difficult to substantiate.

It is in this area, where words still have a particular, though not precise, value attached to them, that complex linguistic moves become possible. For shifts and changes in meaning and value are not always the wholly unconscious consequences of social change. Men are, or at least aspire to be, as much manipulators of their conceptual as of the material and social world. Innovators have two distinct strategies available to them. They can brazenly and openly introduce new ideas, explicitly provoking conflict with traditional ideas and values, or they can attempt to appropriate an established, and 'commended' but suitably 'fuzzy' idea on which to graft their new meaning. Almost invariably we find the latter chosen. Most societies have their version of the English 'ancient constitution' argument, a conservative tradition of presenting the new in the guise of the old. More closely related to our problem is the situation where particular words with positive overtones are persuasively redefined in order to endow a new or otherwise unpalatable notion with the goodwill earned by the appropriated concept. It is this move that Karl Popper accuses Plato of committing, when, in Book I of *The Republic* he rejects commonly accepted notions of justice in order to substitute his own more unpalatable prescriptions.[11] Such a move is imputed to the revisionist democratic theorists by their critics.[12] But the illegitimacy of such a move depends not simply on demonstrating that 'democracy' is a praising word, but in showing that the particular kind of qualities in virtue of which it is, or has become, a praising word, are being neglected or negated. To revert to our previous example: the word 'gentleman' does not simply praise, it praises in respect of certain specific qualities; its evaluative potential is not adequately characterized as 'performing the speech act of commending'. This specificity with respect to the values invoked in praising is true of all but the most general of our evaluative vocabulary. The point up to which this argument is leading is that the failure to specify the values invoked in the use of 'democracy' and their supposed relationship to the empirical criteria governing its use renders incomplete the analysis of the supposed 'ideological move' committed by revisionist theorists. As already pointed out, traditional theorists cannot be expected to have given trans-historical institutional criteria by which to determine correct usages of 'democracy'. However, they did give reasons for thinking that rule by the people was a good thing, and the acceptance of such reasons must be related to the change in the speech act performed by using the word 'democracy' from one of condemnation to one of commendation.

One possible way of making a charge of ideological redefinition stick would be to show that the empirical conditions now presented as embodying 'rule by the people', are incompatible with the original values which democracy was supposed to realize, especially if in addition it could be shown that revisionist theorists still claimed democracy was desirable for those same reasons. In the first case we might be entitled to consider such usage at least an extension, and possibly a perversion, of historically established meaning; in the second case the usage would be incoherent in that the referring and commending components of the meaning would be incompatible.

It is important to stress that democracy has only recently become a good thing. In the seventeenth century Filmer wondered: 'why all our modern politicians, who pretend themselves Aristotelians, should forsake their great master, and account democracy a right or perfect form of government when Aristotle brands it for a transgression, or a depraved or corrupted manner of government.'[13] Filmer's judgement of his contemporaries was ahead of his time; not even the Levellers claimed to be democrats, although some of their opponents tried to brand them as such. Even in the next century, the best states, like the best hives,

> . . . were not slaves to tyranny
> Nor rul'd by wild *Democracy*;
> But Kings, that could not wrong, because
> Their power was circumscribed by laws.[14]

Assertors of democracy in late eighteenth-century England had to contend with polemical and eventually physical opposition.[15] This opposition was hardly surprising in an oligarchical society, but it provoked a number of justifications of democracy which appealed to the values which the implementation of 'rule by the people' in the form of manhood suffrage would supposedly realize. How otherwise, argued Cartwright:

. . . can we give the poor man such an attachment to the constitution, such a respect for the land, and such a love of his country; such a desire for public peace, and such a satisfaction of his own personal condition, as by leaving him the proud and pleasing consciousness that even he has a voice in electing the rulers of the land.[16]

John Thelwall put it more brusquely: 'If you wish people to be humanised you must restore to them the privileges of humanity.'[17] The illocutionary force of 'democracy' as a term of commendation in our language was generated by these early radicals' justifications for the implementation of what *they* understood as rule by the people.

Now whether the institutions they proposed are in fact capable of realizing the values they invoked is ultimately an empirical question. There are at least two levels of analysis here: one asks 'What kinds of values were, as a matter of historical fact, claimed for democracy by its protagonists, were instrumental in gaining for democracy commendatory connotations, and are, as a result, connected with its meaning today?' This line of investigation seeks to explain the relationship between historical movements and ideas in the past, and the resulting connotations of the language we have inherited.

But there is another level of analysis which is concerned not with the historical links between social changes and the language and values asserted in the past on behalf of forms of government. It is concerned instead with either the logical propriety or the practical plausibility of the links so claimed. The historically acquired associations between institutions and values, between the descriptive and the evaluative sides of words like democracy, may in fact turn out to be logically incompatible. Our early 'democratic' theorists may have simply been wrong in thinking such a dramatic moral rebirth possible as a result of instituting universal suffrage, or their prescriptions may have been at the least incomplete.

However, even at our first level of analysis, to say that calling a system democratic both describes some of its empirical characteristics and praises it, is not to say enough. For 'democracy' gained its capacity to praise in respect of *particular values* which its institutional provisions were popularly supposed to realize.

If contemporary 'democratic' systems do not realize these ideals it may be that the early theorists were simply wrong in asserting a relationship between a certain institutional arrangement and certain values. We might be stuck with an historically acquired linguistic connection between the form and values of democracy which practice and later historical experience has invalidated. Alternatively it may be that the institutional arrangements which constitute popular rule are today so attenuated as to make the realization of such values impossible. If we have to choose, do not the *values* invoked by 'democracy' have as much claim to the true 'meaning' of the word as the *institutions* which have failed to realize them? On this view there would be justification for criticizing any theorists who still claim classical ideals for models derived empirically from contemporary states.

One example of a value which has been sacrificed in most accounts of contemporary democracy is participation, a characteristic widely attributed to classical models. Clearly if revisionist theorists claim a high degree of apathy is compatible with, or even essential to democracy, there is something incongruous in their claiming for such systems values which are related to a high degree of citizen participation. Of course the belief that one can legislate for usage is an illusion, and whilst we might want to claim that correct usages of 'democracy' had to demonstrate entitlement to at least some of the values or qualities for which 'democracy' originally became a term of praise, the best that can be hoped for is that such analysis will at least shift the argument away from the more sterile areas of linguistic propriety and onto more substantive issues.

One of the more telling points to be made against critics of empirical and classical theories alike is that they seldom refer their criticisms to identifiable individual theories. Clearly the case outlined in this paper depends on identifying the characteristics and claims of individual theories. This is a detailed task for which there is not scope here. A good beginning is the attempt made by Alan Ryan to compare the values and institutions advocated by James Mill as against those of his son John Stuart Mill. However Ryan uses the contrasted theories merely, as he puts it, 'to illustrate a wide thesis concerning two contrasting images of the nature of politics'.[18] What is suggested here is that these political paradigms can be presented as historical phenomena influencing the development and connotations of such words as 'democracy'. For the two particularly revealing and historically prominent models of political life within which the term 'democracy' was much deployed are the economic or market model and the developmental conception of political activity. The former model sees politics as essentially instrumental, a means for achieving some other non-political end. The latter sees it as an activity that is in some sense constitutive of human social life, and certainly a prerequisite to the full development of individuals' personalities.

William Godwin argued a case for democracy on these essentially developmental grounds in the last decade of the eighteenth century, when 'democracy' was emerging from scholars' tomes on the 'mixed constitution' and appearing on the streets. Godwin's developmental ideal of political life rested on the unlikely foundation of the sensationalist psychology of the eighteenth century. In common with writers of that school he argued that 'everything within [man] that has a tendency to voluntary action, is an affair of external or internal sense, and has relation to pleasure or pain'. Godwin also held the more extreme Hobbesian position that, at least in origin, all our actions are determined by our desire to avoid our own pain, and maximize our own pleasure. Godwin avoids the extreme egoism that would seem to follow from this by arguing that the intellect's ability to abstract from the particular to the general, affects not only the thinking but the sensing mind, and this enables the cultivated individual to be moved by utilitarian considerations of the *total* pleasures and pains resulting from his action rather than only by his own: 'That which gives the last zest to our enjoyments, is the approbation of our own minds, the consciousness that the exertion we have made, was such as was called for by impartial justice and reason.'[19] For Godwin the intellectual pleasures that result from knowing that our act increases the sum of pleasures in the world becomes the motive force of the developed human being; and the generalizing capacity of the mind is what enables it to escape the determining force of our own particular physical experiences. Godwin thus attempts a highly rationalist explanation of the move from individual hedonism to utilitarianism as a principle of action. But it is only when the individual has arrived at his convictions through the exercise of his own understanding that they are effective and reliable guides to his behaviour. Here is where Godwin perceives the effect of a class-divided society. Deference prevents the exercise of individual judgement, and class (and indeed national and cultural) divisions prevent us from allowing full rein to our capacity to abstract from our own particular situation and consider the needs of others as equal to our own. The evil of monarchical and aristocratic societies is essentially that in them 'the basis of all morality, the recollection that other men are beings of the same order as himself is extirpated.' The argument that men are imperfect and imperfectible beings is itself the product of a radically deformed society: 'In the estimate that is usually made of democracy one of the sources of our erroneous judgement, lies in our taking mankind such as monarchy and aristocracy have made them . . . [these] . . . would be no evils, if their tendency were not to undermine the virtues and understanding of their subjects.'[20]

The progressive improvement of mankind can take place only through individual criticism and reflection resulting in the dispersal of ignorance, deference and unthinking adherence to traditional patterns of behaviour. Theories of human nature which place emphasis on the historically acquired 'prejudices' so beloved by Burke, or on any purely causal account of behaviour, are themselves a part of the evil apparatus that prevents men from realizing their true natures. Nothing can be done until we 'consider the human mind as an intelligent agent, guided by motives and precepts presented to the understanding, and not by causes which have no proper cognisance and can form no calculation'. Democracy is for Godwin both a precondition for the full flowering of these conditions and a political system which embodies them.

Democracy restores to man a consciousness of his values, teaches him, by the removal of authority and oppression, to listen only to the suggestions of reason, gives him confidence to treat all other men with frankness and simplicity, and induces him to regard them no longer as enemies against whom to be on his guard, but as brethren whom it behoves him to assist.[21]

Such a creative picture of the relationship between a human agent and his social environment is obviously behind what a lot of writers want to claim as essentially 'democratic' values; when the editor of an American anthology urges that 'a primary concern for the peculiar powers and dignity of the fragile and ephemeral human individual belongs essentially to the meaning of democracy', and Benn and Peters claim, less inflatedly, that the effect of democracy is to 'moralise politics'.[22] It lies behind criticisms that empirical theories 'have fundamentally changed the normative significance of democracy'. Classical theories were 'concerned above all else with human development, the opportunities which existed in political activity to realize the untapped potentials of men and to create the foundations of a genuinely human community'.[23] Clearly such theories as those put forward by Godwin appeal to such values; furthermore, although this is a matter for historical demonstration, views such as Godwin's were influential in the change that occurred in the connotations of the word 'democracy'.[24]

However, even if it can be demonstrated that such a 'developmental' conception of man and politics was attached early to the connotations of 'democracy' rendering them commendatory, there are still two arguments open to empirical theorists. They can still argue that they are not claiming these particular values for the systems they describe and praise. As noted above, it is not always clear exactly what values are being claimed for systems praised as democratic, a point made by Dahl in the course of his exchange with Walker: 'I do not share Professor Walker's confidence that he can divine the implicit or explicit normative assumptions of the writers he has tried to summarise.'[25] Yet implicit in most of Dahl's own work, and occasionally explicit, is a strong revisionist ethic which seems to justify the fears of the fundamentalists whilst recognizing that some fundamental value shift is taking place: 'Attractive as such ideals as equality are, to continue to demand that they be fulfilled in the conditions of modern society only leads to cynicism about democracy itself.'[26]

Yet perhaps Dahl himself, in making the revision explicit, is conceding too much, for there is another democratic tradition, almost as old, but with an equal claim to historical influence and which shows much more congruence with empirical theories of democracy: that of radical utilitarianism. Here politics is valued not for itself, but as an instrument in the pursuit of other goods, mainly economic, which it can safeguard. James Mill's *Essay on Government* is the clearest exposition of the extreme version of this view, which sees popular rule, not as valuable in itself, but as the only way to evaluate the demand for and ensure the production of such goods. The value of democracy is not intrinsic to the activity of politics itself, but only as a means; indeed, political activity is itself a cost incurred in the course of such efforts.

Mill's view in the *Essay* is that the desirable goods of life are produced by the undesirable expenditure of labour. Men are assumed to be selfish, and the political order exists to ensure that rewards are distributed equitably. The assumption of egoism, however, extends also to governors, and consequently the only form of government that can guard against exploitation is democracy. Since time spent on politics is considered a cost, a distraction from intrinsically valuable activity, some method must be found of minimizing the amount of political activity in a community. Representative government provides a general answer to this difficulty, but the problem is to find the optimum point beyond which increased political activity imposes greater costs than it prevents by checking exploitation on the part of rulers.

Notoriously, Mill finds this point where the franchise excludes men under forty, women and children.[27]

As emphasized, the justification for democracy here is essentially instrumental: if other political arrangements produce the same ends, it becomes at least plausible to suggest that they realize democratic values and can count as 'democracies'.

Clearly the implications of this view of politics are the cessation of all political activity when no-one feels he can marginally improve his position for any given expenditure of effort. Indeed, the absence of significant political action by minority groups has been claimed as evidence of their political satisfaction. The utilitarian model is, in broad outline, and in some cases in detail, similar to economic, empirical and elite theories of democracy spawned by American and in some cases British political science since the war.[28] Any relative judgements that we might care to make between the development and the instrumental models are beside the present point, it should at least be clear that both possess good *prima facie* claims to historical importance in endowing 'democracy' with its potential for commendatory illocutionary performances.

Just as there is no democratic theory, but only democratic theories, so there are democratic values rather than a single value to democracy. Particular theories generate and are congruent with particular sets of values. The champions of that snarklike creature, the Classical Theory of Democracy, which turned out to be more hydra than snark, were perhaps over-hasty in accusing the empirical theorists of 'abandoning a whole tradition of political thinking'. One major classical tradition of democratic thought has in them its true contemporary heirs. The values attached to such theories are not those that are most often claimed for 'democracy', but they are values deeply embedded in liberal society. It is tempting to go further, and suggest that developmental values have been more intimately connected with the protagonists of democracy, whilst the more instrumental, utilitarian paradigm belonged strictly to nineteenth-century liberalism.[29] Historical grounds for this could be found in the early nineteenth century, with the split between the largely middle-class libertarian, and utilitarian philosophical radicals, and the still natural-rights-based radicalism of the working-class democrats and republicans who carried on the earlier tradition of the 1790s.[30] It is possible too that these historical grounds could be paralleled by a logical case, and that, as Alan Ryan argues elsewhere in this volume, a democratic theory based on natural rights entails different outcomes from one based on utilitarian premises. A full demonstration of either the logical or the historical point is obviously beyond the scope of this modest essay, which is more in the tradition of the Lockean philosophical 'underlabourer'. I wish merely to point out some levels of analysis which have not been acknowledged in this debate.

Classical theories

4

Mill and Rousseau: utility and rights

ALAN RYAN

In this essay I attempt two rather different things. The first is to elucidate some differences between rights-based and utilitarian defences of democracy; the second is to illustrate my account of these differences by reference to Mill and Rousseau. The account I give of Mill and Rousseau, however, is to some extent subversive of the account I give of the differences between rights-based and utilitarian justifications of democracy, and the resolution of this apparent contradiction forms the conclusion of this essay. I begin with a few remarks about recent treatments of Mill and Rousseau, to set the scene for what follows.

Over the past two decades, the names of Mill and Rousseau have often been coupled. They have been seen as theorists of 'participatory democracy', defenders of a classical ideal of citizen virtue and public spirit, who could still teach us something about the point of democratic government.[1] The invocation of their names was part of a revolt against an excessively 'realistic' style of theorizing which owed much to Joseph Schumpeter on the one hand and to the first students of American voting behaviour on the other.[2] 'Democracy' was defined in terms drawn from the practice of British and American politics as 'that institutional arrangement for arriving at political decisions in which individuals acquire the power to decide by means of a competitive struggle for the people's vote'.[3] When most people most of the time turn out to know little about politics beyond the name of the party they propose to vote for – they know little about the policies of their party, they have few views about the issues of the day – this need not impugn the democratic credentials of the political order; so long as teams of would-be decision makers present themselves to the voters, and incumbents leave office quietly in the event of defeat, we have a stable democratic order. Indeed, it was plausibly argued that the political quiescence of the common man was all to the good; he could not be expected to master complexities in the way professional politicians and administrators did, and if his views were allowed to determine policy too directly, policy would surely be too simple, too crude, and too clumsy. His proper task was to register a general satisfaction or dissatisfaction with the professionals in government, and this he could do through the ballot box every four or five years.[4] Some darker fears were raised by the contemplation of a more active citizenry. The common people were less tolerant, more authoritarian, more prone to anger and resentment, than were the better off, better educated, more practised political classes; their direct entry onto the political stage would cause disasters of a kind, if not on a scale, familiar from Nazi Germany.[5]

Mill and Rousseau seemed to offer grounds for optimism in the face of these anxieties and this 'realism'. It was true that the demands they made on the ordinary man – and ordinary woman, so far as Mill though not Rousseau was concerned – were much greater than the demands the 'realists' made on the American voter. But this did not mean that Mill and Rousseau were simply wrong about 'democracy'. Mill and Rousseau were critics of reality; the political sociologists had simply endorsed it. If present-day voters fail to live up to the standards of democratic citizenship set by Mill and Rousseau, we may criticize the voters and the present political system rather than Mill and Rousseau.[6] Of course, if we could show that nobody *could* meet the requirements of Mill and Rousseau, we should be obliged to admit that their ideals were unrealistic; but both Mill and Rousseau have a great deal to say about the training citizens must get if they are to meet their requirements, as well as about the social and economic system which their political ideal presupposes.[7] If these views are well founded, current practices may properly be condemned as not fully democratic, but there is no reason to despair of the common people.

Even if their *political* ideals are not fully realizable – if the modern nation state is simply too large and too elaborate for intelligent political participation by the mass of the population – they may provide us with participatory and democratic ideals in other areas of life, in the school, factory or office, for instance.[8] With regard to Rousseau especially, we may well think that the price he would want us to pay for political participation is too high, that he would deny us the tolerance, the variety and the prosperity of modern liberal societies; but we may also think that much of what he wanted is acceptable elsewhere.[9]

This is not the only interpretative possibility, however. Further reflection on the contrast between the demands made on the citizenry by Mill and Rousseau on the one hand and by modern writers on the other may make us doubt whether Mill and Rousseau were unequivocal democrats at all. They too recognized that the time, patience, commitment, strength of character and the rest that we seek in those who devote their whole lives to political activity cannot be found in everybody. 'Were there a people of gods', says Rousseau, 'their government would be democratic. So perfect a government is not for men.'[10] In practice, authority will and must gravitate towards a small number. 'It is unimaginable that the people should remain continually assembled to devote their time to public affairs, and it is clear that they cannot set up commissions for that purpose without the form of administration being changed.'[11] The whole people cannot devote its time to discussions of legislative and administrative detail, inevitably some specialization will occur, and the people at large will play a more passive role in public affairs. For all human purposes, an element of aristocracy is required in government, and of the three sorts of aristocracy he distinguishes – the natural, the elective and the hereditary – Rousseau says firmly: 'The first is only for simple peoples; the third is the worst of all governments; the second is the best, and is aristocracy properly so called.'[12]

That Rousseau defends elective aristocracy as the best form of government seems, moreover, to put him in Mill's company on this reading as firmly as did the 'participatory' reading first suggested. For Mill's *Representative Government* is in many respects an extremely 'elitist' or aristocratic work; the duty of the average man and woman is not to try to govern themselves directly, but to elect those who will govern better than they could themselves. Mill, of course, goes further in insisting that even when we have elected our representatives to parliament, they, too, should exercise a great deal of self-restraint and should avoid interfering with the detail of administration. 'There is a radical distinction between controlling the business of government and actually doing it.'[13] What is essential to representative government is that by law and by the positive morality of the state in question, the people through their deputies *can* dictate what the administrators may do. Government is, if you like, practically aristocratic, though morally democratic; since this aristocracy is answerable to the people through the electoral system, it is properly characterizable as an elective aristocracy.

This view of Mill and Rousseau as defenders of the same system of elective aristocracy will strike many readers as suspect. For there is one large contrast between them which it does not take into account. Mill's treatise is entitled *Considerations on Representative Government*; like his father, Mill regarded representative institutions as one of the most important political inventions of the modern world. They bridged the gap between our desire to have the same grip on our governors as the citizens of Athens and Rome had on theirs and our sense that large, complex, pluralistic societies simply could not put the clock back and adopt the institutions of the city state.[14] But Rousseau denies that the people can have representatives:

The deputies of the people, therefore, are not and cannot be its representatives: they are merely its stewards and can carry through no definitive acts. Every law which the people has not ratified in person is null and void – is, in fact, not a law. The people of England regards itself as free; but it is grossly mistaken; it is free only during the election of members of parliament. As soon as they are elected, slavery overtakes it and it is nothing.[15]

The premise from which he deduces this result is that

Sovereignty . . . cannot be represented; it lies essentially in the general will and will not admit of representation: it is either the same, or other; there is no intermediate possibility.[16]

The reply to this appears between the lines in what follows. The outline of the answer, however, is simple enough. There is a strong case to be made on Rousseau's side, and one which is all the stronger if we insist on taking his talk of 'the will' quite seriously and literally. For then it must be true that no law is law – that is, it has no morally binding force – except to those who have actually assented to it. *My* assent cannot be given by anyone other than *me*; the community's assent cannot be given by any body other than the community. To this it might be replied that Rousseau is by no means clear in his use of the concept of the will, and that little in the way of popular participation is required for the general will to be exercised. Until we have become clearer about the role of deliberative assemblies in Rousseau's scheme, we cannot be sure that he and Mill are wholly at odds, since we cannot be sure that what Rousseau says cannot be represented is anything that Mill thinks *can* be. However, it is time to turn to the general problems of rights-based and utilitarian theories of democracy in order to show how this problem arises.

                                        I

A rights-based theory of democracy must be concerned above all else with questions of legitimacy and authority rather than with consequentialist questions. That is, a defence of democratic institutions in terms of rights must claim that a democratic government is uniquely legitimate rather than that a democratic government is more likely than any other kind of government to maximize utility. That this *is* the central issue for democratic theories founded on a doctrine of rights emerges both where writers think they *can* show that democratic governments are legitimate and where they despair of doing so. Thus, Professor Dworkin derives the legitimacy of the liberal democratic state from our fundamental right to be treated with 'equal concern and respect';[17] and Professor Wolff, though he fears that the anarchist has the last word and that *no* government is legitimate, thinks that only 'unanimous direct democracy' is compatible with individual moral autonomy.[18] We shall see a little later that Rousseau *does* think that there is something special about democracy, but not that it is the only legitimate government – indeed, we shall see that Rousseau thinks that governments are legitimate or illegitimate only at second hand. What is legitimate or not is the legislative power and its laws. This is enough to ensure that Rousseau is in the mainstream of the argument connecting a concern for rights and the defence of democracy, since the question we can frame is this: 'Under what conditions can I be obliged to obey laws, consistently with my natural right to perfect freedom?'

The obvious reply to this is that laws are (morally) obliging if they are made by a person or a procedure – or by persons acting under the terms of a procedure – which we have ourselves authorized. Each person starts with the right to act as he chooses, subject only to not infringing that right in others – infringing that right in others would presuppose that we already possessed the right to dictate how others should act, and the whole point of a natural rights theory is to deny that such a right exists by nature. If we all possess authority over ourselves and over nobody else, political authority must be the result of compact or quasi-compact. If authority over me exists only by grant from me, the binding force of law and the authority of those who make it must be traced back to my consent. To the extent that democracy is a form of polity in which either the laws, or the power to make laws, are assented to by everyone, democracy is uniquely legitimate.

It is clear that Rousseau began from these premises: 'Since man has no natural authority over his fellow, and force creates no right, we must conclude that conventions form the basis of all legitimate authority among men.'[19] *Making* others do what we wish is infinitely far from having the right that they should do as we say, and Rousseau mocks writers like Hobbes and Grotius who try to derive authority from *de facto* power. But the question which the natural rights theorist faces is this: '*How* do we consent, and to *what*?' On the face of it, the answer must be that first we consent to there being a political community of which we are members – in effect, there is a club and we are its members bound by its rules. The sense in which what there is is not a state, or possesses no sovereign, if we do not all consent seems to be only that a political community which has *de facto* control over those within a given territory can treat as *members* only those who have consented to its authority over them; others under its control may be treated as harmless strangers or, if necessary, as enemies. Only members stand in relations with the community which raise questions of legitimacy. It is not that my refusal to recognize the British state, say, automatically deprives it of legitimacy; but it does mean that its dealings with *me* do not raise questions of legitimacy. However it treats me, I cannot complain that its acts are *ultra vires*. This does not mean that it has no moral obligations towards me at all, though. It has duties under the law of nature, but not under the laws of its own constitution.

Thus far, we might find ourselves in the company of Hobbes and Locke as much as of Rousseau; and we should find ourselves in the company of untutored common sense, too. States are artificial legal communities constituted by the allegiance of their members. Laws are morally binding on all those and only those who accept the state's authority; or, to put it more stringently, only those who accept the state's authority can *treat its say-so* as a sufficient reason to regard its laws as morally binding. Others must look to other considerations.[20] That the state does not in practice enquire into the consents of those to whom it applies its laws is easily explained; so long as the laws are required for the safety and well-being of the people, it is right to insist that all those whose obedience is needed should obey them. To require non-consenters to obey is not tyrannical; indeed, it is a mild demand, since the state could without displaying a merely neurotic fear of subversion claim that the absence of their consents makes it reasonable to suspect that they will evade the law when they can and makes it reasonable to impose fiercer penalties and a narrower scrutiny on them than on citizens.[21]

None of this, however, yields the conclusion that the only legitimate form of government is democracy. Indeed, since we have been keeping company with Hobbes, it seems that the argument thus far must legitimate absolute monarchy as readily as democracy.[22] The way in which it does so is clear enough; once we have consented to there being a state, the positive constitution of that state is whatever we unanimously declare it to be, and the law thereafter is whatever the constitution entitles us to call law. Thus, if we agree to be one political community and lay down that whatever the king-in-parliament declares to be law *is* law, thereafter we are morally bound to take as the rule of our actions whatever the king-in-parliament lays down.[23] If we are to tie consent to democracy in the required fashion, we need some way of avoiding these Hobbesian conclusions. The obvious way to do this is to deny that we can hand over the power to make law in such a comprehensive way. That is, we must deny that we can renounce in perpetuity the right to decide whether a law is legitimate; Hobbes, in effect, claims that once we have authorized the sovereign to make law, whatever he makes is genuinely and bindingly law. The test for the legitimacy of law is the test for the legitimacy of the lawmaker; if we made him sovereign by our consents, he is and remains sovereign. Rousseau's view, the view of anyone who wants to argue for something other than an absolute monarchy, is that the people must ultimately be sovereign; even if there is a temporary dictatorship, its authority exists only by concession and the concession is revocable.[24] The grounds for this view are to be found in the initial question; only if people are responsible moral agents can there be any point in asking whether governments are legitimate and their laws morally compelling. Hobbes' answer destroys the point of the question by asserting that people were *once* able to legitimate a government but that in doing so they lost the power to do so again. But *ex hypothesi*, it is just because we *cannot* have lost that power that we are able to ask the question.

So we reach the position that some sort of continuing consent to law is required; to put it more dismayingly, we reach the position that some way of preserving unanimous support for the laws is required.[25] This conclusion is dismaying, since it seems unlikely that we could operate anything but the smallest and simplest of groups on a consensual basis like this. It is this which leads Professor Wolff to concede the case to the anarchist; if these are the requirements of legitimate legislation, they cannot be met.[26] There is perhaps more room for manoeuvre than he supposes, however. At all events, what seems to connect democracy and unanimity is an interpretation of the nature of majority voting which is owed to Rousseau, and which is not obviously fallacious.

Law requires the continuing consent of every member of a community if it is to be valid law. This is not, of course, to say that laws must be proposed by everyone, but that they must be assented to by everyone. We may leave their preparation to a small number of people, but we cannot leave their ratification to this small number; law is the command of the general will, and unless ratified by the general will it is invalid.[27] The general will is by definition one will and not several, so the dictates of the general will cannot be anything other than unanimous; the interesting question is then what procedures reveal the dictates of the general will. If it can be argued that voting procedures of the sort we normally associate with democracy do, uniquely, reveal the general will, we may then claim that we have reconciled the demand for unanimity with the exigencies of everyday life. Since I do not think that Rousseau was an unequivocal or wholehearted democrat at all, I do not want to suggest that the argument I offer now is completely his or the only argument he offers. As I shall show later, Rousseau's twin tests for the general will – voting on the one hand and the tendency of the legislation in question to promote the general interest on the other – pull in different directions. But there is an argument of a respectable sort to connect majority voting, unanimity and the criteria for legitimacy, and it owes something to him.

The voting test is a procedural test, hence its connection with the individual's will. What we suppose is that individuals all will their continuing membership of a political community founded to protect everyone's interests. They need a procedure to take decisions about what is in everyone's interests; the question is what it is to be. It is important to stress that what everyone votes on is the question of what will promote the interests of everyone; only if everyone votes on that question can we accept that where things go badly this will be the result of ignorance rather than wickedness.[28]

What makes majority voting attractive is this. If we ask questions like, 'What penalties for murder, fraud or burglary would be in the general interest?' we should be unlikely to achieve unanimity. People who genuinely try to answer such questions with an eye to the welfare of everybody and not just of themselves will still disagree with one another. We expect, however, that although there will be nothing close to unanimity at this first stage, the decision to which the community, or the assembly, comes at this point will subsequently receive unanimous support. Once the decision has been taken, the question each person asks himself is no longer what he or she independently thinks is for the best, but whether he or she should support the measures decided on. In short, if we are eager to achieve unanimity, what we adopt is a majoritarian procedure for taking what we might call provisional or prima facie decisions, although what would make them really binding was that they were, or could properly be, endorsed unanimously. But the claims of the procedure depend on our belief that the procedure has been used properly, that is, that those who were in the majority were attempting to answer the right question in a disinterested spirit.

If we are to remain at the level of an argument from procedure, we must claim that what majority voting achieves is the giving to each voice its fair and equal share in determining the outcome. I have *no* right to use any procedure whatever to try to grab a greater share of the general prosperity for myself; that is, I have no right to treat voting as a kind of moderated fight in which we are all out for what we can get for ourselves. It is only if I am trying to answer the right question that I can claim that my moral standing is impugned if my view is not taken exactly as seriously as that of anyone else. But if I am asking the right question, then my opinion must carry as much weight as anyone else's. It is worth noticing that on one interpretation this argument is an argument *against* seeking unanimity; though on another, unanimity retains its attractions. That is, if our aim was to give each person equal influence on an outcome, anything other than simple majority voting seems to give an unfair degree of influence to the minority.[29] At its extreme, a unanimity rule would mean that the one person whose consent was necessary for a law to pass could exercise over its passage as much power as the whole of the rest of the society. If we are engaged in a rather different enterprise, something other than a simple majority is more defensible. If voting is like voting by members of a jury, the pressures for something better than a bare majority become obvious. The point of demanding something better than simple majority is partly that if there is a question with a genuine answer being asked, we are more likely to find an overwhelming majority in the right than a bare majority; even if we are somewhat sceptical about the objectivity of the answer we are looking for, an overwhelming majority among *disinterested* voters is morally persuasive. If we are in a tiny minority, and we trust the serious intentions of the majority, we are likely to agree that the odds against our being right are so high that we must go along with the majority view.[30]

It is time to turn to a utilitarian view of these issues; but I must draw attention to what I have left dangling here. In Rousseau's employment of an argument much like the one I have just sketched, the question which voters are to ask is not exactly whether 'the people approves or rejects the proposal, but whether it is in accordance with the general will, which is their will'.[31] Because the general will is an objective entity, the connection between voting and the general will is not the connection of procedural fairness we might infer from much of the above; it could be argued that a measure manifestly in the general interest is manifestly required by the general will, and that voting is at best the most reliable way of discovering whether something is in the general interest. There may well be other means, and if they are reliable enough, democratic procedures lose their peculiar attractions. It is on this point that we shall ultimately have to rely to show what departures from both democracy and a strictly rights-based theory of government Rousseau makes.

The argument from utility to democracy is briefer; it is essentially an *external* argument in the sense that there is no attempt to connect the legitimacy of a government with its possessing a democratic constitution. Indeed, in my view, utilitarian political theory has no place for the notion of legitimacy, strictly speaking. Whether a government is the lawful government of a territory is a factual question, that of whether it gets a habitual obedience from the overwhelming bulk of the population of that territory. A person in that territory knows which body of persons possesses sovereignty by applying that test. For himself, he has to make up his own mind whether and in what way the lawfulness of the government affects his duty to obey the laws it promulgates. A good utilitarian always seeks only one thing, which is the maximizing of the general utility, and in the light of that he makes up his mind how much claim on him the laws have. If he is a twentieth-century utilitarian and has been reading R.M. Hare, he will be scrupulous about not taking unfair advantage of other people's compliance with the law, too.[32] But the existence of government is a fact external to the *concept* of duty with which he works.

What, then, justifies democratic government? The answer is that only a government which is answerable to the whole population through some such device as periodic elections can be relied on to govern in the general interest and not in the interests of the members of the government alone.[33] A crude version of this doctrine is argued in James Mill's *Essay on Government*. Its premises are that each of us needs security of person and property to have either the prospect of happiness for ourselves or an incentive to work and co-operate with others. This requires the creation of government, to organize the power to suppress those who would otherwise invade the persons and properties of the rest of us. The creation of government, however, poses a problem just as it solves one; since we need government to fend off the results of selfishness, what is to stop those who possess the power of government from employing it to exploit their subjects? James Mill's answer is that since only power can check power, the only acceptable form of government is one where the community has the power to dismiss its rulers.[34] The way to do this in a modern society is by electing representatives who may be turned out if they govern us badly.

In this account of democracy, as much as in a rights-based theory, the acceptability of the people's vote as a way of determining policy and law depends upon everyone casting his vote with an eye to the interest of the public, rather than with an eye to his own private interest.[35] There is, of course, a decided difficulty about this requirement, at any rate in the context of James Mill's *Essay*. The premises which make democracy necessary appear to make it inconceivable – we must have democracy, because we cannot trust our rulers to govern disinterestedly, but democracy is only acceptable if we can trust the voters to vote disinterestedly. On the face of it, if virtuous voters are obtainable, we might hope for virtuous rulers, and if we may not do so, it suggests that virtuous voters are not obtainable.

James Mill's reply to this is obscure, but in essence it amounts to supposing that the people at large do not suffer from the same temptations as their rulers; power corrupts, rather than human nature. However, what this all suggests is something quite important. For James Mill, the value of democracy is that it secures that the government is answerable to a body whose interests are identical with the general interest. But, we can now draw two inferences from this. The first is that if we were able to find a government which, for reasons other than the restraints imposed by elections, pursued the general interest, it would be as good as a democratic government. The implications for the British in India hardly need to be spelled out.[36] The other is that we do not need anything like *universal* suffrage to achieve the effects James Mill wants. So long as the electoral body is large enough to stop 'sinister interests' gaining too much influence, it is large enough to ensure that its interests and the general interest agree. It is from this observation that James Mill drew his notorious inference that women could safely be left off the electoral rolls, as could young men (those under 40, that is), and the propertyless.[37] The point is simple enough; on the utilitarian view governments exist to protect our interests, and so long as our interests are protected we can have no reason to participate in government. Because questions of legitimacy are not at issue, there is no pressure to ensure that each person has a voice in making decisions; because outcomes, assessed by the principle of utility, are all that is at issue, procedural issues are not directly relevant, and individuals are not supposed to be concerned about the connection between outcomes and their own consents.

II

I began by saying that Rousseau and Mill threatened to upset my account of
the connection between rights and democracy and utility and democracy. I
now turn to showing that threat – in essence by showing Rousseau as a
nostalgic republican, but less of a democrat than I first suggested, and by
showing Mill as more of a democrat and more concerned to argue that
democracy has special claims on our allegiance than I have hitherto suggested
that utilitarian theory allows.

Rousseau has already been quoted to the effect that elective aristocracy is
the best form of government, and yet I have also invoked him to argue that a
writer obsessed, as he was, with questions of legitimacy is pushed towards
defending democracy. Now, one thing that is worth noticing is that Rousseau
is explicit that *government* is not founded on a contract, though the
legitimacy of law is.[38] What Rousseau has in mind is that there is no pact of
obedience and protection between subject and ruler; rather the sovereign
legislates as to the form of the government, and then those who are to fill the
appropriate niches are chosen.[39] Rousseau is much exercised by the problem
of reconciling the choice of personnel with what he has earlier said about the
generality of law and the requirement that laws should not refer to particular
persons; and this gives democracy one rather peculiar claim to be special: 'It
is, indeed, the peculiar advantage of democratic government that it can be
established in actuality by a simple act of the general will. Subsequently, this
provisional government remains in power, if this form is adopted, or else
establishes in the name of the sovereign the government that is prescribed
law; and thus the whole proceeding is regular.'[40] That is, all that could be the
object of an acceptably general law is 'that there should be a government of
such and such a form'; appointment to office is a governmental act, and we
seem to face the paradox that we need a government *in* existence to bring a
government *into* existence. In the unique case of a democratic form of
government the people constitutes itself the government in the act of deciding
that there should be a government of that form. Rousseau thinks there is
nothing extraordinary about the people switching from legislation to
executive action, and cites the way in which the House of Commons can act
as a committee of the whole house and then report back to itself.[41]

The upshot of this, though, is that although democracy occupies a special
place, other forms of government may be constituted as legitimately as it; all
governments get their legitimacy by grant from the people, but it is a matter
of prudential calculation what sort of government to create by such a grant of
authority. At this point, Rousseau is actively hostile to democracy, for
democracy is more riven with factions than any other form of government,
demands tremendous public spirit and self-control in its citizens, and will

only work if the state is small, economic equality maintained, and issues kept simple so that the ordinary citizen can understand them, vote on them, and administer the laws he has helped to make. These observations are in line with the claims made by Montesquieu and others. They suggest that for all practical purposes the best form of government is elective aristocracy; although Rousseau follows Montesquieu in thinking that large countries need monarchs, and that large countries with hot climates are all but doomed to despotic governments, it seems that there is *some* scope for choice in constitution building, and that where there is, elective aristocracy is what is wanted.[42]

This raises the question of the role of the people under such a regime. It is unclear to me how we should integrate Rousseau's remarks about the Roman Republic into the main argument of the *Social Contract*; however, I suppose that we should not simply leave Rousseau's arguments about legitimacy and his borrowings from Machiavelli's *Discorsi* to jangle against each other. If not, we reach, I think, the following view. Republican governments are the best form of government; they maximize the number of citizens, and they achieve liberty. That is, they are ruled by law, not by the whim of one man or one class; and they are ruled by their *own* laws. Moreover, their laws are the reflection of the general will. Now, in saying this, we are not claiming that the ordinary man plays an active political role; we are not claiming that he is to initiate legislation, or take part in discussions of the merits of legislation; nor are we arguing for *la carrière ouverte aux talents*, for social mobility or for an open, democratic society in the twentieth-century sense.[43] The general will is realized, less because of what anyone wills than because the society is one with a clearly defined common interest, and because those who wield the initiative do so in the interests of the whole society and not of themselves alone. Rousseau's talk of the will is slightly deceptive – or, perhaps, 'will' is not an altogether apt rendering of *volonté*. At all events, a society possesses a *volonté générale*, not in virtue of acts of the will of individuals, but in virtue of being a coherent community with enough shared interests to enable it to function. It follows that a law which is in the interests of all members of the society, treating all of them fairly, in accordance with policies which would make the average person as happy as possible over the long run, is what the general will requires. Whether we have the wit to see it is a separate question.[44]

This raises the obvious question of why republican Rome seems almost uniquely desirable as a political solution. The answer is that the system of mutual checks, the place allowed for leadership, the happy match of the economic and political circumstances of the country, and the high state of citizen morale all conspired together to ensure that for a very long time at least the government did invariably act in the general interest. The people played their proper role in such a system; they acted as a check upon corruption.[45] For the people to play this role they needed to be properly organized, too: 'it is impossible to be too careful to observe, in all such cases, all the formalities necessary to distinguish a regular and legitimate act from a seditious tumult . . .'[46] The Roman people could play their role of checking the ambitions of their rulers only because they were provided with wise leadership. Given wise leadership, the people at large are more or less infallible in their opposition to corruption, since they do not have the ambitions that would lead them to try to make alliances to subvert the constitution, and if affairs are simple, their lack of sophistication is not likely to lead them into being bamboozled. Indeed, Rousseau suggests that the unsophisticated are likely to see through wiles which would take in the educated.[47]

Republican Rome was not a democracy; it was a mixed popular government, in which birth and wealth were given advantages, but not so many advantages that a few rich men could outvote the rest of the population. It was not a democracy in twentieth-century terms, or in Rousseau's. There was no commitment to formal political equality, no thought that formal civil rights needed to be complemented by equality of opportunity or 'welfare rights'. It was a government in which the people played an indispensable but relatively passive role. Whether it was a government which has any twentieth-century analogy or any twentieth-century message is arguable. On the whole, admirers of it are likely to stress what we have lost rather than to suggest how we might recapture it; and since Robespierre most commentators have taken a cautious view of the prospects for a revival of republican virtue.[48] The only points I want to emphasize, however, are these: Rousseau's conception of the general will appears not to require democracy, and if we could show that the average citizen of the modern state is not hopelessly corrupted by affluence, his political passivity need not alarm Rousseau. The absence of occasions for plebiscitary endorsement of the constitution might do so; but if we could display a system of checks and balances working with tolerable efficiency, we might find Rousseau prepared to accept more of the modern state than we should expect at first sight.

If Rousseau is less of a democrat than my initial account of rights-based defences of democracy suggested that he ought to be, J.S. Mill turns out to be rather more of a democrat than my account of the relatively loose connection between utilitarianism and democracy suggested he ought to be. I do not wish to deny that there are strongly aristocratic strains in *Representative Government*; that some men and women are simply *better* than others is not a proposition Mill flinches from. What I want to suggest is that Mill does what I denied that utilitarians could plausibly do – that is to take seriously the thought that democratic governments are uniquely legitimate.

The primary claim made for representative government by Mill is that it is the most progressive form of government; it makes more demands on its citizens than any other, and these demands are educative. It makes as much use as possible of existing abilities and promotes as much as possible the development of new abilities. On the face of it, this is a utilitarian argument, even if one which stresses the development of character as much as the satisfaction of more obvious interests. But it is a utilitarian argument which makes the possession of a capacity for self-government central.

Thus, if we turn to Mill's discussion of benevolent despotism, we find Mill arguing that it 'is a radical and most pernicious misconception of what good government is' to suppose that 'if a good despot could be ensured, despotic monarchy would be the best form of government'.[49] On the contrary, says Mill, a good despot would simply deprive his subjects of energy, intelligence and public spirit; and a mild despot would prepare the way for a less mild one by making his subjects too passive to resist. To suppose that a good despot might preserve the spirit which democracy produces is incoherent; it can only be done by giving people the right to discuss public issues, to organize, protest and all the rest. This, then, raises the question of whose will is to prevail if the despot and public opinion are at odds; if public opinion prevails, we have an inadequate constitutional monarchy, and if not, we have a sham which cannot achieve the advantages of a government whose subjects enjoy genuine liberty.[50]

Can there be circumstances in which democracy is not a good thing? For Mill the answer is certainly yes; quite apart from temporary dictatorships in advanced societies, 'despotism is a legitimate mode of government in dealing with barbarians, provided the end be their improvement, and the means justified by actually effecting that end'.[51] But when people are sufficiently advanced to be able to manage their affairs by discussion between free and equal citizens, then only one form of government is legitimate. The arguments in favour of forms of government of a non-democratic kind presuppose that democratic governments have a special status; all other forms of government are warranted to the extent that they inculcate the necessary self-discipline, public spirit, good order and the rest to allow democracy to operate. The argument was employed at its clearest when Mill set out to justify the East India Company's management of Indian affairs; the Company's record, said Mill, was one of *improvement*. He freely admitted that it was a despotic government in that it was neither chosen by the Indian people nor directly answerable to them. He justified this by a principle which offered a new and different version of a 'good despot' from that discussed above; the East India Company itself ran on the principles which ought to animate a democracy – answerability and antagonism of opinions – but in the Indian context its role was to put itself out of business by teaching its Indian subjects how to govern themselves.[52] Once India *could* practise self-government, the East India Company's rule would be illegitimate.

Representative government, then, is defended on the grounds that it is self-government; persons at a certain level in human development are, essentially, sovereign agents, who have a right to govern themselves and whose rights are violated when they are kept in leading-strings any longer than necessary. The same message is reiterated in many of Mill's essays; the essay on *The Subjection of Women* is a long argument to the effect that the moral equality of women and men means that women must enjoy the same legal and political liberties as men. Moreover, since the argument relies on the assumption that no people which has attained liberty will sell it at any price, the conclusion must be that a society in which men and women are equal will also be one in which every man and woman will have an equal vote in political matters.[53] In *The Principles of Political Economy*, workers' control emerges as the only form of industrial organization compatible with the modern workers' striving after citizenship and self-government. There may in future be some peculiarly feeble or obtuse labourers who will be content to work for a capitalist employer, but for the most part, assumes Mill, self-respect will forbid it.[54] This is consistent with, indeed it rests on, Mill's belief in the superiority of some men and women to their fellows. The point, rather, is that self-respecting men and women will obey those whom they choose to govern them, especially since they will choose them on the ground of their superior ability to see what the general interest requires, or their superior sense of where progress lies; they will not obey those who lay claim to authority on grounds of birth or wealth.[55] A final point which needs to be brought into the account is that Mill thinks of representative government as above all else government by discussion. Conflicting opinions must be sought and argued through; a constant lively questioning of what is done is what lies between a genuine representative democracy and the tyranny of the majority.[56]

If this is an accurate account of Mill it strongly suggests that democracy is not only a good form of government inasmuch as it secures the compliance of governments to the people's wishes, but that it is a quite special form of government, as being uniquely one in which individuals are treated as fully responsible adults, with duties to their country, and rights to the whole range of civil and political liberties. Only in such a system can they rightly feel that the government is *their* government.[57]

III

I began by admitting that Mill and Rousseau would provide a certain amount of trouble for my account of the differences between rights-based and utilitarian defences of democracy; for, on my account of it, rights-based theories should be concerned with legitimacy rather than consequences, democracy should be defended as uniquely legitimate, and other forms of government accepted, if at all, very much as a *pis aller*. Rousseau, it goes without saying, is a rights theorist. Conversely, utilitarian theories may give us good consequentialist grounds for approving of democracy, but there is no attempt to argue that democratic procedures are themselves special for anything other than consequentialist reasons. J.S. Mill, it goes without saying, is a utilitarian. Yet Rousseau seems to prefer something other than democracy; Mill seems to be more deeply committed to democratic procedures than pure utility warrants. Either they employ their own moral schemes oddly, or I have misrepresented the resources of the two theories.

The answer to this challenge is not altogether simple, but in essence it involves pointing to the utilitarian and prudential elements in Rousseau's theory of government and to the role of individual rights in Mill's utilitarianism. Some of this has been done already, but we can now summarize the results. So far as Rousseau is concerned, we have to bear two things in mind, the difference between the Sovereign and the government on the one hand, and the twofold nature of the general will on the other. The nature of sovereignty is the nature of law, and Rousseau says firmly that 'I therefore give the name "Republic" to every state that is governed by laws, no matter what the form of its administration may be; for only in such cases does the public interest govern and the res publica rank as a reality. Every legitimate government is republican.'[58] In this sense, a constitutional monarchy is a republican form of government, but an absolute monarchy not. If a state is governed by laws, so that there is nowhere in it merely personal power, it is for Rousseau a republican government, and it can appeal to the legitimacy of its authority in dealing with its subjects.

Governments, therefore, are merely ministers of the law, creatures of the constitution; we seem to have a doctrine which is what one might call a constrained version of Hobbes. The constitution is legitimate if we all consent to it; the government exercises legitimate power if it is operated in accordance with the constitution; the difference between this doctrine and Hobbes's is that the constitution cannot give absolute, arbitrary and irrevocable power to anyone. But so long as the government is governed by a constitution, it need not be democratic in form. Moreover, Rousseau's account of why government is instituted at all is heavily indebted to the utilitarianism underlying Hobbes's account. Individuals have conflicting interests, and they have shared interests; conflicts of interest make government necessary, shared interests make government possible.[59] Competing traders have conflicting interests in the outcome of their competition; they share an interest in the maintenance of order and the administration of a sensible system of property law. So long as the law is concerned with their common interests and not concerned to favour one against the other, the law articulates their common will. Legitimate governments are those which promote the welfare of the anonymous man. Rousseau's emphasis on equality and simplicity can be seen as ways of uniting a broadly utilitarian goal with individual commitment; a government which favours nobody, sacrifices nobody to anyone else, and operates in a generally benevolent way will, in the long run, do as much as it can for the average man. But a society in which there are great inequalities is one in which few people will have a close identification with the average man. This is why Rousseau's desire for a good deal of uniformity is not *only*, even if it is quite largely, a nostalgic and sentimental plea for the ancient Romans.

Now, if it is true in addition that what makes the general will a general will is not so much the number of people who will it as the object to which it is directed, we come close to saying that a government which operates according to the rule of law, and is concerned always to promote the welfare of all its subjects to the extent that it can do so without sacrificing any of them to the rest, *is* a legitimate government. Whether its form is democratic or aristocratic or even monarchical is not essential; what it aims at and how it does it is essential. This, to be sure, weakens the contractual element in Rousseau's theory to the point where it is equivalent to Kant's understanding of the social contract:

It is in fact merely an idea of reason, which nonetheless has undoubted practical reality; for it can oblige every legislator to frame his laws in such a way that they could have been produced by the united will of the whole nation, and to regard each subject, in so far as he can claim citizenship, as if he had consented within the general will. This is the test of the rightfulness of every public law. For if the law is such that a whole people could not *possibly* agree to it, it is unjust.[60]

What we are left with is the hypothetical contract, an intellectual device which reconciles utility and justice by encouraging us to ask whether legislation is such that we should have assented to it in ignorance of how it would affect us individually; the pursuit of the general welfare on terms fair to all is what ought to emerge from such a thought-experiment.[61] To the extent that there is still in Rousseau's work a decided favouring of something more participatory than this, it comes, not from the bare argument from legitimacy, nor from the analysis of the concept of a general will, but from a commitment to achieve the civic liberty of the classical republics rather than from a commitment to have a republican – that is, a constitutional – regime at all.[62] As a defender of democracy in the modern world, Rousseau would need to be taken seriously but cautiously.

The case of Mill is rather different. For Mill's defence of representative government raises, rather, the question of whether he does not slip from utilitarian to rights-based arguments, or more generally, whether he does not tailor his utilitarianism to make democracy special – in particular, by crediting people with a desire for self-government and improvement which means that democratic politics produces a special degree of utility. There is no short answer to this question. Moreover, it is a question which bears as much upon the understanding of *On Liberty* as on the understanding of *Representative Government*. All the same, something along the following lines seems to catch the sense of what Mill requires. To argue from what he terms 'abstract right' would commit us to a doctrine about legitimate authority which invoked the idea of a social contract, and such an idea is unhelpful.[63] All the same, even if societies are not founded on a contract, the scope of legitimate authority may be understood as if they were; what men and women would not rationally contract into cannot be a legitimate form of authority. Employed as it is employed in *On Liberty*, this subverts the 'tyranny of the majority' by insisting that however social rules are made, there are some things they cannot be made about at all. And this in turn is a way of discovering what rights people ought to have recognized.[64] The difficulty with this argument is obviously that it seems to rest on something more than utility alone, since what it appears to invoke is something closer to the *injustice* rather than the disutility of ignoring some voices in the determination of the law. In many places in his work, Mill lays it down as an axiom that modern society is impossible except on terms of equality. This, of course, gives us a rights-based account of why the burden of proof now rests with those who wish to *limit* voting rights, or to restrict access to office; what is less clear is that it gives us a utilitarian account.[65]

At this point, all one can do is point out that Mill's utilitarianism possesses an unusual but not unpersuasive property, that of giving an account of the conditions under which committed utilitarians would recognize one another as possessing rights which no utilitarian considerations ought to override. In essence, we can admit both the suggestions offered above – that Mill appeals to consideration of rights and legitimacy, and that his utilitarian arguments presuppose something close to a desire for self-government among those whose welfare is at issue – but deny that this amounts to a weakening of his case. For his case would be that what we might call the tailoring of his account of utilitarianism to justify democracy is better described as a discovery about the full resources of the doctrine of utility. The simpler version of utilitarianism espoused by James Mill would have little room for the thought that democracy is uniquely legitimate, and its justification of democracy would be external and consequentialist alone, in the way we saw before. A more developed utilitarianism has a more complex view of the individual and his rights and a more elaborate view of what motivations he acquires in the appropriate political environment.

I hope, to sum up, that this at any rate suggests that the claim that rights-based defences of democracy are distinctive, partially non-consequentialist, and concerned with legitimacy, while utilitarian defences are the reverse, survives the examples of Mill and Rousseau. For, on my view of it, each employs the language of individual rights in a context where legitimacy is at issue, and where democracy emerges as a special solution to problems of legitimacy, and each allows utilitarian considerations to make a difference to what institutional arrangements we practise – though they do so in very different ways, since it remains true that Rousseau's ethics are fundamentally the ethics of natural right and Mill's are fundamentally utilitarian. I shall not try to decide whether they are or are not unequivocal democrats, nor whether their defences of citizenship have an obvious purchase on our present anxieties; I hope, indeed, that I have shown how rash it would be to plump for simple answers and how cautious we must be in invoking the shades of Mill and Rousseau in a twentieth-century context.

5

'Classical' images of democracy in America: Madison and Tocqueville

RICHARD W. KROUSE

Contemporary discussions of democracy, both by elite theorists and their participatory critics, often refer to a single, static body of 'classical' democratic theory. By examining two 'classical' images of the American polity, James Madison's contributions to the *Federalist* and Alexis de Tocqueville's *Democracy in America*, this essay will attempt to demonstrate that classical democratic theory is not single and static but diverse and discontinuous and that 'the' classical theory was in fact revised several times and in several ways prior to the advent (with Schumpeter *et al.*) of self-styled contemporary modes of revisionist democratic theory.

The point of departure for this analysis will be the classical republican, or 'civic humanist', concept of democracy,[1] specifically as articulated by Montesquieu, since Madison and Tocqueville both construct their theories of democratic republicanism by way of a more or less explicit dialogue with his theories. Madisonian republicanism breaks sharply with this traditional understanding, whereas Tocqueville finds in American democracy the means of adapting classical democratic republicanism to the circumstances of modern politics and society. In revising a prior 'classical' understanding, the *Federalist* and *Democracy in America* enunciate two sharply competing conceptions of the nature, principle, and preconditions of a democratic republic – two sharply competing 'classical theories of democracy'.

Each of these competing classical visions bears a strong affinity to one of the two major strains, elitist and participatory, in contemporary democratic theory. Hence, we can illuminate our understanding of contemporary theories of democracy through a fuller understanding of the diversity and discontinuity of actual 'classical' theories, and the parallels (usually unacknowledged) linking these theories with their contemporary descendants.

I Montesquieu: classical republicanism versus modern history

According to Montesquieu, each of the three major types of political regime – republic, monarchy, and despotism – possesses a distinctive *nature* and a distinctive *principle*. The nature of a regime is defined by two variables: the number of individuals holding sovereign power, and the manner in which it is exercised. The principle of a regime is its spring of action, the human passion driving it forward. To sustain its distinctive nature and principle, each form of regime must meet certain social preconditions.

Virtuous republics

Classified by its nature, a democratic republic is for Montesquieu a regime in which the many, the demos, hold sovereign power and in which citizens participate *directly* in deliberative and judicial functions, as in the assemblies and courts of the ancient city-state.[2] Direct democracy, or participatory republicanism, is in Montesquieu's view compatible with the preservation of wise and virtuous leadership (in the form of elected magistrates and a senate or council composed of the regime's leading citizens), but its constitutive feature remains the investment of sovereign authority in a community of participating citizens.

The principle of democratic republicanism is civic virtue, a passionate love of the republic and the strict subordination of private and particular interests to its common good or general will. Where the people rule themselves, the repression and restraint required by civil society must of necessity be *self*-repression and *self*-restraint.

The democratic republic, therefore, is for Montesquieu a difficult and demanding form of rule, imposing singular restraints upon natural selfishness. Hence it must satisfy several spartan preconditions: a comprehensive and continuing process of political education, including both the formal schooling of the young and ongoing public supervision of private manners and morals (for example, institutions of censorship, civil religion, sumptuary laws, strong authority distinctions in society); the equality-in-frugality of a (normally) rural-agrarian society and economy, to insure the expenditure of passions upon public objects; and a state of small territorial scale, to permit the direct citizen participation and intimate social life necessary to support civic virtue and republican political education. Only under these conditions of cultural consensus and social homogeneity will the individual subordinate his selfish impulses to the general will and participate in the life of the political community, and only then will the republic escape the corruption that constantly threatens its nature and principle.[3]

Though Montesquieu felt genuine (if ambivalent) admiration for the ancient republic, he clearly viewed the virtuous republic as an anachronistic political form, a phenomenon of the classical past increasingly irrelevant to modern man.[4] The democratic republic requires active citizenship and the severe repression of private interests: the modern world, in Montesquieu's eyes, offers the abdication of citizenship and the aggressive pursuit of private interest. The democratic republic requires smallness, a frugal equality, and austere civic discipline: modernity offers centralized, bureaucratized nation-states and loose, luxurious commercial societies. Montesquieu does admit the possibility of commercial republics, regimes in which trade, inequality, and wealth are reconciled with civic virtue by a bourgeois protestant ethic. But for a viable modern form of liberal and moderate government, Montesquieu turns to European monarchy and the English variation on that theme.

Glorious monarchies

Monarchy is the good and lawful form of one-man rule – in contrast to despotism, the bad and unlawful form. Classified by its nature, monarchy is a regime in which one man rules according to fixed and fundamental law. The principle of monarchy is honor. Its key precondition is a network of intermediary social structures standing between crown and people.[5]

The principle and precondition of monarchy prevent its degeneration into despotism. Aristocratic honor and *esprit de corps* protect the autonomy of the intermediary bodies, and therewith the fundamental law of the realm. By indulging these passions, men unconsciously advance the public good. Because honor replaces virtue in this way, monarchy need not require great probity of its subjects: 'In monarchies policy effects great things with as little virtue as possible . . . The state subsists independently of the love of our country, of the thirst of true glory, of self-denial, of the sacrifice of our dearest interests, and of all those heroic virtues which we admire in the ancients, and to us are known by tradition.'[6]

This economy of political form suits monarchy peculiarly well to the moral and political climate of the modern age. The virtuous republic depends for its success upon direct citizen participation and a powerful process of political education. Modern monarchy dispenses with these requirements. It permits and even encourages political apathy and privatization, and obviates the need for careful and comprehensive institutions of political education. Nor is monarchy in any way threatened by the centralized nation-state, since it can extend its territorial horizons without threatening the integrity of its nature or principle, or by modern commercial society, since it has nothing to fear from luxury and inequality.[7]

When Montesquieu turns to real-world regimes, he finds his preferred alternative in modern, commercial England – a regime dedicated neither to virtue nor honor, but to liberty. This liberty is secured by the constitutional separation of powers, superimposed upon a *mixed* regime.[8] English government resembles the monarchical type in its continued reliance upon aristocratic privilege and one-man rule, and the republican type in its popular foundation (though with the decisive advantage over the latter of participation through exclusively representative forms).[9] But if in its *nature* English government is a mix or hybrid, in its spirit or animating *principle* it is much closer to the monarchical than to the republican form. English liberty and prosperity rest not upon virtue, which is as deficient as in purely monarchical regimes, but instead upon the uninhibited pursuit of selfish private interest in both polity and economy. England is for Montesquieu the quintessentially modern society – a regime in which avarice and ambition have become the moral foundation of politics, not its deadly enemies.[10]

Hence powerful affinities unite Montesquieu's models of monarchy and of contemporary England, separating both from his democratic republic. Neither requires the republic's civic virtue, active citizen participation, or careful political education. In both regimes an invisible hand is at work: politics transforms separate private interests into a common public good through the institutionalized competition of selfish groups and private factions. The republic rests upon the virtue of citizens; these regimes rely upon the cunning of institutions.

It is clear that Montesquieu finds constitutional monarchy of the European or English variant, however bereft of the shining republican virtues, at least *as* conducive as democracy to moderate and liberal government (perhaps more so).[11] Hence he is able to accept with equanimity the seeming obsolescence of participatory republicanism, and to embrace with enthusiasm the virtues of these modern nonrepublican alternatives – regimes far better adapted to a world of large nation-states and luxurious commercial societies than the small, virtuous democracy.

Faced with a conflict between the demands of his own 'classical democratic theory' and the movement of modern history, then, Montesquieu responds by *rejecting* the 'classical model' of democracy in favor of frankly nonrepublican alternatives. For two competing efforts to *revise* Montesquieu's classical democratic republicanism to accommodate the dispensation of modern history, we turn first to Madison and then to Tocqueville.

II Madison: classical republicanism attenuated

It was the fate of Montesquieu, whose influence upon the political thought of the period was profound, to be quoted by federalist and anti-federalist alike in the debate over the Constitution.[12] James Madison's theory of democratic republicanism, given classic expression in *Federalist* 10, reflects this ambiguous legacy. On the one hand, Madison rejects the full range of assumptions held by Montesquieu concerning the nature, principle, and preconditions of republican rule. On the other hand, Madison's transfigured republicanism reproduces the logic of Montesquieu's theory of monarchy and mixed government: in the process of 'revising' the orthodox or classical republican concepts, Madison produces a theory of popular rule that is in important respects closer in spirit and even substance to Montesquieu's glorious monarchy (or its English variant) than to the virtuous republic.

Republicanism and illusion

To summarize a familiar argument as succinctly as possible: for Madison, the central problem of politics is *faction*.[13] We may remove the causes of faction, or control its effects. But the latent causes of faction, being sown in the nature of man, neither should nor can be removed. Hence we must instead control its effects.

The propensity of a minority faction to sacrifice the interests of the majority can be controlled by the republican principle of popular sovereignty. But the forms of popular rule provide no such automatic restraint upon majority faction: 'to secure the public good and private rights against the danger of such a faction, and at the same time to preserve the spirit and form of popular government, is then the great object to which our inquiries are directed' (p. 132).

It is important to understand how artfully Madison's arguments in *Federalist* 10 are designed to explode the categories of orthodox democratic republicanism; they amount to nothing less than a frontal assault upon that tradition. Classical democratic republicans such as Montesquieu and Rousseau had sought to cope with political faction not by controlling its effects but, through social homogeneity and moral consensus, by *removing its causes*. It is on precisely this point that Madison joins the issue. 'Theoretic politicians, who have patronized this species of government,' he writes in *Federalist* 10, 'have erroneously supposed that by reducing mankind to a perfect equality in their political rights, they would, at the same time, be perfectly equalized and assimilated in their possessions, their opinions, and their passions' (p. 133). Against this position, Madison repeatedly insists upon the inevitability of faction. In an important letter to Jefferson, he writes

We know, however, that no society ever did, or can consist of so homogeneous a mass of Citizens. In the Savage state, indeed, an approach is made towards it, but in that state little or no Government is necessary. In all civilized societies, distinctions are various and unavoidable. A distinction of property results from that very protection which a free Government gives to unequal faculties of acquiring it. There will be rich and poor; creditors and debtors; a landed interest, a monied interest, a mercantile interest, a manufacturing interest . . . . In addition to these natural distinctions, artificial ones will be founded on accidental differences in political, religious, or other opinions, or an attachment to the persons of leading individuals. However erroneous or ridiculous these grounds of dissention and faction may appear to the enlightened statesman or the benevolent philosopher, the bulk of mankind, who are neither statesmen or philosophers, will continue to view them in a different light.[14]

We cannot, then, remove the causes of faction through the creation of a harmonious, homogeneous society in which every citizen has identical interests. But despite Madison's claim, orthodox republicans had never believed it possible to give men 'precisely the same interests.' That is why they emphasized the moral consensus that flows from careful political education in common civic virtues. Madison himself occasionally supported this view, asserting that the virtue and intelligence of the citizenry must be the ultimate foundation of a republic.[15] But the main thrust of his argument is decisively in the opposite direction. Just as Montesquieu consigns republican virtue to the remote past and bases his theory of modern politics upon psychological axioms not dissimilar to those of Hobbes or Hume, so does Madison (and the other authors of the American Constitution) reject civic virtue as a possible foundation for nonoppressive popular government. Madison and the other authors of the second American founding saw American society (and civilized society in general) much as Montesquieu saw Great Britain – a world animated by ceaseless self-interested motion, a restless striving after power and profit. The moral axis of such a political universe is interest, not virtue. If a majority is united by a sinister interest, Madison puts the matter most succinctly in *Federalist* 10, 'we well know that neither moral nor religious motives can be relied on as an adequate control' (p. 133). Neither enlightened attachment to the commonwealth nor civic virtue nor religious scruple will deter such sinister interests: these traditional republican remedies, based upon an erroneous political psychology, are raised only to be dismissed.

Hence we can neither unify society nor rely upon virtuous citizens to transcend their competing interests. We must, instead, construct a polity that accepts as given the ambition and avarice of factions and then works to deflect these selfish impulses in the direction of a common, public good. How, on republican principles, can this be done?

The extended republic: towards a democratic leviathan

We may begin with redefinitions. The genus popular government, according to Madison, can be divided into two species: democracy, which is 'a society consisting of a small number of citizens, who assemble and administer the government in person'; and republic, which is 'a government in which the scheme of representation takes place' (p. 133). This semantic gambit contains an important political move. Earlier theorists, such as Montesquieu, had employed the phrase 'democratic republic' or used the two terms interchangeably; the defining formal-legal characteristic (i.e. the nature) of such a regime, they held, is *direct* citizen participation in sovereign decision. By differentiating between lawful and lawless democratic-republics, they had maintained the feasibility (confirmed by appeal to history) of rule that is *both* participatory *and* legitimate or nonperverted in the Aristotelian sense. By redefining his terms in this way, Madison in effect transfers the full pejorative connotation still, on the whole, carried by the term 'democracy' in eighteenth-century political discourse to all participatory regimes, while assigning the more favorable term 'republic', conversely, to *exclusively* representative forms. By implication, democracy (now always direct) becomes the corrupt or vitiated form of popular rule; republicanism (now always representative), its good or lawful counterpart.[16]

Employing this distinction, Madison argues that democracy is intrinsically incapable of alleviating the mischiefs of faction. In a small, participatory regime, 'A common passion or interest will . . . be felt by a majority of the whole; a communication and concert result from the form of government itself; and there is nothing to check the inducements to sacrifice the weaker party or an obnoxious individual' (p. 133). Just and liberal democracies constitute, as it were, an empty set. All actual regimes of this nature, history testifies, are unjust and illiberal. For classical republican theorists (including Americans writing in this tradition), the popular regimes of classical antiquity are magnificent spectacles of patriotism and civic virtue. For Madison, by contrast, 'such democracies have ever been spectacles of turbulence and contention; have ever been found incompatible with personal security or the rights of property; and have in general been as short in their lives as they have been violent in their deaths' (p. 133).

Fortunately, the cure for these democratic vices can be found in the republican form of popular government. 'The two great points of difference between a democracy and a republic are: first, the delegation of the government, in the latter, to a small number of citizens elected by the rest; secondly, the greater number of citizens, and greater sphere of country, over which the latter may be extended' (pp. 133–4). We may control the effects of majority faction by replacing direct democracy in a small society with representative republicanism in a large society.

Representative rule, first of all, serves 'to refine and enlarge the public views, by passing them through the medium of a chosen body of citizens . . .' (p. 134). Here Madison agrees profoundly with Montesquieu in his nonrepublican mode: the advent of representative forms capable of attenuating the excesses of direct democracy is one of the key contributions of the new science of politics to the art of moderate and liberal government.

But representation alone is not a sufficient safeguard against the evils of majority faction. The key is an *extended republic* – that is, a regime of social pluralism. The smaller the regime, the greater its social homogeneity; and the greater this homogeneity (short of perfect consensus, which is impossible), the greater the likelihood of majority tyranny. Conversely, the larger the regime, the greater its social heterogeneity and the smaller the likelihood of majority tyranny (p. 135). Far from being a social vice, political fragmentation has now become *the* republican virtue. Security of private rights and of the public interest must rest not upon virtuous participation in an intimate political community, but upon the clash of selfish interests in an atomized political society: 'Divide et impera,' Madison writes in a telling phrase, 'the reprobated axiom of tyranny, is under certain qualifications, the only policy by which a republic can be administered on just principles.'[17]

Madison is here engaged in a self-conscious reversal of the traditional association, exemplified by Montesquieu, of republican government with restricted territorial scope. The structure (i.e. nature) of republican political institutions is now defined not by the presence of direct citizen participation, but rather by the employment of exclusively representative forms; the spirit (i.e. principle) of republican political culture is now defined not by public virtue but by private interest. Hence the restricted territorial scope previously thought essential to republican political participation and political education is now neither necessary nor desirable; rather, extended territorial scope is now a necessary precondition of the pure representative and pluralist politics essential (given the *inevitable* absence of social homogeneity and moral consensus) to control the effects of majority faction. And hence, Madison argues repeatedly, 'the inconveniences of popular states, *contrary to the prevailing Theory*, are in proportion not to the extent, but to the narrowness of their limits.'[18]

The theorists whom Madison attacks were not unaware of the difficulties posed by their preference for small territorial scale. 'If a republic be small, it is destroyed by a foreign force, if it be large it is ruined by an internal imperfection.'[19] Montesquieu's solution is a 'confederate republic,' a regime which 'has all the internal advantages of a republican, together with the external force of a monarchical government.'[20] But his confederate republic, though reasonably vigorous, is still a limited association for limited purposes. The constituent states owe their external survival to the confederal association, which permits them to achieve the international vigor of monarchy. But they owe their *republicanism* to their internal smallness. And this is precisely how Montesquieu was understood by those opposing a strong national government in the debate over the Constitution, who cited him again and again on the impossibility of republican rule in a consolidated national regime of extended territorial scope.[21]

In *Federalist* 9, Hamilton addresses his argument to those who cite Montesquieu in opposition to the proposed Constitution. The proposed Constitution, he argues, is in no way inconsistent with Montesquieu's confederal republic: it, too, is a means of reconciling the virtues of republicanism, based on smallness, with the vigor of monarchy.[22] Hamilton's rhetorically convenient position is, however, fundamentally at odds with the logic of Madison's argument for an extended republic. For Madison's argument in fact rests upon a complete repudiation of Montesquieu's republican perspective: only a *radical* centralization of political decision, a sovereign national government of truly continental scope, can assure non-oppressive popular rule. A republican leviathan is necessary to secure life, liberty, and property from the tyranny of local majorities. The extended republic is not simply a means of adapting popular rule to new political realities, but an inherently desirable corrective for deep intrinsic defects in the politics of the small popular regime. The republic owes to this device its very status as a lawful and legitimate form of government.

It might be said, therefore, that Madison simultaneously accepts and rejects Montesquieu, or rejects him because he accepts him. Madison recognizes that the general spirit of American society, in Montesquieu's sense, calls for popular government. Yet, with Montesquieu, he feels that republican citizenship and civic virtue are illusory goals under modern conditions. Applying to his analysis of popular government assumptions resembling those employed by Montesquieu in his discussion of monarchy and mixed regimes, Madison proceeds to turn the earlier theory of the democratic republic on its head: features which had previously defined its nature, principle, and preconditions – direct mass participation, public spirit and political education, small territorial scale – are now impossible or undesirable or both; instead, *precisely opposite* features – pure representative rule, interest-group liberalism, extended territorial scale – have now become necessary conditions of lawful republican rule. The small republic, animated by the practice of direct democracy and the principle of civic virtue, is replaced by a remote representative regime driven forward exclusively by the ambition and avarice of competing factional groupings – a regime whose nonparticipatory nature and interest-oriented principle bear at least a family resemblance to Montesquieu's frankly nonrepublican alternatives.

By transforming historical necessities into theoretical virtues, Madison thus effects a sweeping and fundamental revision in the traditional theory of democratic republicanism, bringing it into closer correspondence with the imperatives of modernity by abandoning those values – above all, common participation in the life of the political community and the cultivation of public spirit through political education – comprising the essential core of the older theory. For an effort to modernize the classical republican vision without abandoning these civic humanist commitments, one based upon an alternative reading of Montesquieu, we must turn to Alexis de Tocqueville's vision of democracy in America.

III Tocqueville in America: classical republicanism modernized

A new science of politics?

'I confess that in America I saw more than America; I sought there the image of democracy itself, with its inclinations, its character, its prejudices and its passions . . .'[23] For Tocqueville, democratic equality is the dispensation of a providentially decreed future which neither can nor should be reversed, but which can and should be directed by the agency of autonomous human will. In order to comprehend the contours of this inexorable fate, and subject it to control within these confines, he claims to focus his attention upon the actual society in which its tendencies are most advanced. Jacksonian America thus becomes the empirical basis of 'a new science of politics for a world itself quite new' (I, 5).

It is significant that in reconstructing the theory of democratic republicanism, Tocqueville turns his eyes westward in space rather than backwards in time. American democracy represents the wave of an inevitable future; the republics of classical antiquity, the echoes of an outmoded past. The former cannot be understood or evaluated in terms of the latter: the distance is altogether too great. Theoretical efforts, so central to the classical republican heritage, to comprehend and criticize modern politics and society through concepts derived from ancient politics and society only confuse the issue:

Comparing the republics of America to those of Greece and Rome, one thinks of the libraries full of manuscripts but the rude populations of the former, and of the thousand newspapers which plow the latter and the enlightened people who live there. When one comes to think of all the efforts made to judge the latter in the light of the former, and by studying what happened two thousand years ago to predict what will occur nowadays, I am tempted to burn my books in order to apply none but new ideas to such a new social state (I, 316).

Thus, participatory republicanism has been progressively supplanted by representative democracy in the modern world: the 'pure democracies of Switzerland belong to another age; they can teach us nothing useful for the present or future . . . they live only in the past,' while 'the representative democracies of Switzerland are the off-spring of the modern spirit.'[24]

It is important to note that this movement, while inexorable, is progressive as well. Every form of rule, Tocqueville argues, has its own peculiar vice; that of democracy is to give all power to the people (i.e. to the majority that rules in the name of the people). This has two broadly unfortunate consequences: first, ignorant and incompetent rule, from a lack of enlightened leadership; secondly, as Madison had warned, the political tyranny of the majority. The representative mechanism provides a partial corrective for both of these unfortunate tendencies. Like Madison (and Montesquieu in his discussion of England), Tocqueville understands representation in the strong sense: not as a second-best substitute for direct democracy, but as a means of counteracting its intrinsic defects. He sees the movement from direct to representative forms of popular rule as a decisive improvement upon classical republican theory and practice.[25]

In this and other important respects, therefore, the new political science of *Democracy in America* resembles and builds upon the new 'science of politics' praised in *Federalist* 9. With the authors of the *Federalist*, which he had read and admired, Tocqueville appears to call for a radically revised theory of popular rule, a decisive break with the central presuppositions of classical democratic republicanism; he is tempted to 'burn his books' to avoid reproducing the 'chaos of the republics of classical antiquity'.[26] But Tocqueville cannot simply be taken at his word here. It is most significant that Tocqueville *resists* this temptation: that, unlike Montesquieu in one mode and Madison in another, he does not simply burn his bridges behind him. Despite his own best efforts to disentangle himself from the classical theory of republican politics, he finds himself powerfully attracted to its underlying vision.

Several times in his private correspondence, Tocqueville compares the moral and political assumptions of pagan antiquity with those of Christianity. He argues the decisive superiority of Christian over pagan morality in every respect save one: 'The duties of men among themselves as well as in their capacity of *citizens*, the duties of citizens to their fatherland, in brief, the public virtues . . .'[27] This one defect is, however, a profoundly serious one. It is serious because, for Tocqueville as for the ancients, man is by nature a political being; he is most fully human in the autonomous exercise of moral and political responsibility. And he must love his fatherland more than his merely private self; Christians

. . . also belong to one of the great Human Societies which God has formed, apparently to show more clearly the ties by which individuals ought to be mutually attached – societies which are called nations, inhabiting a territory, which they call their country. I wish the clergy to instill into their very soul that everyone belongs much more to this collective being than he does to himself; that towards this being no one ought to be indifferent, much less, by treating such indifference as a sort of languid virtue, to enervate many of our noblest instincts; that everyone is responsible for the fortunes of this collective being; that everyone is bound to work out its prosperity, and to watch that it be not governed except by respectable, beneficient and legitimate authorities.[28]

This, to Tocqueville, is the moral and political lesson to be learned from appeal to the classical republics. It is a lesson that was transmitted to him through the medium of an identifiable tradition of discourse. While composing the second volume of *Democracy in America*, Tocqueville wrote to a friend 'I pass a short portion of every day with three men, Pascal, Montesquieu, and Rousseau.'[29] From the tension between the democratic republicanism of the latter two theorists, whose books he did not burn, and the empirical realities of democracy in America, as he perceived them, Tocqueville evolved a brilliant and creative theoretical synthesis – a new science of politics differing decisively from Madison's in its continuing subscription to the civic humanist values of this classical republican vision, now extended to the circumstances of 'a world itself quite new.'

Bourgeois versus citizen: the marriage of democratic individualism and democratic despotism

According to Tocqueville, political democracy, for all its admitted defects, has at least two major advantages over other forms of rule. First, democratic government tends to promote the greatest good of the greatest number. Here Tocqueville's argument resembles Madison's for the 'republican principle' of majority rule. But, unlike Madison, Tocqueville has a second major reason for favoring popular rule. *Political* democracy is in Tocqueville's eyes the only possible cure for the deep-seated maladies of *social* democracy: 'I maintain that there is only one effective remedy against the evils which equality may cause and that is political liberty' (II, 112). What, briefly, are these evils?

The central defining feature of an egalitarian society for Tocqueville is its tendency to dissolve the corporate structures of an aristocratic society into a mass of isolated, private individuals. Democratic society atomizes as it equalizes, sanctifying individual reason as the sole basis of opinion and belief and concentrating thought and action upon narrowly self-centered, narrowly self-interested personal ends. Lost in the crowd, with no coherent loyalties of neighborhood or class or profession to sustain them, individuals retreat into the idiocy of an all-encompassing private life.

'Individualism' – atomism, materialism, and privatism – is therefore the characteristic vice of democratic societies. But, unlike most orthodox French social theorists, Tocqueville does not fear that the dust and powder of individuality will issue in moral and intellectual anarchy or social and political disintegration.[30] To the contrary: his fear is that the atomized individualism of an acquisitive bourgeois society will engender oppressive new forms of social and political domination. Democratically dissociated individuals, bent on destroying all forms of aristocratic inequality, naturally tend to invest unlimited authority in a mass society and state. The moral and intellectual consequence is social conformity to the tyranny of mass opinion. The political consequence is a powerful tendency, not towards the equality-in-liberty of democratic republicanism, but rather towards the equality-in-slavery of democratic despotism.

This movement towards the concentration of social and political power, caused by the atomic individual's passion for equality and love of conformity, has attained such momentum because it has also been supported by materialism and privatism, the other defining features of democratic individualism. The crucial way in which these impulses encourage despotic power is by fostering political apathy. Apathy completes what political centralization and the will to social conformity have begun. Absorbed in their material and private concerns, democratic men are too busy to be free. In a passage that might have come from the pen of Rousseau, Tocqueville observes:

There is no need to drag their rights away from citizens of this type; they themselves voluntarily let them go. They find it a tiresome inconvenience to exercise political rights which distract them from industry. When required to elect representatives, to support authority by personal service, or to discuss public business together, they find they have not time (II, 147).

Into this vacuum of the public spirit, Tocqueville warns in the bleak concluding pages of his second volume, rushes the modern leviathan-state.

The structure of freedom: pluralist democracy and participatory republicanism

For Tocqueville, it is the supreme virtue of American democracy to have avoided this dehumanizing fate through the organization of a participatory political life. He sees America as Marx saw France: the land of political culture. It is, he writes, almost impossible to overestimate the place occupied by political concerns in the life of an American:

The cares of politics engross a prominent place in the occupations of a citizen in the United States; and almost the only pleasure which an American knows is to take a part in the government, and to discuss its measures . . .
   In some countries, the inhabitants seem unwilling to avail themselves of the political privileges which the law gives them; it would seem that they set too high a value upon their time to spend it on the interests of the community; and they shut themselves up in a narrow selfishness marked out by four sunk fences and a quickset hedge. But if an American were condemned to confine his activity to his own affairs, he would be robbed of one half of his existence; he would feel an immense void in the life which he is accustomed to lead, and his wretchedness would be unbearable (I, 253–4).

A passion for politics is the animating spirit of Tocqueville's America.
   How does this intensely public life, this frenetic political motion, organize

and express itself? What institutional forms does it assume and what is the principle or spirit which sets it in motion? And how, more specifically, does it work to mitigate the individualism of a democratic society?

The crucial dilemma of a democratic society, we have seen, is the atomization and privatization of its individual components. Individuals are weak and isolated, hence vulnerable to the encroachments of power. In aristocracies, powerful individuals and institutions form a natural barrier against the tyranny of the prince; democracy by nature possesses no such restraints. Therefore, Tocqueville argues, men must cultivate the art of *voluntary* political and social cooperation. Through such cooperative activity, independent and weak individuals together can create intermediary structures functionally equivalent to those of aristocratic society. Thus, Tocqueville has taken Montesquieu's *aristocratic* intermediary bodies and – in the interests of preventing despotism, which was precisely their original aim – advocated their reconstitution on a *democratic* basis.

For Tocqueville there are two places where a democratic society can seek to organize its intermediary bodies: (1) provincial liberties and municipal self-government, and (2) voluntary political and civil associations. He sees administrative decentralization and a tradition of associational activity, distinctive characteristics of American democracy, as essential restraints upon the despotism both of the majority and of the central government. Municipal bodies and county administrations are 'like so many reefs retarding the flow of the popular will' (I, 274); voluntary associations function, in like manner, as 'dikes' (I, 198) which stem the flow of majority or minority tyranny.

It would, however, be wrong to focus exclusively upon the purely negative and protective functions of these institutions, upon the strictly defensive dimensions of Tocqueville's pluralism. An equally crucial feature of these intermediary bodies is their *internally* democratic organization of authority. They have become, for Tocqueville, functional equivalents for the participatory structures of classical *republican* theory and practice.

The magnitude of Montesquieu's influence upon Tocqueville, the continuing indebtedness of his new science of politics to the categories of orthodox republican analysis, is nowhere better revealed than in Tocqueville's discussion of the proper size of a popular regime. His arguments are straight from the *Spirit of the Laws*. The United States is able to have popular rule on a continental scale, Tocqueville maintains, because it is a confederal rather than a consolidated republic. Through federalism, 'The Union is free and happy like a small nation, glorious and strong like a great one' (I, 167). In reverting to the categories of Montesquieu, Tocqueville has tacitly repudiated Madison's republican revisionism. The regime owes its survival to the federal device; it owes its continued republicanism, however, *not* to its extended territorial scope, or its centralization of political decision, but rather to the incompleteness of that centralization – that is, to the survival of the local autonomies that Madison (in 1787) had sought to diminish. 'America', Tocqueville maintains, 'is *par excellence* the land of provincial and township government' (I, 413). The Madisonian leviathan has as its necessary foundation a Jeffersonian infrastructure of ward and township republics:

It is indeed incontestable that in the United States the taste for and practice in republican government were born in the townships and provincial assemblies . . . it is that same republican spirit, those same mores and habits of liberty, which, having come to birth and grown in the various states, are then applied without any trouble in the nation as a whole. Public spirit in the United States is, in a sense, only a summing up of provincial patriotism. Every citizen of the United States may be said to transfer the concern inspired in him by his little republic into his love of the common motherland (I, 166).

The virtue of this local democracy is that it permits *direct* citizen participation in the common affairs of everyday life. The New England town meeting, Tocqueville maintains, preserved a genuinely participatory democracy. With precisely the backwards-looking glance whose legitimacy he elsewhere denies, Tocqueville observes that: 'The New England towns adopted no representative institutions. As in Athens, matters of common concern were dealt with in the market place and in the general assembly of citizens' (I, 39–40; also I, 56). He returns to this theme again and again: in the New England township there is no representative system; the sovereign people meet in open assembly to formulate law and control the policies of the government. Political activity is not confined to the occasional act of voting for representatives; man participates as citizen on a continuing basis.

The spirit of freedom: the bourgeois citizen

For Tocqueville, the virtue of the direct democratic participation, which defines the *nature* of the American regime, is that it forms a process of practical political education which works to sustain the *principle* of that regime. Political education consists above all else in the experience of political action: 'It is by taking a share in legislation that the American learns to know the law; it is by governing that he becomes educated about the formalities of government' (I, 318). Practical intelligence and public spirit – that is, the *moeurs* essential to healthy republicanism – can emerge only from the activity of actually working free institutions. Republican political education consists primarily of the *praxis* of citizenship.

Cultivation of the values of citizenship through the processes of local and associational democracy has enabled the Americans to counteract the centrifugal impetus of democratic individualism. A national representation alone would never suffice to counteract the deep-rooted maladies of this individualism. The general affairs of state may keep the political elite occupied, but they leave the average citizen passive and indifferent. The only mode of participation realistically available to this citizen, voting for representatives, is too occasional and attenuated to have any lasting effects; and the issues are in any case too remote, too removed from pressing matters of daily concern, to draw him out of private life. But things are different when the opportunities and issues are closer to home.

It is difficult to force a man out of himself and get him to take an interest in the affairs of the whole state, for he has little understanding of the way in which the fate of the state can influence his own lot. But if it is a question of taking a road past his property, he sees at once that this small public matter has a bearing on his greatest private interests, and there is no need to point out to him the close connection between his private profit and the general interest (II, 111).

Liberties on this scale and of this nature are most likely to draw democratically dissociated individuals out of private isolation and into public life.

By these means, the Americans have partially resolved the antinomy of bourgeois versus citizen – creating, from the impulse of private interest, a republic of bourgeois citizens. In Tocqueville's travel journals and notes for *Democracy in America*, he returns several times to one theoretical perplexity: the *principle* of a republican regime, according to Montesquieu and others, is civic virtue ('The principle of the republics of classical antiquity was to sacrifice private interests to the general good. In that sense one could say that they were virtuous.').[31] However, the Americans – a bourgeois people – are hardly virtuous in this classical sense. Only one common bond unites the different parts of this huge body politic: *interest*. And yet they are free. Does this constitute a refutation of Montesquieu? Does it call for a Madisonian transfiguration of republican theory? Not at all:

One must not take Montesquieu's idea narrowly. What that great man intended to say was that republics can only be sustained by the action of society itself. What he means by virtue is the moral power which each individual exercises upon himself, and which prevents him from violating another's right.

When that triumph of man over his temptations . . . is the result of weakness or of a calculation of personal interest, it does not constitute virtue in the eyes of a moralist; but it comes within Montesquieu's idea for he is talking much more of the effect than of its cause.[32]

This is how the Americans can be free. Virtue is not strong, but temptation is weak; disinterestedness is not great, but *interest is well understood*. Here is the key: the Americans have substituted interest for virtue as the principle of their regime, but they have derived the consequences of virtue from an enlightened understanding of interest. Interest is the *principle*, but it is interest rightly understood. 'So then Montesquieu was right, although he was speaking of antique virtue, and what he said about the Greeks and Romans is still applicable to the American.'[33]

This is how bourgeois man is induced to participate in politics, and why opportunities for direct participation at the local and associational levels play so crucial a role in Tocqueville's theory. Only through participation in matters of close and intimate concern – a road past his property – can an individual absorbed in the satisfaction of private life and the pursuit of material gain comprehend the nexus between selfish and public interests. Through this self-interested participation on this order, bourgeois man learns – so Tocqueville claims – that his real as opposed to apparent, long-run as opposed to short-run, interest lies in his private share of the public good. He apprehends his selfish interest in being an active citizen and thus becomes capable of the moral self-restraint, the repression of passional impulse, that republicanism – in the traditional understanding – demands. *L'intérêt bien entendu* becomes the functional equivalent of republican virtue.

The doctrine of enlightened egoism thus works by turning 'private interest against itself' (II, 129). But it can readily be seen that if this doctrine works by the action of interest upon itself, it does so in a peculiarly non-Madisonian way. Tocqueville's theory of republican egoism, his effort to extract the consequences of public virtue from the impulse of private selfishness, relies both upon the emancipation and enlightenment of egoism and upon its partial transformation and transcendence. Individuals come to politics as the bearers of private, egoistic concerns; but this initially self-interested participation is, through a gradual process of moral and political education, insensibly metamorphosed into something more genuinely unselfish and public-spirited. Americans pretend to consistent egoism when in fact they are, on occasion, genuine altruists: 'At first it is by necessity that men attend to the public interest, afterward by choice. *What had been calculation becomes instinct.* By dint of working for the good of his fellows, he in the end acquires a habit and taste for serving them' (II, 112). The egocentric impulses of bourgeois individualism are qualitatively (though only partially) transformed, not merely deflected. Interest becomes, as it were, the mechanism of its own (again partial) self-transcendence: it is *aufgehoben*. In this way democratic man becomes more than *mere* bourgeois: he becomes, in part and on occasion, a genuinely public-spirited republican citizen as well.

This, then, is why the fervent political life which exists in America is democracy's greatest benefit. The only cure for the ills of social democracy, Tocqueville believes, is more political democracy. For a truly participatory democracy is more than a Madisonian pluralism of faction; it is first and foremost a process of political education generating the intelligence and public spirit, the *moeurs*, necessary to sustain a republican polity – and, by that very process, creating wiser and better human beings. By cultivating our 'noblest instincts', in sum, it moves beyond individualism to complete man's nature as a political being.[34]

IV Conclusion: 'revisionism' in classical and contemporary democratic theory

Madison in *The Federalist* and Tocqueville in *Democracy in America*, then, present two competing classical theories of democracy and two competing approaches to the revision of political ideas. We find in their opposing classical images of democracy in America precisely the two concepts of politics and democracy – 'instrumental' versus 'developmental' for short – that underlie the opposition between contemporary elite and participatory theories.[35] Madison conceives of republican rule purely as a mechanism for the protection of private rights and the satisfaction of antecedently-given, subjectively-determined wants. Tocqueville conceives of republican rule as a public stage upon which prior, private wants are transformed according to a conception of essential human need, namely, the development of man's rational and moral capacities as a social and political agent. Madison emphasizes the *protective* or defensive purpose of politics and democracy, seeking to diminish participation wherever elite rule will better serve these purposes. Tocqueville emphasizes the *educative* or developmental purposes of politics and democracy, seeking to expand participation wherever it will enhance these purposes.

Moreover, this basic difference of underlying theoretical perspective between Madison and Tocqueville conditions their respective approaches to the revision of political ideas – that is, of a prior 'classical' tradition. Both theorists claim to be modifying and adapting to the circumstances of American politics the classical theory of democratic republicanism. Yet their approaches to this revisionary activity – exemplified by their competing uses of Montesquieu – differ markedly. Madison offers a republican theory which, in its non-participatory *nature* and interest-oriented *principle*, resembles Montesquieu's glorious monarchy (or its English variant) more closely than it does his virtuous republic: a 'revision' that borders on a *rejection* of all that the republican concept had traditionally connoted. Tocqueville, despite his pretensions to a radically discontinuous new science of politics, offers an extension of Montesquieu's republican paradigm to cover a society and polity not anticipated by that 'great man': a revision of classical democratic republicanism that does not tacitly repudiate, but instead seeks to preserve, the essential spirit of that tradition. And, here again, these competing approaches to the revision of political ideas – of a received 'classical model' – find intriguing (if unacknowledged) parallels in contemporary democratic theory.

Contemporary implications

In recent years, political theorists and social scientists have attempted to assess the contemporary relevance and validity of the 'classical theory of democracy' discussed in this essay. There has been extensive debate as to whether this theory has in some sense been undermined by the evidence of modern social science, with some arguing for a drastic revision of the 'classical' model and others strenuously resisting this move as ideologically illicit.

The opposed parties in this debate commonly assume the existence of a *single* and *static* classical theory of democracy. This classical theory of democracy is now seen as undergoing serious and substantial confrontation with the empirical realities of politics (as embodied in the evidence of modern social science). And from this assumption there then follows a sharp dichotomy between an orthodox classical theory of participatory democracy and the contemporary 'revisionist' theory of elite democracy.

As the competing approaches of Madison in *The Federalist* and Tocqueville in *Democracy in America* suggest very clearly, however, this 'classical model' of democracy is neither single nor static, but a diverse and discontinuous body of ideas revised several times and in several ways prior to the advent of contemporary modes of 'revisionist' democratic theory. That classical democratic theory was *itself* revised in these several ways surely suggests that the contemporary theory of democratic elitism is not the only possible approach to the revision of this legacy.

The issue can be framed by examining a series of parallels between classical and contemporary democratic theory. Just as Montesquieu, Madison, and Tocqueville were all in different ways forced to confront a growing discrepancy between the classical theory of democratic republicanism and the actual developments of modern history and society, so have twentieth-century theorists – beginning with 'classical elitists' such as Mosca, Michels, and Pareto – been forced to confront a perceived discrepancy between the prescriptive demands of 'classical democratic theory' and the descriptive evidence of modern social science. The two central tendencies that twentieth-century theorists have been forced to confront are: (1) the domination of large-scale political systems and social organizations by elites, and (2) the apathy and ignorance of mass electorates when measured against a 'rationality-activist' model of citizenship. Just as earlier theorists responded very differently to the tension between classical republicanism and modern history, so likewise have twentieth-century theorists responded very differently to the challenge posed to 'classical democratic theory' by these developments.

A classical elite theorist such as Mosca, for example, responds to this perceived discrepancy in a manner not dissimilar to Montesquieu's earlier response. Just as Montesquieu implied the obsolescence of meaningful democratic republicanism, so does Mosca assert the impossibility of meaningful democracy and the inevitability of rule by an elite or political class under conditions of modern society. And just as Montesquieu made peace with monarchy and English mixed government because their pluralism guaranteed liberal and moderate rule, so did Mosca in his later years come to defend parliamentary government – that is, rule by *plural* elites and *multiple* social forces – as preferable to the autocratic rule of a single, closed elite. Both ultimately *rejected* a received 'classical' concept of democracy in favor of a liberal elite pluralism.[36]

The revisions in 'classical' democratic theory carried through by Schumpeter and his followers are, likewise, interestingly and importantly similar to the Madisonian transfiguration of classical democratic republicanism. In both cases, what were the necessary preconditions of democracy on an earlier view are no longer essential; indeed it is the presence of features previously considered subversive of democratic rule which is now held to be necessary. Apparent social necessities become positive theoretical virtues, and the earlier 'classical' concept is stood on its head, transformed out of all recognition, in the process of being revised.

This has been the fate visited upon the 'classical' theory of representative democracy put forward by Tocqueville (and others, for example, J.S. Mill) by the contemporary revisionist theory of democratic elitism. Central features of that theory – a high degree of citizen participation in political life at both local and national levels, the democratization of associational life – are dismissed as unfeasible and/or undesirable in the light of current empirical knowledge about human nature in politics or the structure of modern society. In fact, *precisely antithetical* conditions – mass apathy, the domination of politics and social organization by remote elites – are now promoted as valuable features of a liberal-democratic polity, even as necessary to democratic stability. Just as Madison's revised theory of republicanism bore a family resemblance to Montesquieu's defense of monarchy and mixed government, so have Schumpeter *et al.* constructed a 'revised' theory of democracy strikingly similar to the formally antidemocratic Mosca's defense of a liberal and pluralist system of elite rule.

In both instances, the commendatory force hitherto attaching to the terms 'republic' and 'democracy' respectively is, through an act of persuasive (re)definition, transferred to a reality shot through with oligarchical elements.[37] And in both instances, the victim of this conceptual moderniz-ation is the civic humanist perspective – as articulated by classical republican theorists, or as revised by Tocqueville (and, for example, Mill) – that had stood at the heart of earlier 'classical' understandings.

But, as the earlier example of Tocqueville suggests, other approaches to the revision of political ideas are theoretically possible. Those who wish to affirm the educative or developmental values sacrificed by elite versions of revisionist democratic theory must, like Tocqueville, seek a newly-revised, empirically-viable theory of contemporary democracy that retains the notion of participation at its heart. Just as Tocqueville sought to overcome the apathy and acquisitiveness of bourgeois man by grounding participation in the immediate routines of daily life, through the politics of self-interest rightly understood, so must such a newly-revised theory seek to overcome the apathy of mass man and woman. And just as Tocqueville sought, to this end, to build representative democracy in the nation-state upon local and associational democracy, so now must his vision of a participatory society be modernized – above all, through its extension to hierarchical structures of power and authority in economic and social life.[38]

That work has already begun, and it is carried forward by the essays in this volume.[39] It is enriched by the awareness that classical democratic theory was revised several times and in several ways prior to the advent of a contemporary 'revisionist' theory of elite democracy. By delineating two prior modes of revisionism in classical democratic theory, this essay has attempted to contribute to that awareness.

6

Marxism and democratic theory

MICHAEL LEVIN

In the mid-nineteenth century the term democracy was used with an imprecision that has not yet been overcome. However, in its broadest sense it connoted more than a particular constitutional system and extended to the general trend undermining inherited privilege. This tendency was variously perceived as resting upon an ineluctable and ascertainable process of historical change, the spread of rationality into social and political affairs, and the extension of political influence to larger sections of the population.

In the mid and late 1840s Marx and Engels associated themselves with a democracy which they saw as the egalitarian movement necessarily leading to socialism. 'Organ of Democracy' was the sub-title of the *Neue Rheinische Zeitung* under Marx's editorship; 'Mr Engels, from Paris, a German democrat' was how the author of a French newspaper article referred to himself in 1846. His colleague he was pleased to designate as 'Mr Marx, German democrat and one of the vice-presidents of the Brussels Democratic Association'.[1]

The first great democratic battles which Marx and Engels experienced were the series of uprisings that exploded across the major cities of Europe in 1848. Participation in actual struggle served to differentiate the heterogeneous elements that constituted the broad democratic tendency and place them in a condition of mutual suspicion. Henceforth Marx and Engels ceased to regard communism and democracy as synonymous. The term 'democracy' came to designate the petty-bourgeois radicals caught in the midst of the political struggle. Such 'democrats' wished to overthrow autocracy and establish representative institutions within a capitalist society, but were wary of allowing power to descend to the working classes. Democracy is thus seen as the highest form of the capitalist state, to be supported as a progressive demand against autocracy but condemned if seen as an ultimate aim. Thus the 1875 unity programme between the leading sections of German socialism was criticized for making 'purely democratic demands'.[2] The point of this objection gets more extended treatment in Engels' comments on an article in *Sozialdemokrat*:

The only rotten thing there is that he invokes the 'concept' of democracy. The concept changes every time the Demos changes and so does not get us one step further. In my opinion what should have been said is the following: The proletariat too needs democratic *forms* for the seizure of power but to it they are, like all political forms, mere means. But if today democracy is wanted as an *end* one must seek support in the peasantry and petty bourgeoisie, i.e. in classes that are in process of dissolution and *reactionary* in relation to the proletariat as soon as they try to maintain themselves artificially . . . And yet the democratic republic always remains the *last* form of bourgeois rule, that in which it goes to pieces.[3]

If, for the moment, we disregard the teleological aspect, we find that Marx and Engels arrived at a designation of a democratic political structure not far removed from contemporary Western notions. Thus it is marked by an emphasis on constitutionalism, civil liberties, and representative government based on universal franchise. From the liberal perspective such a structure provides a satisfactory means of ascertaining and implementing the will of the majority. For Marx and Engels, on the other hand, its real existence made a mockery of its pretensions. The failure was not merely one of political morality – that selfish and corrupt politicians misused democratic structures for their own aggrandizement, for the formal values of liberal constitutional-ism were flawed even in their basic assumptions. This realization derived not just from theoretical works, such as Marx's critique of Hegel's *Philosophy of Right*, nor from his historical studies of the French Revolution, but from direct political experience. Editorship of a newspaper taught Marx the limits of free speech. In wood theft laws he uncovered class justice; in the Frankfurt parliament the difference between formal and real power; and in the actions of parties and governments the gulf between ideology and practice.

II

In summer 1843 Marx undertook an extended investigation of Hegel's *Philosophy of Right*. Hegel, like Herder and Schiller, had been troubled by the basic divisiveness of modern society and was haunted by the supposed wholeness of Greek civic life. Marx, too, shared this concern, but not Hegel's response to it. 'It shows Hegel's profundity that he feels the separation of civil from political society as a *contradiction*. He is wrong, however, to be content with the appearance of this resolution.'[4] Hegel, then, whom Marx regarded as a representative of the modern state, had presented the state as the highest point of reconciliation between the individual and society, and saw particularity as being overcome by the institutions of monarchy, embodying the universal essence, and bureaucracy as a universal class. To Marx, in contrast, the powers granted to the state strengthen not its universality but its particularity. This was especially so when its personnel were recruited from an exclusive stratum, for in Hegel's system the landed gentry was 'summoned and entitled to its political vocation by birth without the hazards of election'.[5] State power, rights and privileges are exclusive to it and are thus implicitly defined as just those that the people do not possess. Thereby the disunity of modern society is reinforced rather than resolved, and instead of identifying with the Universal as full citizens, subjects are condemned to the narrow idiocy and competitiveness of private existence. The state in fact represents an alienation of the powers of the whole community which will only be resolved when it no longer exists and society administers itself on a basis of full equality. Thus where liberal theory sought to separate the state from society, Marx looked for the hidden linkages. 'Everywhere it requires the guarantee of spheres which lie outside it. It is not realised power. It is *supported* impotence, it is not power over these supports but the power of the support. The support is the paramount power.'[6] From this realization it was just a short step to the notion of the class state. The state bureaucracy, courts, police and army appear henceforth not as neutral arbiters standing above social divisions and maintaining general law and order, but as partisan instruments in capitalist society of bourgeois law and order.

Another less acknowledged emphasis allows the state relative autonomy. However this also, in a different way, still detracts from any notion of neutrality, for now the state becomes a mammoth, powerful yet parasitic excrescence on society with a primary commitment to itself. In the Rousseauist sense it is a particular grouping likely to develop a particular will. Either way, as class state or particular interest, it is still a barrier to popular power, neither neutral and objective, nor the passive executor of the wishes of the legislature.

Here already, in their notions of the central political institution, we have the core of Marx and Engels' whole critique of bourgeois democracy. It is that the state, parliament and the entire political sphere do not occupy neutral ground in which success is obtained purely on the basis of cogent argument and numerical appeal. Instead, for the working class, the whole terrain of formal politics is enemy territory. This does not mean that one should abstain from entering it. On the contrary, it presents valuable opportunities, but they can only be maximized by those aware of the traps and pitfalls that accompany the endeavour.

The illusion accompanying the liberal theory of the state also characterizes other aspects of liberal ideology. Just as a particular interest was presented as a universal benefit, so are restricted rights announced as general freedoms. In the name of freedom the French Revolution tore asunder a system that for centuries had bound men to a fixed place within the social order, but in destroying one particular form of community it appeared to decimate community as such. In terms of liberal theory man was set free, released from onerous communal obligations and left to roam isolated, selfish and carnivorous through the competitive jungle that society had become. But this nominal social anarchy had the state as its support, and its constitutional guarantees it called 'The Declaration of the Rights of Man and of the Citizen'. Marx immediately recognized the significance of a conceptual duality that expressed the duality of bourgeois society itself. 'Who is *homme* as distinct from *citoyen*?' The latter is universal man conscious of an affinity with his species but 'the so-called *rights of man* . . . are nothing but the rights . . . of egoistic man, of man separated from other men and from the community'.[7] So the new social freedom is not so much one that men share with each other but one they guard against each other. The threat to the narrow, isolated individual is seen to come from other individuals, and bourgeois society is exposed as 'officially antisocial in theory'.[8] In its implementation abstract freedom emerges as bourgeois freedom. Seek for the content behind the form and this freedom reduces itself to private property and free trade. It is not men who are set free but capital. 'Liberty, Equality, Fraternity' was the appealing battle-cry of the French Revolution, but its definition of liberty precluded its attainment of equality and fraternity. Equality could not be achieved alongside the freedom of exploitation, nor fraternity derived from the postulate of natural selfishness.

Similarly, the declared rights of liberal constitutionalism emerge in the form that allows their negation in practice. Marx's analysis here is so central to his distrust of bourgeois rule that it is worth quoting at some length.

> For each of these freedoms is proclaimed as the *absolute* right of the French *citoyen*, but always with the marginal note that it is unlimited so far as it is not limited by the '*equal rights of others* and the *public safety*' . . . that is, the safety of the bourgeoisie, as the Constitution prescribes. In the following period, both sides accordingly appeal with complete justice to the Constitution: the friends of order, who abrogated all these freedoms, as well as the democrats, who demanded all of them. For each paragraph of the Constitution contains its own antithesis, its own Upper and Lower House, namely, freedom in the general phrase, abrogation of freedom in the marginal note. Thus so long as the *name* of freedom was respected and only its actual realisation prevented, of course in a legal way, the constitutional existence of freedom remained intact, inviolate, however mortal the blows dealt to its existence *in actual life*.[9]

It was not just that the rights nominally pertaining to the political sphere were not realized even there, for even were this remedied their scope would still be restricted, for the political itself was too narrowly defined. As just one more aspect of the division of labour, politics was accepted as a specialist task practised only by the few. Political freedoms only related to the formal political sphere which itself formed only a segmented part of the social totality. Thus 'just as the Christians are equal in heaven, but unequal on earth, so the individual members of the nation are *equal* in the heaven of their political world, but unequal in the earthly existence of *society*'.[10]

For Marx and Engels the reality of liberal democracy appeared systematically to curtail its pretensions; the class state for the neutral arbiter; paper freedoms for real political freedoms; and restricted political freedoms for general human emancipation. A similar characteristic applied to the prevailing theory of democratic political choice. Traditional Social Contract theory depicted political forms as originating from the unconstricted choice of rational individuals. Tom Paine presented the French Revolutionary epoch as signifying the Adam of a new world. So, even later, according to Marx, the naive theory of democracy assumes that any decision can be implemented merely because parliament has so determined. Anything is possible. This notion of political omnipotence overplays the significance of will and neglects the force of constraining circumstances. 'Are men free to choose this or that form of society? By no means',[11] Marx informed Annenkov in 1846. Ripeness as well as willingness has to prevail. On this issue the breach occurred with Willich, Schapper and numerous other members of the Communist League in the early 1850s. Marx complained that 'the revolution is seen not as the product of the realities of the situation but as the result of an effort of will'.[12] In the aftermath of the defeats of 1849, Marx and Engels looked primarily not to the opinions of radical leaders but to the economic crisis that would indicate a revolutionary situation. They were, surprisingly and unjustifiably, fearful of attaining power prematurely and finding themselves in a contradictory situation. This concern found its way into Engels' articles on *The Peasant War in Germany*.

The worst thing that can befall the leader of an extreme party is to be compelled to assume power at a time when the movement is not yet ripe for the domination of the class he represents . . . he necessarily finds himself in an unsolvable dilemma. What he *can* do contradicts all his previous actions and principles and the immediate interests of his party, and what he *ought* to do cannot be done . . . he is compelled to represent not his party or his class, but the class for whose domination the movement is then ripe . . . He who is put into this awkward position is irrevocably lost.[13]

In addition to illusions concerning the possible, Marx also laid stress on what was necessary. Here we find a notion of immanent destiny which is a teleological variant of Rousseau's theory of the general will. According to Rousseau such a will exists 'constant, unalterable, and pure'[14] whether people actually will it or not. It was, one might say, a people's real, rather than their expressed, will. It denotes what was true rather than what might, at any random moment, be actually desired, and is what people would will if they conceived of themselves rationally as citizens rather than selfishly as private individuals. In its Marxist form this notion of representation runs directly counter to the usual liberal democratic concern to ask people what they want. At one level Marxism appears to have democratic credentials because of its claim to represent the majority class of capitalist society. But in respect of the destiny of that class its terminology is often one of pure necessity and obligation rather than of expressed preference. 'It is not a question of what this or that proletarian, or even the whole proletariat, at the moment *regards* as its aim. It is a question of *what the proletariat is*, and what, in accordance with this *being*, it will historically be compelled to do.'[15] As a corollary to the belief in one immanent will we find the notion of it being articulated and organised by one party, the real party of the proletariat. Although the *Manifesto* described the communists as 'the most advanced and resolute *section* of the working-class *parties* of every country'[16] later writings show this situation to be acceptable only during the early stages of the movement. Properly there can only be one party. Others are moments towards it, but such 'sects and amateur experiments'[17] are bound to disappear in the process towards class maturity.

Owing to the presumption of knowing the real interests of the proletariat the liberal concern for the means of seeking and expressing consent appeared superficial. Marxism, then, marks the point at which the major strand of radical thought dispensed with consent theory. The belief in a science of society led to the view that one could postulate class interest without the need to actually test opinion. Objective interest was taken as the real; mere opinion as its shadow, which like all shadows, contains varying degrees of distortion. At first the gulf between proper and actual will did not seem to pose too great a problem. Their life experience was such that the proletariat easily attained consciousness of their necessary task. In *The Holy Family* Marx and Engels confidently asserted that 'There is no need to explain here that a large part of the English and French proletariat is already *conscious* of its historic task and is constantly working to develop that consciousness into complete clarity.'[18] This simple confidence did not endure. In *Capital* Marx noted that the proletariat too are suffused with bourgeois assumptions.[19] The danger here is that the Party might become a kind of clerisy charged with the task of educating the proletariat to an understanding of their destined role.

The aims of the working class, then, are a function of their social position. The contradictions of the class structure find expression in political antagonisms that have to be fought out to the end. Thus the liberal democratic notion of politics as compromise appears fraudulent, involving the leadership's betrayal of the class interests they are supposed to represent. Time and again Marx and Engels bemoaned the use made of working-class power by other interests which, having once securely established themselves, then deny the workers any fruits of victory. Sometimes objective circumstances made the durability of proletarian power impossible. Thus in 1848 the French workers had the power to help make the February revolution but not the position to benefit from it. They were the instruments rather than the immediate beneficiaries of social progress. At other times, as with the English labour leaders' servile adherence to the Liberals, real opportunities appeared lost through simple lack of vision or understanding of what was required.

Coalitions are always precarious, for their natural tendency is to blur and distort the separate real aims of the classes involved. This does not, however, mean that they are to be rejected, for at various historical stages they present the only means of progress. Compromise of ultimate class aims is what Marx and Engels most feared, but coalition without compromise is attainable between different social groupings who may for a limited period share the same immediate interest. During the 1840s Marx and Engels assumed an alliance of all the progressive forces. In Germany the communists even 'fight *with the bourgeoisie* whenever it acts in a revolutionary way, against the absolute monarchy, the feudal squirearchy, and the petty bourgeoisie'.[20] All progressive groupings are to be supported, but an ultimate aim for a marginal class will be merely a transitional one for the proletariat. Alliance without illusion, coalition without compromise, and unity without proletarian subordination were to be aimed for. Only the most oppressed class fights through until all oppression is removed. Thus the proletariat should never fall under the ideological or organizational sway of classes with limited aims and, as the most unequivocally radical grouping, should always assume the leadership of any progressive alliance. 'The French peasants', Marx noted, 'suffer an exploitation that differs only in *form* from the exploitation of the industrial proletariat'.[21] 'Hence the peasants find their natural ally and *leader* [emphasis added] in the *urban proletariat*, whose task is the overthrow of the bourgeois order.'[22]

In a parliamentary context the priority of long-term aims over immediate tactics becomes particularly hard to maintain. As forums of compromise where labour leaders were too easily seduced into adopting the 'respectability' of their 'betters' parliamentary life was bedevilled by two particular dangers. The first concerned the question of consciousness, and the replacement of basic transformation by piecemeal reform. Vision is shortened, imagination is lost, and the grievances of the working classes are tackled by palliatives that give only slight and temporary relief. The second danger is to mistake parliamentary influence for basic social power. This illusion, termed 'parliamentary cretinism', was given its fullest clarification in Engels' account of the ill-fated Frankfurt parliament which, apparently, talked without being listened to, in the happy conviction that the outside world awaited its every declaration with bated breath, whereas in reality it was merely a consultative body which only met when the King so decided, and eventually sank without leaving even a ripple of attention or regret.

Exaggerated self-importance, the occupational hazard attending the closed world of bourgeois democracy, can be countered by a strong organic link between the masses and their representatives. Otherwise it continues unabated until 'some fine day the left may find its parliamentary victory coincides with its real defeat',[23] as happened to the French parliament of 1851 which voted to depose Louis Bonaparte but was 'finally led off in the custody of African sharpshooters'.[24] The general implication is that the bourgeoisie intend both parliament and the universalistically defined liberties for their own class use. When other classes attempt to share these rights the whole hard-won liberty package is redefined as 'socialistic' and thrown overboard. Liberty thus sinks below the surface so that political influence may rise out of reach above it. The bourgeoisie then cling all the more tenaciously to their economic and social power, and align themselves with upper-class reaction. In the France of 1850, 'Universal suffrage declared itself directly against the domination of the bourgeoisie: the bourgeoisie answered by outlawing universal suffrage.'[25] For them, democracy was a means, a convenient form for the maintenance of class rule at a certain stage of the class struggle, to be used as and when and in so far as it served that more basic purpose.

By intimation a somewhat similar approach was enjoined upon the working class. The notion that a revolutionary party has no interest in a bourgeois parliament finds no confirmation in the writings of Marx and Engels. For them the parliamentary and revolutionary paths were not mutually exclusive. Neither criticized the Chartists for the strongly electoral and parliamentary basis of their demands. Indeed, in 1874 Engels complained that English labour leaders had fallen below the level of political maturity achieved by the Chartists a quarter of a century earlier. Universal suffrage was first seen as a guarantee of socialism itself. Later it was regarded as providing a useful measure of strength, and a means of gaining a public platform for revolutionary views. From the 1870s the value of parliament appeared still greater as the franchise had been extended to some of the male workers in England and to the whole male proletariat for German Reich elections. The tenor of Marx and Engels' pronouncements shifted perceptibly. In 1872 Marx considered the possibility of America, England and, perhaps, Holland achieving socialism by peaceful means. Were that to happen it would still remain the exception, for 'in most continental countries the lever of our revolutions will have to be force'.[26]

A sharper breach with their earlier emphasis came in Engels' 1895 reconsideration of the lesson of the Paris Commune. Now the old insurrectionary tactics appeared antiquated. The fire power at the disposal of the military was such that any popular uprising would be courting disaster. The extension of the vote to the working classes gradually gave them better opportunities within the prevailing legal framework. 'Slow propaganda work and parliamentary activity are . . . the immediate tasks of the party.'[27] This, however, did not exclude revolution when the time was ripe for it and victory could be assured. Marx and Engels thus accepted parliamentary tactics as *one part* of class struggle. Theirs was a vigorous, radical, suspicious parliamentarism, without illusions concerning the attendant dangers, and involving no renunciation of other forms of struggle.

III

Marx and Engels accepted the Enlightenment ideal of citizenship as a participatory activity but saw it as ultimately incompatible with a parliamentary model which viewed politics as a specialist activity restricted to a relatively harmless sphere. In his *Critique of Hegel's Doctrine of the State* Marx noted that 'Properly speaking *executive power*, e.g., rather than legislative power, the *metaphysical* state function, must be the goal of popular desire. The *legislative* function is the will not in its practical but its theoretical energy.'[28] Parliament still provided the proletariat with valuable opportunities, but belonged essentially to the later stages of the class state. As political parties represented different material interests so, logically, a classless society would not reproduce party politics. Neither would a society that had overcome the division of labour allow administrative tasks to become the monopoly of any particular grouping.

The Paris Commune of 1871 provided, in Marx's view, an actual indication of 'the political form at last discovered under which to work out the economic emancipation of labour'.[29] Here we find that the whole panoply of state power, its specialist functions, physical might, elevated status and wealth and its caste mentality, have been dissolved. Rather than being a power which sets itself above society, it has had its repressive functions removed and its legitimate ones integrated back within society. All its officials were elected for short periods of time on a basis of universal suffrage and paid at workmen's wages. Even 'magistrates and judges were to be elective, responsible, and revocable'.[30] The standing army was suppressed and replaced by the armed people, while the previous ideological arm of the state, the priests, 'were sent back to the recesses of private life, there to feed upon the alms of the faithful in imitation of their predecessors, the Apostles'.[31]

The commune would, Marx hoped, serve as a model for the rest of France, thus facilitating the dissolution of the excessive centralization that had flourished under bourgeois rule. Power would devolve to the various provincial localities, and the real unity of the nation would actually be enhanced by the destruction of the old state. Whether that would have happened became a matter of conjecture following the bloody suppression of the Paris Commune in May 1871. Its two-month existence, however, has fired the imagination of socialist writers ever since. Twenty years later Engels saw in it the dictatorship of the proletariat, the first stage of post-revolutionary rule. This, as Neil Harding recently explained, does not make sense.[32] The dictatorship of the proletariat is a state form, the one which follows the proletarian revolution, but precedes the final disappearance of all class distinctions. It is the transitional arrangement in which the state, rather than being an instrument used by the bourgeois minority to oppress the

proletarian majority, becomes that by which the victorious proletariat
secures its domination over the expropriated bourgeoisie. This, however, is
not what the Commune appears to have been. As Marx presented it, the
Commune was a political form closer towards the actual withering away of
the state. Rather than being an instrument of repression it appears primarily
as one of popular participatory expression. In Marx's private view this was
one of its mistakes. He felt it to have been insufficiently authoritarian in that it
did not crush its enemies. This comes closer to the view that in fact the
Commune should have been more of a dictatorship of the proletariat. Its
exact status and many of the problems associated with post-bourgeois rule
were given only the most scanty consideration by the founders of modern
communism. For a fuller analysis we must turn to Lenin's *State and
Revolution*.

For Lenin 'Democracy is a form of the state, one of its varieties.'[33] As such
it is a particular form of organized violence. The liberal state is the
dictatorship of the bourgeoisie, but because of its democratic representative
character 'it signifies the formal recognition of equality of citizens'.[34] It thus
points to a future in which the ideals associated with democracy could be
manifested through the removal of restrictions that the wider social context
imposed. Under bourgeois democracy the majority decide which section of
the bourgeois minority is to oppress them for the next few years. Proletarian
democracy, on the other hand, is the form whereby the proletarian majority
use the state apparatus to suppress what opposition remains from the
expropriated bourgeoisie and their supporters. It is synonymous with the
dictatorship of the proletariat. That democracy can be identified with
dictatorship makes sense, if at all, only if emphasis is placed virtually
exclusively on the majoritarian aspect. The prerequisite of free expression is
downgraded because opinion is presumed to be known simply by reference to
social location. Representation remains, but in the manner suggested by the
Paris Commune, that is without parliamentarism 'as a special system, as the
division of labour between the legislative and the executive, as a privileged
position for the deputies'.[35] Bridging this gulf is one of the main ways in
which Lenin's theory pursues a fuller development of political participation
than exists in the liberal parliamentary system. The combination of
proletarian rule and modern scientific developments is assumed to facilitate
the gradual withering away of the state through the performance of necessary
administrative tasks by the community in general. There are echoes of both
Rousseau and Paine in Lenin's assumption that government would appear
straightforward, simple and uncontentious in a society without basic
divisions, when honesty prevails and personal ambition and pride are
curtailed. In essence the mystique of power hides an activity that is not

inherently complicated. The difference in Lenin's position is that he placed this apparently utopian scheme of universal participation upon a materialist basis. Capitalism

itself creates the *premises* that *enable* really 'all' to take part in the administration of the state. Some of these premises are: universal literacy, which has already been achieved in a number of the most advanced capitalist countries, then the 'training and disciplining' of millions of workers by the huge, complex, socialized apparatus of the postal service, railways, big factories, large-scale commerce, banking, etc., etc.[36]

In sum the accounting and control necessary for

the correct functioning of the *first phase* of communist society . . . have been *simplified* by capitalism to the extreme and reduced to the extraordinarily simple operations – which any literate person can perform – of supervising and recording, knowledge of the four rules of arithmetic, and issuing appropriate receipts.[37]

As for the law and order function of the state, Lenin assumed that it would be performed simply and expeditiously by the armed people, and that the problem is considerably reduced by the cessation of class struggle. Separate 'bodies of armed men' are necessary for the ruling class to oppress subservient classes, but the adoption of equality creates a situation where no one section of the population is placed in structural antagonism to any other. No longer is conflict built into the social fabric.

In this situation the state form as previously known has disappeared. As democracy is one of its variants, it also has disappeared. In his rather narrow sense Lenin appears to be working for the disappearance of democracy, but in fact through the transcendence of formal parliamentary rule he hoped to achieve in fuller form many of the ideals that liberal democrats claim as their own. Consensus politics he pursued not by appeal to a common rationality but through the basis of a common and equal life situation. The full flowering of human freedom, pursued through constitutional safeguards in classical liberalism, is, according to Marxist theory, a consequence of transcending the division of labour; that is by greater choice in the daily work situation rather than in occasional general elections.

Chapter 7 of *The State and Revolution* breaks off after just two sentences. A postscript written in November 1917 notes that the final section 'will probably have to be put off for a long time. It is more pleasant and useful to go through "the experience of the revolution" than to write about it.'[38] The close proximity of the Bolshevik revolution and the writing of *State and Revolution* indicates that precisely at the point of taking power Lenin foresaw a future that, even on liberal democratic grounds, had much to recommend it. The most fundamental objection concerns not so much its democratic aims as its feasibility.

IV

'Leninism', writes Marcel Liebman, 'came to power under conditions that were as unfavourable as they could possibly be for the carrying out of its tasks.'[39] In spite of the appallingly unpropitious combination of civil war, foreign intervention, blockade and famine, Communist rule has endured, but only at the cost of rendering the original ideals increasingly hollow. The reasons for this failure are various, complex, and matters of considerable dispute. To some the flaw lies in Marxism itself. Milovan Djilas, for example, believes that those who mistake a social ethic for a scientific truth are bound to be intolerant of other viewpoints, and thus, once in power, inevitably find themselves repressing contrary opinions.[40] To others, such as the 'orthodox' German Marxist, Karl Kautsky, the basic failure stems from the premature introduction of socialism to a country that had not even fully consolidated its bourgeois revolution. A third view questions whether the combination of advanced technology, transcendence of the division of labour, high political mobilization and direct participation in administration can ever be success-fully maintained.

On achieving power the Bolsheviks had inherited arrangements worked out under Kerensky for establishing a Constituent Assembly. This they chose to abolish in January 1918, almost as soon as it had convened. 'The Constituent Assembly', wrote Trotsky, 'placed itself across the path of the revolutionary movement, and was swept aside.'[41] This was criticized by Rosa Luxemburg who declared that if the Assembly 'reflected the picture of the vanished past'[42] the simple and appropriate remedy consisted in the calling of fresh elections. This, however, misses the Marxist point that the pure Soviet form is considered a higher mode of democratic expression, 'a form of democracy without parallel in any other country of the world'.[43] The issue, theoretically at least, was not between democracy and dictatorship, but between parliamentary, representative democracy on the one hand, and direct participatory democracy on the other. In practice this was not the operational distinction, as access to the Soviets was restricted to those 'who procure their sustenance by useful or productive work'.[44] This rather elastic definition was so applied as to make the Soviets associations of those who supported the revolution. They were now no longer instruments of direct democracy but of, at best, direct class dictatorship. In March 1919 Lenin conceded that 'the Soviets, which by virtue of their programme are organs of government *by the working people*, are in fact organs of government *for the working people* by the advanced section of the proletariat, but not by the working people as a whole'.[45] Was this, then, the much proclaimed 'dictatorship of the proletariat'? How could it be that when, as a result of famine and devastation, the proletariat had virtually ceased to exist and only the peasantry maintained a clear continuity with their pre-revolutionary class existence? What, then, was to be the policy of the party ruling in the name of the almost non-existent working class? To relinquish power after the difficulties involved in obtaining and consolidating it was unthinkable. Besides, Russia's setbacks were regarded as transitional and, hence, temporary. Revolution in the more advanced industrial countries of western Europe was expected to rescue her from isolation and backwardness. Meanwhile Bolshevism established a dictatorship over society while attempting to create the material conditions for the transition to socialism. For Marx proletarian revolution came after the capitalist system had created the basis for general plenitude. Now Trotsky spoke of the need for 'primitive socialist accumulation', a revealing adaptation of Marx's description of emergent capitalism. The party, meanwhile, was placed in the unenviable position of representing a class that barely existed, committed to a social order not yet attainable. It had to hold power until conditions were ripe for its exercise. Its responsibility was thus to the future rather than its present, and so the question of its contemporary consensual level was somewhat devalued. The party hoped to rule so that society might become fit for its rule. In this situation people with political or social aspirations or, perhaps, a concern for their own security, sought entry to the Bolshevik party. Initial optimism at the rapid growth of the party soon declined as the revolutionary 'Old Guard' saw their ideals engulfed in a wider inchoate radical and careerist mêlée. The first purge occurred in 1921, and was the forerunner of many more, as the self-destructive attempt was made to achieve a Marxist purity that the wider social environment could not provide. Gradually the defence of Bolshevik values was transformed into the defence of the defenders. The ideals became distorted or irrelevant and the state came to function as an end in itself.

This tendency was one already feared by Lenin. Expertise proved to be less widespread and more necessary than he had assumed. Large sections of the Czarist bureaucracy had to be retained although the attempt was made to control them through a system of 'workers' and peasants' inspectors'. Lenin foreshadowed many later criticisms of the Soviet Union when in 1921 he described it as a 'workers' state with bureaucratic distortions'.[46] These 'distortions', rather than being merely a transitory phenomenon, later became more pronounced, just as the relative freedom of the immediate post-revolutionary situation was transformed into the oppressive coarseness of Stalinism. The overseers, the self-proclaimed guarantors of orthodoxy, ruled over society rather than allowing society to rule itself. This was, quite simply, because more democratic expression would have endangered Bolshevik rule. Their ascent to power was facilitated by a short-lived rush of support based on their policy of ending the war and giving land to the peasantry. When this tide of approval ebbed, the party was driven to what Trotsky called 'measures of revolutionary self-defence'[47] to provide a power base that the masses no longer supplied. The breach with democracy thus made was never to be healed, and was to engulf many of its erstwhile supporters.

The operational assumption is that 'state power must be identified with, or at least based upon, a political organization that knows no rival'.[48] Thus, although certain of the forms of parliamentary practice are maintained, the genuine participatory content is almost entirely extinguished. Some time ago Moscow Radio was good enough to explain to *The Times* its argument for a one-party system. The core of its analysis was the following:

If one is to apply the British yardstick to the Soviet electoral system, one has to visualise conditions in Britain resembling Soviet conditions. Supposing you in Britain had a party completely representative of the entire people – so representative in fact that nearly 100 per cent of the electorate cast their votes for it year after year. I think it reasonable to say that no one in Britain would consider such a state of affairs undemocratic. Yet this would mean that in the actual elections you would have one candidate in a constituency.[49]

In Marxist theory a party must represent a particular class interest. For one party to represent virtually the 'entire people', for there to be only one interest, there must be only one class, or rather, since class is a function of social division, society must be classless. But for Marx classlessness resulted from overcoming excessive division of labour and from different relations to the ownership of the means of production. Unless this occurs different material interests necessarily arise. Not having overcome the division of labour, nor the unequal control over the social product, Soviet society must be assumed to produce different material interests. Thus, on their own logic, one must assume either or both of the following: that certain interests are not granted recognition, and that the Communist Party, rather than being simply the formal representative of the consensual popular will, provides instead the context within which certain material conflicts obtain restricted expression.

There is, then, a wide gulf between Soviet ideology and practice. Marx's negative critique of bourgeois democracy is maintained, but his positive alternatives are barely contemplated. Bourgeois democracy, it seems, is easy to criticize but difficult to improve upon. Soviet attainment of even the much derided bourgeois political freedoms would be an immense step forward in a democratic direction. As for Lenin's conception of proletarian democracy and the withering away of the state, it is impossible to believe that either are being pursued by the Soviet government or any of its East European satellites. The epithet 'formal democracy' has as its Soviet counterpart a 'formal Marxism', which functions as a mode of legitimation rather than description.

V

Why is it, then, that in attempting to go beyond the modest participatory levels of liberal democracy, communism has fallen far short of them? Rather than concentrate on particular factors such as Russia's material and political backwardness at the time of the Bolshevik Revolution, we shall instead mainly turn to some more general problems pertaining to Marxism and the institutionalization of democracy.

Democratic structures provide a necessary pre-condition for popular control but are not in themselves sufficient. Their aim is only manifested when widespread participation actually ensues, i.e. the opportunity has not only to be there, it has to be continuously taken up. For most people, however, political concerns are far from predominant and rank behind economic pursuits, kinship obligations and even leisure activities. From our Western perspective, fuller democratic control of political power would require, among other things, a level of public involvement that our type of society does not ordinarily produce. On the one hand there is a passive public who, grumble though they might, want the 'experts' to get on with it; on the other, a bureaucracy for whom public indifference is highly convenient. Between them is placed the thin layer of 'politicals' whose activity helps to legitimise the system in terms of its apparent participatory possibilities.

From a Marxist perspective levels of political participation do not derive from the 'nature of Man' but from the character of a particular social and political system. The narrow conception of politics as parliamentary thereby assumes it to be a specialist activity. Division of labour designates politics as the concern of others. A Marxist view is that this situation is overcome by economic crises which increasingly politicise formerly dormant sections of the population. This creates a revolutionary situation which eventually leads to the establishment of a socialist system which both relies on and facilitates the fullest possible popular participation.

This is what the Paris commune of 1871 and the Russian soviets of 1905 and 1917 seem to have promised. However, the commune form has yet to prove its durability. What Marc Ferro has called 'a state of permanent mobilization'[50] has, paradoxically, never been more than temporary. It is, however, its permanence that revolutionary, participatory theory assumes.

A post-revolutionary decline of political fervour can be attributed both to weariness after years of heightened activity, and to the changing nature of the immediate tasks. The stage of gallant heroics passes by; and in 1920 Lenin emphasized the need for 'day-by-day, monotonous, petty and workaday effort'.[51] Whatever precise weighting one puts on particular suggested causes, 'the depoliticization of the Soviet working class'[52] was the result. Rather than facilitating a participatory society, communism has created an enforced passivity *vis-à-vis* a well-nigh unchallengeable bureaucracy.

What evidence, then, does modern political experience provide as to the possibility of direct popular participation as a permanent system of government? The answer is not encouraging, for it seems that capitalism does not produce it; communism does not allow it; and revolutionary upheavals do not sustain it.

A further difficulty is that even were high participation to prove durable, democratization would still be endangered by what Rousseau saw as the likelihood of a particular will forming at the very centre of power, or what Michels later termed 'the iron law of oligarchy'. The general problem here is the tendency for the executive to emerge from their nominally passive role and to formulate a will of their own. They develop a distinct political interest in virtue of their distinct position. From an approach that initially coincides with that of their electors they develop into a separate power over those to whom they owe their elevation. Their position gives special knowledge which is transformed into an overriding claim to have their opinions respected and their suggestions implemented.

The Marxist defence against this danger is based on the fairly rapid circulation of executive tasks among the population, thus ensuring that an isolated caste, with high salary, power and status, does not emerge. The main presuppositions behind this aspiration are that political problems are actually so straightforward that anyone can understand them, and administrative tasks so simple that all can perform them. The only problem about relevant knowledge is assumed to be its distribution rather than its inherent complexity. Engels wrote of the government of people being replaced by the administration of things, as if these were the only alternatives, but surely the absence of class government would remove neither the need for decision taking nor much of the difficulty of ascertaining the optimal path. Theodor Roszak has vividly portrayed the intellectual demands of contemporary political involvement.

Nothing is any longer simply and straightforwardly accessible to the layman. Everything – economics, foreign policy, war and peace, city planning, education, environmental design, business administration, human psychology – now requires the benefit of professional training to be comprehensible . . . Does our democracy not continue to be a spectator sport in which the general public chooses up sides among contending groups of experts, looking on stupidly as the specialists exchange the facts and figures, debate the esoteric details, challenge one another's statistics, and question one another's prognostications?[53]

Here, as so often, the particular difficulties might be attributed to the adverse consequences of capitalism – that science is too specialized an activity, and that educational levels are below what they could be if social priorities were different. Such answers have a measure of truth but contain an even larger dose of evasion. Not only must we assume a highly participatory motivation as a generalized attribute of 'socialist man', so also we must add to it a polymathic intelligence. As the necessary attributes mount up in terms of knowledge, ability and purpose, the result defies commonplace credibility.

It becomes as truly stupendous as it appears increasingly distant. It is not that we bound the objectively attainable within the modest horizons of our own sceptical age, but rather that the widening gulf between contemporary aspirations and the Marxist ideal militates even further against the chances of the contemporary working class actively committing themselves in its pursuit. In short, for a goal to be pursued it has to be conceived as attainable. Certainly the paucity of aspiration is one of the most depressing aspects of current politics. In the language of Herbert Marcuse, capitalist society seems to have created a one-dimensional mentality unable to envisage any alternative to what currently prevails. And yet history does not stand still. 'If Sparta and Rome perished, what State can hope to endure for ever?'[54] Unlike the optimists of the French Revolutionary period, whose heir Marx was, we do not presume to know what the future holds in store. However, we may feel sure that in response to whatever developments ensue, the most critical and the most optimistic aspects of the Western intellectual tradition will once more come to the fore. A Marxism aware of its history, and hence, sensitive to the dangers of Stalinist degeneration, is emerging as part of this process.

Part of Marxism's contemporary appeal derives from its portrayal of liberal democracy as both narrow and fraudulent. We know too much about manipulated consent and secret government naively to accept the rationalist individualist assumptions behind liberal democratic practice. Its constriction of politics to the certified party experts comes through all too clearly when a national newspaper can declare that 'The only day of action that counts in a democracy is polling day.'[55] Related to this restriction, assumptions that are accepted as normal in respect of formal political power – one person, one vote – for some reason appear dangerously heretical when applied to the workplace. And yet the notion of management/labour parity, scarcely yet achieved, is monstrously unbalanced even in its assumptions. If one is motivated by the demands of people rather than of capital, of democracy rather than plutocracy, labour and management would exert influence in proportion to their respective numbers, and thus the former would prevail overwhelmingly.

Marxist theory thus broadens the area perceived as political and extends democracy into the economic and social domains. It thereby pursues a much fuller democracy than that envisaged in liberal theory. However, its negative strength, that of critique, has not been matched by alternative positive achievements. Its failures pose a challenge not just for advocates of Marxism but for anyone committed to the values of democracy itself.

7

Consensus and community: the theory of African one-party democracy

PAUL NURSEY-BRAY

The departure of the colonial powers from Africa left the newly independent states, rough-hewn from the old colonial empires, with many customs, institutions and ideologies that were tokens of the pervasive influence of the colonial culture. From bewigged judges to boulevard cafés, from university syllabuses to a passion for football, the Africa that had been shared out in so cavalier a manner in the nineteenth century had suffered a sea change by the time of independence. Many of the introduced norms and institutions were already so accepted or absorbed as to be, apparently, part of the established order. But many of the outward manifestations of colonial influence, particularly the political institutions of the multi-party liberal-democratic model, rapidly established by the colonial powers prior to their departure, underwent an early assault. Out of this critical rejection of European cultural norms and the legacy of colonialism was born the theory of African one-party democracy.

As C.B. Macpherson notes in his excellent essay on democracy in the undeveloped world, there are 'in a newly-independent country . . . strong pressures against a liberal-democratic system'.[1] In the African context these pressures stemmed, in part, from a broad effort to enunciate genuine African values, as against the oppressive and racist views of the colonizer. It was the Négritude movement that began this search for an authentic African identity and which was thus the progenitor of the theory of African democracy.

Based on the work of two West Indian intellectuals, Léon Damas and Aimé Césaire, and one West African writer, Léopold Senghor, Négritude, through poetry and literature, sought to counteract the negative image of the African that was all too manifest in European culture. Ultimately the project was to replace the value-structure of the European with one more directly linked to the aspirations of the African people. Césaire, Damas and Senghor began to publish in the 1930s, and by the 1940s and 1950s their work had found echoes in Anglophone Africa, especially in the theories of Kwame Nkrumah and his ideas on African personality.

The Négritude writers adopted two main forms of expression. On the one hand they criticized, by ridicule, the major taunts of the Europeans by unashamedly claiming, as their own, qualities the Europeans derided. Thus the blackness of African skin was celebrated and the movement named. Aimé Césaire produced perhaps the best example of this side of the Négritude philosophy in his *Cahier d'un Retour au Pays Natal*, in which the idea of Négritude was launched, when he mockingly proclaimed that the absence of technical inventiveness, held by European writers to be the *sine qua non* of civilization, was something of which the African could be proud.

> Heia for the royal Kailcedrate!
> Heia for those who have never invented anything
> those who never explored anything
> those who never tamed anything
>
> those who give themselves up to the essence of all things
> ignorant of surfaces but struck by the movement of all things
> free of the desire to tame but familiar with the play of the world
>
> truly the eldest sons of the world
> open to all the breaths of the world
> fraternal territory of all breaths
> undrained bed of the waters of the world
> flesh of the flesh of the world pumping with the very movement
>   of the world.[2]

The latter lines of this stanza speak to the other side, and perhaps the key aspect, of the movement's philosophy, the assertion of the uniqueness and value of African experience. It is an experience associated with uniquely African institutions and norms that are held to derive from pre-colonial African society, the traditional society of the village, the age group and the family.

There were, of course, many differences between the various pre-colonial village communities of Africa, in terms of culture, of economy and of social mores. However, many basic characteristics were shared. For the most part they were engaged in production for immediate consumption and, while there were some inequalities of wealth, no significant economic classes existed. The members of the villages were linked not only through the village structures, but through kinship and often complex age-group arrangements that served to reinforce the sense of equality and community. While political systems and formal leadership patterns varied, nonetheless there was a sense in which a basic political democracy functioned. At village meetings, or informally, people were consulted in the decision-making process. The tribal elders might make the decisions, but they would be decisions that reflected the consensus.[3] In short there were in existence communities that correspond to Ferdinand Tönnies' definition of Gemeinschaft, 'characterised by the social will as concord, folkways, mores and religion'.[4] The alien world, represented by the colonizer, was the world of social differentiation and liberal-capitalist individualism, the world of Gesellschaft.

Drawing on these historical sources African traditional society is en- visaged as an ideal communal society where equality and care for others is the norm, where land, work and produce are shared, and where decision- making, while informal, is essentially democratic. This conceptualization of an ideal pre-colonial society had far-reaching significance. First introduced by the Négritude writers, it became the foundation of those specifically African political philosophies that emerged in the 1950s and reached their ascendancy in the heady days of early independence. In fact the concept of traditional society performed the same function in the creation of African political theory as the concept of the state of nature had done in the Western tradition. It was an analytic concept on which fruitful speculation could be based. Yet its presumed historical existence, as a set of general characteristics attaching to African traditional society in general, was of crucial importance. It gave the concepts derived from it polemical force in opposition to introduced norms and mores, and it legitimated their use in the construction of a future society. The project of African political theory as it emerged from this quest for a new identity was the reconstruction of an idealized past as the basis for present and future political activity.

The two major theories that sprang from this source were African socialism and African democracy. Although our prime concern is with the latter tradition, they cannot be easily separated, since they share a common ancestry and depend on similar assumptions regarding the essentially communal nature of African society. Léopold Senghor (b. 1906) and Julius Nyerere (b. 1922), both poet-presidents and political theorists, best set out the characteristics of this society in a way that distinguishes it from its European counterpart. Senghor contrasts the communal nature of African society with the collectivism of the European. The African traditional society, he asserts, elevated sharing, and the integration of the individual into the communal whole, into its key values. This contrasts favourably, in his view, with the individualism of European society, which makes of society an aggregation of discrete individuals, a collective, rather than a community.

For Senghor it is the African family that is at the very heart of the communal nature of African society. It is the 'centre and source, the hearth that maintains the flame of life, the "vital force" which increases and intensifies as it is manifested in the living bodies of a multiplying and prospering people'. Moreover, Senghor emphasizes that the African family is turned not only to the past; it is 'also turned towards the future. Indeed, it is the past with the traditions that prepares the future.'⁵ It is these traditions that enshrine the communal character of African society, where property and work are shared. 'In Africa . . . traditional Africa . . . there is almost never *property* in the European sense of the word, objects, that is, which can be "used or abused", destroyed or sold. The general means of production . . . the land and its wealth, the wealth of the soil and subsoil . . . cannot become property.'⁶ Thus in the traditional society labour is unalienated and the spirit of community triumphant.

Senghor uniquely carries this opposition between European and African culture one stage further by the assertion that they are characterized by quite different approaches to reality. While the European approach, he asserts, is rational and intellectual, the African's is affective and inductive. Senghor accepts the European's taunt that the African is irrational and translates it into a positive value, giving to the African a special claim to the integrated, emotionally participative life of the community. '"I think therefore I am," wrote Descartes, the European *par excellence*. The African might say, "I smell, I dance the *Other*. I am" . . . *Classical European reason is analytical and makes use of the object. African reason is intuitive and participates in the object.'*⁷

Nyerere adopts a similar stance towards the character of African traditional society, although he does not venture into epistemology. Traditional society was, he believes, a social system operating on the basis of love, family ties, unity and equality. The organized pursuit of selfish ends was alien to this society. Everybody was a worker and the proceeds of labour were shared.

Both the 'rich' and the 'poor' individual were completely secure in African society. Natural catastrophe brought famine, but it brought famine to everybody – 'poor' or 'rich'. Nobody starved, either of food or of human dignity, because he lacked personal wealth; he could depend on the wealth possessed by the community of which he was a member. That was socialism. That *is* socialism.⁸

Senghor and Nyerere also agree on the factor that disrupted traditional society. The alien values of the European colonizer engendered divisions and created problems. In particular the capitalist system and its ethos of greed for private rather than communal advantage shattered the old mores, mutated the prevailing environmental influences and destroyed the original unity. 'The unity of society', Nyerere asserts, 'has been weakened because the equality of its members has been broken.'⁹ In essence it is asserted that African traditional society was classless; class division and its attendant evils is a European product, a problem foreign to African experience. 'In spite of what certain abstract theorists have said,' Senghor proclaims, 'we had no classes before the European conquest.'[10] Nyerere makes a similar claim in his assertion that in 'traditional African society *everybody* was a worker. There was no other way of earning a living for the community.'[11]

On the basis of this vision of the traditional society as classless and communitarian, its development rudely interrupted by the introduced vices of capitalism, both Senghor and Nyerere embrace socialism while rejecting Marxism. Nyerere's adoption of this position is the more significant since he was to commit his country to a programme of socialist development. Marx's theories are irrelevant because the class struggles they address are not native to Africa and will, in the optimistic view of Senghor and Nyerere, disappear along with other malign effects of colonialism as the salutary effects of political independence are felt. The task for African leaders, at least as set out in these writings of the 1950s and 1960s, is the rediscovery of the genius of the African people and the creation of a socialist future by the recreation of a socialist past. The somewhat ingenuous belief in the regenerative effects of independence this suggests was typical of the period.

From a Marxist point of view this standpoint is, of course, essentially ahistorical, and places Senghor, Nyerere, and other exponents of the theory of African socialism in the camp best described as utopian. Yet it is a utopian socialism quite distinct from its European counterpart. The utopians of the nineteenth century, both admired and reviled by Marx and Engels, saw them-selves as creating an entirely new society, whether it be a New Lanark or a Phalanstère. The African utopians at one and the same time recognize history and yet deny its force. Their vision, while ahistorical and utopian, draws on history both for the design of the new society and for its claim to legitimacy.

It is not our task to rehearse the arguments, now legion, as to the enduring values, or otherwise, of the theories of African socialism and the political programmes they engendered. But it is important to understand the nature of the assertions made about traditional African society in order to appreciate the basis for the theory of African democracy with which it is intrinsically linked. For the communal nature of African traditional society was held to have engendered a distinct style of democratic practice. In essence it was a form of democracy that encouraged discussion and participation among the community and which produced a consensus, without factional divisions. Senghor describes this communal democracy in these terms:

Europeans, from the West and from the East, often speak to us of democracy, each in his own way. Yet we have our own conception of democracy, the African conception, in no way inferior to that of Europe. We would do well to go back to it. It is founded, at least among the Negroes and Berbers, on the 'palaver'. 'Palaver' is a dialogue, or rather a discussion, where everyone speaks, taking his turn, expressing his opinion. In the past, even the dead were consulted. But once everyone had expressed his opinion, the minority followed the majority so that there was unanimity. And the unanimous opinion was rigorously enforced.[12]

Nyerere's vision is very similar. His views are set out in his early writings, in particular in the essays 'One-Party Government'[13] and 'Democracy and the Party System'.[14] He quotes with approval Guy Clutton Brock's description of the political process in traditional society where people 'sat and talked under the tree until they agreed'. He notes in 'One-Party Government':

Basically democracy is government by discussion as opposed to government by force, and by discussion between the people or their chosen representatives as opposed to a hereditary clique. Under the tribal system whether there was a chief or not, African society was a society of equals, and it conducted its business by discussion.[15]

Thus we have an account of democratic practice within traditional society which, when taken together with the other postulates regarding that society, becomes a theory of democracy that can inform contemporary practice. As Senghor notes, 'What we have to do is to restore, under a modern form of course, this democracy.'[16] It is a theory of democracy that, based as it is on a communal vision, emphasizes participation, discussion and consensus. In doing so it self-consciously distinguishes itself from the liberal-democratic model bequeathed by the colonial powers. Such a model, it is argued, is inadequate and inappropriate to African needs, since it reflects and reinforces divisions in society. Thus, the theory of African democracy is centrally located in a certain conception of the character and future role of African traditional society. It is indissolubly linked to the idea of society as a community, and to a rejection of forms of property that promote division and inequality.

Rousseau: the general will and the community

Western political thought has few examples of a theory of democracy associated with the notion of community, although its influence is extensive. The ideas of Winstanley, Rousseau and the early Marx are examples of a developed theory of the community and its attendant political forms. The ideas of the latter two theorists in particular provide a useful comparative basis for a discussion of African experience. It is to the theory of Rousseau that one is immediately drawn because of the striking parallels between his ideas and those of African theorists.

There is no evidence that Rousseau's ideas have been directly borrowed, but that his political theory had an influence on the Western-educated proponents of African democracy is indisputable. Kwame Nkrumah, at a state dinner to celebrate Ghana's independence in March 1957, noted that '. . . here today the work of Rousseau, the work of Marcus Garvey, the work of Aggrey, the work of Casely Hayford, the work of these illustrious men who have gone before us, has come to reality at this present moment'.[17] As earlier commentators, discussing the link between Rousseau's ideas and

Africa noted, Nkrumah was here invoking the spirit of revolution as exemplified by Rousseau.[18] But there is also a sense in which, as Thomas Hodgkin claimed, Rousseau was the 'spiritual ancestor' of African popular nationalism.[19]

Rousseau's primitivist vision of the noble savage is a direct parallel of the euphoric praise of the simplicity of the traditional society that characterizes the work of the theorists of African democracy. Indeed, for both Rousseau and the latter theorists, there is a sense in which the natural, the primitive, is given a moral force which elevates it above existing practice. Rousseau's attack on modernity and its effect on contemporary morals in his *Discourse on the Arts and Sciences* finds an echo in the attack by the Africans on the introduced norms of colonialism. There is also an echo of Rousseau's emphasis on the role of human emotion and passion in Senghor's statement regarding the affective attitude of the African to reality. The latter's depiction of the African's apprehension of reality has many similarities to the epistemology of European romanticism. Moreover, in his description of the emergence of social man from natural society, Rousseau describes one stage of society, prior to the development of metallurgy and agriculture, which quite clearly, in its character as a society of equals engaged in simple production, parallels the traditional society of the African writers.

Rousseau and contemporary African theorists share a conviction that democracy is only possible in a community that is not factionalised through the dominance of private over public interests. He believes with them that selfishness and faction are produced by inequality which in turn stems from an unequal access to, and command of, the society's resources. In the *Discourse on the Origins of Inequality* Rousseau gives an almost satirical account of the type of civil contract described by Locke, where the original parties to the contract that establishes society are concerned, in the main, with the preservation of property, or rather with the maintenance of an unequal division of property.

This type of society, in its essentials a liberal-capitalist model, is rejected by Rousseau. Its institutionalization of inequality which 'bound new fetters on the poor, and gave new powers to the rich', gives rise to a society where competition and the pursuit of private interest are paramount.[20] For Rousseau the point of contrast is natural society where, he argues, complete liberty and equality exist. The task he sets himself is to design a society that will preserve both these virtues; a task that issues in the theory of the 'general will'.

Nyerere's complaints regarding the evils of capitalism essentially make the same point. 'For it was from those overseas contacts,' he laments, 'that we developed the idea that the way to the comfort and prosperity that everyone wants is through selfishness and individual advancement.'[21] Thus, while Rousseau is protesting against the growing influences on civil society of a nascent, yet strengthening, bourgeois society, Nyerere is protesting against the effects of the global expansion of its influence. He, like Rousseau, rejects this influence in an attempt to translate the values of what is the equivalent in moral terms of Rousseau's natural society, the African traditional society, into a modern idiom.

Having dedicated themselves to the task of formulating a blueprint for a functioning community, Rousseau and the African theorists face the same difficulty; it is easier to describe a consensus than to design one. In a community, whether it be the idealized communities of Ancient Greece or an African traditional society, a consensus exists because the community exists, producing a community interest that binds its members. The mechanical, political means by which this consensus is manifest are not as important as the underlying features of the society that ensure its continuing existence. If a consensus exists in a genuine community it will find a means of expression. If it does not, it is unlikely that it can be manufactured by the political procedures adopted. Rousseau recognizes this and is careful to set out the ground rules for his political community. There must be a basic equality, economic as well as political. While private property and some differences in wealth may exist, they must not be so great as to create class divisions in society.[22] There must be a commitment to consensus in the form of the general will where 'Each of us puts his person and all his power in common under the supreme direction of the general will, and, in our corporate capacity, we receive each member as an indivisible part of the whole.'[23] Finally the political community must be small so that all may participate in the business of governing and being governed. Representation is barred and large states an impossibility. Despite the establishment of these prerequisites, Rousseau still faces problems when he attempts to describe how a consensus emerges from the deliberations of the general will. His problematic discussion of voting procedures as the basis for the general will, and of the way in which the minority, should one emerge, will be constrained to acquiesce totally in the decisions of the majority, illustrate the peculiar difficulties that attend attempts to describe how a complete, rather than limited, consensus can be produced by a formal political process.

The theorists of African democracy, while subscribing to a similar ideal, adopt a more pragmatic approach towards implementation. The community democracy of the traditional society is not seen as a model that can be directly put into practice. No case is made for the return to small self-contained communities. The nation-state and representation are seen as unavoidable political realities. The idea of the traditional society is used within this framework to legitimize certain communitarian values, and it is the one-party system itself that, in practical terms, is seen as the vehicle of consensus.

It is Nyerere in particular who has attempted to translate the broad theory drawn from the idealized practice of traditional society into guidelines for a functioning democratic society. To his elaboration of the theory we must now turn our attention.

Nyerere and one-party democracy

Nyerere's theory of democracy is, as we have noted, based on ideas of consensus and community and on decision-making as a process involving agreement among a community of equals. But as Nyerere is interested in drawing, from this ideal, guidelines for practical action, he is forced to make accommodations to the reality of the large and complex territorial state bequeathed by the colonizer. While direct democracy is preferable, represent-ation is an acceptable alternative.

Moreover, not only does Nyerere accept a democratic scheme based on representation, but he also accepts a parliamentary system where the elected representatives can give voice to the interests of their constituents. What then is to prevent the emergence of factional divisions that could create rifts within the consensus? If there are to be parliamentary divisions, with formal voting and the crystallization of interests, what is to prevent a division into parties? At one level the existence of a genuine community of interests in Tanzania is clearly held to be a safeguard. Indeed one argument for the introduction of one-party democracy in 1965 was the fact that the Tanganyika African National Union had won all of the seats in the previous elections. More importantly, at another level, the one-party system itself is an institutionaliz-ation of consensus; a formal arrangement that allows for division while setting it within strict limits. The two levels are reciprocally linked. The consensus within the community allows for a one-party system to exist in a democratic manner, while the task of the party is to organize, orchestrate and maintain the consensus.

The notion of consensus underlines any democratic scheme of govern-ment. In liberal-democracy there must be a basic agreement as to the rules of the political game. There is division and a conflict of interest, but it is accepted that these conflicts are not so basic that they cannot be channelled through the election system and manifest themselves within a parliament as an opposition between representatives or parties. If the divisions within the society are sufficiently great then this system, whereby a plurality of interests is represented, can break down and the opposing groups may reject the electoral process in favour of other forms of conflict. But the consensus regarding majority rule and minority right is normally sufficient to in-stitutionalize competition and prevent a violent resolution. Nyerere, by contrast, requires a much higher level of consensus. It must be a consensus that minimizes division to the point where there is no longer the need for a representation of differences by contending parties. The divisions that advocates of liberal-democracy believe can be usefully expressed, but safely contained, within the multi-party system, are seen by Nyerere not as healthy manifestations of differing views within a broad consensus, but as either the outcome of selfish and mischievous factional interests, or as representative of fundamental and antagonistic social divisions.

Consequently Nyerere argues, in 'Democracy and the party system', that not only is it possible for consensus government to operate democratically on the basis of the one-party system, but '. . . where there is one party, and that party is identified with the nation as a whole, the foundations of democracy are firmer than they ever can be where you have two or more parties, each representing only a section of the community.'[24] Thus Nyerere rejects the two-party system as one alien to African experience, a foreign system that reflects the European society in which it was born. In the European context the multi-party system functions as an expression of opposed class interests. It is a system that turns the discussion of important national issues into a 'football match' of factional disputants. The one-party system proposed by Nyerere will, he believes, not be prone to such evils, since it is 'identified with the nation as a whole'.

In fine, Nyerere rejects the multi-party system as both the institutional manifestation of the feuding of selfish factions or classes and as an unsatisfactory way of disguising and defusing a lack of national purpose and unity.

Now my argument is that a two-party system can be justified only when the parties are divided over some fundamental issue; otherwise it merely encourages the growth of factionalism. Or, to put it another way, the only time a political group can represent the interests of a section of the community, without being a faction, is when that group fights to remove a grievous wrong from society. But then, the differences between this group and those responsible for the wrong it fights, are fundamental; and there can therefore be no question of national unity until the differences have been removed by change. And 'change' in that context is a euphemism, because any change in fundamentals is properly termed 'revolution'. What is more, the reason why the word 'revolution' is generally associated with armed insurrection is that the existence of really fundamental differences within any society poses a 'civil war' situation, and has often led to bloody revolution.[25]

This statement illustrates both the absolute necessity of national unity, of a consensus within the community of the nation, for the one-party scheme to operate democratically, and also the potential rigidity of the scheme. Nyerere's statement poses abrupt alternatives. Either the society is sufficiently united to allow of democratic one-party rule, truly identified with the nation as a whole, or we are faced with a divided society operating on the basis of a multi-party system. If it is divided over minor issues the effect is seen as the manifestation of petty factionalism. If the issues are fundamental, then we have a civil-war situation. The potential for the accommodation of differences, frequently produced by conflicting economic interests, assumed by the theorists of the multi-party system, is absent, as too is the accompanying flexibility. Nyerere's scheme of democracy needs as its *sine qua non* a community of interests based on a relatively equal access to resources.

With the emphasis on unity and consensus it may be thought that the individual would, in Nyerere's scheme, be allowed less scope for dissent or purely eccentric behaviour than in a Western liberal-democratic model. Nyerere denies this. While each person will be constrained by the norms that maintain the community by maintaining equality, nevertheless there is a place for non-conformity and for a critical attitude towards the *status quo*. In terms that echo those of Mill, Nyerere praises the virtues of the non-conformist. 'It is here that the value of the "eccentric", the non-conformist in society, comes in. He it is who by the irritation he causes, stops society from ceasing to think, forces it to make constant re-evaluations and adjustments.'[26] Nyerere's disclaimer of a lack of tolerance is indicative of a problem that bedevils all theorists of community democracy. The search for consensus and unity appears from the liberal-democratic viewpoint to threaten individualism. Thus it is that Rousseau suffers the fate of being pilloried as a totalitarian, while, in truth, his concern was, as Cobban has noted, to 'hold the balance between the individual and the community'.[27] For a true totalitarian the individual's weight is so slight that the question of balance does not arise.

Clearly the maintenance or creation of a unified society is crucial to Nyerere's theory of democracy, which is why it is linked to his proposals for the development of *ujamaa* socialism,[28] a socialist experiment founded on *ujamaa* villages, the aim of which is to maintain or, where necessary, recreate the virtues and values of traditional society.

The continuing arguments regarding the success or failure of Tanzania's socialist experiment are involved. On the one hand stand the supporters of *ujamaa* socialism, who argue that, given the constraints imposed on Tanzanian society by its position in the world economy, important achievements have been accomplished since Nyerere set a course for a unique species of socialism in the Arusha declaration of 1967.[29] They point to the nationalization programme, the education programme aimed at general literacy, the equalization of wages, the establishment of *ujamaa* villages and the general egalitarian ethos as evidence of an important departure from the development experience of other African nations. Given that Tanzania is one of the poorest nations on earth what more can be expected, they ask, in the time span involved? Tanzania is not yet socialist, as Nyerere himself admits. He insists, however, that she is still on the road to socialism. The critics, particularly those of the Marxist school, argue that despite some social welfare achievements the attempt to create socialism has failed.[30] They argue that the *ujamaa* villagization scheme has failed to create experiments in communal living and has degenerated into a mechanism for increasing the production level of cash crops; that the nationalization programme has failed to prevent the penetration of foreign capital; that the nation remains dependent on foreign aid; that the economy displays the same features of distortion as other peripheral capitalist states, with a heavy dependence on cash crops and with industrialization geared to processing and import substitution rather than capital goods. Most significantly, it is charged that, overall, despite an equalization of income structures class formation has occurred, both in the rural areas with a growing division between rich and poor peasants, and in the urban areas, where, it is alleged, privileges and positions are aggrandized by a growing state bureaucracy. Indeed, one commentator has gone so far as to describe the bureaucratic stratum as a ruling class and given them the title of 'the bureaucratic bourgeoisie'.[31]

This is not the place to rehearse these arguments and to attempt to reach a conclusion regarding their relative merits. But the effects on the theory of the one-party system of these different characterizations of the evolution of Tanzanian society is within our brief. In broad terms, given the two views of the progress of Tanzanian socialism, two conclusions can be reached. If, on the one hand, the Tanzanian experiment is deemed to be at least partially successful as its proponents claim, then this success will help to maintain and reproduce equality, the unity and the community of interests necessary for the democratic functioning of a one-party system. Even so the system, while democratic, will still be several removes from the model of community democracy on which it is based. Tanzanian democracy is the outstanding success story of African politics, with regular contested elections – contested between opposing members of the same party – held every five years since 1965. Also, there is abundant evidence that these are free and fair elections within the one-party format, with genuine contests that have seen the departure of more than one cabinet minister, and with a real representation of constituency interest at the national level. The gap between this system with its real democratic content and the blueprint drawn from traditional society widens rather than closes, however. The movement away from a close contact with the people increases as the complexity of governmental functions and the accompanying growth of the bureaucracy erect even greater barriers between government and people. In the view of commentators like Saul and Samoff the domination of bureaucracy and the distance between the government and the people has meant a substantial diminution in the quality of democracy.[32] Rousseau, of course, would have regarded this conclusion as inevitable once the attempt was made to adapt the model to a large-scale society where representation replaced direct democracy.

If the bureaucratization of the system poses a danger to its democratic operation, an even more severe threat lies in the possibility of class formation and of growing divisions within society, suggested by the critics of *ujamaa* socialism as an accurate description of the current situation. If divergent class interests are emerging, and there is strong evidence to suggest that this is the case, then the democratic operation of the one-party system will indeed be under siege. Without the flexibility to allow for the representation of these differing interests through a multi-party system, the bleak alternative, according to Nyerere, will be a civil-war situation. Such a resolution is less likely, however, than the equally bleak alternative of enforced compliance to the dictates of the party and an end to the life of a democratic system. Some of Tanzania's critics have charged that there is already evidence of a movement in this direction.[33]

Faced with this problem the Tanzanian experience in the attempted operation of a community-based democracy demonstrates the relevance of Marx's thoughts on the issues of class, community and political democracy.

Marx and the political community

In 'On the Jewish Question' Marx takes up the issue of the creation of a political community in the face of an unequal division of property. His specific concern is to demonstrate that political and religious emancipation, in the form of the institution of a liberal-democratic system, falls far short of human emancipation. In doing so he addresses many of the problems of establishing a democratic community that we have already touched upon.

What Marx is concerned to establish is the partial nature of a community established by political democracy alone. In essence, it creates a divided persona. Man as a member of a political community is an equal with his other citizens sharing equal rights and duties. Here he has a life in a 'political community where he is valued as a communal being'.[34] But, simultaneously, the same person is a member of a civil society based on private property, acquisition and competition, where his activities are far from co-operative and moral. In 'civil society where he is active as a private individual [he] treats other men as means, and degrades himself to a means and becomes the plaything of alien things'.[35] This divided state leads to alienation and to the betrayal of the ideals of the community, and thus of human emancipation. The much vaunted rights of man, Marx proclaims, are in essence merely the way in which the political persona, man in a putative community, is used to protect the partial interests of the individual as an economic agent in bourgeois society.

> . . . the political community, is degraded by the political emancipators to a mere means for the preservation of these so-called rights of man, that the citizen is declared to be the servant of egoistic man, the sphere in which man behaves as a communal being is degraded below the sphere in which man behaves as a partial being, finally that it is not man as citizen but man as bourgeois who is called the real and true man.[36]

Marx's critique of liberal-democracy echoes that of Rousseau in the latter's *Discourse on the Origin of Inequality*.[37] For both the solution to the problem is the creation of a genuine community. At this point Marx speaks, in terms still influenced by Feuerbach, of the need for the reunification of the divided persona.

The actual individual man must take the abstract citizen back into himself and, as an individual man in his empirical life, in his individual work and individual relationships become a species being; man must recognise his own forces as social forces, organise them and no longer separate social forces from himself in the form of political forces.[38]

In fine we have a somewhat more abstract statement of a conception that parallels Rousseau's general will. Later, of course, Marx situates the same conception of a community within the parameters of his materialist conception of history, and of his analysis of the working of the political economy of the capitalist mode of production. Once he has forged the tools of his materialist analysis then the conception of the community, or communism, departs markedly from that of Rousseau. At the same time it can serve as a touchstone for an evaluation of the ideas of the theorists of African one-party democracy.

The later Marx sees his model of a community as the consummation of the historical development of class-divided societies. The community can only exist as a viable entity, its basis of equality, sharing and unity, is only a possibility, once class struggles have ceased to hold sway. Thus, until we have achieved a classless society by a supersession of class struggles through revolution and the socialization of the means of production, there is no end to the objective basis for the opposition between public and private interest, and the idea of a community, while a desirable ideal, is ahistorical and utopian. Thus Marx, unlike Rousseau or the African proponents of the traditional society, is not looking back to the halcyon days of pre-capitalist communities, although there is a certain sympathy evinced for primitive communism. Generally, however, Marx looks forward to a post-capitalist situation where the essential preconditions for a community and for a democratic structure based on that type of association, have been established.

African one-party democratic theory is illuminated by this account, and its utopian character revealed. A vision of traditional African society can serve as a source of values for theorists searching for authentically African norms. But an attempt to re-create the conditions for the revival of African traditional society and its associated political customs is fraught with difficulties. While it is true that the colonial powers did disrupt traditional social and economic practices by the introduction of the capitalist mode of production, it is utopian to believe that this process can be reversed by an act of political will alone. Commodity production and wage-labour are not so easily removed. In short, the task of creating a community is more daunting than the African theorists would have us believe. The creation of a new community needs those socio-economic prerequisites that make community life possible, especially a basic economic equality in terms of both production and distribution. Given the existence of capitalist influence, both internal and external, the establishment of the necessary preconditions predicates a long period of social change, not to say revolution.

The genius of the Tanzanian experiment in democratic *ujamaa* socialism is its recognition of this link between the nature of the political process and the socio-economic character of the society. Its weakness lies in the extent to which it partakes of the utopian vision attaching to African political society, thereby discounting the very real obstacles that stand in the way of the implementation of this vision. Certainly Nyerere's view of the problem has matured since his writings of the earlier sixties. There is, in more recent work, a greater appreciation of the problems of class formation in Tanzania. But the experiment in socialism is in a critical state and the bases of community democracy remain to be created.

In addition to these problems there remain difficulties that result from any attempt to create a community without giving ground to the issue of population and territorial size. It is a problem that Nyerere has avoided, but at some cost to the credibility of his scheme. Marx answers the problem only at a level of abstraction that makes no concession to practical guidelines. Only Rousseau has faced the question squarely and given uncompromising answers. Ultimately the question of the creation of a community, in the face of modern large-scale organization, must carry us towards the solutions suggested by theorists of the anarchist tradition in their emphasis on decentralization, equality and the need to remove all traces of statism. But this lies outside the scope of the present paper.

However, despite these practical deficiencies of African one-party democratic theory which it shares with other theories of community democracy, it also shares with them certain important strengths. All such theories establish a clear link between the political process that they propose and the socio-economic characteristics of the society for which it is designed. As such they distinguish themselves from liberal-democratic models that are frequently purblind on this question. The tension between political freedom and economic equality, which so often bedevils liberal-democratic debate, is clearly faced and an answer is at least essayed. The theory of the community, and of its proposed democratic process, thus has a revolutionary potential under auspicious circumstances. Under less favourable circumstances this potential will, perhaps, appear more utopian than practical, but the importance of the theories as critical theoretical benchmarks remains.

It is in this light that the final judgement on the theory of African democracy should be made. As a guide to practice it faces many obstacles. But these are no more numerous, certainly, than those faced by theories of democracy, based on notions of community, that exist within the Western tradition. In the same way in which the latter have been accepted, if not celebrated, as an important contribution to the traditions of Western political thought, so the theory of African democracy and its attendant ideas on community life must be seen as a basic element in the creation of an authentically African political thought. It has a valid contribution to make to a specifically African vision regarding political life and the processes of government.

Revisions and critiques

8

Democracy: American style

MICHAEL MARGOLIS

But there are also cases in which, though not averse to a form of government – possibly even desiring it – a people may be unwilling or unable to fulfill its conditions . . . Thus, a people may prefer a free government, but if, . . . they are unequal to the exertions necessary for preserving it; . . . they are more or less unfit for liberty; and though it may be for their own good to have had it, even for a short time, they are unlikely long to enjoy it.
                                                                                    J.S. Mill[1]

I The problem of democratic citizenship

One thing political science tells us about citizens of the United States is that most don't know much about their governmental institutions. Another is that they neither know nor care very much about most political leaders, current issues, and public policies. For most citizens the day-to-day concerns of family and work-place demand far more attention than the concerns of politics. Were questions of governmental policy put directly before the people instead of before their representatives, the modal response would be 'no opinion'.[2]

While these findings are common knowledge among students of politics, the average citizen they picture does not comport with that pictured by the so-called 'popular image' of American democracy. The average citizen, according to this popular image, is the modern equivalent of the eighteenth-century yeoman: a hard-working individual of modest means and in-dependent mind, attentive to public affairs, protective of his own interests but fair in balancing those interests against the interests of others and of the polity in general. This image of a mythical rational citizen, traceable to the writings of such democratic theorists as Locke, Bentham or Jefferson, highlights the virtues of individualism in contrast to the values embodied in the existing societies the theorists sought to alter.[3] And even though the theorists exaggerated the citizens' abilities in order to serve the purposes at hand, these exaggerations have become muddled with representations of reality:

The man of broad common sense, mixing on equal terms with his neighbors, forming a fair unprejudiced judgment on every question, not viewy or pedantic like the man of learning, nor arrogant like the man of wealth, but seeing things in a practical businesslike, and withal kindly spirit, pursuing happiness in his own way, and willing that everyone else should do so. Such average men make the bulk of the people, and are pretty sure to go right . . .[4]

Needless to say, we Americans have been happy to accept this inflated estimate of our virtues. It complements the chauvinistic view most of us hold regarding our country's place in the world. The land of opportunity, the focal point of world commerce and industry, the fount of scientific discovery, the heart of the Western alliance, America is the exemplar of democracy – Watergate and other warts on the body politic notwithstanding:

America has been and continues to be one of the world's most democratic nations. Here, far more so than elsewhere, the public is allowed to participate widely in the making of social and political policy. The public is not unaware of its power, and the ordinary American tends to be rather arrogant about his right and competence to participate . . . The people think they know what they want and are in no mood to be led to greener pastures.[5]

Despite their sophistication, American political scientists have not been immune to the beguilement of the popular image of democracy. How could they resist when most grew up in the United States, exposed to beliefs in the wisdom of American political institutions and the goodness of the American people? Among other things the political history of the United States was presented to them in school as the epitome of progressive democratization of the political process. The expansion of the franchise, the direct election of the Senate, the introduction of primary elections, and the institution of initiatives and referenda – to name just a few progressive developments – all presumed a citizenry capable of deciding in some detail upon questions of public policy. 'All the ills of democracy can be cured by more democracy', we say.[6]

To be sure, critics had called into question the unbounded faith in the citizen projected in the popular image. The founding fathers themselves were not at all enamored with pure democracy, and they designed certain constitutional features, such as the system of the checks and balances and the indirect elections of both the President and the Senate, to curb the citizens' tendencies toward democratic excess. Foreign observers like Tocqueville and the younger Mill had fretted over the dangers of conformity and suppression of minority opinion as American society democratized in the nineteenth century, and domestic critics like Mencken and Lippmann had suggested that people were incapable of deciding in a rational manner upon most questions of twentieth-century politics.[7] But for every instance of irrational or suppressive behavior cited by the critics, defenders of the popular image could cite examples of rational democratic behavior.

The advent of systematic polling based upon probability sampling, coupled with the general adaptation of empirical methods of the natural sciences to political science, however, produced incontrovertible evidence that Lord Bryce's 'average man' was by no means average at all. By the late 1940s American political scientists, who professed faith both in scientific methods of social research and in democracy in the United States, found themselves facing a dilemma. Either they had to admit that most Americans failed to live up to the high standards of democratic citizenship, a shortcoming that John Stuart Mill had warned would lead to the loss of liberty; or else they had to declare that, notwithstanding claims to the contrary, the United States simply was not a true democracy. Needless to say, most found neither of these alternatives palatable.

To avoid this dilemma American political scientists developed a third alternative: they revised the theory of democracy to conform to American praxis as they had discerned it. The theory they developed laid emphasis on particular institutional features, which sufficed to make up for the individual citizen's shortcomings. A 'plural-elite' model of democracy emerged, in which the distribution of powers and of values among separate sets of groups, parties and leaders provided the basis for democratic governance.

II Democracy: American style

Fundamentally democracy is rule by the *demos*, the common people. But how such rule can be realized in a modern mass society, where the people cannot possibly meet face to face to debate and resolve public issues, presents a problem. The common solution, of course, is to institute representative democracy in lieu of direct democracy. The people's elected representatives meet face to face, instead of the people themselves. Through periodic elections and rotation of office the common people maintain ultimate control over their representatives and hence the ultimate (though indirect) control over the public business.

Difficulties arise, however, when scientific evidence begins to indicate that individual citizens appear to lack the basic knowledge of the political institutions, public questions, and public policies deemed necessary to provide general guidance for their representatives. When an index of political predispositions based upon socio-economic characteristics or a party membership measure based on subjective partisan self-identification are better predictors of the vote than sentiments on substantive political issues – indeed, when the most common sentiment is 'don't know' – how are the people to rule?[8] Classical statements of liberal democracy, however exaggerated by their popular image, had nonetheless taken for granted the general capability and rationality of the individual citizen. Scientific studies of the citizen's actual capacities and behaviours suggested that these presumptions were wrong.

Even though, as we shall see, there are reasons to dispute the above interpretation of the scientific findings, many American political scientists, fancying themselves as realists, readily accepted its validity. It not only laid to rest presumptive claims of the empirical accuracy of the popular image of democratic citizens, but it also demonstrated the utility of applying scientific techniques of observation and measurement to empirical representations of theoretical concepts. The logic itself was appealing: (1) If the democratic citizens of the popular image abound, they have the following empirically measurable characteristics: x, y, and z; (2) Here is a random sample of citizens whose characteristics we shall measure; here is another; and another; (3) Behold! Time and again the sampled citizens lack characteristics x, y, and z; (4) Therefore, the popularly imagined democratic citizens do not abound; they are rare birds indeed.

It did not follow, of course, that the absence of numberless good democratic citizens necessarily required substantial revisions of classical statements of liberal democracy. One first had to demonstrate that classical theorists had in fact postulated the presence of such ideal citizens. As things stood, what scientific studies actually proved was that if one accepted the validity of their measurement, then the popular image of citizens postulated by vulgarized versions of liberal democratic theory was unsupportable in the face of empirical evidence.

Nevertheless, such considerations did not stop empirically-minded political scientists from developing revised theories of democracy, which they argued took more realistic account of the capacities and behaviors of the general citizenry than had classical theories. These revised theories, which attempt to merge democratic theory and practice, fall under the general rubric of plural-elite theories. They take three apposite forms: group theories, party theories, and leadership elite theories. We shall examine each of these in turn.

Group theories of politics have a long pedigree. The idea that democratic forms of government can be achieved through the appropriate balance of powers among groups with separate interests can be found discussed in works as ancient as those of Aristotle and Polybius. The twentieth-century impetus for group theories, however, can be found in Arthur Bentley's landmark study, *The Process of Government*, first published in 1908.[9]

Bentley's work was particularly suited to the needs of revisionists of democratic theory, not only because of its emphasis on the active roles of groups in politics, but also because of its admirable attempt to measure activity in a quantitative scientific manner:

If a statement of social facts which lends itself better to measurement is offered, that characteristic entitles it to attention. Providing the statement does not otherwise distort the social facts, the capacity of measurement will be decisive in its favor. The statement that takes us farthest along the road toward quantitative estimates will inevitably be the best statement.[10]

Of Bentley's intellectual disciples David B. Truman had the greatest direct impact on group-based revisions of democratic theory. In his *Governmental Process*, first published in 1951, Truman moved beyond using the pattern of group activity as an explanation of American politics by raising open competition among interest groups to a normative principle of government.[11] In his view twentieth-century democracy consisted of a pluralistic struggle among diversified interest groups. The United States was a democracy, therefore, by virtue of the fact that no small set of the multifarious interest groups controlled a dominant share of public policy decisions. For Truman the behavior of individual citizens *per se* was not crucial, for the virtues of groups would make up for the failures of individual citizens to conform to the popular democratic image.

If the citizens were ignorant of the political issues that affected their interests, the relevant interest groups would protect them. If individual citizens lacked the wherewithal to make their wishes known, the relevant groups would pool their resources, aggregate their separate concerns, and articulate them to the appropriate decision-makers. The groups would also discourage intolerance and extremism by forcing moderation of demands among their own members in order to achieve a common front and by negotiating with opposing groups in order to achieve an accommodation of interest.

Truman's work was followed by a slew of studies which used the interaction of multifarious groups to orient their analyses both empirically and normatively. These included works by such prominent (or soon to be prominent) political and social scientists as Gabriel Almond, Robert Dahl, William Kornhauser, Earl Latham, Charles Lindblom, Seymour M. Lipset, Nelson Polsby, and Aaron Wildavsky.[12] While these works differed in the subject matter and in the particular emphases of their interpretations, they shared a common group-based plural-elite model of democracy.

As mentioned above, the key characteristic of this model of democracy was that no single group or minority coalition of groups dominated in all important areas of political decision. In fact, for group theorists like Robert Dahl, modern democracy itself could be operationally defined as a process of governance by which minorities – plural – rule.[13] In order to effect such rule, the theorists postulated an open political system, one in which all citizens had the legal opportunity and the economic resources to organize and to pursue their interests in the political arena. Normal politics consisted of the resolution of conflict among groups, preferably through stable channels of communication between citizens and public officials provided by established groups. As most citizens lacked the competence to govern directly, even if that were practical, democracy worked better when citizens governed indirectly through membership in or identification with groups that supported their interests.

The democratic quality of this group-based model of the political system was preserved not just by the great diversity of competing groups but also by the greater commitment to democratic principles which studies had found among group leaders and activists in comparison with the general public.[14] Governing consisted of little more than taking account of differing demands and facilitating their resolution through bargaining and compromise. That there might be some higher collective or public interest over and against the policies resultant from this process of bargaining and compromise was largely discounted. The closest thing to a public interest was a general consensus regarding the rules of the political game. If this general consensus were seriously threatened or violated, group theorists expected 'potential interest groups' to organize and through mobilization of slack resources to act to defend or restore the democratic status quo.[15]

Friendly critics of the group model of democracy tended to focus upon two main shortcomings. First, the critics suggested that the model placed government in too passive a role. Surely political institutions did more than mediate group conflicts and then register the outcomes as law. At the very least political institutions became associated with particular interests which their occupants, the public officials, sought to promote and defend. Secondly, the critics pointed out that a politics based upon interest groups was probably too exclusive to be described as democratic. The same sorts of studies that had revealed the inadequacy of the democratic characteristics of the average citizen in comparison with the popular image had also indicated that significant proportions of the citizenry – by some estimates a majority – belonged to no voluntary associations whatsoever. Moreover, most of the associations to which citizens did belong had little or nothing to do with politics. And to make matters worse, those who did participate in political associations tended to be atypical of the general population, drawn in disproportionately large numbers from those whose socio-economic status was above average.[16]

An alternative plural-elite theory that rectified these problems placed emphasis on political parties instead of interest groups. As political parties ran candidates for office and those candidates in turn took responsibility in the names of their parties for running the government institutions to which they were elected, parties were accountable more clearly and directly to the general citizenry than were interest groups. Moreover, whereas approximately half the citizenry had little or nothing to do with interest groups, nine out of ten adult Americans readily identified themselves as Democrats or Republicans. Thus, instead of relying upon the support of potential interest groups to preserve democratic principles and procedures, party theorists argued that democracy could be preserved and defended by responsible parties whose leaders respected the constitutionally defined rules of the political game, and whose followers comprised the great majority of the American electorate.

Responsible parties acted like supereminences, aggregating the interests of lesser groups into party platforms and articulating those platforms to the electorate and to the appropriate governmental authorities. As successful party candidates assumed positions of authority, they could be expected to employ the official powers of governmental institutions to implement their parties' platforms. At the same time, however, the socialization of successful party candidates to the values associated with their governmental positions was likely to cause them to take account of interests broader than those of their party alone.[17] A good Democrat like Harry Truman might also become a good democratic statesman.

American political scientists were wont to point to the British party system as the principal example of the 'responsible parties' theory of democracy in action. Samuel Beer suggested that the British system of 'collectivist democracy,' which rested upon government by responsible parties representing broad but differing class interests, was 'as practicable a solution as one is likely to find' to the problem of how 'to combine a substantial degree of popular participation with a system of power capable of governing *effectively* and *coherently*'.[18] Beer's interpretation of British democracy was consistent with the American Political Science Association's Committee on Political Parties whose *Toward a More Responsible Two-Party System* had argued the necessity of responsible parties for democratic governance.[19] The Committee's position in turn bore the stamp of its chairman, E.E. Schattschneider, who had previously defined competition between parties as the essence of democracy.[20]

Even though the 'responsible parties' model of democracy could assure greater involvement of the general public and greater consideration of what some would call the public interest than could the interest group model, it did not gain general acceptance. The individualistic ideology associated with the popular image of the democratic citizen stressed the virtues of the independence of elected officials from their parties. Moreover, sober analysis of the Constitution and the *Federalist Papers* indicated that the separation of powers and the checks and balances among political institutions were designed to discourage the formation of 'majority factions', which, in contemporary terms, translated to 'broad-based mass political parties'. Nor was it necessary to rely upon historical arguments. Political scientists like E. Pendleton Herring argued that lack of discipline among legislators and party leaders and a consequent lack of coherence among party policies were highly functional responses to the demands of the great diversity of interest groups in American society.[21] In contrast to the British experience, disciplined parties could not accommodate such diversity in the United States. Were strict party discipline imposed upon the Democratic and Republican parties, they would soon splinter into a confusing array of small narrowly-focussed political parties, none of which would stand any serious chance of assuming responsibility for governing in its own name.[22]

In place of either the interest group or 'responsible party' theories of democracy, therefore, a third form of plural-elite theory was developed, one which stressed competition among leaders who were socialized to uphold a democratic electoral process. Theorists like Joseph Schumpeter, who emphasized the importance of this leadership elite, averred that the essence of modern democracy was to be found in the 'institutional arrangement for arriving at political decisions in which individuals acquire the power to decide by means of a competitive struggle for the people's vote'.[23] This system of governance depended for its success primarily upon the quality of the competitively elected leaders, not upon the coherence of the parties nor the rationality of the citizenry. Voter awareness of the candidates' public policy positions was irrelevant. Democracy could flourish as long as voters managed to elect good leaders, regardless of the reasons for their election.

Implicit in this theory was a strong faith in the democratic commitment of most leaders who competed to attain the power to formulate and implement public policy. Yet this faith was soon vindicated by systematic studies in the burgeoning field of political socialization. These studies provide ample evidence of the benign influence that major social institutions exerted to instill democratic *bona fides* into American political leaders.[24] Better still, the socialization process helped create a general feeling of support for American political institutions among the populace.

According to 'leadership elite' theorists the ongoing process of political socialization was crucial to the development of diffuse support for political institutions and processes and for the development of an identification with and support for the broader political community or the people as a whole. In the United States the inculcation of political values was accomplished through a combination of mutually reinforcing agencies, most importantly, the family, church, school, and mass media. Parents acted as a stabilizing influence passing along traditional patterns of political behavior and party loyalties. The churches tended to encourage acceptance of civil authority tempered by notions of individual worth and toleration of individual differences within the broad spectrum of the Judaic–Christian tradition. Schools reinforced the incipient socialization received at home and church while the mass media reflected rather than questioned dominant political values. Destabilizing influences might be encountered among peer groups, especially during a citizen's youth, but most social intercourse – even among rebellious youth – remained virtually devoid of explicit political content. The greasy hairstyles and noisy rock-and-roll of the 50s were not viewed as indicative of any more political protest than the bobbed hair, Dixieland jazz, and swing music of the 20s.[25]

America was blessed with a civic culture, a bundle of attitudes held by its citizens that allowed democracy, as defined by leadership elite theorists, to flourish. According to Gabriel Almond and Sidney Verba the American civic culture was an 'allegiant-participant' culture.[26] Even though citizens failed to live up to the expectations of the Enlightenment, they nonetheless supported the political institutions and processes that encouraged such high standards of behavior among political leaders. And if most American adults failed to participate directly in the policy process, they expressed their general approval or disapproval of those policies with their votes, and most expressed confidence in their abilities to gain sympathetic hearings and desired actions from public officials if they chose to exert themselves. By and large, however, the inactive citizen was a happy citizen, apathy a tacit expression of satisfaction.[27]

This view was concordant with the influential post-war statement of the plural-elite thesis that had been developed by Bernard Berelson and his collaborators in the concluding chapter of their classic study, *Voting*.[28] Having demonstrated that the average citizens they surveyed had failed to satisfy the requirements of the popular image of democratic citizens, Berelson *et al.* went on to argue that even if citizens were to participate with all the zeal they were supposed to show, the results would be unsatisfactory. The sad truth was that persistently high levels of political participation produced deadlock at best and social breakdown at worst, for such participation inevitably centered about emotionally charged issues that polarized large blocs of citizens. Better to strive for a balance – a few highly motivated leading citizens; a few apoliticals. The rest should form an Aristotelian middle class, a moderate center whose members concerned themselves only sporadically with special political issues, but who supported the processes and institutions of the polity.

Amen, said such leading lights as Herbert McClosky and V.O. Key. McClosky demonstrated afresh the superior commitment to democratic principles of political party leaders in comparison with ordinary citizens.[29] And Key, after a thorough-going analysis of the empirical political literature of the fifties, concluded:

The longer one frets with the puzzle of how democratic regimes manage to function, the more plausible it appears that a substantial part of the explanation is to be found in the motives that actuate the leadership echelon, the values that it holds, in the rules of the political game to which it adheres ... and perhaps, in some objective circumstances, both material and institutional, in which it functions.[30]

Better indeed to place faith in the democratic predilections of the leaders than in the whims of the people.

III Responses to the revised theories

Whatever their specific emphases plural-elite theorists in common viewed democracy as procedure. Democracy called for open competition among interest groups, political parties, and freely chosen political leaders. It was actualized through appropriate arrangement of political institutions, and everyone knew that the United States was about as democratic a nation as one might expect to find. If American citizens failed to fulfill the expectations expressed in classical theories of democracy, then the classical theorists, who lacked the advantages of modern scientific observation of political behavior, were mistaken in those expectations.

The implications of these revised theories were revolutionary. They suggested that on the basis of new scientific evidence some 200-odd years of liberal democratic theory stemming from the Enlightenment ought to be severely modified or discarded. This radical claim was very bad news, and many mainstream political theorists first responded with all the wisdom of the ancient Greeks: they decided to put the messenger – scientific method – to death.[31]

Scholarly invectives condemning 'scientific' and 'behavioral' methods of the study of politics streamed from their pens. Among other things, these theorists argued that human behavior was so complicated that efforts to develop systematic theories about it would prove fruitless, and if they didn't prove fruitless, they would prove dangerous, providing potential dictators with the information needed to establish oppressive regimes. Besides, the really important questions of political science – the nature of freedom, justice, morality, and the organization of the good society – could not be answered by scientific methods, which, as employed by social scientists, were applicable only to concepts directly measurable in accordance with some crude tenets of logical positivism.[32]

When they finally got around to criticizing the substance of the plural-elite theories, anti-revisionists did manage to point out that the form in which liberal democratic values like equality and liberty had been incorporated into the new theories remained unexamined. Moreover, the behavioral analysis supporting plural-elite theories of democracy relied heavily upon a rather narrow notion of participation, namely, the voting act alone. But these points tended to become lost amidst the larger more strident tracts, which inveighed against the whole scientific enterprise. At their most extreme these impassioned critiques degenerated into attacks on the work of Harold Lasswell and Arthur Bentley that bordered on the *ad hominem*.[33]

As the tone of these critiques rendered them more polemical than scholarly, defenders of scientific method had little difficulty in dismissing them: whether or not scientific study of politics is trivial must be judged by examination of the resulting research, not by fiat; obviously, knowledge of human behavior can be used for evil as well as for good, but to forgo pursuing such knowledge for fear of its evil consequences would be more characteristic of the Inquisition than of modern scholarly inquiry; finally, empirical findings would bear directly on the empirical questions of how to secure justice, freedom and the good society.[34]

Virtually unscathed by these attacks, empirical methods adapted from the natural sciences emerged as the dominant research paradigms in American political science.[35] And as they were purportedly derived from the results of the new wave of scientific studies, the plural-elite theories of democracy were carried along like smart-looking baggage. Actually, the Panglossian tone of the theories – the United States was the best of all possible modern democracies, the common good sure to emerge from the clash of democratically led parties and interest groups – made them popular with students of politics and with the general public. By the mid-60s these theories under the broad label of pluralism had become the dominant interpretations of American democracy presented in major textbooks.[36] But while the scientific study of politics has remained dominant, plural-elite theories of democracy have been tarnished by events and battered by philosophical critiques penned by theorists well-versed in scientific methods. They have proved to be inadequate regarding both democratic practice and democratic theory.

The empirical inadequacies of the revised theories of democracy became manifest by the mid-60s. If every interest really had a fair chance to make its case, then why did minority racial groups, women, the poor and others have to struggle so to achieve even a semblance of equality in such diverse areas as housing, health care, educational and employment opportunities? And why did demonstrable inequalities in these areas persist? If the political system was sensitive to each group's needs, then what led blacks in the ghettoes to riot? If organized political activity was the *sine qua non* of plural-elite democracy, then why did both the Johnson and the Nixon administrations treat organized opposition to the increasingly unpopular war in Vietnam as though it were illegitimate? If the faith and trust in political institutions and processes bred through political socialization were necessary to sustain democracy, then did the precipitous decline of trust in these institutions following the 1964 election signal a crisis?[37]

C. Wright Mills had been one of the earliest critics to attack the plural-elite theories of democracy in their own terms.[38] By the mid-60s his loosely documented allegations of the antidemocratic influence of a 'power elite' were being battened down with hard facts. There was no longer any denying that Congress, the elected representative branch of government, had become overshadowed by the executive and its vast bureaucracy. Moreover, as the wealth of the country became ever more concentrated in the assets of the 'Fortune 500', and as the military's size and budget grew with American involvement in Vietnam, it became increasingly difficult to dismiss the allegation that the military–industrial complex controlled sufficient resources to have its way in most important areas of public policy.

In truth, nothing in the plural-elite theory of American democracy led political scientists to anticipate the upheavals of the 60s. According to this theory, Americans who took to the streets should have been able to have made satisfactory representations by working through established political organizations or by forming new organizations that worked through accepted institutional channels. That young people socialized in the American political system should suddenly show so little trust in government was both surprising and inexplicable.[39]

Despite the inexactness of its empirical measures, however, Mills' work provided a ready explanation. Many intelligent citizens had finally recognized that the American political system was unconcerned about their interests:

. . . the images of the public of classic democracy which are still used as working justifications of power in American society . . . are not adequate even as an approximate model of how the American system of power works. The issues that now shape man's fate are neither raised nor decided by the public at large. The idea of the community of publics is not a description of fact, but an assertion of an ideal, an assertion of legitimation masquerading . . . as fact.[40]

It slowly dawned on the American political science community that their orientation to the scientific study of politics, which looked mainly for explainable regularities in the present political system, tended toward conservatism. This search for regularities within a presumably democratic political system could limit the scope of inquiry to incremental changes and adjustments in established public policies. As a result, scientifically oriented researchers could fail to recognize – let alone analyze – those political problems which governments ignored, and they, along with interests entrenched within and without government, might view with suspicion any social movement that threatened to disrupt the regularities in the system. In short, there were biases in the application of 'objective' scientific methods after all.[41]

And as there were empirical difficulties with plural-elite theories, so too there were philosophical ones. The theories lacked the traditional liberal democratic concern for the individual citizen achieving self-improvement through political participation. Instead the theories asserted that with proper institutional arrangement the virtues of political leaders could be substituted for the virtues of the people. Were citizens too indolent or too indifferent to decide intelligently upon questions of public policy? No matter: the leaders of the interest groups protecting them would decide. Were citizens ignorant of the major issues of the day? No matter: the political parties would reduce all complexities to a simple choice among alternate slates of candidates. Were the citizens motivated only by selfish concerns? Were majorities intolerant of all who disagreed? No matter: the leadership elite would protect everyone's rights and privileges. Such an empty political life bore little resemblance to the rich one envisioned by democrats like Jefferson, Rousseau or Mill.

This impoverished conception of citizenship stemmed from an emasculated conception of democracy itself. For the plural-elite theorists the United States, along with other Western nations, already operated as a democracy. Their concern, therefore, became how to *preserve* democracy rather than how to *achieve* it. Yet it would seem that a central concern of liberal democratic government should be to make available the widest possible range of options and values for its citizens to choose. Not only should there be no premature closure of alternatives, but any selected set of public policies should be viewed as impermanent, constantly open to challenge. Change, not preservation, was the watchword of liberal democracy, and change should be radical or incremental depending upon the nature of the problems faced and the preferences of the citizens concerned.

Democracy was not achieved merely by arranging political institutions to facilitate competition for public support among elites. Democracy involved substantial participation by citizens in the formulation, adoption and implementation of public policy, and democracy's success must be measured by citizens' satisfaction with the results as well as the processes of politics. Liberal democracy involved faith in the ultimate rationality of the citizenry, and it presumed that the knowledge and abilities of the citizens would improve through political participation. If the scientific research of plural-elite theorists found insufficient empirical basis for this faith in the American people, then the sad fact was that the United States of America simply was not a liberal democracy.[42]

But did the results of scientific research lead inevitably to the conclusion that the political behavior of American citizens lacked sufficient rationality to provide a base for democratic politics? If, as scientific studies also showed, the most powerful organized interests generally consisted of large manufacturers, utilities, bankers, defense contractors, organized labor, and large farm producers – groups which tended to exclude citizens of lower socio-economic status – then why was it irrational for such citizens to remain apathetic? On the average those of lower status possessed neither the resources nor the forensic skills that effective participation in such groups required. It could be argued that apathy was a rational and effective response to the alternative of fruitless participation in such a biased nexus of interest groups.[43]

Even though parties could represent those interests neglected by the powerful, American political parties had failed utterly in this task: so much so that by 1972 the Survey Research Center of the University of Michigan found that four out of ten citizens in their national sample saw no differences between the Democrats and Republicans regarding the most important problem they thought the American government should act upon.[44] Small wonder, then, that voting turnout was dropping and that increasing proportions of the electorate were calling themselves political independents. Again, it could be argued that apathy was a perfectly rational response to an electoral system dominated by two parties whose stands on issues of vital concern to the citizen were indistinguishable or irrelevant.[45]

By a similar token distrust and disaffection with political leaders seemed like a perfectly rational response to the bitter experience of the Johnson and Nixon years. Too many leaders, in whom Americans had lately placed their faith, not only had lied, cheated or stolen, but had also tried to suppress those who had found them out.[46]

The upshot of the new critiques was that considerable doubt and discredit were cast upon plural-elite theories of democracy. As the critics now included prominent political scientists like Peter Bachrach, William Connolly, Henry Kariel, Lewis Lipsitz, Theodore Lowi, Charles McCoy, Grant McConnell, and Jack Walker, many of whom had employed the newer scientific methods in their own research, their arguments could not be dismissed as anti-scientific reactionism.[47] Their arguments had impact on the professional activities of political scientists as well, for most of these critics became associated with like-minded colleagues in the newly formed Caucus for a New Political Science, a group active within the American Political Science Association, which had the avowed aim of turning the discipline's attention once again toward research bearing on fundamental questions of liberty and justice. Unlike earlier critics, however, the Caucus avoided prejudging the methods that might be required in order to carry out such research.[48]

The press of events coupled with this internal pressure produced discernible changes in American political science. By the early 70s unexamined acceptance of plural-elite assertions of the openness and even-handedness of the American political system had disappeared from most mainstream textbooks in American Government, and a new wave of textbooks skeptical or highly critical of the democratic quality of American politics had appeared.[49] Whereas the older textbooks had read like pan-egyrics on American society, with a few caveats appended concerning the plight of the 'Negro,' the newer texts viewed the documented denials of equal opportunity to blacks, American Indians, women, and other underprivileged groups as something more than minor aberrations. Respectable political scientists even began to consider seriously questions about the undemocratic features of American political life that had been raised by such unorthodox 'new left' groups as the Students for a Democratic Society.[50]

By the mid-70s American political thought had come nearly full circle regarding modern democracy. In the 50s and early 60s plural-elite theorists, claiming that democratic theorists had failed to measure how well citizens conformed to the behavioral assumptions of their theories, had attempted to reconcile democratic theory with scientific findings concerning democratic practice. In the late 60s and early 70s their critics had demonstrated that this attempted reconciliation was inadequate: not only did it misinterpret some of the scientific findings, but, more importantly, its reliance on the virtues of interest groups, political parties and leadership elites compromised utterly the traditional liberal democratic concerns for the benefits individuals were supposed to derive from political participation. Unfortunately, after having exposed the inadequacies of the plural-elite theories of democracy, and having reaffirmed the importance of traditional democratic values, the critics seemed to have run out of ideas. They offered no realistic statement about how political institutions and processes might be arranged so that citizens could cope democratically with the responsibilities of modern governance.

IV Where do we go from here?

It would be pleasant to report that since the mid-70s American political scientists have managed to develop restatements of democratic theory that are both philosophically sound and behaviorally plausible. Sadly, this is not the case. The major contribution of recent statements has been to make us aware of how the shrinking availabilities of natural resources and the attendant dangers of environmental pollution serve to limit the possibilities of achieving satisfactory levels of socio-economic equality among citizens through continued economic growth.[51] But no consensus has been reached concerning political processes or institutional arrangements that any satis-factory theory must take into account.

Plural-elite theories have not been interred, their critics' efforts to bury them notwithstanding. Instead, as shown in David Miller's essay (below), efforts have been made to demonstrate their connection to the classical democratic tradition.[52] And while such theories of democracy are admittedly less than ideal, their defenders argue they have two important virtues: (1)

their empirical basis leads to realistic assessments of citizens' abilities to govern; and (2) their emphasis on procedures to assure open competition among elites leaves citizens with a wide range of choices for leadership. Plural-elite theorists still rely upon democratically elected leaders to develop agreement upon particular programs or specific goals.

Critics, including myself, remain unconvinced that procedural safeguards that assure competition form an adequate foundation for democracy. Modern societies contain powerful new actors, whose presence cannot be ignored, and they face serious environmental constraints, which cannot be dismissed. It would seem that in addition to assuring competition among elites a satisfactory theory of modern democracy would need to (1) devise ways for the elected legislature, the central institution of liberal democracy, to control the huge public bureaucracy; (2) limit the military's control of the budgetary resources and technical information that allow it to manipulate public policy in its favor; (3) limit or control the great concentrations of wealth, income, and employment opportunities found in the large private corporations; (4) devise ways to increase or redistribute society's resources so that traditionally underprivileged groups like racial minorities, women, and those of lower socio-economic status get sufficient shares to allow them opportunities to participate in politics with their compatriots on a substantially equal footing; (5) manage to achieve all of the above within the limits of natural resources available for development at reasonable economic and environmental cost.

Building upon work of both the plural-elite theorists and their critics some American political scientists have developed possible, though not necessarily practical, restatements of democratic theory that meet several of the above criteria. Within the limits of this essay, we have room only to summarize the major features of a few of these.

Decentralization is a recurrent theme in these recent restatements of democratic theory. Citing evidence as diverse as citizens' feelings of greater efficacy regarding control of government and local problems in comparison with national ones, to Rousseauian arguments that the larger the polis the less possibility of achieving expression of the general will, theorists as diverse as Wilson Carey McWilliams, Frederick Thayer, Robert Wolff, (a reformed) Robert Dahl and myself have advocated decentralization of governmental and/or private organizational units to facilitate direct control of crucial policy decisions by citizens or their elected representatives.[53]

Going against this train of thought, however, Theodore Lowi has argued that the way to achieve legislative control over the public and private sectors is through careful definition and formalization of universal standards. Whereas decentralization, particularly in the noxious form of 'interest group liberalism', fosters injustices by avoiding questions of fairness and equity and parcelling out privileges to various and sundry private parties instead, 'juridical democracy' forces codification of standards of justice which can be universally and equitably applied.[54] Without necessarily agreeing with Lowi's unique solution, others like Samuel Beer and Hugh Heclo also argue that problems of democracy in the United States more often stem from too much rather than too little decentralization of policy-making.[55]

Socialization of the private corporation either through public ownership or public control is another recurrent theme. Whether they advocate traditional forms of public ownership as do Michael Best and William Connolly, or whether they recommend public input by other means, such as public representatives on corporate boards or formal consultation on corporate plans with public bodies, as do Peter Bachrach, Robert Dahl, and others, all seem agreed that the ostensibly private decisions of these corporations, concerning economic investment and planning, have so much impact on the public sphere that the public must have some say in them if the polity is to call itself a democracy.[56]

Some, like Ithiel de Sola Pool and myself, have focussed on the necessity of making relevant information available to responsible decision-makers. Accordingly, I have proposed elsewhere to enhance citizen control through public access to the otherwise proprietary files of large bureaucracies, both public and private, by means of a nationwide computerized information network linked via cable television. Such an information network, reinforced by institutional arrangements that encouraged responsible whistle-blowing by publicly-minded bureaucrats, would form the foundation for intelligent and selective direct participation by citizens in public policy formulation.[57]

Finally, the liberal democratic theme of individualism has been stressed in various forms as the basis of democracy. Frederick Thayer has suggested that democracy can only be achieved when the hierarchical authority to make decisions binding upon others is replaced by cooperative networks of individual decision-makers who meet in groups of 5 or 6. Henry Kariel despairs of traditional liberal democratic solutions, seeking instead a romantic expressive politics in which political actions need not be instrumentally directed toward some concrete goal. Wilson Carey McWilliams advocates an Aristotelian–Rousseauian sort of individualism in which realization of true human freedom and dignity is possible only when the individual comes to feel part of and conforms to the general will of a small tightly knit community.[58]

That none of these restatements fulfills the five criteria listed above is daunting but hardly surprising. The task of linking principles of democratic theory to practices of democratic governance has always been difficult, and it has been rendered even more difficult in recent times as governments have been asked to expand greatly the scope of their public policy concerns.

Whereas classical principles of democracy may endure, it is questionable whether or not the eighteenth- and nineteenth-century political institutions traditionally associated with these principles can be made to respond successfully to the complex problems of the late twentieth century.

The plural-elite theorists attempted to make virtues out of the shortcomings of these institutions. They supplemented the presumed (but not observed) policy linkages between citizens and representatives, realized through the electoral process, with indirect linkages, realized through interest groups, political parties and leadership elites. Their critics pointed out that government based upon such practices violated too many democratic principles. The critics have failed, however, to develop an alternative that remains true to democratic principles yet viable in practice.

While we can only speculate on the directions American democratic theory is likely to take in the future, it appears that the failure of vision on the part of the critics combined with the loss of faith in the federal government and many of its programs have produced circumstances encouraging a neo-conservative theory of democracy not greatly different from the plural-elite theories of the 60s. Neo-conservatives emphasize the limits of government, the fact that government is not capable of solving all our public problems even when democratic majorities desire it to do so.[59] Like Reaganite conservatives they favor getting the federal government off the citizens' backs in numerous areas of public policy, and like plural-elite theorists they favor strengthening voluntary associations, particularly broad-based political parties and interest groups.[60] Indeed, if President Reagan's social and economic policies should succeed, the next wave of American democratic theory will probably be decidedly more conservative, once again translating the features of American practice into democratic principle. Conversely, if they fail, we can expect a resurgence of theories critical of current practices, once again emphasizing the importance of implementing public policies that conform to democratic principles.

9

The competitive model of democracy

DAVID MILLER

There are many possible ways of classifying democratic theories, but for the purposes of this chapter one particular contrast between views of democracy is of paramount importance. On one view, democracy is essentially a protective device, a mechanism which obliges rulers to pursue policies in line with the wishes of their subjects. Elections are the lynch-pin of the machine, serving to punish, by loss of office, leaders who have failed to satisfy the people's aspirations and to select a new leadership who seem likely, by virtue of campaign promises or past performance, to do better in the future. On the other view, democracy is essentially a means whereby the people's will is translated into public policy. The people, by debate and discussion, reach certain conclusions about what ought to be done politically. In the most radical version of the second view, this popular will becomes law directly: the people assemble together and enact legislation. In a less radical version, the people choose delegates who meet to enact what they have been mandated to enact. Elections are the transmission belt whereby the people's will is communicated to the smaller number of persons who actually make law.

It is not hard to find examples of the two views in the democratic theory of the past couple of centuries. James Mill's *Essay on Government* may serve as a paradigm of the first, and Rousseau's *Social Contract* as a paradigm of the second.[1] More commonly, however, one finds elements of the two perspectives combined in a single piece of theory – as in John Stuart Mill's *Considerations on Representative Government*, for instance – and this should come as no surprise, since each rests on a distinct, yet appealing, set of values.[2] I shall return to this conflict in underlying values in the final section of the chapter. Now I want to observe that the competitive model of my title is best seen as a modern development of the first view of democracy identified above. It belongs squarely in the tradition which sees democracy as a device for forcing rulers to pay attention to the people's wishes. This observation exposes two complementary errors made respectively by the friends and the enemies of the competitive model, both of which can be avoided by seeing the continuities between modern and 'classical' accounts of democracy. The friends' error is to regard the model as providing a realistic or up-to-date account of democracy to replace an exploded 'classical theory'. The enemies' error is to complain that the model is merely a description of the practices of Western liberal democracies, and therefore no substitute for the prescriptive theories of democracy found in older writers.[3]

What, then, in bare outline, is the competitive model of democracy? The model envisages a population roughly divided between a small group of political leaders and a large mass of ordinary citizens, with perhaps an intermediate section of more active citizens who transmit demands and information between the mass and the leadership. The leaders form themselves into two or more parties and develop political platforms on which they stand at periodic elections, the victorious party forming the government in the subsequent period. The core of the model is an analysis of the way in which the platforms developed are adjusted to take account of the preferences of the electorate. Competition is crucial here. The competitive process, it is argued, forces the parties to draw up and follow programmes which reflect, more or less faithfully, the wishes of the people, whatever the private desires of the leaders themselves.

This claim encapsulates the model's democratic credentials. We should observe, however, that the mechanism of democracy here is an indirect mechanism. There is no sense in which the people's will is translated directly into law, as in the second view outlined above. Adherents of the model stress that legislation itself is wholly a matter for the political leadership. But this leadership is obliged to respond to the electorate's preferences *by antici-pation*. Both the legislation enacted when a party is in power and the platform on which it fights an election are drawn up with an eye to the ensuing contest. Now there is no reason to suppose *a priori* that such an indirect mechanism will be less effective than a direct mechanism in producing legislation in accordance with the people's wishes. This is an open issue which needs to be explored by looking both at the logic of the model as developed by its adherents and at the empirical reality to which it will be applied.

There is an obvious parallel here with the basic argument used to justify a market economy. In so far as the market serves to satisfy consumers' desires, it does so indirectly; producers are primarily interested in making profits, not in satisfying desires, but are forced by the competitive process to make things that consumers are willing to buy. To some people it seems self-evident that such a system must be less efficient than one in which producers aim directly at satisfying desires (hence the talk about 'production for use' rather than 'production for profit', as if these were mutually exclusive). But it is really far from self-evident, and indeed there are powerful arguments for the superior efficiency of the indirect mechanism.

This parallel has without a doubt influenced the construction of the competitive model. Its two leading proponents – Joseph Schumpeter and Anthony Downs – were both economists by training, who saw it as part of their task to transfer assumptions that were commonplace in economics to the seemingly recalcitrant territory of political theory. They did so in particular by modelling the behaviour of political leaders competing for votes on that of entrepreneurs competing for custom in the market. The basic insight that social ends might be served indirectly, by individuals seeking their private advantage under competitive conditions, was expressed by Schumpeter in a passage that, according to Downs, 'summarizes our whole approach to the functioning of government'.[4]

In observing human societies we do not as a rule find it difficult to specify, at least in a rough commonsense manner, the various ends that the societies under study struggle to attain. These ends may be said to provide the rationale or meaning of corresponding individual activities. But it does not follow that the social meaning of a type of activity will necessarily provide the motive power, hence the explanation of the latter. If it does not, a theory that contents itself with an analysis of the social end or need to be served cannot be accepted as an adequate account of the activities that serve it. For instance, the reason why there is such a thing as economic activity is of course that people want to eat, to clothe themselves and so on. To provide the means to satisfy those wants is the social end or meaning of production. Nevertheless we all agree that this proposition would make a most unrealistic starting point for a theory of economic activity in commercial society and that we shall do much better if we start from propositions about profits. Similarly, the social meaning or function of parliamentary activity is no doubt to turn out legislation and, in part, administrative measures. But in order to understand how democratic politics serve this social end, we must start from the competitive struggle for power and office and realize that the social function is fulfilled, as it were, incidentally – in the same sense as production is incidental to the making of profits.[5]

It can be seen from this passage that Schumpeter (and this holds of Downs as well) conceives of his task as primarily *explanatory* in nature: he wants to explain how democratic systems do in fact work, as opposed to how they are supposed to work according to the familiar rhetoric of democratic politics. In both writers there is an urge to demystify, to give 'realistic' and perhaps even cynical accounts of the motives of politicians in a democracy. But this should not blind us to the fact that the models developed are normative as well as explanatory; for if, to put the point simply, a model shows how the pursuit of private ends may lead under the appropriate conditions to social goals being achieved, then anyone who shares those goals must endorse the model – at least pending an alternative theory which shows how the goals in question may be achieved more effectively.[6] If competition between leaders entails that policies in line with the people's wishes are pursued, then other things being equal democrats must approve of the competitive system. So, whatever Schumpeter's and Downs's stated intentions, it makes no sense to divorce the explanatory and normative aspects of their theories; indeed no one reading their books can really doubt that they are morally committed to the system they are analysing.

At the same time it is perfectly proper for the critic to focus on one or other aspect of the model. He may primarily be interested in the ways in which the model fits or fails to fit the actual competitive process in Western democracies; or he may take the logic of the model as given, and use various evaluative criteria to assess the way in which different constellations of individual preferences are translated into social outcomes by the competit-ive mechanism. Most effort so far has gone into the former task, but if we want to assess the model as democratic theory, we need to take on both. For the model to be acceptable we need to be satisfied (a) that the formal relationship it establishes between the wishes of the electorate and the policies pursued by the governing party meets our criteria of democracy; (b) that the model corresponds reasonably closely to the way that competitive systems work in the real world. I say 'reasonably closely' because the model is, after all, a model – an ideal representation derived from certain axioms concerning human behaviour, not a depiction of any one political system or indeed a composite picture drawn from several. What we must ask is whether party competition in contemporary liberal democracies works basically in the way that the model requires, or whether it departs systematically from the model; and if the latter, whether the departure is remediable or not – for if one believes in the virtues of the model, one may try to alter the political system so that it approximates more closely to the model's requirements. This is the point at which the democratic theorist and the political scientist wishing to use the model as an explanatory device part company – although up to that point they have much to learn from each other.

In the remainder of this chapter I shall make a start on this task of assessment. In sections II and III I outline the two versions of the model developed by Schumpeter and Downs – for it will turn out that there are significant differences between them. In section IV I examine the main empirical criticisms of the model and ask how damaging they are from the perspective of democratic theory. Lastly in section V I consider the normative claims that can be made for and against the model and reach a final verdict on its democratic credentials.

II

Schumpeter's account of democracy constitutes a small part of a much larger study of the transition from capitalism to socialism in the advanced societies. He delivered it in response to a particular question, namely whether democracy and socialism were compatible with one another, and the account is under-elaborated in many respects. Indeed it is an exaggeration to speak of

Schumpeter as offering us a model, for all he gives us is a bare definition of the 'democratic method' together with a number of remarks about how the method works in practice. Nevertheless Schumpeter's account is well worth examining in some detail for, apart from inspiring several later versions of the competitive model, he gives in their boldest form the reasons for preferring this model to other versions of democracy.

He begins with an attack on what he calls 'the classical doctrine of democracy'.[7] The doctrine under attack is an unwieldy composite of Enlightenment rationalism, utilitarianism and Rousseauian ideas, and Schumpeter has often (and rightly) been criticized for erecting a straw man which he then proceeds to demolish. But if we drop the idea that Schumpeter had his sights on anyone in particular, and if indeed we abandon (as we should) the whole idea of a 'classical doctrine', we are left with a sustained attack on the second view of democracy that I identified at the beginning of this chapter, the view which sees democracy as a means for expressing the popular will. This confrontation between views of democracy has, to repeat, nothing essentially to do with the contrast between 'classical' and 'modern' theories, and everything to do with conflicts over underlying values, views of human nature, and so forth.

Schumpeter's attack proceeds in three stages. He argues first that no amount of rational argument will bring about a consensus on policy that would form the basis of an all-embracing general will. The reason is simply that people differ in their basic values, or even if they happen to agree, they will inevitably hold different opinions about which particular policies realize these values best. This attack appears to be directed against 'popular will' theories of Rousseauian pedigree which envisage an enlightened population coming to unanimous agreement over questions of policy. Although such theories undoubtedly have a certain appeal – for one thing they abolish the problem of discontented minorities at a stroke – it does not seem integral to a popular-will view of democracy that agreement be unanimous. A more realistic view is simply that the popular will is the will of the majority. Here Schumpeter deploys his second argument. Even if the people taken separately have clear preferences on issues, the democratic process does not guarantee an overall outcome that corresponds to 'what people really want'. He produces an example – the religious settlement engineered by Napoleon Bonaparte in France – where a generally satisfactory outcome was achieved by dictatorial means that could not, Schumpeter claims, have been achieved by democratic processes as understood in the 'classical' model.

The exact nature of Schumpeter's argument here is hard to discern, but I think that what he has in mind is roughly as follows: the settlement that Napoleon achieved was essentially a package made up of a number of policies each of which, taken separately, was strongly opposed by an important section of French society, and so would have been rejected by a democratic decision-making process (say a series of referendums). The whole package, however, was acceptable because each group gained more on balance from it than they lost. Clearly, then, the overall settlement would have been successful if put to a democratic vote. Schumpeter's claim must be that the linking of the different elements could only have been achieved dictatorially; that a democratic body would have insisted on disaggregating the package and voting on each element individually. This would occur if each group believed that by doing so it could achieve the overall settlement *minus* the element that it found particularly objectionable. Thus reconstructed Schumpeter's argument points to a flaw in direct democracy with majority voting that I shall return to in section V. He is correct to say that such a system may not produce results that, over a number of separate issues, correspond to 'what people really want'.

Schumpeter's third and most famous argument, however, undercuts the very idea of a 'popular will'. Using the evidence of crowd psychology and the effects of advertising on consumers, he claims that individuals' preferences are for the most part neither independent nor rational. They are formed by outside influences, most notably by the arts of advertisers and other persuaders; and the preferences that result are not necessarily for things which in the long run serve their possessor's interests best. It looks here as though Schumpeter is about to abandon a cornerstone of all conventional economics: the sanctity of consumers' preferences. But he partially retrieves the situation by introducing an important distinction. In some fields, he suggests, the individual decision-maker is able to learn by his own mistakes. However persuasively it is advertised, a product that fails to satisfy the consumer will not be bought repeatedly. 'The picture of the prettiest girl that ever lived will in the long run prove powerless to maintain the sales of a bad cigarette.'[8] But in other fields, and particularly in politics, there is no such direct feedback. The decision-maker cannot assess the results of his decision; they are long-term, they are hard to quantify, and they are strongly influenced by what other people decide. If I vote in a referendum on nuclear energy, for example, I am unlikely to experience the costs or benefits of my decision directly, as I do when I decide to buy a new car. This, Schumpeter claims, leads to a failure of responsibility. A citizen asked to participate in such public decisions will not trouble to inform himself properly about the issues, will give vent to irrational emotions, and so on.

Thus the typical citizen drops down to a lower level of mental performance as soon as he enters the political field. He argues and analyzes in a way which he would readily recognize as infantile within the sphere of his real interests. He becomes a primitive again. His thinking becomes associative and affective.[9]

The conclusion Schumpeter draws is that even though a democratic process designed to evoke a 'popular will' might succeed in doing so, what was called forth would lack the qualities that make this view of democracy attractive. It would be made up of poorly-informed and emotionally-distorted individual wills; and it would to a greater or lesser extent be 'manufactured', since large numbers of people would be swayed in their decisions by powerful groups of persuaders.

The defects of the doctrine of democracy that he calls 'classical' lead to Schumpeter's alternative view: democracy should be understood as a system in which the electorate's role is confined to that of choosing between alternative teams of leaders. This view recognizes a distinction between a relatively small political class, who are responsible for choosing policies and enacting legislation, and a much larger class of ordinary citizens, who are not expected to be informed in detail about matters of policy, but who periodically pass a verdict on the performance of the party in office. Democratic regimes are distinguished from non-democratic regimes by the fact of electoral competition. In sum 'the democratic method is that institutional arrangement for arriving at political decisions in which individuals acquire the power to decide by means of a competitive struggle for the people's vote'.[10]

While recognizing that there is an analogy to be drawn here between teams of party leaders competing for votes and entrepreneurs competing for customers in the market, Schumpeter acknowledges that the appropriate model is not that of perfect competition as understood in classical economics. This must be acknowledged, given what he has already said about the non-independence of the citizen's preferences. He admits, in other words, that the desires expressed when the citizen votes are *to some degree* manufactured desires – manufactured both by the competing parties themselves and by various pressure groups who agitate in favour of specific policies. A more appropriate model is that of oligopolistic competition in which a small number of established enterprises compete for customers who are man-ipulated into supporting one or other competitor. But clearly this line of thought cannot be pushed too far without destroying the model's democratic credentials entirely. There is a danger that the powerful arguments marshalled by Schumpeter against the 'popular will' theory will rebound upon him by showing that electoral competition is really pseudo-competition. To avoid this he needs to establish that at least some of the citizen's preferences are neither wholly manipulable nor wholly irrational.

Schumpeter's case relies here on a distinction being drawn between the electorate deciding on matters of policy – which he holds they are generally incapable of doing – and their choosing between teams of leaders offering alternative policy platforms. Such a distinction is not absurd. It is possible to decide whether the governing party has performed satisfactorily during its term of office – say on the basis of its success in stimulating economic growth – without having opinions about which kind of economic policy (Keynesian or monetarist, say) is most likely to produce this result. Essentially we are distinguishing here between the electorate's basic preferences, say for an increase in living standards, and its policy preferences, say for monetarism. The former may well be less manipulable and more rational than the latter. But although this distinction helps to save Schumpeter's position, it is clearly a fine line that we are drawing. Unless the electorate has *some* ideas about economic policy, how can it tell whether a poor record in economic growth is attributable to the governing party rather than to world events outside its control? And how can it rationally decide that the alternative team is likely to perform better?

The tension in Schumpeter's account is visible in the conditions he lays down for the competitive system to work successfully.[11] These are, first, that the political leadership should be made up of men of sufficiently high moral and intellectual quality – a hereditary ruling class such as the English aristocracy seems to be his ideal. Secondly, the scope of political decision should not be too wide. Party competition should, in other words, take place within a relatively restricted range, bounded by consensus on the major parameters (both constitutional and substantive) of the system. Thirdly, the government should be able to command the services of a professional bureaucracy which plays a major role in the policy-making process, to compensate for the amateurism of the politicians themselves. Fourthly, everyone in the system must exercise what Schumpeter calls 'democratic self-control': parliamentary oppositions must refrain from attacking the government too violently, and the electorate must 'respect the division of labor between themselves and the politicians they elect'. In particular, they must avoid putting pressure on their representatives to take up particular policy stands – say by 'bombarding them with letters and telegrams'.[12]

The picture of Schumpeterian democracy that emerges is of a system where party leaders compete electorally on terms that they largely set themselves. Ideally the parties should be closely aligned in matters of policy, and should stand on their respective records in achieving shared ends such as economic stability and growth. Being 'responsible', they will refrain from competing on issues likely to inflame the electorate's irrational prejudices – the current tacit agreement between the major British parties to keep the race and immigration issues off the electoral agenda might serve as an example. It looks very much as though democracy has been sacrificed to liberalism here – the political class being regarded as the repository of liberal values.[13] (We should recall that Schumpeter was writing with the rise of Nazism in Germany in mind. He believed that the Weimar Republic had collapsed because it failed to produce political leadership of sufficient calibre, allowing irresponsible power-seekers to campaign on platforms that appealed to the population's baser instincts.) But having said this we should also recognize the model's two main claims to be democratic. First, the parties are forced to respond to the demands of organized minorities, for pressure groups play a major role in forming citizens' preferences. Here Schumpeter anticipates the later development of pluralist theory, though without the pluralists' focus on the role of pressure groups in influencing government *between* elections. Secondly, where the electorate have stable preferences for goods that can be produced politically, the parties are obliged to respond to these preferences: if the people want economic growth, for example, each party must adopt policies that aim at this objective. Electoral competition can only be fixed within limits.

Schumpeter's work points up a basic dilemma for the competitive model. In order to make a convincing case for a competitive system, rather, say, than a referendum democracy, it seems necessary to postulate a political leadership which is more competent to make political decisions than the remainder of the population. But if this is so, how can the people at large make an adequate assessment of the competing parties at election time? Schumpeter's solution, reduced to its essentials, is that a lesser degree of rationality is required to choose a team of leaders than is required to decide directly on policy. This solution is clearly vulnerable to critical attack. But it must be defended, or else some other way found of justifying the competitive model.

III

Although Anthony Downs acknowledges an intellectual debt to Schumpeter, the model of democracy that he develops is in several respects at odds with the latter's. To begin with, while Schumpeter has sometimes (though wrongly) been criticized for merely describing the political system as it has evolved in the West and calling it democracy, Downs is only too clearly building an abstract model whose relationship to the real world is questionable. Furthermore, while both use economic analogies to illuminate the workings of party competition, Downs (unlike Schumpeter) borrows the orthodox assumptions of neo-classical economics. In the Downsian model voters are depicted as rational maximizers of their utility, who calculate how much satisfaction they are likely to derive from each of the policy packages offered by the parties at election time, and vote accordingly. Parties, on the other hand, are characterized as unified teams of men whose sole aim is to win office and to reap the rewards thereof, identified as 'income, prestige and power'; they do not, in other words, have ideological commitments, and are prepared to adopt whatever policy platform seems most likely to win elections.[14] The system itself is assumed to be fully competitive in the sense that there are no financial or other barriers preventing a new party from forming and entering the competitive struggle for votes. These assumptions may seem unrealistic, but Downs asks us to suspend judgement until we can see how successful the model is in explaining real-world party competition.

The behaviour of the voters in the model raises certain difficulties that need to be addressed at once. First, Downs states that all voters are assumed to be selfish, i.e. to be aiming at the maximum satisfaction of their personal desires (for wealth, status, etc.) alone. This assumption is quite unnecessary. All the model requires is that the voters have preferences which are independent of the behaviour of the parties, and that their voting behaviour is instrumental – i.e. that they act so as to achieve the greatest future satisfaction of their preferences. It does not matter whether the preferences themselves are selfish (e.g. for a higher level of personal income) or altruistic (e.g. for an increase in the foreign aid budget). Secondly, Downs has to face the problem that an instrumental voter is unlikely to vote at all whenever voting is costly (which it will be in the sense that it requires time and effort to take oneself to the polling booth). The reason is that the voter decides how to vote (in the two-party case) by comparing the utility that he expects to derive from Party A's being in power during the next period with the utility he expects to derive from Party B (the difference being his 'party differential'); but then multiplies this differential by the chance that his vote by itself will be decisive in determining which party holds office. Since in a large electorate this latter chance is infinitesimally small, the expected pay-off from voting also shrinks to near vanishing point. So the rational voter will abstain whenever the costs of voting are at all significant. Downs tries to avoid this implication of his model (clearly at odds with the actual behaviour of voters) by arguing that the voter also values the democratic system itself, and will vote to ensure that the system remains in operation. But, as critics have pointed out, this addition to the model faces a difficulty analogous to the original one, namely that a rational voter will vote only if he thinks that *his* vote is likely to be the one that saves democracy.[15]

It seems, therefore, that to explain voting at all, we have to assume that the voter is motivated differently – either he obtains some kind of expressive satisfaction from the act of voting, or he votes from a sense of duty ('the system only works if everyone does his bit, so I ought to do mine . . .'), or something similar. Although this exposes Downs's mistake in assuming that the model can work if everyone is egoistically motivated, there is nothing formally wrong with explaining the decision to vote in one way and the choice of party in another. Indeed Downs tacitly makes the same kind of move when he postulates on the one hand that party leaders are self-interested power-seekers but on the other that they play by the rules of the democratic game. The deeper question, however, is whether voters who decide to go to the polls on non-instrumental grounds are likely (as a matter of empirical fact) to be wholly instrumental in their choice of party. If a political system can command moral allegiance, why not a party as well? We shall return to this question later.

Downs's main interest is in how parties will respond to a given distribution of electoral preferences. In his initial development of the model, he assumes that voters are perfectly informed about party platforms. Suppose that there are two parties, that in a given period there are N issues that divide the electorate, and that on each issue there are just two positions one can hold (for example, one is either for or against capital punishment). Parties fight elections by offering platforms which contain a stand on each of the N issues. It is easy to see that in these circumstances both parties will gravitate towards the majority position on every issue. For suppose Party A, currently in power, takes a minority line on some issue. Party B can ensure its electoral victory by taking the majority line on that issue and matching A's policies in every other respect. Does this imply that the parties will reach a stable equilibrium with both adopting the majority view on all N issues? Not necessarily, for it may be possible for one party to win by adopting a 'coalition of minorities' strategy. Suppose that A follows the majority line on all issues. B adopts a platform containing 2 minority planks (but otherwise following the majority line) – say it declares for abolishing immigration controls and in favour of devolution. It can win if the pro-immigration minority regard *this* as a more important issue than devolution, while the pro-devolution minority take the opposite view. Provided that the two minorities together add up to more than half of the electorate, Party B will win. But next time round it can be trumped itself by A switching policy on one or other of the two issues (for then the electorate will decide entirely on the basis of the remaining issue and A, holding the majority view, will win). In these circumstances there is no equilibrium position, and the parties perform a kind of merry-go-round on the contested issues. But so long as the voters agree over the relative importance they attach to the various issues, the coalition-of-minorities strategy cannot get off the ground. Downs sums this up as 'the rule of the passionate majority': 'in a two-party system, both parties nearly always adopt any policy that a majority of voters strongly prefer, no matter what strategies the parties are following'.[16]

All of this analysis, however, is based on the rather unrealistic assumption that voters are perfectly informed about the parties' platforms. In his revised model Downs abandons this assumption by introducing the idea that information is costly to acquire. Most voters will then not find it worthwhile to become well-informed about party policy. The parties themselves will respond to this state of affairs by developing *ideologies* – general pictures of the good society, together with some not-too-specific recipes for getting there. The voter's task is now made much simpler, for he can reach his decision merely by comparing the ideologies of the competing parties with his own basic ideological commitments, and choosing the nearest fit. So Downs reverses the conventional assumption that politicians with ideological convictions try to win office to implement their ideologies, and postulates instead that office-seeking politicians develop ideologies in order to win votes.

To model the behaviour of parties under these conditions, Downs assumes that voters can be arranged across an ideological spectrum from left to right (he suggests that the left end of the spectrum might be identified with a commitment to complete state control of the economy and the right end with a commitment to complete *laissez-faire*). Assume that voters are distributed normally across this spectrum, and that everyone votes. It is not difficult to show that competing parties will reach an equilibrium when their platforms represent ideological stances fractionally to the left and right respectively of the centre of the spectrum (more generally, with other distributions of voters, to the left and right of the median voter). Suppose we begin with the parties positioned as in Diagram I. According to Downs's assumptions, all voters to the left of A vote for A, all voters to the right of B for B, and the voters in between vote for the party whose position is closer to their own. If X represents the point midway between A's position and B's, all those between A and X will vote for A and those between X and B for B. B captures all the votes in the shaded area, and wins the election.

To fight back A must move ideologically towards the centre. Suppose it positions itself as in Diagram II. A will now capture all the votes to the left of Y and win. The process will repeat itself until A and B are lined up just to the left and right of the mid-point of the spectrum, neither having any incentive to move outwards.

Since parties in the real world do not always adopt such centrist policies, Downs tries to inject some extra realism into his model by introducing the possibility of abstention. The basic idea is that as party A moves toward the middle ground, voters on the extreme left may begin to abstain, as in Diagram III. A's votes, represented by the shaded area, are now fewer than B's, and A may increase its votes by moving to the left, if the number it loses in the centre is more than compensated by the number it gains at the extreme. Downs argues that, with abstention, the equilibrium position for the parties will depend on the distribution of the electorate across the spectrum. With a normal distribution, as shown, the equilibrium will have the parties still quite close to the centre; but if the voters cluster at the ends of the spectrum, the parties will settle much farther apart.[17]

But why should voters begin to abstain when the parties congregate at the

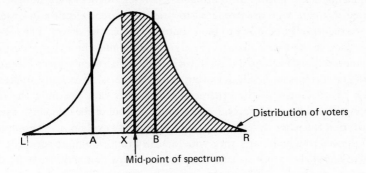

Diagram I

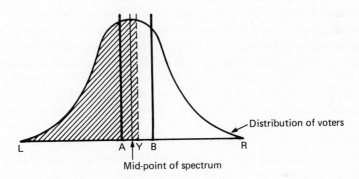

Diagram II

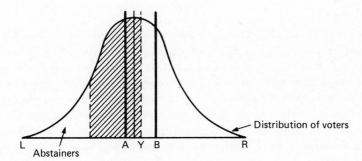

Diagram III

centre? Downs suggests two explanations, neither of them particularly convincing. One is that abstention is a strategy deliberately adopted by extremist voters who are prepared to lose the current election in order to induce their preferred party to move outwards from the centre. The other is that when the parties converge closely, the extremists find that their party differentials have become too small for it to be worth their while to vote. But strategic abstention is self-defeating unless there is an equally numerous block of extremists at the other end of the spectrum pursuing the same strategy;[18] and Downs's second suggestion falls foul of the difficulty, already noted, that the party differential cannot in any case explain *why* people vote (as opposed to which party they vote for). So I think we must conclude that Downs's model is more successful in showing how competitive forces drag parties towards the centre of the political spectrum than in showing why, despite these forces, they may remain apart. Some possible causes of the latter effect will be considered in section IV.

If the centripetal forces operate unhindered, however, we can derive one result of importance to democratic theory: a competitive party system will tend to produce a government whose policies satisfy voters' preferences to the greatest possible extent. It can easily be shown that the central position on the spectrum is the policy position which maximizes voters' utility, provided that voters are distributed symmetrically around the centre, and assuming that utility is a function of the ideological distance between the government's policy and the voter's own preferred policy.[19] Since competition drives the parties to the centre, it forces them to adopt voter-satisfying policies, even if the party leaders themselves are interested only in winning office. This is the main normative claim of the competitive model, and Downs provides the logic to support it.

IV

I turn now to an empirical assessment of the Downsian model. We are looking here for aspects of party competition which make it unlikely to work in the way that the model would predict. It is important to separate these from adjustments which the model can accommodate without difficulty. For instance, it is obviously a gross over-simplification to assume that ideological competition between parties occurs along only one dimension; but one can incorporate multi-dimensional competition into the model without changing its basic structure. Other criticisms of the model are, however, less easy to accommodate.

First, the model presupposes that voters' preferences are independent of the behaviour of the parties; in other words it excludes the possibility that parties may succeed in manipulating the voters into taking up policy standpoints that correspond to the parties' own.[20] The model does not require that voters' preferences should be unaffected by wider social and cultural forces; nor does it require that they should be invariant over time. But it does demand that they should be taken as fixed for the purposes of party competition in any electoral period, otherwise the parties will be able to choose between a strategy of adapting to the voters' preferences and one of moulding the voters to the party's preference, and the whole nature of the model changes.

The evidence indicates, however, that parties actively try to alter voters' opinions on issues, and that these attempts are sometimes successful. A suggestive piece of evidence is that, when voters are interviewed repeatedly over a period of time, their policy preferences are much less stable than their party preferences.[21] Much will of course depend on the kind of issue involved.[22] In the context of British politics, voters appear to have relatively fixed views on matters such as capital punishment and coloured immigration, and are not open to political persuasion. On a question such as membership of the E.E.C., however, involving arcane economic considerations, opinion is volatile and party propaganda can make a considerable impact. While the voter is not completely malleable, therefore, he is persuadable to an extent that compromises the Downsian model.

Secondly, we cannot ignore the related phenomenon of party identification. There is evidence that a large percentage of voters acquire an emotional loyalty to one or other of the established parties, and vote accordingly, without any real appraisal of the policy package that is being offered at election time.[23] It is again important to see what the Downsian model can accommodate and what it cannot.[24] A Downsian voter is not required to make a full calculation of his party differential at every election; to save on information costs, it may be rational for him to vote routinely for one party, only occasionally checking to see that his decision remains valid. If, for example, in a two-party system, the parties compete mainly along one ideological dimension, a voter near to the end of the spectrum will probably need only to be sure that the parties have not switched positions before casting his vote. But party allegiance as a time-saving device is not the same as emotional loyalty to a party. A Downsian voter would be able to give the reasons for his allegiance in terms of ideology or of issues, and this many real-world voters cannot do. Party loyalty is acquired as a kind of identity, often inherited from parents. If a substantial proportion of voters are identifiers in this sense, the competitive process is liable to be distorted, since the party can shift its position without provoking any reassessment on the part of many of its supporters.

It is possible, however, that the importance of party identification as an explanation of voting behaviour has been exaggerated. Voters may have better reasons for supporting parties than they are able to produce in interviews; and the reasons they do give are open to alternative interpretations. As Plamenatz once remarked, electors who vote for a party because its image associates it with the class to which they belong may be behaving more reasonably than if they allowed themselves to be swayed by tangential arguments about policy.[25] Moreover, recent research shows that, in Britain at least, party identification is in decline.[26] So perhaps the electorate is becoming more Downsian, more willing to make voting choices on the basis of ideology or issues rather than traditional party allegiances.

The remaining criticisms of Downs's model focus on the parties. The third difficulty is that Downs, in assuming that the parties act as perfect competitors, overlooks the possibility of collusion between their leaders. Collusion takes the form of agreeing not to compete on certain issues, even though the views of the electorate may differ from the current policy of the parties, so that a party which broke ranks could expect to benefit electorally from doing so. It need not be undertaken from disreputable motives. Party leaders may be moved by a sense of moral responsibility not to bring potentially inflammatory issues (such as immigration) into the political arena. At a somewhat more down-to-earth level, they may appreciate that the policy which makes best sense when they are in government is not the one calculated to win most votes, so they tacitly agree to keep the issue off the electoral agenda. Downs overlooks the fact that winning elections is not the final goal of politicians: they also have to govern in the period that follows.

In the Downsian universe, the mechanism which prevents collusion is the threat of new parties emerging. If the established parties repeatedly adopt policy X where the electorate prefers Y, a new party that adopts Y but otherwise mirrors the current incumbents will win the next election. But this supposes that the cost of entering the competition is very small. In the real world there are two formidable barriers: the financial cost of setting up a new party, and the difficulty of convincing the electorate that the new team is competent to govern. These barriers to entry create the space in which the established parties can collude.

Fourthly, party leaders are not on the whole men and women whose sole political aim is to win office. They have their own ideological commitments which they hope to fulfil once in power. Now, so long as such leaders are instrumentally rational – i.e. they act so as to maximize their chances of achieving their goals – they may not behave any differently from pure office-seekers. Suppose a party leader has personal ideological beliefs that put him well to the left of centre. If he is faced with a choice between losing an election standing on his own preferred policies and winning an election standing on more moderate (but still left-of-centre) policies, he must choose the latter course: half a loaf is better than no bread. So electoral logic will force even ideologically committed leaders towards the position of the median voter.

But this identity of behaviour will be upset if we suppose that the party leaders are uncertain about the distribution of opinion in the electorate, or alternatively that there are some voters who choose on the basis of the government's success or failure in (say) managing the economy over the last period of office. On either assumption ideological leaders will stay away from the median point, since their aim is not simply to win office, but to win at the least cost to their convictions. If they think that they can win while still standing away from the centre, they will do so; and there is evidence that parties which believe themselves to be electorally strong (on the basis of the incumbents' unpopularity, say) may take advantage of this fact to stand on a more radical (left or right) platform.[27]

Fifthly, Downs ignores the important distinction between party leaders – those who may be elected to parliament, and especially those who hope to form the government – and ordinary party members, who contribute funds, campaign for the party and so forth. It clearly makes no sense to suppose that the latter are motivated by the desire to win office. Unless their motive for working for the party is purely social, they must be acting for ideological reasons; and, unlike the leaders who also have the spoils of office to think about, these reasons will be unmixed. Moreover, supposing that party activists are drawn evenly from the spectrum of those who support the party, the median activist will be well to the left (in the case of a left-wing party) or right (in the case of a right-wing party) of the median voter. So we should expect that the activists' preferred policies will always be more extreme than the electorate's policies. In so far as ordinary members are able to influence the formulation of party platforms, they will draw them away from the centre of the political spectrum.[28]

To this it might be replied that instrumentally rational party members must face the same calculation as party leaders, discussed above: whatever their preferred ideological stance, the party still needs to win elections. But here the real world obtrudes in two respects. To begin with, ordinary activists are not likely to be wholly instrumental in outlook – indeed perhaps they cannot be, since an instrumentally rational man would not be an activist for the same reason that he would not be a voter.[29] Activists must, in other words, enjoy the business of campaigning, attending party meetings, and so on. But this enjoyment derives from the sense of promoting policies that are believed in, not policies adopted for reasons of electoral expediency. Additionally, activists appear more likely than party leaders to believe that opinions in the electorate correspond to their own commitments. The reason for this is unclear, but it may be that activists are more likely than leaders to live in a closed informational circle, receiving messages only from other activists. They can then press for the adoption of their preferred policies without being conscious that they are sacrificing instrumental rationality.

To sum up, I have outlined five ways in which party competition in existing

liberal democracies differs from the Downsian model. First, voters' preferences can to some extent be formed by the parties themselves. Secondly,
voters are liable to identify with a particular party prior to assessing its
policies. Thirdly, parties may collude to keep certain policy options away
from the electorate. Fourthly, party leaders may have ideological convictions
which divert them away from a pure vote-maximizing electoral strategy.
Fifthly, ordinary members will be even more strongly inclined to keep party
policy away from the median position.

The first three points indicate that Schumpeter's oligopolistic model is
more likely to be accurate as an analysis of party competition than Downs's
perfectly competitive model. Indeed the processes we have described – voter
manipulation, party identification, collusion – are all explicitly recognized by
Schumpeter as ingredients of democracy. The last two points in a way suggest
that matters are even worse than Schumpeter supposed: it is as though
oligopolistic producers not only used the standard techniques for manipulating the market to increase their profits, but positively believed in the product
they were selling, refusing to alter it in response to consumers' tastes. From an
explanatory point of view, therefore, the Downsian model has to be modified
considerably to fit the processes that occur in the real world; which is not to
say that the model is completely lacking in explanatory power.

From a normative point of view, our response must be more complex. We
must ask first what normative claims can be made on behalf of Downs's
model *qua* model of democracy. But we must also ask how far features of
party competition as it actually occurs undermine these claims, and whether
these features can be eliminated. For if the model is normatively acceptable,
we may try to alter the world to fit the model more perfectly. To these issues I
turn in the final section of the chapter.

V

To assess the competitive model from a normative point of view, it is useful to
compare it with the alternative model of democracy outlined at the beginning
of this chapter, the 'popular will' model. In the competitive model, leaders
initiate policies and the mass of the people respond to what is offered through
the ballot box; in the popular will model, the people initiate policies, and
leadership is at most a channel through which this will is expressed. There are
three main variants of the second model: assembly democracy, where the
people meet face to face to enact legislation;[30] referendum democracy, where
policy is decided by mass vote; and delegate democracy, where the people
elect representatives but mandate them to follow specified lines of policy.
These variants can be combined in several ways, and the third can obviously
shade into the competitive model by degrees. The basic contrast between the
two models is nevertheless clear enough.

Which model is to be preferred in the light of basic democratic principles? It is important here to distinguish two ways in which democracy may be justified. *Instrumental* justifications value democracy for the way in which it translates the people's wishes into government policy: democracy is desirable because it produces outcomes that satisfy wants most efficiently. *Intrinsic* justifications value democracy for the benefits that the act of policy-making confers directly on the participants: democracy is desirable either because political participation is an intrinsically worthwhile activity or because it develops qualities of character – moral qualities, for instance – that are valuable in other areas of life. These two types of justification may pull in different directions – if, for instance, a group of people enjoy making decisions democratically yet are so incompetent that the decisions made are invariably bad ones – but most democrats would, I imagine, want to include both as reasons for having democracy.[31]

Taking the intrinsic justification first, it is apparent that the popular will model is preferable to the competitive model. The popular will model envisages the people actually taking part in the making of policy–informing themselves, debating, and so forth – whereas in the competitive model the people's role is more passive: the leaders propose and the people respond. Of course the latter model does not stipulate that people should *not* take an active interest in political issues, and indeed the Downsian version requires the electorate to have considerable political knowledge; but the model's rationale is in part that it incorporates an efficient division of labour between a professional leadership and an amateur electorate, the assumption being that it takes greater expertise to draw up policies than to choose between two or more policy packages. The popular will model requires extensive participation, whereas the competitive model is designed to work with limited participation, so on the intrinsic grounds identified above the former must be preferred.

How do the two models compare on instrumental grounds? We can approach this question by asking why, first of all, the popular will model might fail to produce efficient policies ('efficient' being understood to mean 'maximally want-satisfying'). There are two broad reasons, both canvassed in Schumpeter's critique of the model. The first is simply that a badly-informed population might decide on a policy that did not produce the outcomes it intended (think of alternative policies for reducing inflation). The second is that the procedure for converting votes into policy might be inefficient. This is the possibility I want to consider here.

Unless we envisage an assembly which continues debating issues until there is unanimous agreement, decisions under the popular will model are likely to be made by majority vote. This will produce efficient results whenever everyone stands to gain roughly the same amount from having his preferred policy adopted, but not when members of the successful majority gain less than members of the defeated minority lose. Thus suppose 60% of the population vote to prohibit sport on Sundays and 40% to allow it. The 60% are religious people who feel slightly more comfortable for knowing that the Sabbath is being kept holy (gaining, say, 10 units of satisfaction each) while the 40% are frustrated sportsmen (losing, say, 20 units of satisfaction each from the decision). The decision results in a net loss of 20 units of satisfaction per hundred people. This is known in the literature as the 'intense minority' problem.[32]

How might the popular will model try to solve the problem of intense minorities? Two avenues may be followed. One, deriving from Rousseau, is to suppose that the people, when making decisions, do not ask 'which policy do I most prefer?' but 'which policy is in the general interest?' It is easiest to envisage this in the context of assembly democracy. Using our example, churchgoers and sportsmen both deploy their arguments in the debate, then each person tries to assess how much a decision to prohibit Sunday sport will benefit churchgoers and harm sportsmen respectively before casting his vote. This solution is clearly vulnerable in two respects: it requires participants to vote with perfect good will, and it requires them to be well-informed both about the numbers on either side of the issue and about how strongly each side feels. These difficulties are equally clearly magnified when we pass to referendum or delegate democracy.

The second avenue is more realistic. It looks for ways in which the decision-making procedure may be modified to give additional weight to intense minorities. An informal method is the practice of logrolling, whereby minorities on two issues agree to support one another in their respective causes. Suppose that the devolution of power is an issue in the same legislative session as Sunday sport, and that again 60% of the population mildly oppose devolution while 40% strongly favour it. Provided the devolutionists do not overlap too extensively with the sportsmen, they can successfully form a pact to vote in favour of both policies – some sportsmen swallowing devolution (which they dislike) to get Sunday football and vice versa. Thus logrolling restores efficiency. But for it to occur, each minority group must know the other's mind, the two must be able to co-ordinate their behaviour, and they must establish mutual trust. Logrolling is therefore a phenomenon of small, well-informed assemblies, and not a mechanism that is likely to work in mass publics.

A more formal method of reaching the same result is to give each voter a number of votes that he is allowed to distribute as he chooses over the issues in any legislative session. The assumption is that he will use up more of his votes on those issues about which he feels strongly. Thus suppose that only Sunday sport and devolution are being decided in a particular session, and that each participant has five votes to distribute. A sportsman who is opposed to devolution may choose to cast four votes for Sunday sport in the sport poll and one vote against devolution in the devolution poll. Again this is likely to avoid inefficient outcomes, because minorities can register the intensity of their preferences. But there are at least two serious problems: the decisions reached will depend on which issues are grouped together in a session, for the purpose of allocating votes, and the system is open to strategic voting, where voters calculate that they can do best by *not* distributing their votes according to the relative strength of their feelings about issues.[33]

So we have to conclude as follows: where intense minorities exist (virtually certain in a culturally plural society), the popular will model using majority voting will produce inefficient outcomes; and although there are mechanisms which might avoid this, it is unlikely that they will operate consistently and successfully in a large society.

This gives us a toehold from which to build a defence of the competitive model. For if we could show that the competitive model is more likely to avoid the intense minorities problem than the popular will model, we would have proved that the former model is preferable on instrumental grounds (though intrinsic arguments still of course favour the latter). Consider the question first in the context of the Downsian model. If the electorate are divided over several issues or along several dimensions, the parties will clearly consider both the number and the intensity of those standing on either side before drawing up their platforms. Each party is interested in attracting the maximum number of voters, and knows that the voter in reaching his decision will weigh each plank in the platform according to the intensity of his feelings. Unfortunately it does not follow simply that where an intense minority exists, both parties will take the minority view. As we saw above,[34] under perfect information a party can combine two intense minorities to defeat a majority-policy party. In effect a party that does this is logrolling on the voters' behalf. But we also saw that this does not produce a stable equilibrium. Where information is imperfect, it is still harder to reach definite conclusions. But informally one can see why parties will be reluctant to include in their platforms planks that are opposed by intense minorities. Suppose the election will be fought on a number of issues, one of which is Sunday sport, and that opinion on that issue is divided as in our earlier discussion. Which stand will party leaders decide to adopt on Sunday sport? They are likely to reason as follows: if we oppose Sunday sport, we shall probably lose the votes of almost all the 40% of people who are strongly in favour of sport, since it is unlikely that our combined platform on the other issues will be sufficient to win them back. On the other hand, we *may* win the votes of the 60% opposed to Sunday sport, but since they don't feel strongly about the issue it is more likely that they will choose on other grounds. On balance, therefore, it will be safer to support Sunday sport in our manifesto.

In short, whenever parties feel that a policy will certainly lose some votes but possibly win more, they will be reluctant to adopt the policy. And this prediction of Downs's model is borne out in practice, in so far as a complaint that is frequently levelled at governments in liberal democracies is that they take more notice of vociferous minorities than of 'silent majorities'.[35]

I conclude that the competitive model is likely to be preferable on instrumental grounds to the popular will model. Whereas the system of voting embodied in the latter is insensitive to the strength of feeling on issues (and theoretical remedies for this are unlikely to work in practice) competing parties will take account of intensities of preference. Or to put the point differently, parties will informally undertake the logrolling between minorities that is unlikely to occur in large-scale popular democracies.

There are still two serious problems for the model. One is that it ignores the intrinsic arguments for popular participation; the other is that real-world competition is Schumpeterian rather than Downsian, so that the system is actually less efficient than the instrumental argument suggests. I want to end by proposing a reform that (optimistically) may meet both of these difficulties at once. It involves inserting elements of the popular will model into the competitive model.

My suggestion is that we should aim for a political framework that combines competitive democracy at the national level with participatory democracy at the local and industrial levels. In other words we should retain something like the present system of elections and competing parties for national government while handing over local government to popular assemblies and transferring firms to workers' control. There are several things to be said in favour of this proposal. First, people would enjoy the benefits of participation in a forum, or a series of fora, which is small enough to make participation meaningful – since the effectiveness of participation is inversely proportional to the number of co-participants.[36] Secondly, small assemblies are more likely to avoid the inefficiencies associated with direct democracy, as we saw above. Thirdly, even if this failed, dissatisfied minorities would have the option of moving to a different jurisdiction, which is clearly a more viable option than its equivalent at national level (namely emigration). Fourthly, the experience gained in local and industrial democracy would help to produce a more competent electorate, and so make the competitive system work more efficiently. This is the point at which the two halves of my argument come together. There are two main factors which make the competitive system less than wholly efficient: a malleable electorate, and a rigid and unresponsive party system. If voters, through the experience of participation, become better informed and firmer in their views, the greater difficulty is removed. We need then only look for contingent ways of lessening the rigidity of the party system, such as facilitating the entry of new parties and improving the flow of information to party leaders about voters' preferences.

I therefore end on a note of reconciliation. There is more to be said, normatively speaking, for the competitive model than is usually admitted in the literature of democratic theory. However distasteful, at first glance, a gaggle of political entrepreneurs competing for electoral custom may seem, the model must be judged dispassionately, and its instrumental advantages recognized: the competitive mechanism is likely to produce better results on balance than a system which attempts to translate the people's will directly into policy. But the model is seen at its best when combined with elements of the popular will model. Direct democracy at grass-roots level would provide the intrinsic benefits of participation, and at the same time improve the efficiency of the competitive system.

10

Marcuse and autonomy

VINCENT GEOGHEGAN

In the Europe ushered in by the Congress of Vienna of 1815, it was felt by many that, for better or worse, a 'full' (i.e. adult male) extension of the franchise would lead to fundamental socio-economic change. In their struggle with the restored autocracy, sections of the bourgeoisie might pose as champions of democracy but, as the events of 1848 were to show, they shared with their autocratic opponents the fear that universal suffrage would result in the catastrophe of rule by the masses. In this they were at one with a tradition dating back to ancient times in which 'democracy . . . was defined as rule by the poor, the ignorant, and incompetent, at the expense of the leisured, civilised, propertied classes. Democracy, as seen from the upper layers of class-divided societies, meant class rule, rule by the wrong class. It was a class threat, as incompatible with a liberal as with a hierarchical society.'[1] It was above all in the most advanced capitalist nation of this period, the United Kingdom, with its increasingly self-confident working class, that the fears and hopes surrounding suffrage reform were most apparent: fear expressed by the liberal Bagehot that 'both our political parties will bid for the support of the working man . . . both of them will promise to do as he likes'[2], hope in the words of the Chartist leader O'Connor: 'six months after the Charter is passed, every man, woman and child in the country will be well fed, well housed and well clothed'.[3] Disraeli's partial extension of the suffrage in 1867 and all the subsequent extensions, both in the United Kingdom and internationally, revealed just how groundless such fears and hopes had been – the social fabric remained intact, Jerusalem was not built. The failure of universal suffrage to usher in socialism was to give impetus to those on the left who maintained that the fetishization of suffrage reform was based upon the false assumption that the majority of individuals in capitalist societies could be relied upon to use democratic institutions effectively. Erich Fromm, looking back over a hundred years to the optimism of O'Connor, indicated the shift to which, he maintained, the dashing of such hopes had given rise. 'It became clear that the problem of democracy today is not any more the restriction of franchise but the manner in which the franchise is exercised.'[4]

Fromm's strictures on liberal democracy are permeated by a highly unflattering concept of the individual in capitalist society: a concept of a heteronomous individual who is fundamentally different from the autonomous citizen assumed in liberal democratic rhetoric; an individual whose inability to control his or her life consciously belies the supposed *modus operandi* of liberal democratic political systems. 'How', asks Fromm, 'can people express "their" will if they do not have any will or conviction of their own . . . ?'[5] This scepticism concerning the capacity of individuals to act as rational, political actors in liberal democracies, with its sharp contrast between the ideal and the reality of such democracies, can be characterized as the dominant trend in democratic theory this century and *in this respect* Fromm can be seen as the rather unlikely bedfellow of Schumpeter (whose low estimation of the democratic individual is quoted appreciatively in Fromm's *The Sane Society*), Berelson and the other democratic revisionists. If, however, the theoretical roots of Fromm's critique of the 'autonomous' individual are examined, then the true nature of the dissimilarity between his critique and that of the democratic revisionists can be perceived, and it is to an examination of these roots that we shall now turn our attention.

The modern antecedents of the critique of the 'autonomous' individual can be found in the work of Hegel, in particular in his conceptions of history and cognition. History, for Hegel, is a law-governed process whose mode of progression and ultimate purpose has remained hidden from the individuals who have made it, and his famous dictum that 'The Owl of Minerva spreads its wings only with the falling of the dusk' expressed the conviction that full comprehension of the process of historical development only occurs at the end of that process. In the case of cognition, its lower, inadequate forms develop into higher and more adequate ones as the straightforward and commonsensical is revealed to be a partial and mystified experience. Common to both conceptions is the image of the mystified individual, engaged in activity whose actual contours are not perceived, an individual unable to grasp the essential through and from the apparent.

Marx's critical appropriation of the Hegelian heritage provided the theoretical framework for the critique of the 'autonomous' individual. Hegel's opaque historical process, his 'cunning of reason', was transformed into Marx's historical progression of modes of production, in which as in Hegel's system, history is made by actors who, be they nations, classes or individuals, are not conscious of the true character of their acts: England is 'the unconscious tool of history' in its destruction of traditional Indian society, the bourgeoisie misconceives its labour contracts as the very essence of freedom, and Adam Smith in his writings spoke of society but described capitalism. As Seliger has pointed out,[6] although Marx did not use the term 'false-consciousness' (though Engels did use it after Marx's death), he did use kindred terms such as 'incorrect', 'twisted', 'untrue', 'abstract', 'illusion', 'block' and '*idée fixe*' to denote this phenomenon of mystified consciousness, consciousness which, it should be added, was historically specific to and conditioned by particular modes of production and was not a universal attribute of humanity itself. As a consequence of his conception of mystified consciousness, Marx was aware of the danger of asserting that there was any simple linkage between universal suffrage and human emancipation. True, he considered that universal suffrage could, under special circumstances, be used as a weapon by the working class, but, these comparatively rare circumstances aside, he saw bourgeois democracies as establishing the sovereignty of the corrupt, uncivilized, unsocial individual.

Marx's conviction that, in bourgeois democracy, the 'autonomous citizen' concealed the heteronomous individual is fundamental to the work of the thinker who is the subject of the rest of this essay – Herbert Marcuse. In an analysis of Gracchus Babeuf's defence at his trial, for example, Marcuse sympathetically presents the French Revolutionary's distinction between the sovereign people and the apparent sovereignty of the people: 'the people who vote for their constitution and their representatives are not necessarily the sovereign people . . . their expressed will is not necessarily their autonomous will'.[7] 'The people', the shining centrepiece of democratic theory, are simply not to be found in advanced capitalism, the actual denizens of which are a highly impoverished breed: 'the masses'. 'The masses', Marcuse insists, 'are not identical with "the people" on whose sovereign rationality the free society was to be established.'[8]

Though Marcuse uses the word 'autonomy' time and again throughout his voluminous writings, nowhere does it receive a systematic definition. It is most often used in the sense of a goal to be achieved, that whole and happy, free and rational condition which has perennially informed socialist theorizing about the good society. Heteronomy, in contrast, characterizes the contemporary state of the individual – fragmented, incapable of genuine happiness, enslaved, irrational. Marcuse's particular reworking of this dualistic commonplace has little to say about the socio-economic structures of a future 'autonomous society' and his work will, as a consequence, prove disappointing to those concerned with the nature of collective control of the productive forces or of the institutional forms of decision-making in such societies. He is above all concerned with the instinctual and cognitive aspects of autonomy (a highly personal amalgam of Marx and Freud principally), with why such a state is suppressed by the current conditions (the 'one-dimensionality' thesis) and with the counter-tendencies to this suppression. This points to a second usage of the word 'autonomy' in Marcuse's work where it indicates anticipations in the present of the full autonomy to come – those embryonic forms of autonomy located in such varied modes of thought and behaviour as sexuality, artistic production and critical thought. These are the lifeline to the future for, as Marcuse insists, 'the slaves must be free for their liberation before they can become free . . . the end must be operative in the means to attain it'.[9]

The pivotal concept in Marcuse's analysis of the modern heteronomous individual is that of technological rationality; this concept reveals the influence of Weber, whose account of the 'rationalization' which accompanies industrialization is appropriated critically. In a 1941 essay entitled 'Some social implications of modern technology', Marcuse charts the catastrophic triumph of technological rationality – or in other words, charts the emergence of the modern heteronomous individual. In the sixteenth and seventeenth centuries the conception of the individual promoted by the militant bourgeoisie was, according to Marcuse, that of the rational autonomous individual ('individualistic rationality') – a conception appropriate to free market, mercantile and industrial capitalism. This conception lost its grounding as the mode of production mutated over time. The whip of the market revolutionized productive instruments, economic organizations and, as a consequence of the latter, undermined the position of autonomous individualistic rationality in favour of heteronomous technological rationality (Weber's formal rationality). In the new, rationalized world individuals think and act as efficient units in an efficient whole – the efficient individual is the new hero whose

performance is motivated, guided and measured by standards external to him, standards pertaining to predetermined tasks and functions. The efficient individual is the one whose performance is an action only insofar as it is the proper reaction to the objective requirements of the apparatus, and his liberty is confined to the selection of the most adequate means for reaching a goal which he did not set.[10]

The pernicious effect of technological rationality is not simply confined to the consciousness and behaviour of the workplace but has spread beyond this to affect all areas of human experience, informing the way individuals see, act upon and even rebel against their environment and each other.

Marcuse is at pains to suggest that technological rationality includes in its definition a substantial proportion of a further meaning of the term reason – namely reasonableness. Advanced capitalist society is such a reasonable society, making so few demands on individuals yet supplying so much, that it is the individuals who wish dysfunctional freedom, and not those who are content to be recipients of the good life, who are being unreasonable. Such a society 'is not only perfectly rational but also perfectly reasonable . . . There is no room for autonomy.'[11]

Marcuse's 1941 account of the pervasiveness of technological rationality lacks any detailed analysis of the psychological dimension of this process. His Frankfurt School colleagues, notably Horkheimer and Fromm, had sought in the 1930s to fill the undoubted lacuna of psychological explanation in Marx's work with insights drawn from the work of Freud. It was, however, not until the 1950s and 1960s that Marcuse introduced a Freudian element into his own account of the contemporary heteronomous individual. With respect to the history of the species, Marcuse pointed to the conservative function of the superego as the repository of the values of repressive societies, and developed the notion of a 'psychic Thermidor' to suggest an internal resistance in individuals to radical activity which had so often resulted in the betrayal of revolutions. Turning to contemporary developments he maintained that the Freudian concept of the individual possessed of a conscious and sovereign ego *vis-à-vis* the demands of the unconscious and external reality had been undermined by the internal development of advanced capitalist society. The 'reification and automatization of the ego', as Marcuse calls this development, is characterized by the replacement of conscious confrontation on the part of the ego with 'immediate, almost physical relations in which comprehending consciousness, thought and even one's own feelings play a very small role'.[12] Since, for both Freud and Marcuse, the individual ego is formed in the Oedipal struggle with the father, the origins of the decline of the ego must be sought in a contemporary transformation of the Oedipal conflict. Marcuse maintained that such a transformation had occurred as a result of the development of monopoly capitalism and its ubiquitous and all-powerful technical, cultural and political apparatus. Family socialization, centred upon the paterfamilias, has given way to extra-familial socialization which has grown in effectiveness at the expense of the traditional family, whose economic base has been undermined by monopoly capitalism. The 'ego ideal', the standard of perfection which traditionally resulted from the individual's ultimate identification with the father, is now systemically embodied. Not the father, but the concrete apparatus as a whole, provides the standards of behaviour and it does this not after a process of creative struggle between the individual and reality but in a pre-emptive strike which renders the individual passive and malleable. So successful is this process that the possibility of autonomy produces anxiety in most individuals, who consequently multiply the channels by which the systemic cues can be communicated: 'The antenna on every house, the transistor on every beach, the juke-box in every bar or restaurant are as many cries of desperation – not to be left alone, by himself, not to be separated from the Big Ones, not to be condemned to the emptiness or the hatred or the dreams of oneself.'[13]

The various strands of Marcuse's analysis of the contemporary individual were brought together in his 1964 work *One Dimensional Man*: the rise of technological rationality, the centrality of the productive process in that rise, the indoctrination promoted by the good life, the deep penetration of the individual (and of the mass of individuals) by external norms and the stifling of autonomous thought and behaviour. It is worth quoting at length a passage from the above work, which admirably sums up Marcuse's thesis:

The productive apparatus and the goods and services which it produces 'sell' or impose the social system as a whole. The means of mass transportation and communication, the commodities of lodging, food and clothing, the irresistible output of the entertainment and information industry carry with them prescribed attitudes and habits, certain intellectual and emotional reactions which bind the consumers more or less pleasantly to the producers and, through the latter, to the whole. The products indoctrinate and manipulate; they promote a false consciousness which is immune against its falsehood. And as these beneficial products become available to more individuals in more social classes, the indoctrination they carry ceases to be publicity; it becomes a way of life. It is a good way of life – much better than before – and as a good way of life, it militates against qualitative change. Thus emerges a pattern of one-dimensional thought and behaviour in which ideas, aspirations, and objectives that, by their content, transcend the established universe of discourse and action are either repelled or reduced to terms of this universe. They are redefined by the rationality of the given system and its quantitative extension.[14]

In the light of these analyses Marcuse arrives at a number of damning conclusions about liberal democratic societies. First, the apparent rationality and reasonableness of such societies conceal essential relations of domination and so castrate the political impulse, for under the sway of the myth of the classless society (where of course only technical problems remain), the disadvantaged majority fail to adequately conceptualize the dominant elites and the political stance required *vis-à-vis* these elites, and fail in fact to see that they occupy a political terrain. Since a failure to conceptualize the actual nature of the social world extends to the elites also, authentic political debate is precluded. Secondly, the formation of mass society does not abolish the social atomization so inimical to genuine democratic politics but actually consolidates it, for the 'mass' is an oppressive aggregate of isolated units and not a genuine community. At the political level (in the narrow sense) this manifests itself on the one hand in the dependence of the masses on leaders for authoritative guidance to fill the vacuum not filled by autonomous in-dividuality and on the other, in the channelling of the consequent deep instinctual frustration into outbursts of mass extremism – of which governments are partly the cynical controller, partly the helpless prisoner. Finally, and to sum up, where autonomous thought and activity are not possible, one has the democracy of the blinkered, democracy in the conditions of Plato's cave. In *One Dimensional Man*, Marcuse makes no attempt to conceal his conclusion:

In the last analysis, the question of what are true and false needs must be answered by the individuals themselves, but only in the last analysis; that is, if and when they are free to give their own answer. As long as they are kept incapable of being autonomous, as long as they are indoctrinated and manipulated (down to their very instincts), their answer to this question cannot be taken as their own.[15]

Before turning to the question of strategy and tactics, a couple of clarificatory remarks concerning the possibility, and locus, of autonomy within liberal democratic societies are necessary. In what follows, Marcuse points to areas in which, he believes, autonomous thought and behaviour are possible in such societies. However, he rejects any suggestion that the autonomy possible in capitalism is equivalent to the full autonomy which is possible only in a transformed society in which all individuals can lead an authentic existence. Secondly, as suggested in a number of earlier remarks, Marcuse's references to governing elites, leaders, privileged and powerful strata are not meant to imply that these groups possess a greater autonomy than the bulk of the population. The undoubted manipulative skills and cynicism of these elites are not to be confused with autonomy, being as much the polluted fruit of advanced capitalism as the (usual) passivity of the conservative majority.

Controversy has been generated over the precise nature of the strategy and tactics deemed appropriate by Marcuse in liberal democracies – much of it focused on his 1965 piece 'Repressive Tolerance' (published as one contribution to a collection of essays by different authors entitled *A Critique of Pure Tolerance*). Cranston sees in the work 'a vein of impatience, intolerance, and the will to violence' and sees significance in the fact that it was published 'in a peculiar format, bound in black like a prayer book or missal and perhaps designed to compete with *The Thoughts of Chairman Mao* as devotional reading at student sit-ins',[16] whilst MacIntyre says of the ideas in the work that whereas Lenin and the Jacobins believed 'in a temporary dictatorship of the majority over counter-revolutionary minorities . . . it was left to Marcuse to profess a belief in a dictatorship by a minority'.[17] Or again Vivas, who maintains that the essay clearly shows Marcuse to be 'a Torquemada of the left'.[18] Let us therefore begin our analysis of Marcuse's account of authentic political behaviour in liberal democracies by looking at his essay 'Repressive Tolerance', which generated so much disapproval.

The provocative conclusion of the work is stated in the very first paragraph: 'The conclusion reached is that the realization of the objective of tolerance would call for intolerance toward prevailing policies, attitudes, opinions, and the extension of tolerance to policies, attitudes, and opinions which are outlawed or suppressed'.[19] The tolerance operative in liberal democracies is divided by Marcuse into two types – passive tolerance and abstract tolerance. Passive tolerance tolerates the intolerable; it is the unacceptable tolerance of the unacceptable. Palpably evil phenomena (amongst others Marcuse mentions nuclear weapons, neo-colonial massacres, deceptive advertising, planned obsolescence) are tolerated when what it actually required is their total extirpation: 'Tolerance is extended to policies, conditions, and modes of behaviour which should not be tolerated because they are impeding, if not destroying, the chances of creating an existence without fear and misery.'[20] Tolerance instead of being a partisan practice by the autonomous people is experienced passively by the heteronomous masses – they are not its authors, its controllers. This is complemented by abstract toleration, which is toleration (within broad limits) of all shades of opinion and behaviour but in a context where, owing to thoroughgoing and continuing socialization, certain opinions and behaviour have the prior 'preference' of the underlying population:

Under the rule of monopolistic media . . . a mentality is created for which right and wrong, true and false are predefined wherever they affect the vital interests of the society. This is, prior to all expression and communication, a matter of semantics . . . Other words can be spoken and heard, other ideas can be expressed, but at the massive scale of the conservative majority . . . they are immediately 'evaluated' . . . in terms of the public language – a language which determines 'a priori' the direction in which the thought process moves.[21]

Marcuse uses as an example a U.S. magazine printing simultaneously a positive and a negative account of the F.B.I., thereby seeming to act even-handedly when in fact mere parity consolidates the built-in advantage of the positive account, given popular internalization of the official image of that agency.

Universal, pure tolerance can only become a reality in conditions of socialist democracy, and this necessarily involves the reactivation of liberating intolerance against the reactionary forces protected by the 'impartial' but effectively partial tolerance of liberal democracies. There is some confusion in 'Repressive Tolerance' concerning the subject to whom the work is addressed, since Marcuse moves at various points in the essay from addressing a governmental subject – this is basically a heuristic device – to addressing radical minorities, which are his principal concern. The intolerance of these radical minorities in liberal democracy is legitimated by the possibility of correct, undistorted consciousness.

In Plato's allegory of the cave, individuals who have spent their lives in one fixed position, able only to see directly ahead, necessarily mistake the shadows cast by objects on a wall facing them for the objects themselves. One individual, however, is able to demystify his experience by investigating the cave, seeing the immediate source of the shadows and finally emerging from the cave itself into the reality beyond. Plato rejects any relativist interpretation here; both experiences are not equally valid, for one is mystified while the other is not, and though the people remaining in the cave reject the account of the man who saw the sun, it is they who are mistaken and not he.

Marx's concepts of science and ideology represented a modern reformulation of this Platonic distinction, in which science adequately grasps what is inadequately understood in ideology. Like Plato, Marx was able to ground a normative political theory on this epistemological base.

As 'Repressive Tolerance' makes clear, Marcuse is firmly in this tradition: 'In the interplay of theory and practice, true and false solutions become distinguishable';[22] or again, 'the distinction between true and false tolerance, between progress and regression can be made rationally'.[23] Given that the value-judgement 'human life is worth living, or rather can be and ought to be made worth living'[24] is not rejected, and that reality can be examined objectively, then it is possible to establish ways and means, based on the current level of material and intellectual resources, of achieving a truly human existence. Absolute certainty, the desire for which reflects a theological illusion, cannot be guaranteed; what can be guaranteed however is sufficient certainty – 'the certainty of a reasoned and reasonable chance'[25] to legitimate political action based upon such analysis.

Marcuse is acutely aware of the arguments of what he terms 'the theoreticians of educational dictatorship' – particularly Plato and Rousseau, and in 'Repressive Tolerance' and *One Dimensional Man*, he can be seen wrestling with them. In *One Dimensional Man*, for example, he says of the argument that in conditions of material and intellectual immaturity, liberation has to be the work of force and administration by an elite body: 'it is easily ridiculed but hard to refute because it has the merit to acknowledge, without much hypocrisy, the conditions (material and intellectual) which serve to prevent genuine and intelligent self-determination'.[26] These thinkers were not afraid to discuss the problems of achieving liberation in societies where the majority are passively enslaved and where the process of liberation commences outside this majority.

However, Marcuse adamantly sets his face against the concept of an elitist or dictatorial revolution: 'the alternative to the established semi-democratic process is *not* a dictatorship or elite, no matter how intellectual and intelligent'[27] (Marcuse's emphasis). Only a truly popular, democratic movement can usher in a free society which cannot be established or sustained by Jacobin, Blanquist or vanguardist elites – there is simply no short cut that can avoid the uphill struggle of facilitating the development of genuine autonomy in the population at large. However, before examining precisely how Marcuse envisages this facilitation process it is necessary – given their importance to his strategic and tactical considerations – to examine his account of a number of other areas in which autonomous activity, although possible, is in fact blocked by liberal democratic societies; these are the spheres of art and sexuality.

For Marcuse, art had historically been a vehicle for aspirations repelled in the prevailing social conditions, and served to indict the unrealized potential of those conditions. This critical and anticipatory function rendered art a realm in which the individual either as artistic producer or consumer could experience the autonomy denied in other realms:

There is an element of earthly delight in the works of great bourgeois art . . . The individual enjoys beauty, goodness, splendor, peace and victorious joy . . . He experiences liberation . . . Reification is transpierced in private . . . The world appears as what it is behind the commodity form: a landscape is really a landscape, a man really a man, a thing really a thing.[28]

Art provided an 'Archimedean point', an expanse of 'mental space' outside and beyond the heteronomous conditions of everyday life.

This mental space had been obliterated in the triumphal progress of technological rationality. Whereas in the heyday of bourgeois culture, art was fundamentally divorced from everyday affairs (the very ritualization of behaviour at cultural occasions, special costumes, precise etiquette and so forth serving to project the individual into another world) in the society that subsequently emerged, art became assimilated, reconciled to the daily grind. The mass marketing of art which makes it available to all occurs necessarily at the expense of its other-worldly character: 'the integration of cultural values into the established society cancels the alienation of culture from civilization . . . The result: the autonomous, critical contents of culture become educational, elevating, relaxing – a vehicle of adjustment'.[29]

With respect to the widespread sexual freedom, the widespread desublimation operative in liberal democratic societies, Marcuse argues that this is more a token of the absence of autonomy than of its prevalence and, consequently, coins the phrase 'repressive desublimation'. The erotic drive as an essentially critical force has championed the autonomous creative impulse against the repressive character of human society to date; it has, to use Marcuse's terms, championed the pleasure principle against repressive reality principles. The very historical restriction of the sexual expressions of Eros (the taboos on non-procreative, non-heterosexual, non-'normal' eroticism) was a measure of the latter's link with human fulfilment. The modern liberalization of sexual mores has effectively managed the conflict between the pleasure principle and the reality principle by harnessing libidinal energy to the status quo. Sex, like art, has exchanged its role of distancing the individual from society for that of binding the two together more firmly. In the libidinal realm 'was the surreptitious freedom, the dangerous autonomy of the individual under the pleasure principle . . . with the integration of this sphere . . . society has enlarged, not individual freedom, but its control over the individual'.[30]

As regards prospects for fundamental political change, the first half of the 1960s witnessed the most pessimistic presentation of Marcuse's one-dimensionality thesis; his book *One Dimensional Man* and the essays 'Repressive Tolerance' and 'The Obsolescence of the Freudian Concept of Man' are notable products of this period. In the advanced societies (of which the U.S.A. is the most advanced example), where 'a comfortable, smooth, reasonable, democratic unfreedom prevails',[31] oppositional centres were considered to be few and impotent, existing only above and below the overwhelming popular consensus – critical intellectuals on the one hand, and on the other 'the substratum of the outcasts and outsiders, the exploited and persecuted of other races and other colours, the unemployed and the unemployable'[32] who are not integrated into the good society, and probably never will be.

The gloom began to disperse after this period, as Marcuse claimed to perceive more pronounced oppositional forces, which thus enabled him to outline more specifically his current conception of the battle for democracy. We shall concentrate on three dissenting forces highlighted in his work of this time – the students, the drop-outs or hippies and the blacks. In the case of the students, their involvement in the U.S. civil rights movement and subsequent participation in the Vietnam War protests were the events which, for Marcuse, marked the emergence of the student body as a dissenting force in the United States, a development which seemed to reveal ways in which the one-dimensional world of advanced capitalism could be combated. In their own sphere, that of education, students were both attacking links between the academies and the military–economic complex and demanding the replacement of the pseudo-neutrality of the curriculum with a genuinely critical content; at the same time anti-universities and other alternative educational centres were being established as islands of demystified consciousness. In pursuit of a genuinely democratic upsurge the student body had to establish (and in Marcuse's opinion, were to a limited extent actually establishing) links with the conservative majority: 'If the student opposition remains isolated and does not succeed in breaking out of its own limited sphere, if it does not succeed in mobilizing social strata that really will play a decisive role . . . then the student opposition can play only an accessory role.'[33] The concept used by Marcuse to define this process tended not to be 'vanguard' – with its connotation of a mass bureaucratic party and authoritarian leadership (though he was not totally consistent in this at the terminological level) – but 'catalyst', the communication of ideas and experience as a trigger to the latent autonomy of individuals.

The 'drop-out'/hippie phenomenon contained an existential dimension of protest. The rejection of, and withdrawal from the good society created free space where autonomous thought and behaviour could develop whilst the erotic renaissance of this marginal group (and of the young generally) heralded the emergence of the instinctual basis of freedom which was qualitatively different from the repressive desublimation of conventional sexuality. For Marcuse, these individuals bore out in practice his long held belief that the life instinct (Eros) was the ultimate source of all truly civilized existence. In *An Essay on Liberation* it is argued that specific moral values are rooted in the deepest layers of the human organism (the work speculates about an 'erotic drive to counter aggressiveness') and that it is legitimate to talk about an instinctual or 'biological' foundation for socialism. As an example of the political potential of this eroticization, Marcuse recalled a demonstration he had witnessed where serried ranks of armed police confronted a large body of demonstrators:

After two or three scary minutes the thousands of marchers sat down in the street, guitars and harmonicas appeared, people began 'necking' and 'petting', and so the demonstration ended. You may find this ridiculous, but I believe that a unity spontaneously and anarchically emerged here that perhaps in the end cannot fail to make an impression even on the enemy.[34]

As regards the black ghetto population of the U.S.A., Marcuse was particularly impressed with what he considered to be a critical linguistic and aesthetic practice. In the linguistic sphere, the language of technological rationality is undermined by splitting the totalitarian unity of object, term and meaning, as when the unconscious progression: uniformed individual/policeman/legitimate authority is interrupted by substituting 'pig' for 'policeman', or when 'soul' is detached from white culture and incorporated into black parlance. Black music, as authentic non-repressive desublimation, unlike the affirmative works of bourgeois culture, connects directly with the instinctual roots of autonomy:

The black music, invading the white culture, is the terrifying realization of 'O Freunde, nicht diese Töne!' – the refusal now hits the chorus which sings the Ode to Joy, the song which is invalidated in the culture that sings it . . . In the subversive, dissonant, crying and shouting rhythm, born in the 'dark continent' and in the 'deep South' of slavery and deprivation, the oppressed revoke the Ninth Symphony and give art a desublimated, sensuous form of frightening immediacy, moving, electrifying the body, and the soul materialized in the body.[35]

The struggle for democracy in liberal democracies therefore extends beyond the political institutions and traditional political practices of these societies. In an important respect for Marcuse, the very act of using such institutions and practices reinforces the position of one-dimensional society by implicitly draping the semi- or defectively democratic with the mantle of democracy itself. However, the liberties of liberal democracies are not to be mocked, for they provide the freedom essential for the building of the democratic alternative, an alternative which would not dispense with such liberties but which would embody them more effectively. Similarly action outside the conventional usages of liberal democracy does not preclude the use of conventional institutions by those who have no illusions as to their effectiveness but who nevertheless feel they can supplement the struggle on other fronts.

On the question of violence, Marcuse distinguishes between the violence which may become absolutely necessary in the creation of a free society, which is justified by that goal in those conditions, and violence in the service of human degradation. The former kind of violence may become necessary because of the covert and overt violence which is institutionalized in liberal democracies, and its practice, although inhuman (as is the practice of all violence, and never to be glorified as some revolutionary thinkers have done), can, unfortunately, not be rejected a priori. To totally eschew violence against a violent opponent (as opposed to rejecting it for tactical reasons) is to betray one's own cause – this is the bitter truth Marcuse sees in lines which he quotes in 'Repressive Tolerance' from Sartre's introduction to Fanon's *The Wretched of the Earth*:

Try to understand this at any rate: if violence began this very evening and if exploitation and oppression had never existed on the earth, perhaps the slogans of non-violence might end the quarrel. But if the whole regime, even your non-violent ideas, are conditioned by a thousand-year-old oppression, your passivity serves only to place you in the ranks of the oppressors.[36]

The events of Paris in May–June 1968 appeared to Marcuse as signalling great popular revulsion against one-dimensional society. As he wrote excitedly at the time:

for one reason or another the time had come when hundreds of thousands and, as we can see now, millions of people didn't want it any more. They didn't want to get up in the morning and go to their job and go through the same routine and listen to the same orders and comply with the same working conditions and perform the same performances. They simply had enough of it.[37]

The events (which he does not naively ascribe to purely non-economic causes) seemed to vindicate his conception of the struggle for democracy, particularly with respect to the catalytic role of the students. In his account of the aftermath of the first battle between students and police (notwithstanding his own use of the words 'order', 'followed' and 'avant-garde'), he clearly envisaged the relationship between students and workers to be quite different from that between a Leninist vanguard and the working class: 'Their young leader, Daniel Cohn-Bendit, who organised the barricades and was with them all the time till six in the morning, when the street battle was lost, said, "Now there is only one thing to be done: the General Strike." The following Monday the strike order was followed 100%.'[38] The lesson was clear:

it should once and for all heal whoever suffers from the inferiority complex of the intellectual. There isn't the slightest doubt that, in this case, the students showed the workers what could be done and that the workers followed the slogan and example set by the students. The students were literally the avant-garde . . .[39]

The explosion of the autonomous on the streets of Paris manifested itself, for example, in the breakdown of the traditional division between the aesthetic and the political: 'The graffiti of the "jeunesse en colère" joined Karl Marx and André Breton: the slogan "l'imagination au pouvoir" went well with "les comités (soviets) partout"; the piano with the jazz player stood well between the barricades; the red flag well fitted the statue of the author of Les Misérables . . .'[40] In short, these events signified, for Marcuse, the emergence of the instinctual transformation he had longed for, a transformation in which the life instincts came to the fore and autonomy became possible. 'A utopian conception?', he asks in *An Essay on Liberation* when describing such a possibility: 'It has been the great, real, transcending force, the "idée neuve", in the first powerful rebellion against the whole of the existing society, the rebellion for the total transvaluation of values, for qualitatively different ways of life: the May rebellion in France.'[41]

As 1968 receded and normality returned Marcuse began to reiterate his old theme of the absorptive power of liberal democratic societies. Although weaker than in the early 1960s, one-dimensional society was still a formidable force and when asked in an interview in 1973 whether the Paris events had shown *One Dimensional Man* to be too pessimistic as regards the possibility of autonomous political action, he replied: 'It seems to me that unfortunately what I said in my book has been corroborated. Unfortunately!'[42] The 'Marcuse phenomenon', his elevation by the media to prophethood seemed to him to add weight to this conclusion. Even in late 1969, when asked how he analysed his international status, he replied: 'I think my own self-analysis is a simple one. By which I mean that there is nothing in heaven or on earth which publicity is unable to integrate into the established system.'[43]

In summing up Marcuse's strategic and tactical considerations, it can first be said that the charge that he advocates minority dictatorship cannot be sustained, being quite alien to his whole outlook; demystification may well start with minorities but free societies must be the creation of autonomous collective action. Secondly, the struggle for autonomy extends far beyond the narrowly political into areas such as art and sexuality. Thirdly, notwithstanding Marcuse's broad conception of struggle and his critical view of the function of liberal democratic institutions and usages, he does see both strategic/tactical validity and universal validity in the hard-won liberties of such societies. Fourthly, violence is considered to be at best a necessary evil; no attempt is made to glorify it. Finally, although Marcuse's concern with Paris 1968, for example, now seems dreadfully dated, we should not lose sight of the general perspectives behind these remarks. He was well aware of the historical specificity of strategy and tactics, and of the danger of legislating for the future by universalizing these; he saw his task as identifying and encouraging the universal in the particular.

What then are we to make of Marcuse's critique of liberal democracy? Let us commence our assessment with an exploration of possible avenues of criticism – starting with his concept of autonomy.

His characterization of the liberal democratic individual as lacking autonomy might be rejected on the grounds that he has narrowly defined autonomy in specific – one might argue idiosyncratic – political and cultural terms. The possibility, for example, that satisfaction with the status quo might itself be a token of autonomy is not seriously considered; nor is there any suggestion that fundamental political and cultural disagreement might not be explicable in terms of autonomy versus heteronomy. His account of the blunting of critical forces by one-dimensional societies might provide another line of attack. Is it the case that the popularization and marketing of critical sources dissolves their critical function to the extent suggested by Marcuse? For example, are the progressive features of sexuality really cancelled in repressive desublimation? Did not the erotic renaissance of youth, so welcomed by Marcuse in the late 1960s, have something to do with the liberalization of sexual mores so criticized in *One Dimensional Man* some years earlier? Does Bach as accompaniment to the washing-up (to use a further example) really not have the same distancing effect as in the cultural temples of the past? The importance of Freud in Marcuse's account of the pervasiveness of heteronomy suggests a further avenue of criticism. It is undoubtedly the case that Marcuse accepts without question the clinical findings on which Freud based his theoretical speculations; also, although he revises Freud's account of the contemporary relationship between the principal components of the psyche (the id, ego and superego) he nonetheless appropriated this model and Freud's later metapsychology wholesale. This prompts the question – is Marcuse too uncritical of Freud, and does he as a consequence derive an impoverished (or over-fanciful) model of the in-dividual from this source? Furthermore, it could even be argued that Marcuse did not fully understand Freud, at whose door the blame for the impoverished (or fanciful) model that may have resulted should not be laid.

Turning to the epistemological grounding of Marcuse's social theory, it is surely permissible (many conservatives, liberals and social democrats might argue), given the undoubted problems associated with the grounding of value-judgements or of assessing competing values, theories, perceptions and strategies, to ask whether 'true' and 'false' needs, 'true' and 'false' solutions can be so rationally distinguished as to legitimate fundamental social and political change, including the possible removal of tolerance from, and infliction of violence upon, opponents. If human fallibility is granted, might not politics which (however imperfectly) actually embody pluralism and the politics of gradualism, compromise and tolerance, be preferable to the many dangers involved in trying to achieve an uncertain perfection?

Even those who accept the possibility of a theory of 'true' and 'false' needs might question Marcuse's bleak picture of the integrated masses. Does an exaggerated concept of the total and interconnected character of advanced capitalism, where all facets of life embody the imperfection of the whole, combined with the specific political and cultural definition of autonomy mentioned above, lead to both an excessive focusing on the spectacularly marginal and a superficial analysis of the experience and behaviour of the majority of the population? As evidence, one might point to the lack of predictive power in his work of the 1960s, where political optimism (1968) replaced pessimism (1960 +), only to be ousted in turn by renewed pessimism (1969 +) – and all in the space of ten years.

Finally, one might wish to criticize the lack of detailed speculation regarding the relationships between radical minorities, and between these and the conservative majority. With respect to the first of these relationships, what, one might ask, is the common ground (apart from the rather insubstantial one of fundamental opposition to aspects of the status quo) that would enable hippies and ghetto populations, for example, to unite in political activity? As regards the second, is there not the prospect of friction between critical intellectuals and the bulk of the population not simply before but during and after the initial stage of the democratic revolution, a possibility which clearly haunts Marcuse's tussle with the concept of educational dictatorship and which accounts for a number of ambiguous references which have been seized upon by commentators who are anxious to suggest that (contrary to the whole spirit of his work) he is in favour of and believes in the future necessity of an elite dictatorship.[44] Even if we accept his belief in the specificity of strategies and tactics, greater discussion of these issues might be thought desirable.

Moving from a possible 'prosecution case' to a few closing remarks for the defence, the first observation that could be made is that Marcuse's work represents (amongst other things) a serious attempt to get to grips with the central issue of democratic theory this century – the discrepancy between liberal democratic rhetoric and the reality of such political systems. To this attempt he brought sophisticated conceptualization, rigorous analysis, a healthy eclecticism, boldness and breadth of vision, and great honesty in confronting controversial issues. Although he is as gloomy as the democratic revisionists in his account of the competence of liberal democratic in-dividuals, he does not adopt their solutions of scaling down governmental purposes and practices to fit the poor human material but rather seeks ways in which the individual can become a conscious participant in political and social life. As such, he is a part of the great normative tradition in democratic theory. That he is a democrat should by now be clear. He is critical, though not dismissive, of liberal democracies, because they are not democratic enough and in his rejection of the elite educational dictatorships he makes it quite clear that any transition from the liberal democratic to the truly democratic must itself be democratic in character.

11

Functional representation and democratic politics: towards a corporatist democracy?

ALAN CAWSON

> . . . have we *got* a post-liberal-democratic theory? I shall suggest the answer is no . . .
> do we *need* a post-liberal-democratic theory? I shall suggest that the answer is yes.
>
> C.B. Macpherson[1]

I

Theories of democracy are essentially value-laden but their credibility depends heavily on the degree to which they correspond to the real world. Likewise, theories which aim to explain the political process of what we choose to call democracies are inescapably wedded to a normative position. The gradual rejection of participatory theories by the contemporary political science of democratic politics was at once a claim to better explanation and a call for commitment to the values of stability and moderation. Empirical democratic theory did, for a time, provide a more convincing explanation than participatory theory because it fitted the 'facts' of ignorance and apathy uncovered by survey research.

This essay will not seek to uncover or refute the normative postulates of empirical democratic theory. It will seek to demonstrate that its explanatory claim must now be rejected in favour of a theory which explains power in contemporary industrial societies by reference to concepts of functional representation and group interaction, as well as to the more familiar liberal ideas of individualism and territorial representation.

Following on from this the argument will explore the implications of such an explanation for normative democratic theory. The central conclusion of the essay is that functional representation and group politics are not, as is sometimes argued, incompatible with liberal theory. Indeed, liberal – as distinct from conservative – values can only be protected by giving due weight to functionally derived interests in the political process. For the democrat the vital issue becomes one of finding the means by which democratic politics can be extended into the hierarchical and inegalitarian structures of corporatism.

II

Empirical democratic theory is the offspring of behavioural political science, in the sense that the systematic study of individual voting behaviour produced a more realistic explanation of democratic politics than that implied by the nineteenth-century advocates of participation. Both empirical and elitist theories of democracy involve the application to politics of models of imperfect competition developed by economists; it is no surprise that the most influential early exponent, Joseph Schumpeter, was an economist.[2] Schumpeter's economic analysis of capitalist development traced the gradual disappearance of the individual capitalist entrepreneur and his replacement by the committee or board of the joint-stock company. This for Schumpeter had the striking consequence of eliminating the processes of innovation and 'creative destruction' which were the essential ingredients of entrepreneurial capitalism; indeed, he predicted that capitalism's very successes would create an 'atmosphere of almost universal hostility to its own social order'.[3]

The analysis of democracy as a method, analogous to the economic marketplace, flourished especially in the Anglo-American democracies in the post-war period because the implicit value-stance it contained accorded well with the dominant political consensus of the day.[4] The 'competitive struggle for the people's vote' produced effective and stable government by excluding the anti-democratic mobilization of the masses; elected governments are indeed a bulwark against tyranny so long as they have to be re-elected. Its rapid rise to the status of orthodoxy coincided with the post-war commitment by the victorious democracies to full employment, social welfare and a Keynesian strategy of aggregate demand management.

Empirical democratic theory thus had an economic analogy as its root, but it then flowered as political science rather than political economy. Largely forsaking normative questions, a new sub-discipline emerged which examined the mechanics of the democratic process through statistical studies of voting behaviour. At the local level of democratic systems, its assumptions dominated the study of community power; its central claim here, as elsewhere, was that it provided a better explanation of politics within democracies than did constitutional or normative approaches.

C.B. Macpherson has argued that this version of democratic theory – what he calls 'equilibrium democracy' to emphasize its economic pedigree – is substantially accurate as a description of liberal-democratic societies, although under some criticism as an explanation.[5] He goes on to argue that at a normative level the case for equilibrium democracy rests now upon its function in protecting against tyranny; it 'will remain the most accurate descriptive model, and will continue to be accepted as an adequate justificatory model, as long as we in Western societies continue to prefer affluence to community (and to believe that the market society can provide affluence indefinitely)'.[6]

I want to suggest in this essay that it is now time to reject equilibrium democracy, and thus the dominant orthodoxies of behavioural political science, on descriptive, explanatory and justificatory grounds. The case rests on an attack on the economic model itself, as well as on its application to politics, and the consequence of accepting the argument is to take up the task of attempting to provide a realistic theory of the political economy of democracy, and a plausible strategy by which its democratic character might be defended and extended.

III

Let us examine the essentials of the model of imperfect competition which underlies Schumpeterian democracy, and see if it continues to explain the functioning of the economy in advanced capitalism. The model derives from the work of economists such as E.S. Chamberlin and Joan Robinson, who argued that outside of agricultural production there are very few instances of the perfect competition espoused by the neo-classical economists who followed Alfred Marshall.[7] In the perfectly competitive world, paradoxically, producers do not compete (with each other) at all, for their individual actions cannot affect the behaviour of the market. But under imperfect competition firms can and do exert power: competition in the form of a struggle between firms (rather than against nature) does take place.

Even so, the model of oligopoly is based upon a somewhat modified postulate of perfect competition and a static framework which eliminates the passage of time. But as Schumpeter crisply put it: 'The essential point is that in dealing with capitalism we are dealing with an evolutionary process.'[8] If we accept this point about the economy we are at least entitled to pose the same question about the equilibrium theory of democracy. And, interestingly, whereas Schumpeter's successors have removed the dynamic element from the economic analysis of politics, he himself was deeply concerned with questions of change and exceedingly gloomy about the prospects for the democratic process in the context of capitalist transformation.

Let us take as an indication of the inadequacy of the model of imperfect competition the recent comments of one of its most distinguished erstwhile proponents. Joan Robinson argues that the central problem of economics is what determines the price of a commodity. Neo-classical economics teaches that prices are formed by the interaction of supply and demand; imperfect competition that prices are determined by costs of production. The latter notion 'soon faded out and, in my opinion, was not much of an improvement'.[9]

Apart from 'thought experiment' which 'is all too apt to develop into the idle amusement of setting up insoluble puzzles and then disputing how they might be solved',[10] economics is left with a few plausible hypotheses. These come from questions 'opened up by Keynes and Kalecki' which have been closed once more by being 'shifted back into concepts of equilibrium'.[11]

The essential starting-point for the 'post-Keynesian' alternative to neo-classical economics seems to be an emphasis on explanatory theory rather than normative. As Joan Robinson puts it: 'An economic theory which is seriously intended to apply to reality is neither an ideological doctrine, such as the presumption in favour of laissez-faire, nor a tautology true by definition . . . it is an hypothesis about how an actual economy operates.'[12] Although directed at the neo-classical school, the remark is equally apt in relation to those like Anthony Downs,[13] who have sought to understand democracy through the elegant logic of economic analysis. The test must be whether the theory is capable of exploring the world as it is.

On this count neo-classical theory falls down, and its discomfiture is nowhere plainer than in the realization that the simultaneous appearance of inflation and unemployment contradicted its assumptions that there was a trade-off between these elements. The economists who do have an explanation of 'stagflation' are those who reject the assumption of equilibrium. Instead they argue that 'prices are determined by an historically set wage level, itself the result of class struggle over relative shares'.[14] In doing so they – and this includes Galbraith, O'Connor and Holland, as well as Robinson and the 'post-Keynesians'[15] – are forced to reject the idea of a single theory of *the* firm and *the* economy.

Their alternative theory starts from the premise that the structure of the mature capitalist economy comprises different kinds of markets, some of which may approximate to the model of perfect competition, but most of which do not. Galbraith distinguishes the planning system and the market system; O'Connor the monopoly sector, the competitive sector and the state sector; and Holland the meso-economy, the micro-economy and the macro-economy. The important point to note here is that these authors fundamentally question the orthodoxy of a macro-economy which is kept in equilibrium by myriad acts of micro-economic behaviour. It is not the precise boundaries of the sectors which matter so much as the argument that the different parts function in distinct ways which require separate explanation. None of these authors assumes an equilibrium; all of them are concerned with political economy as a reciprocal set of influences between politics and economics.

The importance of all this for the study of democracy is that since equilibrium theory is increasingly recognized as an inadequate explanation of economic processes, its relevance for the political must be treated from the outset as suspect. We cannot accept that its ousting of prior normative – what Macpherson calls 'developmental'[16] – democratic theory is itself a proof of its superior explanatory power. Constant repetition does not ensure truth, only familiarity. To reinforce this critique of the adequacy of equilibrium theory for explaining political processes, I turn to the examination of competition in democratic politics.

IV

For Schumpeter, as is well known, democracy is an 'institutional arrangement for arriving at political decisions in which individuals acquire the power to decide by means of a competitive struggle for the people's vote'.[17] The part of the definition which can be challenged on descriptive and explanatory grounds is that political decisions, or at any rate the important ones, are decided by those who have been elected in a competitive struggle. That the government is elected is not in dispute; that it alone has the 'power to decide' certainly is.

The problem for Schumpeterian democracy is that the evidence concerning the structure of power in late capitalist democracy does not conform to the assumptions of the definition. Schumpeter recognizes the existence of sectional interests but argues unmistakably that groups which represent them are subordinate to political leadership:

. . . so far as there are genuine group-like volitions at all . . . our theory does not neglect them. On the contrary we are now able to insert them in exactly the role they actually play. Such volitions as a rule do not exert themselves directly. Even if strong and definite they remain latent, often for decades, until they are called into life by some political leader who turns them into political forms. This he does, or else his agents do it for him, by working them up and by including eventually appropriate items in his competitive offering. The interaction between sectional interests and public opinion and the way in which they produce the pattern we call the political situation appear from this angle in a new and much clearer light.[18]

New, certainly; clearer, perhaps – but it is the logical clarity of the ideal type which does not necessarily, or indeed at all, correspond to reality. The post-Schumpeterians who enshrined the mechanism of electoral competition into pluralist theory contended that group interaction, like party politics, was a competitive process tending towards equilibrium: hence Robert Dahl's famous formulation that 'with all its defects, [the American political system] does nonetheless provide a high probability that any active and legitimate group will make itself heard effectively at some stage in the process of decision.'[19] Schumpeter himself would have had grave doubts about this, preferring the formulation that there is a high probability that any active group will be manipulated by political leadership engaged in the competitive struggle. But then Schumpeter was no radical democrat: those who have read *Capitalism, Socialism and Democracy* will be familiar with his eulogy of – or perhaps elegy to – bourgeois values in the face of what he saw as the inevitable collapse of capitalism.

Those (few perhaps) who have read it closely would possibly be surprised by Macpherson's attachment of the label 'equilibrium democracy'. For Schumpeter there was no such thing as equilibrium outside of pure theory:

In the general case of oligopoly there is in fact no determinate equilibrium at all and the possibility presents itself that there may be an endless sequence of moves and counter-moves, an indefinite state of warfare between firms. It is true that there are many special cases in which a state of equilibrium theoretically exists . . . [but] . . . even in these cases . . . [it is] . . . much harder to attain than the equilibrium in perfect competition.[20]

In his specification of the democratic mechanism Schumpeter attached certain conditions, and in later editions of *Capitalism, Socialism and Democracy* he indicated the extent to which they were placed in jeopardy by the constant evolution of capitalism. The five conditions were: the adequacy of the calibre of politicians; the limited scope of political decision; an effective and independent bureaucracy; democratic self-control, and tolerance for differences of opinion. Of these five the key one with respect to economic change is the second: that 'the effective range of political decision should not be extended too far'.[21] What this meant for Schumpeter was that politicians should be content with a measure of overall supervision. He stressed that the limitations were with respect to the '*effective* range of political decision – the range within which politicians decide in truth as well as in form . . . Democracy does not require that every function of the state be subject to its political method.'[22]

What Schumpeter had in mind here was that certain key functions – the administration of justice, for example – should be insulated from political interference. But the important question to which we should be alive is whether the process of political competition rewards successful competitors by parcelling out to them power over the determination of state policies which is no longer subject to effective supervision by elected political leadership.

Clearly the extension of the sphere of public authority in recent years, which in 1949 Schumpeter described as 'the march into Socialism',[23] has tested this condition for successful democracy to the utmost – beyond it if the current preoccupation with 'overloaded government' is to be taken seriously.

Through a (long-run) commitment to the use of Keynesian (short-run) demand management techniques to promote full employment, the positive role of the state has become enlarged to embrace new forms of state intervention, from the attempt to control prices and incomes in the 1960s to the attempt to control the supply of money in the late 1970s. These new strategies of intervention are part of the state function of economic management, itself a recognition of the limitations of the self-regulating equilibrium model of the economy. The important point is that these policies have been largely determined within political structures effectively insulated from parliamentary representation. To what extent is the competitive democratic mechanism adequate for the supervision of such intervention?

V

Parliamentary means of representation which depend on the territorial aggregation of individual interests have proved extremely effective for determining issues on a legal–rational basis. In those areas of policy where a set of publicly-validated rules can govern bureaucracies delivering services or extracting resources from defined categories of individuals, the democratic mechanism has produced a workable concept of the 'public interest'. In these tasks the state is essentially *allocating* – resources or demands upon resources – by means of general rules on the basis of formal rationality.[24] Income tax and social security spring to mind as perhaps the best examples of legal–bureaucratic policy-making where the only justifiable basis of political representation is the individual citizen.

But perhaps the larger part of the contemporary activities of the state do not fall under this head. Pre-eminently in the sphere of economic management, but also with respect to important areas of social policy,[25] state intervention *cannot* follow legal–bureaucratic procedures. Where the state is itself the producer – of schools, hospitals, factory estates and so on – or the regulator of non-individually-based interests – of trade unions, economic sectors and the like in incomes policy and economic planning – the intervention has to be purposive–rational, that is, justified in terms of effective results rather than legitimate procedures.

The question which concerns us is that of the basis on which such interventionist policies are formulated. The establishment of *ad hoc* agencies, deliberately non-bureaucratic, is an indication that parliamentary means of representation are ineffective when the targets of intervention are not individual citizens but interests constituted on the basis of their socio-economic function. That form of state – or better, area of state activity – which fuses representation based on functional interest and intervention justified by its effects has been recently identified as corporatism.[26]

In liberal-democratic systems the means of representation through parliamentary bodies are formally separated from the process of state intervention, in which a set of general rules is administered through legal–rational procedures via the agency of bureaucracy. In corporatism those bodies which represent their members' interests according to their function within the division of labour are also the instruments of policy implementation. For example, in the determination of incomes policies the trade unions are at the same time representing the interests of their members in a bargaining process, and acting as the agents of the state in implementing agreed policies. Whereas in a liberal democratic political process interest group activity takes place outside the institutions of the state, corporatism brings strategically important functional groups inside the state. In effect the political sphere is extended into civil society.

The *extent* of corporatist practice in contemporary liberal democracy has been well-documented, but its *significance* for liberal democratic politics has been barely hinted at. Contemporary political science has been dismissive of corporatist empirical theory, for reasons related to its Schumpeterian heritage, which I will now explore.

Political science and the sub-field of pressure group studies has at its foundation the assumption that the individual is the basic unit of analysis. The 'group' is conceptualized as a voluntary association of individuals who share a subjectively perceived common interest. On this assumption the competitive model of pressure group politics is constructed to fit in with the theory of liberal democracy: groups help to make elected leaders more responsive to the demands of the electorate. It assumes an equilibrium, and a competitive marketplace.

In this scheme the group which takes its identity from the socio-economic function of its membership is no different in kind from any other group. Its members combine for a common purpose; they share a common interest which arises from the division of labour in society. This view is historically plausible, in that trade unions, for example, formed as associations which protected the interests of their members.

But what this approach neglects is the important change in the role of functional groups as state activity expands quantitatively and changes qualitatively. For interventionist goals to be realised, functionally-based groups are given certain structural privileges which transform the competitive market of interest group politics. As the post-war state has become preoccupied with economic management the power of functional groups of producers, of capital and labour, has increased enormously. Just as in section III I argued that we must recognise distinct *sectors* of the economy in late capitalism, and explain their operation in distinct ways, so in the political sphere of liberal democracy we must recognise the existence of a dual polity.

To do this we must take seriously Samuel Beer's argument that: 'It was primarily because government attempted to control or manage the economy that producer groups acquired power to influence policy.'[27] The collective basis of producer groups is quite distinct from that of others: 'The unity of [a functional] stratum is not that of mere voluntary association which stresses common ideas and moral judgements. On the contrary, its integration is seen as arising especially from objective conditions that give its members a function and are the grounds for deeply rooted, continuing – even 'fixed' – interests.'[28]

Thus the association takes its interest and derives its power from the individuals who comprise it. But for the functional group the membership *takes its interest* from the function, and the power of the functional group in part derives from what are the objectives of state policy. Interventionist policies require the co-operation, if not collaboration, of functional groups, and this fact alone helps to explain some of their power.

The political science of pressure group politics has, to its cost, tended to ignore Beer's pioneering analysis and this crucial distinction between individual and functional interest. The methods by which power is studied within a pluralist framework preclude the view that state policy-making gives structural priority to those interests relevant to capital accumulation. For this lacuna to be filled the task of integrating the dualist perspectives on economy and polity becomes paramount.

I shall discuss this problem with respect to the task of formulating a theory of corporatist democracy in the final section of this essay. But before that I want to make some remarks about the implications of this for the explanation of policy-making in a liberal democracy where corporatist practices are becoming commonplace.

First, as Schumpeter feared, the delimitation between the private sphere and the public sphere is more and more difficult to define. Economic and political power are becoming more and more coterminous with respect to the productive activities of the state. Here the corporation itself is becoming increasingly significant, not simply as an economic actor, but in terms of representing by itself its own interests. In the corporate sector of the economy power is exercised within a framework of interests constituted by function, subject to the continuing importance of class antagonisms between functional groups based on the interests of capital and those based on the interests of labour.

Class divisions in society cut across these sectoral or functional cleavages, but both are part of the process of structuring political interests. Marxist theory argues that the division between capital and labour is the fundamental one, which would rule out any possibility of bargains between corporate capital, corporate labour and the state which damaged the interests of competitive capital and competitive labour. But the expansion of the state sector means that an important section of the working class is employed outside of 'pure' capitalist social relations, and has a distinctive set of interests linked to the level of state expenditures. The investigation of how these new sectoral divisions affect the political process in liberal democracies – for example, the structure of political alignments[29] – is only just beginning.

Secondly, for a whole range of state activities concerned with consumption, and with moral and ideological issues, the corporatist mode of interest representation is inappropriate. There is no inevitable progression towards a corporate state – corporatism, as Beer argued, cannot constitute a complete polity[30] – but the emergence of corporate power within society sets up contradictions between the 'liberal' and the 'corporate' within the state. Liberal-democratic politics continues to serve a vital protective function against tyranny. But the shift in power to the corporate nexus sets up both grave problems and unparalleled opportunities for democratic theory, and it is to these that I now turn.

VI

'Corporatism and liberty do not go together' argued Sir Keith Joseph in 1976,[31] repeating the argument that liberty is secured by the functioning of a competitive economic market free of state interference. But in late capitalism, where an important part of the market has been transformed by the development of monopoly, the attempt to recreate the nineteenth-century political economy represents an even greater threat to liberty.[32] Is it necessary to see corporatism as inevitably eroding political liberty? Is functional representation and corporatist negotiation *fundamentally* incompatible with parliamentary democracy?

The answer, of course, is no, because the contemporary state already combines both parliamentarism and corporatism, but in an unstable and volatile mixture. Corporatist practice has developed piecemeal in response to pressing policy problems, but has so far not been accompanied by an adequate justificatory theory. Indeed, with its stress on the sovereignty of parliament, liberal theory presents an obstacle to securing a legitimate place in the democratic order for political institutions not grounded in individualist modes of representation.

It is often argued that liberal freedoms are threatened by trade union power, less often that they are at risk from the economic power of business corporations. The issue for democratic theory is how to extend democratic control over the corporate sector of the political economy whilst at the same time preserving and extending those features of liberal democracy, such as civil liberties and freedom of association, which are an essential part of the competitive political process.

There are two ways of conceiving this problem. One – the liberal way – is to pose the issue as one of how to bring corporatist arrangements within the effective scrutiny of parliament. But, as argued earlier, parliamentary institutions are ineffective vehicles for economic intervention: corporatism is tried because the groups whose co-operation is necessary are not directly represented in parliament. The second, and more radical, way is to argue that liberal democracy must be supplemented by the active and direct participation of members within the corporate groups, so that the political leaders of corporate groups can derive their legitimacy from popular involvement rather than stake their claim to power on the basis of socio-economic leverage.

Functional groups can only claim legitimacy for their role in determining policies if they can demonstrate their commitment to internal democracy. The justification, for example, of the trade union bloc vote within the Labour Party would be that much more acceptable to popular opinion if it could be shown to follow on from prior and effective exercise of democratic choice within the trade unions. And still more important, if less attainable, is the democratic requirement that corporations encourage widespread participation in their internal decision-making. It used to be a persuasive liberal argument that economic power was private, so that non-interference in economic arrangements was an essential pre-condition of political liberty. But concentration and centralisation within the economy have given to corporations a public character and a public purpose. The challenge for radical democrats is to give them a democratic character and a democratic purpose, not to undermine, but to underwrite liberal democracy.

It is often argued[33] that democratic theory must be behaviourally plausible, and this argument still represents a powerful critique of classical theories of participatory democracy. But the process of change in the political and economic landscape of capitalist societies has produced corporate forms which render implausible models of democracy based on competitive individual interaction. If corporatism does open up new opportunities for democratic advance, we need to be able to show from where the impetus for change might come.

In the case of the large corporations, democratic reform via worker participation could form an important part of the planning agreements through which state investment funds would be channelled to the corporate sector under some version of the Labour Party's Alternative Economic Strategy. Unquestionably, corporate capital would not surrender decision-making powers without a struggle, whether to the state or to workers, but in the context of a failure of the monetarist solution to Britain's economic crisis, the leverage of the state over private capital would be greatly enhanced.

Such a combination of circumstances would provide the maximum opportunity, but the impetus for a move towards worker participation would have to come from a Labour Government which recognized the limitations of parliamentary democracy and had secured a commitment from the trade unions to extend their traditional economistic and protective perspective. The current debate within the Labour Party is an indication that such issues are at last back on the agenda, but it is by no means certain that the outcome will be favourable to democratic advance.

Possible futures

12

Human nature and radical democratic theory

GRAEME DUNCAN

At the heart of traditional political theory lies the effort to establish a relationship between human nature and society, on one hand, and reg. lative and political institutions on the other. The inevitable political advocacy, the preferring of certain forms of polity to others, has rested in large part on ideas about the powers and the limitations of individuals and social groups. The classical advocates of democracy (Mill, Rousseau, Tocqueville) – though the nature of their 'democratic' commitment is disputed constantly[1] – clearly supported their political analyses and prescriptions by conceptions of man. But their assertively realistic critics in this century have striven to counterpose an empirically valid account of political behaviour to the ideals and phantoms of philosophy. The explicit purpose of a dismal political science was to demolish the rational and intellectualistic assumptions sustaining the supposedly empty optimism of socialists and democrats. Myths and utopias, often built upon threatening conceptions of man's essential nature, were to be supplanted by a cautious and cooling science.

However, as a new generation of normative critics made clear, the 'realists' had exaggerated both the power and the purity of descriptivism. They, too, assumed that they knew what was best for man. These assumptions were sometimes denied or hidden, and were rarely submitted to hard scrutiny by the authors themselves.[2] The new normative criticisms only confirmed that any account of the kind of democracy which is appropriate to people as they are, or might be, must rest upon judgments about human needs, desires and capacities, and how far they can be satisfied or fulfilled under certain – perhaps possible but absent – conditions.[3] Any theory of democracy contains assumptions about what people can and cannot achieve.

It is hard to define what kind of an object of enquiry human nature is, and the methods and criteria by which a particular account of it might be supported or attacked. Many statements supposedly about human nature are in fact statements about particular human societies or particular human beings – a point brought out strongly by Rousseau, Hume and Marx, amongst many others. Human nature may imply something fixed, settled, static, a permanent human essence. My own commitment, which contains assumptions which will not be defended here, is to the language of potentialities or capacities, which amongst other things draws attention to the difference between actual and possible human behaviours. The central question becomes: 'Of what are people capable, and incapable, in such and such circumstances?' 'Such and such circumstances' calls for a further word. We are interested in certain – if varying – determinate circumstances or conditions, which control, limit, structure or frustrate potentialities. Of course, not all potentialities can be developed: apart from the limits of time, energy and so forth, the development of some capacities closes doors on others. These diverse potentialities, which await specification, may unfold under particular – perhaps remote – circumstances. Their failure to emerge can then be traced to the absence of necessary supporting conditions rather than to inherent deficiences in human nature, though it is neither obligatory nor fruitful to take an either/or position.

Political theory must therefore grapple, not only with the relationship of ideals and values to each other, but also with an apparently imperturbable world outside: the environment of action. Reality imposes sharp limits upon imagined possibilities. In these harsh times, especially, men quickly draw back from that engaging French slogan: 'All power to the imagination'. Hence, although conceptions of human nature are as much inspired by faith, hope and charity and their gloomy opposites as by hard reason, and while the dictates of hard reason itself are accepted by each of us according to our own preferences, principles and paradigms, there are at least three types of limits whose precise impact upon both goals and programmes requires assessment. These limits or conditioning factors are: physiological or genetic limits, set by human biology and anatomy; economic limits, set by the amount and accessibility of material resources; and those limits set by seemingly inescapable – or valuable – social and political routines and arrangements. The first, which must count as part of 'human nature' – though genetic intervention could alter the normal range – would present a problem for a radical democrat if it could be shown, for example, that people as such have basic destructive drives, or are incurably passive. Economic and political limits, which may gratuitously prevent human nature from unfolding in innumerable and conflicting directions, are subject both to different interpretations and to potential control and change. The issue is whether opportunities for wider self-expression or self-realization or participation would be made available through changes in institutional arrangements, modes of distribution, technology and the like.

However, both radical democratic and libertarian theories are commonly assumed to be unrealistic or utopian, if not positively dangerous to established arrangements. The dominant perspectives on human nature and social structure contain different and even conflicting elements,[4] but it is commonly held that people have certain fixed needs and desires which, along with social and other imperatives, makes some utopian visions of organized life unrealizable, if not unimaginable. According to this view, radical social engineers – Oakeshott's Rationalist, Popper's Utopian, Talmon's totalitarian – may be willing to tear ordinary people out of their comfortable and established environments, but tear it will be, given their reluctance to budge and become new people. Recalcitrant human material must be twisted to the desired shape. Radical social engineers wildly exaggerate human capacities, perhaps turning fallen man into God. They simplify society, squeezing out its history, its prejudice and emotions, its distinctions, its division of labour, its necessary inequalities. Guilty of fantasies about man, impatient to realize their absurd dreams, they trample on man as he is, on what Talmon calls 'the sum total of the existing generation'.[5] The message is: 'Trust an empirical epistemology, know the limits and stay within them'. To the liberal pluralist, people can make their way, if they choose, within the incremental, bargaining society. Democracy becomes the stable system of freely competing political elites, checked both by the vote (the limited and occasional involvement of the people) and by the existence of suspicious and weighty rivals. On this view democracy does not require and, indeed, may be inconsistent with, a politically active, public-spirited populace. Impressed by the ability of liberal societies to function with a low level of political participation, the champions of this version of democracy are apt to question both the desirability and the possibility of widespread active citizenship.

Against this background, what credence can be gained for the grand ideals of a society of participating equals, personal autonomy, self-determination, self-government, and the fulfilment of the individual in the community? These ideals often remain obscure and are interpreted differently, resulting in deep and sharp conflicts over the institutional forms which best support them, or in which they are to be embodied. Such ideals are not bare and abstract slogans, or course, but parts of complex theoretical structures which require elucidation before they can be assessed. Although my purpose here is not to examine closely the views of radical democratic theorists,[6] a brief comment on radical democratic goals is unavoidable.

The radical democrat, who may be reformer or revolutionary, has the goal of a fuller democratization of social institutions, which will enable man to shape his own destiny or govern himself. Man is given a dramatically different place in a political universe which is itself more broadly conceived. Radical democratic theory asserts that people have the potential capacity to run their own affairs and, in the right circumstances, the will to do so. Institutions can be devised which overcome the technical or organizational difficulties stressed by empirical political science. The goal may be larger, emphasizing power and control, or smaller, emphasizing influence and participation. The obstacles most commonly recognized in actual democratic societies include elite or oligarchic power, bureaucracy, the mass media and the (political) division of labour. The centre of such a theory is the specification of the relationships, actual and hypothetical, between institutions and processes *and* human motivations and goals. Given a conception of man as more diverse, complex, dynamic and with greater potentialities than the conservative thinker allows, the radical democratic theorist refuses to accept the shrinkage of the political realm and its confinement to small sections of the people. He may go further, following the possibly dangerous path of treating existing democratic citizens and choices as inauthentic, false or other-directed, judged in terms of the rationality and autonomy imputed to the ideal democratic citizen. The grandiosity and vagueness of some of our recent liberating prophets and preachers, especially the men of the sixties, such as Marcuse, Illich, Laing and Goodman has helped give radical thought an aura of irresponsibility. Their generalized critiques of modern society brought out both the oppressive and the alterable character of much of social reality, but avoided what they dismissed as academic petty-mindedness, and usually failed to provide detailed institutional analysis or coherent accounts of the way forward. What, then, might be the lineaments of a more adequate radical theory? How might an ideal radical – hopeful, rigorous and responsible! – respond to ostensibly realistic opponents? How might human nature be described, explained and envisaged, what kinds of evidence and argument might be produced for a more optimistic account of possible futures? In a nutshell, the question is: What kind of evidence is available for radical democratic theories which strive, not merely to describe the existing world, but to criticize and transcend it, while maintaining some roots in it? Theories seeking to reinvigorate an older speculative tradition and aiming to bring out potentialities which are hidden or suppressed, must recognize historical facts. Speculation should be grounded in empirical findings, drawn from studies of actual political systems. But a wide gap between present circumstances and goals must be faced: how is that gap to be explained and bridged or, alternatively, dismissed? Empirical theories of political behaviour, if accurate, only describe things as they are. Once the supposedly empirical theorist challenges the critical and normative one, we enter a complex conceptual world in which judgment, evaluation and prescription mix with descriptive analysis, including readings of history. The elements cannot be easily unscrambled, enabling us to decide between disputed empirical views and then move on quickly to our differences. Valuations penetrate accounts of what is the case, what is feasible, and what the costs of change would be.

Clearly basic differences exist between those who accept – fatalistically or more positively – existing liberal democracies, and those who urge a much fuller and deeper democratization of society. A major area of conflict concerns the capacities of humans in particular circumstances, and the capacities of polities to accommodate them. The broad differences between liberal or conservative and radical theories, allowing ample scope for research and argumentation, include at least the following:

(1) accounts of existing political life, what has happened and is happening. These may contain radical and utopian histories and perhaps new methodologies and modes of classification;

(2) explanations, even granting an overlap of descriptive accounts;

(3) evaluations of existing and alternative or imaginable polities and of the costs and benefits of change;

(4) descriptions of supporting conditions for a different society; historical models of persons and communities who already embody, in some degree, the new and higher level of human achievement; and accounts of strategies, agencies or practices which might convert routines and institutions which are at present pervasive.

These pieces of enquiry may be combined, in political reflection and in practice, by an underlying conception of people as more capable than many accounts of political behaviour and many histories allow, and as having potentialities which altered environments might encourage. The descriptions of men and women in orthodox political science and sociology are easily shown to be inaccurate and incomplete. Existing attitudes and practices may be construed differently e.g. by distinguishing between rationality and articulateness,[7] or by depicting at least some non-participators, not as apathetic, but as intelligent and cynical realists, conscious of their lack of access to or control over the political system, aware of what the vote, letters to the editor, political agitation and so forth can be expected to achieve. But while there may be truth in this – and it is accessible to empirical testing – it is at best a beginning for radical critique.

More substantially, attention can be drawn to hidden aspects of reality, to what is cut off from politics by definitions and classifications as well as by institutions. An act of reconceptualization, perhaps associated with an extension of the notion of politics, will bring previously excluded aspects within its purview. For example, feminist literature portrays the prevailing domestic mode of production (reproduction, child care, housework), not as domestic, private, voluntary and inevitable, but as public, political, coercive and changeable. The personal is political. Relations of power start in the home, and therefore that realm is inescapably politicized. This reconceptualization explodes the careful liberal distinctions between public and private, and denies its common point of application. It exposes the

oppressiveness inherent in domestic relationships: women are as they are
because of their subordination to the power, prestige and freedom which
inhere in male roles, and would be different in different circumstances. The
needless and unnatural repression of women prevents the emergence of real
persons and sharply limits achievements in the traditional political realm. In
addition, political contributions and achievements within this supposedly
non-political, domestic realm are overlooked. The denial of a narrow,
distinctive, fixed political realm as conceived by liberalism casts different
lights and shadows, suggesting that things are not at all what they seem, and
indicating grounds for change.

A good example of a legitimate radical reconceptualization of the past is
provided in Chomsky's essay, 'Objectivity and Liberal Scholarship'.[8]
Radicals have often seen history as a record of criminality, prejudice,
violence, oppression, obstinate illusion, but to some it has a far more
encouraging aspect, though one rarely found in history books. The good is
not only suppressed in fact: it is hidden in or by ideology. Chomsky is
concerned with counter-revolutionary subordination, whereby ideological
closure of a subtle and unconscious kind occurs. He assumes, correctly, that
potentially supporting cases for optimistic social thinking are seen only
through distorting perceptual screens, with the result that history requires
rewriting from a positive or humanistic standpoint. The central object of his
criticism is the liberal perspective on Vietnam and on the Spanish Civil War: it
presents constructive social movements, sources of optimism and hope, as all
muddle, immorality, banditry. Taking issue with Gabriel Jackson's prizewin-
ning book[9] on the early stages of the Spanish Civil War, Chomsky depicts a
largely spontaneous and remarkable social revolution, brought about
through the mass action of anarchist and socialist industrial and agrarian
workers. Chomsky's Jackson, on the other hand, can only comprehend
anarchism from a perspective which is elitist, with 'a deep bias against social
revolution and a commitment to the values and social order of liberal
bourgeois democracy', and a strong distaste for 'the forces of a popular
movement'.[10] From an ideology appropriate to his own orderly world,
workers' control becomes workers abusing their authority, and they are
defeated, not by the force and cynicism of the central government, but
because of 'the complexity of modern society'.[11] He scorns the idealism and
human warmth of the anarchists, and takes them to be naive or primitive or
otherwise irrational. The historian sits heavily upon his more aspiring
subjects. He is the Doubting Thomas of social experimentation. E.P.
Thompson also brings out the constructive or positive elements in radical
social movements of the past, for example in his account of Luddism, in
which he emphasizes the forward-looking element, the shadowy image of a

democratic community, rather than the mindless machine-breaking.[12] The claim here is not that history rather than human nature made people a certain way, but that there are alternative histories, from whose perspectives 'human nature' may appear in novel or unusual forms. Existing silences may be explained by a rigid orientation of the historical vision, or by political interest, or in some other way: the point is simply that history, of a kind which helps sustain more optimistic social outlooks, can be and is being written. Emancipatory histories are made neither better nor worse as histories by their moral possibilities or purposes, or by their success in helping to reinstate 'poor shivering human nature'. That judgment must be made in terms of the ordinary – and disputed – canons of historical interpretation.

The claims that our modes of observation structure and thereby limit enquiries relevant to argument about human nature – of what are people capable in specified determinate conditions? – may gain greater force if the validity of existing research methodologies is denied. Herbert Marcuse, for example, in the course of an attack upon positivism and rationalism, condemns the one-dimensionality of the dominant language and methods of enquiry. He complains that: 'The trouble with the statistics, measurements and field studies of empirical sociology and political science is that they are not rational enough. They become mystifying to the extent to which they are isolated from the truly concrete context which makes the facts and determines their function'.[13] Reality is expurgated, as 'the facts' are detached from their appropriate context, cut off from a theory of society, isolated from the relevant totality, thereby losing their meaning. The failure to see things in their context is a common weakness in social theory, although the isolation or abstraction of certain phenomena or certain patterns, for example in model-building, can be fruitful as long as it is remembered exactly what is being done, and as long as the models are not substituted for reality.

R.D. Laing also demands what appears to be a far-reaching epistemological clean-out. Writing of the so-called mentally ill, he complains of the way crucial short-comings of language (or conceptual categories) prevent us from seeing things in all their ambiguity or manysidedness. 'The choice of syntax and vocabulary are political acts that define and circumscribe the manner in which the "facts" are to be experienced.'[14] The essence of his phenomenological or existential approach is that the established mode of classification, with its settled assumptions, limits and languages, is quite incapable of grasping the relevance and significance of the patient's experience. More concretely, the limitation of 'a basically monadic psychology'[15] is that it has no concept of a unitary whole, which to Laing is the necessary starting-point of analysis. It begins with man or a part of man 'abstracted from his relation with the other in the world'.[16] This artificial isolation from social relationships splits the real, complex and changing individual verbally and conceptually, with a particular aspect separated from its context and presented as him or her. Issues are thus prejudged or predetermined, certain experiences are invalidated at the outset, and no authentic science of persons – treating man as a self-acting agent – can develop.[17] If this were true, the 'patient' of empirical democratic theory may be as little understood as is the patient in orthodox psychiatry, according to Laing. It may be that, fully understood, there is more to him than appears to be the case, or that he is (mal)formed by contingent social processes.

Whether or not one goes the whole distance with Laing or Marcuse – and I do not, finding more possibilities within established modes of discourse and practice than one-dimensional pessimism allows – the critique of simple descriptive methodologies, along with the existence of (often systematically) different selections of past and present facts, throws strong doubt upon such seemingly straightforward claims as that prescriptive or normative theory must be based upon an accurate empirical assessment of the real world. It is not that we throw out any notion of facts or solid realities, or deny that there are more or less rational, well-informed and compelling accounts of the world. But we can and do discover very different things out there. 'Accurate', well-researched, well-considered assessments, and the methods held conducive to such assessments, differ, so that what constitutes 'the sum total of the existing generation', or of past generations, is itself highly disputable.

Any defence of a more optimistic view of human possibilities must confront the conservative dogmatism which often parades as realism. Common beliefs about the permanent impediments set by human nature, or by social imperatives or necessities, to far-reaching social change are reiterated and taken to be clinching, as if the limits to possibility are subject to clear-cut decision. Rigorous summaries of or abstractions from past or present behaviour – perhaps misconceived – may form the ground for generalized laws or axioms of social structure, or for general assertions about human nature. Examples of the first include 'organization means oligarchy', and 'full popular participation in basic decision-making cannot be combined with efficient management of large communities'. Examples of the second include the claim that man is not fit for democracy; that man's apparent rationality and autonomy are illusory (Freud); that 'Homo civicus' is not by nature a political animal (Dahl); that there are basic differences between male and female human natures; that the lack of joiners (of political organizations) and the general lack of interest in intense political activity is 'a fact of human nature' established by empirical study, rather than, say, the effect of a certain kind of political structure or culture (Sartori).

However, even should the situations to which such claims point exist in the present, these situations can be explained by special or transient or changeable institutions and circumstances. To cite existing social facts is to do that and no more. It does not demonstrate that existing structures, or desires, preferences, and even needs, are fixed, or that markedly different societies and people might not emerge in the future. Whatever our views as to the practicability of any particular proposal or programme or goal, the perspective, the assumptions and methods of 'realists' or conservatives themselves require critical examination. They may be taking surrounding behaviour and psychological axioms as universal, and we may find, buried within an ostensibly descriptive vocabulary, a romanticized image of their own society. Hence at present many people may indeed be egotists, acquisitive, possessive individualists, asocial and apathetic in regard to formal politics. But 'human nature' cannot be read off from these widely shared attributes: we are observing people in a particular slab of history, in captivity, the results of what Marcuse calls 'a mutilated, crippled and frustrated human existence'.[18] After all, a remarkable diversity of human beings and human societies exists and changes, and with changing social experience people's moral conceptions and their views of what is reasonable and possible, and what is necessary or inevitable, also change. Existing motives, interests and values are simply not permanent.

An adequate reassessment of man's democratic potential must relate behaviour to particular, contingent social institutions. The basic explanatory categories become culture, economy, social structure and the like, rather than human – or sub-human – nature. Negative phenomena, such as 'the ordinary democratic citizen', are not taken as given, as the more or less fixed basis of politics. Explanations both stop and start at the wrong point. What is created is used to justify that which created it, as Marx argued in relation to the one-sided labourer and the division of labour. By contrast, a social explanation of people's characters and choices, the degrees and forms of their political activity, is offered by the radical democratic alternative. Men and women are 'situated' within a particular social system or a particular lesser environment or series of such environments. Significant causal relationships are sought between social and economic conditions and processes *and* personal attributes and achievements. Examples are the correlations between low socio-economic status and low political participation or a low sense of responsibility, or between poor nutrition and apathy, or between authoritarian family and school structures and a readiness or a need to submit to a tyrant.

To take another kind of example, the logic of Laing's account of mental illness seems to me impeccable, and to provide a useful model for a democratic theorist. Laing places and comprehends real and imagined or ascribed mental illness by setting it within a series of relevant contexts (rising upwards and outwards from smaller through larger to total and all-encompassing, Total World System or total cosmos). Within the new explanatory system, the various elements of the patient's experience make more sense than when perceived in isolation, and that experience also becomes more amenable to change, in that it is no longer seen as 'natural' and can be altered by manipulation of the relevant environments. It becomes comprehensible within its context, and is subject to transformation through change of that context.

In terms of the view which I am outlining, conservative accounts of man's essential or universal nature become abstractions – and as a rule politically useful abstractions – from particular social practices. Many observed deficiencies in people are seen now as the results of damaging but changeable social institutions. The identification of the institutions, arrangements and forces held responsible for man's sorry plight, and of the causal links between the different parts of the total system, is sometimes done with a lack of precision and a degree of inflatedness which reduces its practical – as distinct from theoretical or prophetic – significance. The social explanation of our ills is often undertaken very lightly, with weighty generalizations (society as a vast, embracing category), a lack of clear theoretical and empirical connections, and a picture of people and societies as easily alterable. The grandeur of our social critics allows leaps from the sick individual to a sick world, with little display of the intermediate, connecting links in the process,[19] but the very difficult task of moving between different levels or units of analysis has been taken seriously by some radical democratic theorists.

The explanatory theory developed by the radical is closely linked with a theory of change: it provides grounds for confidence and suggests appropriate political strategies. The approach which I have supported begins with clear and rigorous theoretical accounts of the ways in which deficient educational systems or the division of labour or private property or the state or poverty or whatever, malform people. Then the imagination, disciplined by history and by whatever prefigurative or exemplary forms can be found in the present world, is used to conceptualize societies without the responsible institution or body of institutions. The effect of the amputation of the destructive or deforming cause can then be envisaged. A redirection of energies or appetites in new and constructive ways may be imagined: for example, in Fourier's phalanstery would-be murderers became butchers. Sydney Hook saw the educational processes of a socialist society striving 'to direct the psychic tendencies to self-assertion into "moral and social equivalents" of oligarchical ambition', and thought that this, along with other changes, made quite remote the danger that Michels' 'law of oligarchy' would express itself in the traditional form.[20] Alternatively, the sources of destructive or debased appetites may be removed.

All this, to the conservative, will amount to the removal of basic institutions, with the world crumbling as men's dark drives express themselves in new and destructive ways. Freud, for example, argued that aggressiveness was not created by private property. The abolition of private property would not eliminate male prerogatives in the field of sexual relationships, 'which is bound to become the source of the strongest dislike and the most violent hostility among men who in other respects are on an equal footing'.[21] The claim that such primal drives constitute an imperishable part of human nature commonly underlies the negative generalizations which are counterposed to such ideas as political democracy, equality and socialism. There is no easy or straight road on potentialities. Not all potentialities are positive or good. The unfolding of human nature in innumerable and conflicting directions will not be a process of pure delight nor will a loving, untroubled humanity appear suddenly. The social institutions which frustrate valuable potentialities may also hinder their more vicious fellows.[22] In the absence of restrictive arrangements, problems will remain over decision-making or over evil, or at least inhumanity. The essential radical claim is that people have significant and unrealized potentialities, and could be more than they are with more favourable conditions (more or better material resources, education, information and the like).

Even if the radical and the conservative happened to agree on discrete and isolated parts of the descriptive characterizations of existing societies, for example on the character of democratic voting, their evaluations of both actual and imagined states differ. From a radical perspective, social reality seems systematically misconstrued by lovers of the present world. It is common to count the advantages rather than the costs of living in one's favoured society, and history is full of nostalgic and one-sided invocations of the harmony and beauty of life once upon a time – in pre-revolutionary England or France or Russia – as against the horrors of afterwards. Where the lover sees culture, civilization, the colour and variety of life, stability, or even only comfortable and straightforward banality, the reformer and critic may see inequality, privilege, deformity, misery and oppression. Like Paine, the radical may charge the Edmund Burkes of his day with pitying the plumage and forgetting the dying bird. Costs are counted not simply in terms of overt misery or declared dissatisfaction, but of frustrated needs, lost potentialities, stultified human development, which generally do not arise at all in the rival evaluations. Certainly basic differences exist over how to characterize 'the sum total of the existing generation', which is not nearly as firm and straightforward as Talmon imagined.

Calculation of the costs of maintaining or changing the status quo is a closely related evaluative–descriptive question. There are significant disputes over the amount and manner of change which is compatible with a proper concern or respect for the interests and desires of real, existing people.[23] But it is simply dodging the problem to say: 'leave things as they are, let things be'. Not only is it hard to say what 'things' are, but they are changing continuously anyhow. Most political theorists since the eighteenth century have seen human nature changing because of chance, circumstance, environment, power and so forth, and as being subject, properly, to planned change (or planned defence), through education, legislation, propaganda, agitation and organization, suppression, genetic intervention and so on. Political theory has its share of lobotomists and bullies, ready to ride rough-shod over existing desires, but normally what is proposed is that any remoulding should be in conformity with people's own tendencies or potentialities. While it is necessary to examine any particular proposal on its merits, it is also clear that it is not commonly a choice between remoulding, with all its nasty connotations, *or* leaving people as they are: they are being remoulded, not left as they are, all the time. It is neither natural nor by accident that they are where they are. And it is a matter of evaluation whether hidden but perhaps systematic social moulding and remoulding is better or worse than making a break or planning changes towards defined and chosen ends – which is quite compatible with a recognition of the untidiness and diversity of real people, and does not imply a chess-board approach. One common reply is: 'Why take the risk, given chain reactions and unpredictable effects?' Yet equal risks may apply to letting things be.

Karl Popper, attacking the drastic changes and false methodologies which he associated with 'Utopianism', recommends 'a modest and self-critical rationalism which recognizes certain limitations', and a social technology whose results are testable by piecemeal social engineering.[24] But this attempt to depict the character of decent and proper change confuses political ideals or utopias with political programmes, and falsely assumes that restriction to concrete and proximate ends will save us from the dangers (basic disagreement, irrationality and ultimately violence) to which utopianism is supposedly prone.[25]

It is true that paradise is not attainable here, and to demonstrate that is a salutary reminder to those who believe it possible to build brand-new social systems. But there is no necessary connection, or intimate connection in fact, between radical aspiration or utopianism *and* authoritarianism or a readiness to violate flesh-and-blood men and women. The association may exist, as it may between authoritarianism and a great variety of political ideals. There is good reason for disturbance at Marcuse's response to the one-dimensionality of democratic citizens: that because of their lack of autonomy people cannot give their own answer to what are true and false needs.[26] It is a common implication of the dichotomies between true and false consciousness or needs, real and immediate interests, and so on, that existing desires or claims are inferior, external and not autonomous, created by and confirming the established order, and denying people their potential freedom. To some this provides a warrant for intolerance, for forcing life towards the ideal, though it is both sensible and familiar to distinguish between lower and higher desires or pleasures without seeking to coerce people towards the higher. Against the facile condemnation of certain beliefs as totalitarian, for example the beliefs that some choices are better than others, or that there is a discernible public interest or common good, my view is that an adequate categorization must place these particular ideas within the whole complex of ideas of which they are part, and especially that it must consider the connected notions of leadership, freedom and change. One may not wish to embrace people as they are, may want them to change or be changed, but at their own volition and through processes which are themselves democratic and open, and in which the distinction between the agent of change and the human beings which he or she seeks to change is virtually non-existent.

Finally, the new world itself, deviating so much from what we know, and the model of the new democratic citizen – active, autonomous, communally-oriented – require elucidation. Each must be given some concrete outline. The creation of 'imagined alternatives', resting on views of history, of human nature and of relevant contemporary experience, may produce various kinds of example: past paradises, logical models, particular periods of community and creativity, smaller groupings taken to be prefigurative or constructive. Exemplars may be literary or imaginative, but the new modes may have actual exemplars – liberated or emancipated or many-faceted or co-operative persons, such as Marx's French workers with the brotherhood of man shining on their faces, or the political activists praised in some accounts of the system of competitive elites. There is nothing strange in the fact that people in the same society act, live and dream differently, and that more of the valued potentialities have emerged in some than in others. But what attitude is to be taken to the remarkable diversity of human beings and human societies? The optimist may take the existence of noble individuals in an imperfect present as showing the amazing possibilities given proper education, socialization, social arrangements, distribution of resources, and so on. But on the other hand, how does one explain these occasional successes, these embodiments of virtue, given the bad environment: might it not suggest that much more is possible within its limits and without substantial social change? At least it suggests the implausibility of the one-dimensionality thesis – even this poor life is richer than that! – though it does not challenge optimistic views of what might follow from larger institutional change.

Examples of small constructive communities, novel achievements in particular areas of life, and periods of unusual national harmony and joint activity, can also be introduced, with appropriate theoretical background, not just as a means of embellishment but as indications of what is feasible or what is accessible more generally or more continuously. The vital first question is: What is the particular model intended to do or to show? Small co-operative communities of monks or scholars or simple peasants or hippies, or free schools[27] or workers' councils, show that groupings of an examplary kind – perhaps of an exemplary democratic kind – may exist. But they may be – and may see themselves as – separate, islands or enclaves of virtue within bad or intractable societies, retreats rather than models for all people. Ideal communities may require, for their purity and sense of common purpose, isolation from the world, and even then they often fail and fall apart, and those failures themselves need accounting for. Often they develop in peculiar or unusual circumstances, out of stress, or with crucial material or cultural advantages, for example hippie communes, with regular cheques from middle-class Momma. And models for sustained social life may be derived – misleadingly – from intense and short-lived experiences, such as Paris 1968, or the unusual – more equalitarian or communitarian – social relationships prevailing during the Battle of Britain. Anachronism may lie at the heart of many of our most pleasing images of a democratic community. Pictures are plucked from transient pasts and set before us as possible models, in a very different world.

But models are normally more than dead exemplars. They are usually conceived, within radical democratic theory, as stimulants, transforming agencies, potent means of moral influence and the change of consciousness, sectoral or mini-democracies as foundations for a democratic society at a national level. Mill saw participation in voluntary community activities as a true political education, taking people 'out of the narrow circle of personal and family selfishness, and accustoming them to the comprehension of joint interests, the management of joint concerns . . .'[28] It provided a foundation for a more democratic and participatory political life. Within the anarchist and libertarian traditions the institutions and arrangements which are built to transform the old society already embody, in miniature, the basic features of the new order.[29] David Cooper and R.D. Laing each envisage transform-ation at the intermediate level, with family, school, university, mental hospital, factory, whole areas of industry and education, becoming re-volutionary centres for transforming consciousness.[30] Their argument is unexplored in relation to actual institutions, structures and resources, but it is concerned with a crucial question: the connection between power relation-ships in traditionally non-political spheres and the area of government. More concretely, Carole Pateman[31] argues that there is an interrelationship between the authority structure of institutions and the psychological qualities and attitudes of individuals. She finds – unsurprisingly – that there is a greater sense of efficacy in more participatory, less authoritarian structures. Workers' Councils in Yugoslavia provide her with her most encouraging real-world case. While the point for a democrat is clear – democratize lesser institutions as a necessary support for a democratic society – problems remain.

The vision itself can be stated in broad but clear terms. It is a vision of greater democratization, including institutions, nominally private, which have far-reaching effects upon the public realm. It would involve an enlargement of the political and participatory arena to incorporate immediate areas of work and experience. The result, ideally, would be an interpenetrating network of democratic institutions at all levels. The difficult questions include the following: Are we talking of participation or control? Is it not possible to participate regularly and enthusiastically, but insubstantially, or to have power on the margins of life? How are the different levels connected? What is the nature of the move from economic and social organizations to the traditional political arena, and from specific institutions – factories, families, schools or universities – to all that is comprehended under the concept of citizenship? Are the relationships one-way, and if so, which way? Or are they interactive? One possible misunderstanding can be cleared away at this point. I am not suggesting that the state can be democratic in the sense that lesser institutions or associations might be. The smaller units cannot constitute the appropriate model for the larger. Difficulties for the participatory democrat arise inescapably when large numbers of diverse people live together in a relatively open society. The representative devices which are normally taken as the best means of ensuring responsive government may contribute to the separation or alienation of people from political life. Optimistic democratic theory must confront the genuine problems created by the distance of most people from politics, by bureaucracy, by the iron law of oligarchy or an attenuated form of it, by the distribution of time and expertise. It can best confront them, not through the illusion that participatory democracy can somehow supplant representative democracy (with the polity sharing the attributes imputed to lesser associations), but through indicating how the subsystems might serve to fill out and support democracy at the state level.[32] A democratic society would then be conceived as one which is sustained though not completely constituted by democracy at the lower levels.

At this stage we will probably wish to discriminate between different institutions, and may conclude that political democracy is inappropriate to some of them, for example where the (relative) immaturity or irresponsibility of the subjects, or some of them, suggests more hierarchical or closed structures. Eckstein argues, in this vein, that families and schools can never be run democratically and 'must therefore always be to some extent out of tune with democratic patterns and potentially at odds with them'.[33] The lack of congruence between the different institutional domains certainly constitutes a problem for democratic theory, but although we might concede that a perfect congruence is impossible, and that not all the lesser institutions or units in the state should be conceived simply as supportive structures for democracy at the national level, we can nonetheless evaluate them in terms of the degree to which they encourage or allow self-reliance and otherwise contribute, within their acknowledged limits, to the development of the capacities valued in a democracy.

It may be true that new conditions now support liberation, providing economic, technological and perhaps institutional underpinnings of a new order, in ways anticipated in Marx's account of communism, and in neo-Marxist claims that freedom from poverty and the emergence of a 'postscarcity psychology' may undermine institutions which have hitherto enchained people.[34] But the rivers which feed contemporary liberationist thought, which challenges deeply-entrenched interests and practices, appear to flow less towards a fuller democracy than towards a hedonistic utopia of leisure and indulgence. But more time and more resources could contribute to a potentially constructive change or opening-up of consciousness and to a fuller democratic society, though this would require also the invention of new political institutions and arrangements, more fluid and responsive than those with which we are familiar.[35]

This essay, which is in some respects a broad agenda for research, reflects a particular attitude to social theory. This holds that the social imagination should not float freely, but should be realistic in recognizing obstacles and necessities, and not simply bold and enthusiastic in declaring possibilities. Given a controlled social imagination strategies are more likely to be feasible and people are more likely to be respected as they are, while to combine a study of resources and possibilities with one of limits will still allow the opening-up of genuine but hidden alternatives. If there was such a theory as the anti-elitism presented by Sartori, I would sympathize with his attack. It has, he writes, 'paved the way for a literature that is all ideals and no facts: the supporting facts are not given because they do not exist and facts which fail to conform are simply erased'.[36] No one is named, 'paved the way' is vague, and the modern Newspeak experts hardly seem to be concentrated in leftist political science faculties. But it is a common weakness in radical social theory that it fails to specify and show the relevance of an ideal standard in terms of which a penetrating and constructive critique might be offered: what alternative arrangements and distributions are envisaged, and how are they expected to work? What are we to make both of resource limits, the so-called imperatives of complex industrial societies, and so on, which appear to stand in the way of an equal and even of a more participatory society, and of those insistent and perhaps valuable particularities which, to Rousseau, stood opposed to democratic citizenship?

My goal has been to take issue with the argument, often made by pessimistic democrats, that a fuller democracy must founder on the rocks of human nature. I have argued that a more generous conception of the democratic citizen can be supported by historical argument and by current example – not just by immaculate models or magic moments, but by a deeper exploration of ordinary life. In addition, such an ideal can be supported by critical analysis of reasons why democratic citizens are less than they might be, and by practical, moral and imaginative argument concerned with elucidating the character of a democratic society and establishing means whereby it might be approached. My main substantive claim is that there is no compelling evidence that there are firm limits set by a lack of potentialities or by 'human nature' to visions of radical change. To establish that would be to establish something, and to begin challenging the technical problems posed by size, complexity and tradition. It would lay some groundwork for more than a cynical denial or acceptance of these problems if we could show either that the low conception of humankind underlying conservative political theory and political science was nowhere confirmed by argument and evidence, or that there are good reasons for thinking that men and women in general are capable of sustained and considered political endeavour.

That democracy is most likely to survive and flourish if the mass of citizens are democrats goes without saying. But the path from this observation to the maximization of human – including political – capacities is a hard and treacherous one. The valued potentialities may require preconditions which do not yet exist, or which are not available for everybody, or which presuppose more drastic – and unpredictable – changes than have been contemplated here.

13

Feminism and democracy

CAROLE PATEMAN

A feminist might dispose briskly of the subject of this essay. For feminists, democracy has never existed; women have never been and still are not admitted as full and equal members and citizens in any country known as a 'democracy'. A telling image that recurs throughout the history of feminism is of liberal society as a series of male clubs – usually, as Virginia Woolf points out in *Three Guineas*, distinguished by their own costumes and uniforms – that embrace parliament, the courts, political parties, the military and police, universities, workplaces, trade unions, public (private) schools, exclusive Clubs and popular leisure clubs, from all of which women are excluded or to which they are mere auxiliaries. Feminists will find confirmation of their view in academic discussions of democracy which usually take it for granted that feminism or the structure of the relationship between the sexes are irrelevant matters. The present volume at least acknowledges that feminism might have something significant to say to democratic theorists or citizens, albeit in a token paper by a token woman writer. In the scope of a short essay it is hardly possible to demolish the assumption of two thousand years that there is no incompatibility between 'democracy' and the subjection of women or their exclusion from full and equal participation in political life. Instead, I shall indicate why feminism provides democracy – whether in its existing liberal guise or in the form of a possible future participatory or self-managing democracy – with its most important challenge and most comprehensive critique.

The objection that will be brought against the feminists is that after a century or more of legal reforms and the introduction of universal suffrage women are now the civil and political equals of men, so that feminism today has little or nothing to contribute to democratic theory and practice. This objection ignores much that is crucial to an understanding of the real character of liberal democratic societies. It ignores the existence of widespread and deeply held convictions, and of social practices that give them expression, that contradict the (more or less) formally equal civic status of women. The objection is based on the liberal argument that social inequalities are irrelevant to political equality. Thus, it has to ignore the problems that have arisen from the attempt to universalize liberal principles by extending them to women while at the same time maintaining the division between private and political life which is central to liberal democracy, and is also a division between women and men. If liberal theorists of democracy are content to avoid these questions, their radical critics, along with advocates of participatory democracy, might have been expected to confront them enthusiastically. However, although they have paid a good deal of attention to the class structure of liberal democracies and the way in which class inequality undercuts formal political equality, they have rarely examined the significance of sexual inequality and the patriarchal order of the liberal state for a democratic transformation of liberalism. Writers on democracy, whether defenders or critics of the status quo, invariably fail to consider, for example, whether their discussions of freedom or consent have any relevance to women. They implicitly argue as if 'individuals' and 'citizens' are men.

It is frequently overlooked how recently democratic or universal suffrage was established. Political scientists have remained remarkably silent about the struggle for womanhood suffrage (in England there was a continuous organized campaign for 48 years from 1866 to 1914) and the political meaning and consequences of enfranchisement. Women's position as voters also appears to cause some difficulty for writers on democracy. Little comment is excited, for example, by Schumpeter's explicit statement, in his extremely influential revisionist text, that the exclusion of women from the franchise does not invalidate a polity's claim to be a 'democracy'. In Barber's fascinating account of direct democracy in a Swiss canton, womanhood suffrage (gained only in 1971) is treated very equivocally. Barber emphasizes that women's enfranchisement was 'just and equitable' – but the cost was 'participation and community'. Assemblies grew unwieldy and participation diminished, atomistic individualism gained official recognition and the ideal of the citizen-soldier could no longer be justified.[1] The reader is left wondering whether women should not have sacrificed their just demand for the sake of men's citizenship. Again, in Verba, Nie and Kim's recent cross-national study of political participation it is noted, in a discussion of the change in Holland from compulsory to voluntary voting, that 'voting rights were universal'. The footnote, on the same page, says that in both electoral systems there was 'a one man one vote system'.[2] Did women vote? Unrecognized historical ironies abound in discussions of democracy. Feminists are frequently told today that we must not be offended by masculine language because 'man' really means 'human being', although when, in 1867 in support of the first women's suffrage bill in Britain, it was argued that 'man' (referring to the householder) was a generic term that

included women the argument was firmly rejected. Another recent example
of the way in which women can be written out of democratic political life can
be found in Margolis' *Viable Democracy*. He begins by presenting a history
of 'Citizen Brown', who is a man and who, we learn, in 1920 obtained 'his
latest major triumph, the enfranchisement of women'.[3] Thus the history of
women's democratic struggles disappears and democratic voting appears as
the sole creation – or gift – of men.

Such examples might be amusing if they were not symptomatic of the past
and present social standing of women. Feminism, liberalism and democracy
(that is, a political order in which citizenship is universal, the right of each
adult individual member of the community) share a common origin.
Feminism, a general critique of social relationships of sexual domination and
subordination and a vision of a sexually egalitarian future, like liberalism and
democracy, emerges only when individualism, or the idea that individuals are
by nature free and equal to each other, has developed as a universal theory of
social organization. However, from the time, three hundred years ago, when
the individualist social contract theorists launched the first critical attack on
patriarchalism the prevailing approach to the position of women can be
exemplified by the words of Fichte who asks:

Has woman the same rights in the state which man has? This question may appear
ridiculous to many. For if the only ground of all legal rights is reason and freedom,
how can a distinction exist between two sexes which possess both the same reason and
the same freedom?

He replies to this question as follows:

Nevertheless, it seems that, so long as men have lived, this has been differently held,
and the female sex seems not to have been placed on a par with the male sex in the
exercise of its rights. *Such a universal sentiment must have a ground, to discover
which was never a more urgent problem than in our days.*[4]

The anti-feminists and anti-democrats have never found this 'urgent
problem' difficult to solve. Differential rights and status have been and are
defended by appeal to the 'natural' differences between the sexes, from which
it is held to follow that women are subordinate to their fathers or husbands
and that their proper place is in domestic life. The argument from nature
stretches back into mythology and ancient times (and today often comes
dressed up in the scientific garb of sociobiology) and its longevity appears to
confirm that it informs us of an eternal and essential part of the human
condition. But, far from being timeless, the argument has specific formu-
lations in different historical epochs and, in the context of the development of
liberal-capitalist society, it appears in a form which obscures the patriarchal
structure of liberalism beneath the ideology of individual freedom and
equality.

It is usually assumed that the social contract theorists, and Locke in particular, provided the definitive counter to the patriarchal thesis that paternal and political power are one and the same, grounded in the natural subjection of sons to fathers. Locke certainly drew a sharp distinction between natural or familial ties and the conventional relations of political life, but although he argued that sons, when adult, were as free as their fathers and equal to them, and hence could only justifiably be governed with their own consent, it is usually 'forgotten' that he excluded women (wives) from this argument. His criticism of the patriarchalists depends upon the assumption of natural individual freedom and equality, but only men count as 'individuals'. Women are held to be born to subjection. Locke takes it for granted that a woman will, through the marriage contract, always agree to place herself in subordination to her husband. He agrees with the patriarchalists that wifely subjection has 'a Foundation in Nature' and argues that in the family the husband's will, as that of the 'abler and the stronger', must always prevail over 'that of his wife in all things of their common Concernment'.[5] The contradiction between the premise of individual freedom and equality, with its corollary of the conventional basis of authority, and the assumption that women (wives) are naturally subject has since gone unnoticed. Similarly, there has been no acknowledgement of the problem that if women are naturally subordinate, or born into subjection, then talk of their consent or agreement to this status is redundant. Yet this contradiction and paradox lie at the heart of democratic theory and practice. The continuing silence about the status of wives is testament to the strength of the union of a transformed patriarchalism with liberalism. For the first time in history, liberal individualism promised women an equal social standing with men as naturally free individuals, but at the same time socio-economic developments ensured that the subordination of wives to husbands continued to be seen as natural, and so outside the domain of democratic theorists or the political struggle to democratize liberalism.

The conviction that a married woman's proper place is in the conjugal home as a servant to her husband and mother to her children is now so widespread and well established that this arrangement appears as a natural feature of human existence rather than historically and culturally specific. The history of the development of the capitalist organization of production is also the history of the development of a particular form of the sexual division of labour (although this is not the history to be found in most books). At the time when the social contract theorists attacked the patriarchal thesis of a natural hierarchy of inequality and subordination, wives were not their husband's equals, but nor were they their economic dependants. Wives, as associates and partners in economic production, had an independent status. As production moved out of the household, women were forced out of the trades they controlled and wives became dependent on their husbands for subsistence or competed for individual wages in certain areas of production.[6] Many working-class wives and mothers have had to continue to try to find paid employment to ensure the survival of their families, but by the mid-nineteenth century the ideal, the natural and respectable, mode of life had come to be seen as that of the middle-class, breadwinning paterfamilias and his totally dependent wife. By then the subjection of wives was complete; with no independent legal or civil standing they had been reduced to the status of property, as the nineteenth-century feminists emphasized in their comparisons of wives to the slaves of the West Indies and American South. Today, women have won an independent civil status and the vote; they are, apparently, 'individuals' as well as citizens – and thus require no special attention in discussions of democracy. However, one of the most important consequences of the institutionalization of liberal individualism and the establishment of universal suffrage has been to highlight the practical contradiction between the formal political equality of liberal democracy and the social subordination of women, including their subjection as wives within the patriarchal structure of the institution of marriage.

It is indicative of the attitude of democratic theorists (and political activists) towards feminism that John Stuart Mill's criticism of the argument from (women's) nature, and the lessons to be learned from it, are so little known. The present revival of the organized feminist movement has begun to rescue *The Subjection of Women* from the obscurity into which Mill's commentators have pushed it, although it provides a logical extension of the arguments of his academically acceptable *On Liberty*. The *Subjection* is important for its substantive argument, but also because the ultimately contradictory position that Mill takes in the essay illustrates just how radical feminist criticism is, and how the attempt to universalize liberal principles to both sexes pushes beyond the confines of liberal democratic theory and practice.

In *The Subjection* Mill argues that the relation between women and men, or, more specifically, between wives and husbands, forms an unjustified exception to the liberal principles of individual rights, freedom and choice, to the principles of equality of opportunity and the allocation of occupational positions by merit that, he believes, now govern other social and political institutions. In the modern world, consent has supplanted force and the principle of achievement has replaced that of ascription – except where women are concerned. Mill writes that the conjugal relation is an example of 'the primitive state of slavery lasting on, . . . It has not lost the taint of its brutal origin' (p. 130).[7] More generally, the social subordination of women is 'a single relic of an old world of thought and practice, exploded in everything else' (p. 146). Mill opens the *Subjection* with some pertinent comments on the difficulty feminists face in presenting an intellectually convincing case. Domination by men is rooted in long-standing customs, and the idea that male supremacy is the proper order of things derives from deep feelings and sentiments rather than rationally tested beliefs (and, it might be added, men have a lot to lose by being convinced). Thus feminists must not expect their opponents to 'give up practical principles in which they have been born and bred and which are the basis of much of the existing order of the world, at the first argumentative attack which they are not capable of logically resisting' (p. 128). Mill is very conscious of the importance of the appeal to nature. He notes that it provides no criterion to differentiate the subordination of women from other forms of domination because all rulers have attempted to claim a grounding in nature for their position. He also argues that nothing at all can be said about the respective natures of women and men because we have only seen the sexes in an unequal relationship. Any differences in their moral and other capacities will become known when men and women can interact as independent and equal rational beings.

However, despite Mill's vigorous attack on the appeal to custom and nature he ultimately falls back on the very argument that he has carefully criticized. His failure consistently to apply his principles to domestic life has been noted by recent feminist critics, but it is less often pointed out that his inconsistency undermines his defence of womanhood suffrage and equal democratic citizenship. The central argument of *The Subjection* is that husbands must be stripped of their legally-sanctioned despotic powers over their wives. Most of the legal reforms of the marriage law that Mill advocated have now been enacted (with the significant exception of marital rape, to which I shall return), and the implications of his unwillingness to extend his criticism to the sexual division of labour within the home are now fully revealed. Mill argues that because of their upbringing, lack of education and legal and social pressures, women do not have a free choice whether or not to marry: 'wife' is the only occupation open to them. But although he also argues that women must have equal opportunity with men to obtain a proper education that will enable them to support themselves, he assumes that, if marriage were reformed, most women would *not* choose independence.

Mill states that it is generally understood that when a woman marries she has chosen her career, like a man when he chooses a profession. When a woman becomes a wife, 'she makes choice of the management of a household, and the bringing up of a family, as the first call on her exertions, . . . she renounces, . . . all [occupations] not consistent with the requirement of this' (p. 179). Mill is reverting here to ascriptive arguments and the belief in women's natural place and occupation. He is falling back on the ancient tradition of patriarchal political theory that, as Susan Okin has shown in *Women in Western Political Thought* (Princeton, 1979), asserts that whereas men are, or can be, many things, women are placed on earth to fulfil one function only; to bear and rear children. Mill neatly evades the question of how, if women's task is prescribed by their sex, they can be said to have a real choice of occupation, or why equal opportunity is relevant to women if marriage itself is a 'career'. Mill compares an egalitarian marriage to a business partnership in which the partners are free to negotiate their own terms of association, but he relies on some very weak arguments, which run counter to liberal principles, to support his view that equality will not disturb the conventional domestic division of labour. He suggests that the 'natural arrangement' would be for wife and husband each to be 'absolute in the executive branch of their own department . . . any change of system and principle requiring the consent of both' (p. 169). He also suggests that the division of labour between the spouses could be agreed in the marriage contract – but he assumes that wives will be willing to accept the 'natural' arrangement. Mill notes that duties are already divided 'by consent . . . and general custom' (p. 170) modified in individual cases; but it is exactly 'general custom', as the bulwark of male domination, that he is arguing against in the body of the essay. He forgets this when he suggests that the husband will generally have the greater voice in decisions as he is usually older. Mill adds that this is only until the time of life when age is irrelevant; but when do husbands admit that this has arrived?[8] He also forgets his own arguments when he suggests that more weight will be given to the views of the partner who brings the means of support, disingenuously adding 'whichever this is' when he has already assumed that wives will 'choose' to be dependent by agreeing to marry.

Anti-feminist movements and propagandists in the 1980s also claim that the domestic division of labour supported by Mill is the only natural one. They would not be disturbed by the implications of this arrangement for the citizenship of women but advocates of democracy should be. Mill championed womanhood suffrage for the same reasons that he supported votes for men; because it was necessary for self-protection or the protection of individual interests and because political participation would enlarge the capacities of individual women. The obvious problem with his argument is that women as wives will largely be confined to the small circle of the family and its daily routines and so will find it difficult to use their vote effectively as a protective measure. Women will not be able to learn what their interests are without experience outside domestic life. This point is even more crucial for Mill's arguments about political development and education through participation. He writes (p. 237) in general terms of the elevation of the individual 'as a moral, spiritual and social being' that occurs under free government, but this is a large claim to make for the periodic casting of a vote (although the moral transformation of political life through enfranchisement was a central theme of the womanhood suffrage movement). Nor did Mill himself entirely believe that this 'elevation' would result from the suffrage alone. He writes that 'citizenship', and here I take him to be referring to universal suffrage, 'fills only a small place in modern life, and does not come near the daily habits or inmost sentiments' (p. 174). He goes on to argue that the family, 'justly constituted', would be the 'real school of the virtues of freedom'. However, this is as implausible as the claim about the consequences of liberal democratic voting. A patriarchal family with the despotic husband at its head is no basis for democratic citizenship; but nor, *on its own*, is an egalitarian family. Mill argues in his social and political writings that only participation in a wide variety of institutions, especially the workplace, can provide the political education necessary for active, democratic citizenship. Yet how can wives and mothers, who have 'chosen' domestic life, have the opportunity to develop their capacities or learn what it means to be a democratic citizen? Women will therefore exemplify the selfish, private beings, lacking a sense of justice or public spirit, that result when an individual is confined to the narrow sphere of everyday family life.[9] Mill's failure to question the apparently natural division of labour within the home means that his arguments for democratic citizenship apply only to men.

It might be objected that it is unreasonable and anachronistic to ask of Mill, writing in the 1860s, that he criticize the accepted division of labour between husband and wife when only very exceptional feminists in the nineteenth century were willing to question the doctrine of the separate spheres of the sexes. But if that objection is granted,[10] it does not excuse the same critical failure by contemporary democratic theorists and empirical investigators. Until the feminist movement began, very recently, to have an impact on academic studies not only has the relation between the structure of the institution of marriage and the formal equality of citizenship been ignored, but women citizens have often been excluded from empirical investigations of political behaviour and attitudes or merely referred to briefly in patriarchal not scientific terms.[11] A reading of *The Subjection* should long ago have placed these matters in the forefront of discussions of democracy. Perhaps the appearance of empirical findings showing, for example, that even women active in local politics are inhibited from running for office because of their responsibility for child-care and a belief that office-holding is not a proper activity for women,[12] will be taken more seriously than the feminist writings of even eminent philosophers.

The problems surrounding women's citizenship in the liberal democracies may have been sadly neglected, but the failure of democratic theorists to confront the woman and wife question runs much deeper still. Democratic citizenship, even if interpreted in the minimal sense of universal suffrage in the context of liberal civil rights, presupposes the solid foundation of a practical, universal recognition that all members of the polity are social equals and independent 'individuals', having all the capacities implied by this status. The most serious failure of contemporary democratic theory and its language of freedom, equality, consent, and of the individual, is that women are so easily and inconspicuously excluded from references to the 'in-dividual'. Thus the question never arises whether the exclusion reflects social and political realities. One reason why there is no consciousness of the need to ask this question is that democratic theorists conventionally see their subject-matter as encompassing the political or public sphere, which for radical theorists includes the economy and the workplace. The sphere of personal and domestic life – the sphere that is the 'natural' realm of women – is excluded from scrutiny. Despite the central role that consent plays in their arguments democratic theorists pay no attention to the structure of sexual relations between men and women and, more specifically, to the practice of rape and the interpretation of consent and non-consent which define it as a criminal offence. The facts about rape are central to the social realities which are reflected in and partly constituted by our use of the term 'individual'.

Among Mill's criticism of the despotic powers of nineteenth-century husbands is a harsh reminder that a husband had the legal right to rape his wife. Over a century later a husband still has that right in most legal jurisdictions. Locke excludes women from the status of 'free and equal individual' by his agreement with the patriarchal claim that wives were subject to their husbands by nature; the content of the marriage contract confirms that, today, this assumption still lies at the heart of the institution of marriage. The presumed consent of a woman, in a free marriage contract, to her subordinate status gives a voluntarist gloss to an essentially ascribed status of 'wife'. If the assumption of natural subjection did not still hold, liberal democratic theorists would long ago have begun to ask why it is that an ostensibly free and equal individual should *always* agree to enter a contract which subordinates her to another such individual. They would long ago have begun to question the character of an institution in which the initial agreement of a wife deprives her of the right to retract her consent to provide sexual services to her husband, and which gives him the legal right to force her to submit. If contemporary democratic theorists are to distance themselves from the patriarchal assumptions of their predecessors they must begin to ask whether a person can be, at one and the same time, a free democratic citizen and a wife who gives up a vital aspect of her freedom and individuality, the freedom to refuse consent and say 'no' to the violation of the integrity of her person.

A woman's right of refusal of consent is also a matter of more general importance. Outside of marriage rape is a serious criminal offence, yet the evidence indicates that the majority of offenders are not prosecuted. Women have exemplified the beings whom political theorists have regarded as lacking the capacities to attain the status of individual and citizen or to participate in the practice of consent, but women have, simultaneously, been perceived as beings who, in their personal lives, always consent, and whose explicit refusal of consent can be disregarded and reinterpreted as agreement. This contradictory perception of women is a major reason why it is so difficult for a woman who has been raped to secure the conviction of her attacker(s). Public opinion, the police and the courts are willing to identify enforced submission with consent, and the reason why this identification is possible is that it is widely believed that if a woman says 'no' her words have no meaning, since she 'really' means 'yes'. It is widely regarded as perfectly reasonable for a man to reinterpret explicit rejection of his advances as consent.[13] Thus women find that their speech is persistently and systematically invalidated. Such invalidation would be incomprehensible if the two sexes actually shared the same status as 'individuals'. No person with a secure, recognized standing as an 'individual' could be seen as someone who consistently said the opposite of what they meant and who, therefore, could justifiably have their words reinterpreted by others. On the other hand, invalidation and reinterpretation are readily comprehensible parts of a relationship in which one person is seen as a natural subordinate and thus has an exceedingly ambiguous place in social practices (held to be) grounded in convention, in free agreement and consent.

Political theorists who take seriously the question of the conceptual foundations and social conditions of democracy can no longer avoid the feminist critique of marriage and personal life. The critique raises some awkward and often embarrassing questions, but questions that have to be faced if 'democracy' is to be more than a men's club writ large and the patriarchal structure of the liberal democratic state is to be challenged. The assumptions and practices which govern the everyday, personal lives of women and men, including their sexual lives, can no longer be treated as matters remote from political life and the concerns of democratic theorists. Women's status as 'individuals' pervades the whole of their social life, personal and political. The structure of everyday life, including marriage, is constituted by beliefs and practices which presuppose that women are naturally subject to men – yet writers on democracy continue to assert that women and men can and will freely interact as equals in their capacity as enfranchised democratic citizens.

The preceding argument and criticism is relevant to discussions of both liberal democracy and participatory democracy, but particularly to the latter. Liberal theorists continue to claim that the structure of social relations and social inequality is irrelevant to political equality and democratic citizenship, so they are no more likely to be impressed by feminists than by any other radical critics. Advocates of participatory democracy have been reluctant to take feminist arguments into account even though these arguments are, seen in one light, an extension of the participatory democratic claim that 'democracy' extends beyond the state to the organization of society. The resistance to feminism is particularly ironical because the contemporary feminist movement has, under a variety of labels, attempted to put participatory democratic organization into practice.[14] The movement is decentralized, anti-hierarchical and tries to ensure that its members collectively educate themselves and gain independence through consciousness-raising, participatory decision-making and rotation of tasks and offices.

Feminists deny the liberal claim that private and public life can be understood in isolation from each other. One reason for the neglect of J.S. Mill's feminist essay is that his extension of liberal principles to the institution of marriage breaches the central liberal separation, established by Locke, between paternal and political rule; or between the impersonal, conventional public sphere and the family, the sphere of natural affection and natural relations. Proponents of participatory democracy have, of course, been willing to challenge commonplace conceptions of the public and the private in their discussions of the workplace, but this challenge ignores the insights of feminism. It is rarely appreciated that the feminists and participatory democrats see the division between public and private very differently. From the feminist perspective participatory democratic arguments remain within the patriarchal-liberal separation of civil society and state; domestic life has an exceedingly ambiguous relation to this separation, which is a division within public life itself. In contrast, feminists see domestic life, the 'natural' sphere of women, as private, and thus as divided from a public realm encompassing both economic and political life, the 'natural' arenas of men.[15]

By failing to take into account the feminist conception of 'private' life, by ignoring the family, participatory democratic arguments for the democratization of economic life have neglected a crucial dimension of democratic social transformation (and I include my *Participation and Democratic Theory* here). It is difficult to find any appreciation of the significance of the integral relation between the domestic division of labour and economic life, or the sexual division of labour in the workplace, let alone any mention of the implications of the deeper matters touched on in this essay, in writings on industrial democracy. It is the feminists, not the advocates of workplace democracy, who have investigated the very different position of women workers, especially married women workers, from that of male employees. Writers on democracy have yet to digest the now large body of feminist research on women and paid employment or to acknowledge that unless it is brought into the centre of reflection, debate and political action, women will remain as peripheral in a future participatory 'democracy' as they are at present in liberal democracies.

I have drawn attention to the problem posed by the assumption that women's natural place is a private one, as wife and mother in the home, for arguments about the educative and developmental consequences of political participation. It might be argued that this problem is much less pressing today than in Mill's time because many married women have now entered the public world of paid employment and so they, if not housewives, already have their horizons widened and will gain a political education if enterprises are democratized. In Australia, for example, in 1977 women formed 35% of the labour force and 63% of these women were married.[16] The reality behind the statistics, however, is that women's status as workers is as uncertain and ambiguous as our status as citizens and both reflect the more fundamental problem of our status as 'individuals'. The conventional but implicit assumption is that 'work' is undertaken in a workplace, not within the 'private' home, and that a 'worker' is male – someone who has his need for a clean place of relaxation, clean clothes, food and care of his children provided for him by his wife. When a wife enters paid employment it is significant for her position as 'worker' that no one asks who performs these services for her. In fact, married women workers do two shifts, one in the office or factory, the other at home. A large question arises here why members of enterprises who are already burdened with two jobs should be eager to take on the new responsibilities, as well as exercise the opportunities, that democratization would bring.

The relative importance of the two components of the wife's double day, and so the evaluation of women's status as workers, is reflected, as Eisenstein notes, in the popular use of 'the term "working mother" which simultaneously asserts women's first responsibility to motherhood and her secondary status as worker'.[17] Again, the question has to be asked how workers of secondary status could, without some very large changes being made, take their place as equal participants in a democratized workplace. The magnitude of the changes required can be indicated by brief reference to three features of women's (paid) worklife. The sexual harassment of women workers is still a largely unacknowledged practice but it reveals the extent to which the problem of sexual relations, consent and women's status as 'individuals' is also a problem of the economic sphere.[18] Secondly, women still have to win the struggle against discrimination by employers and unions before they can participate as equals. Finally, it has to be recognized that the workplace is structured by a sexual division of labour which poses still further complex problems for equality and participation. Women are segregated into certain occupational categories ('women's work') and they are concentrated in non-supervisory and low-skilled and low-status jobs. It is precisely workers in such jobs that empirical research has shown to be the least likely to participate.

The example of the workplace, together with the other examples discussed in this essay, should be sufficient to show the fundamental importance to democratic theory and practice of the contemporary feminist insistence that personal and political life are integrally connected. Neither the equal opportunity of liberalism nor the active, participatory democratic citizenship of *all* the people can be achieved without radical changes in personal and domestic life. The struggles of the organized feminist movement of the last 150 years have achieved a great deal. An exceptional woman can now become Prime Minister – but that particular achievement leaves untouched the structure of social life of unexceptional women, of women as a social category. They remain in an uncertain position as individuals, workers and citizens, and popular opinion echoes Rousseau's pronouncement that 'nature herself has decreed that women, . . . should be at the mercy of man's judgement'[19] The creation of a free and egalitarian sexual and personal life is the most difficult to achieve of all the changes necessary to build a truly democratic society precisely because it is not something remote from everyday life that can be applauded in abstract slogans while life, and the subjection of women, goes on as usual. Democratic ideals and politics have to be put into practice in the kitchen, the nursery and the bedroom; they come home, as J.S. Mill wrote (p. 136) 'to the person and hearth of every male head of a family, and of everyone who looks forward to being so'. It is a natural biological fact of human existence that only women can bear children, but that fact gives no warrant whatsoever for the separation of social life into two sexually defined spheres of private (female) existence and (male) public activity. This separation is ultimately grounded in the mistaken extension of the argument from natural necessity to child-rearing. There is nothing in nature that prevents fathers from sharing equally in bringing up their children, although there is a great deal in the organization of social and economic life that works against it. Women cannot win an equal place in democratic productive life and citizenship if they are deemed destined for a one ascribed task, but nor can fathers take an equal share in reproductive activities without a transformation in our conception of 'work' and of the structure of economic life.

The battle joined three hundred years ago when the social contract theorists pitted conventionalist arguments against the patriarchalists' appeal to nature is far from concluded, and a proper, democratic understanding of the relation of nature and convention is still lacking. The successful conclusion of this long battle demands some radical reconceptualization to provide a comprehensive theory of a properly democratic practice. Recent feminist theoretical work offers new perspectives and insights into the problem of democratic theory and practice, including the question of individualism and participatory democracy, and an appropriate conception of 'political' life.[20] It has been hard to imagine what a democratic form of social life might look like for much of the past century. Male-dominated political parties, sects and their theoreticians have attempted to bury the old 'utopian' political movements which are part of the history of the struggle for democracy and women's emancipation, and which argued for prefigurative forms of political organization and activity. The lesson to be learnt from the past is that a 'democratic' theory and practice that is not at the same time feminist merely serves to maintain a fundamental form of domination and so makes a mockery of the ideals and values that democracy is held to embody.

14

Returning the social to democracy

DAVID HARRIS

For many radicals, representative democracy has been a major disappoint-
ment. It has failed to make good its promise to establish democratic control
of society and to engage citizens in creative forms of participation in public
affairs. Citizens remain preoccupied with their private concerns and fail to
develop an awareness of, and commitment to, the wider community.
Representative democracy's failings, however, are not entirely of its own
making. Responsibility lies with capitalism, the framework within which
developed representative democracies work. It is argued that one effect of
capitalism is to undermine political equality and eliminate popular democratic control. This occurs because the concentrations of economic power
found in all capitalist systems can be, and often are, translated into political
influence. Effective power to make decisions lies, not with the weight of
numbers (where each individual has a roughly equal opportunity to influence
the outcome), but with the economically powerful. It is alleged that one
reason why democracy and capitalism are incompatible, is that capitalists
can hold governments to ransom. A second reason is that the dominant
ideology in capitalist societies moulds and influences the ideas and expectations of ordinary people. The effect is that the political agenda rarely
contains items likely to threaten the interests of capital. Capitalism also
accounts for the lack of socially responsible participatory zeal. Capitalism
encourages individuals to narrow the focus of their interest to the pursuit of
private advantage. Individuals are led not only to narrow their vision and
consequently to underplay the significance of the wider social framework as
an influence on their condition and opportunities for action, but also to
conceive of their relationship with other individuals and the world in purely
instrumental terms. Small wonder then that the typical citizen's basic
question about politics is, 'What's in it for me?' And small wonder that when
confronted with the choice of digging his garden or participating in politics,
he chooses the former. 'When I hear the word "politics"', he might remark,
'I reach for my trowel.'

Confronted with these problems, many radicals have concluded that political systems in liberal democracies do not have that degree of independence from the distribution of power within the economic and social system which they would need if directive control was to be exercised through them in a democratic manner. Democratic control is vitiated, in part, because other politically important centres of power are left intact when the political system is democratized. What is required to remedy this defect, it is sometimes argued, is a social democracy. Unfortunately, it is not clear exactly what this means. At the heart of social democracy lies a problem of interpretation, namely how should the relationship between 'social' and 'democracy' be understood? Does the term 'social democracy' refer to a unitary concept? Or are the two elements capable of being independently characterized in a way which allows questions about the connections between the 'social' and the 'democratic' to be formulated? In the first part of this chapter I examine this question and suggest that a focus on connections between the 'social' and the 'democratic' is an essential precondition for developing an adequate theory of a social democracy. The second part uses the framework of the first to examine two specific theories of social democracy, developed respectively by Tawney and Crosland. Finally, I attempt to use the insights of the central section to identify some problems inhibiting the development of a genuinely social democracy in modern society.

Sometimes radical politicians and academics write as if the problem of establishing a genuinely social democracy amounted to no more than the problem of extending democracy to more, most, or all decision-making in society. The argument appears to be that, if there is a decision to take, it should be taken democratically, or alternatively, the decision-taker should be democratically accountable to the (appropriately defined) constituency. 'No power without accountability' makes a good slogan. This suggestion has clear and radical implications. Many concentrations of economic and social power should be 'democratized'. Capitalist managers, previously accountable only to anonymous market forces and a stock exchange, might be displaced by workers' councils issuing directives or taking decisions concerning pricing policy, the allocation of investment, the security of jobs and the nature of work practices, and so on . . . And why not? Workers have a direct interest – indeed a vital interest, since their livelihood depends on their job – in the decisions made by managers. By extending democracy, the opportunity to participate in making decisions that affect one's life is extended. The ability of individuals to control their own lives is enhanced, and the potential for limiting gross abuses of power increased. All are worthy reasons for extending democracy. Extending democracy from the limited political realm, allowing it to penetrate into the economic and social system, might be thought to be tantamount to establishing a social democracy. What is implied here is that what matters in considering whether a society is a social democracy, is the extent of democracy. The essential questions become 'How far does democracy extend?' and 'Are all power centres democratically controlled?'

But is this all that is meant when radicals talk of the need to build a social democracy? Clearly the answer is 'No'. The reason is that nothing has been said about the character or quality of the decisions taken. Consider, for example, the following case. Indem Ltd is a factory managed by its workers. The workers are predominantly white, although a small black minority exists. The workers' assembly meets regularly to allocate jobs. Every one has an equal vote. Anybody can suggest schemes for distributing tasks amongst the workers. At each meeting the blacks argue for a straightforward job rotation. Each worker is to spend x hours in each job within the factory. The whites, however, do not like this for two reasons. First, it means that whites will have to work alongside blacks. This they resent. Secondly, it means that each white will have to spend some time engaged in some extremely unpleasant tasks which are part of the work process of this particular factory. As a consequence the whites propose a scheme under which the blacks are allocated to those tasks. After a long and intense discussion, richly informed by arguments about human dignity, justice and the irrationality of colour as a guide to action, a vote is taken and the blacks return to their sweated labour. What could be more democratic than that? We seem to face the apparent paradox that the simple extension of democracy into the social sphere may generate anti-social consequences.

The difficulty we face with this example of sweated labour is not that democratic procedures have produced *undemocratic* policies. In this case nobody's democratic rights have been abridged. All those affected by the decision are enfranchised, the agenda has not been arbitrarily controlled, votes may be assumed to be secret and equally weighted, discussion free and well-informed, and so on. The problem we face is that an unjust or immoral or anti-social decision has been taken through properly constituted and respected democratic procedures. The reason why this could occur is that a large part of the definition of democracy refers to the *procedures* by which a decision is taken, and not to its acceptability. In other words, it might well be that whether or not a decision has been made democratically will depend not at all on its substantive content, but wholly on the way it is taken.

It seems, therefore, that in giving an account of social democracy, we need to be clear about the connection between democracy and the production of socially acceptable outcomes. Perhaps a lack of an explicit focus on this question, in some radical writings, should not be read as implying the belief that this problem could not exist. Rather it might be an expression of an implicit assumption that in practical terms the extension of democracy would be sufficient to guarantee the production of acceptable outcomes. To some it may be just obvious that, if the injustice and immorality of social life is the product of concentrations of unaccountable economic power or market relationships or whatever, then their eradication and replacement by their opposite, i.e., accountability or democratic planning, is both necessary and sufficient to protect justice and morality. This, however, is a naive and an unwarranted assumption, as a few examples may make clear. Consider the case of an economy in which all centres of power have been democratized. Let us assume that this means that a system of workers' control has been established. What is to guarantee that cases like the sweated labour example would not arise even if in a less dramatic form? What is there to prevent these groups adopting anti-social and exploitative policies *vis-à-vis* the wider community? It is not good enough to suggest, without argument, that they wouldn't. We need to know why not. It is not stretching the imagination very far to suggest that our worker-controlled factories might be just as efficient at evading or avoiding taxes, intended to finance welfare services for the sick and indigent, as any capitalist firm. Nor would it be surprising if underinvestment for the future, coupled with overutilization of present resources, occured, thereby ignoring our responsibility to future generations. Tony Crosland identified some of the potential problems facing participatory democracy in *The Future of Socialism*.

It is not merely that groups may develop . . . extremely disagreeable characteristics – intolerance of dissent, excessive conformity, arbitrary cruelty in the exercise of their ultimate power to ostracise . . . but even if they do not, their purpose or function may be in no way communal or altruistic so far as objectives and institutions outside the group are concerned.[1]

There are a number of distinct reasons why problems of this kind may arise. The first is that just because a decision is made democratically does not mean that the electorate will consider the issue and vote with thoughts of morality or social desirability foremost in their minds. They may just be seeking to pursue their own self-interest. The danger is that the decision might exploit groups within the electorate, for example, where there is an easily identified and persisting minority. The second reason of relevance here is that democracy alone is not sufficient to ensure equality of power, or that any particular individual can exercise control over his life. Mill identified this problem clearly in *On Liberty*.

Such phrases as 'self-government,' and 'the power of the people over themselves', do not express the true state of the case. The 'people' who exercise the power are not always the same people with those over whom it is exercised; and the 'self-government' spoken of is not the government of each by himself, but of each by all the rest.[2]

The key insight here is that, even if democracy is the best approximation to institutionalizing equality of influence, it is at best an approximation and never a guarantee. Those on the losing side of a vote have not made the decision; it is not they who are exercising control. Democratic procedures offer an opportunity to influence the outcome, but an opportunity to exercise influence and actually exercising that influence are quite separate things. Mill's remarks, therefore, raise the spectre that an extension of democracy, far from increasing the control that individuals exercise over their own lives, may, in practice, decrease it. Under certain circumstances democracy may be more of a threat to than an expression of freedom. There is even the possibility that liberal rights, which identify aspects of an individual's life over which he alone is sovereign, may be of more relevance to self-determination than democracy.

The basic point is that a simple extension of democracy into the social sphere is not sufficient to guarantee that socially acceptable outcomes would emerge. It is not, because the new extended democracy may just process the anti-social preferences of the electorate and/or because the democratic rhetoric of equalizing power and establishing accountability may merely conceal new inequalities of power, which are no less invidious than those that existed before. The suggestion is, therefore, that the extension of democracy alone is not enough to establish a social democracy. It is this suggestion that I take up in my discussion of Tawney.

It might be objected to the discussion so far that the questions raised about the social desirability of democracy assume one particular conception of democracy. Under alternative conceptions these problems would not arise. The argument would be that an excessively procedural definition of democracy has been employed. Under this definition, only those outcomes which undercut the rights which define the procedure, for example, the right to vote, assemble and so on, could be classified as undemocratic. Any decisions which left the procedure intact would be democratic, even if they were morally or socially objectionable. The difficulty arises because the use of a procedure alone can not guarantee that outcomes will have a particular substantive character. This difficulty might be avoided, however, if a richer notion of democracy was adopted. Democratic procedures give expression to a range of moral principles and, if the policy output conflicts with those principles, then it could be classified as undemocratic. In other words, only those policies which are consistent with the moral principles encapsulated within democratic procedures could count as being genuinely democratic. For example, democracy might be the only way of taking collective decisions which incorporates a principle of respecting individuals as potentially self-determining agents. If a policy emerged which failed to recognize this principle, then it could be classified as undemocratic. Provided that the moral principles expressed within democratic procedures were sufficiently determinate to identify as democratic only those outcomes which were, at the same time, socially or morally acceptable, then the task of building a social democracy becomes equivalent to establishing a genuinely democratic society.

The attraction of this position is obvious because it simplifies the social democrat's task, focusing attention on one primary aim; democratization. By contrast, adopting the alternative view involves confronting and grappling with the connection between the 'social' and the 'democratic', a connection which may involve both tension and complementarity. There are, however, a number of reasons for believing that a confrontation with these connections is inevitable.

In the example introduced above it was suggested that, if a policy output was inconsistent with a principle of respecting persons as potentially self-determining agents, then that policy could be classified as undemocratic. It is undemocratic because this principle is one which is encapsulated within democratic procedures. For this conclusion to hold, we have to be able to say that respecting persons as potentially self-determining is a distinctively *democratic* principle. Only then would actions transgressing the principle automatically be labelled as undemocratic. But why should we say this? Surely it would be more reasonable to regard 'respecting persons' as a principle which democracy can instantiate. But then so would other forms of action which we would not wish to regard as democratic, for example, respecting property rights or a right to life. The fact that democratic procedures embody a principle does not mean that the principle is, therefore, a democratic principle, nor does it mean that a violation of that principle is undemocratic, even though it may be wrong. Thus, to return to Indem Ltd, we may agree that the treatment of the blacks violates the principle of respecting self-determination and agree that this principle is encapsulated within democratic procedures, but argue that this does not mean that the decision to exploit was undemocratic. The most we could say is that democracy offers an opportunity to respect the principle which is not always realized in practice. We might want to go further, however, and point out how ambiguous a principle like respecting persons is. It could be argued that what the principle enjoins in the context of democracy is only that democratic procedures should not be tampered with. No more and no less. In other words, the principle is respected, as far as its democratic application is concerned, provided that the procedural rights to vote, put forward argument, and so on, have not been abridged.

A further difficulty with expanding the notion of democracy in order to identify unacceptable outcomes as undemocratic may be noted. The strategy relies on pointing to the moral implications of certain values incorporated

within democratic procedures. This strategy works only if the relevant
'reasons why we value democracy' can be read into the procedures.
Sometimes, however, this cannot be done, because the connection between
our reasons for valuing democracy and democratic procedures is a contingent
one. Democracy may be valuable not because it intrinsically expresses certain
values, but because taking decisions democratically increases the likelihood
that certain values will be promoted. Democracy may provide mechanisms
for the peaceful resolution of conflict, but that doesn't mean that democratic
resolution guarantees peace. Similarly, utilitarians may believe that democracy is the best means of maximizing welfare, but this would be true only
if voters knew which policies would best satisfy their desires. The fact that
voters might be ignorant and occasionally make bad choices means only that
democracy might not always be efficient at promoting the general welfare. It
does not mean that the policies chosen are, therefore, undemocratic.

The purpose of the preceding discussion is to suggest that problems related to
the establishment of a more social democracy cannot be subsumed under the
simple heading, democratization. Noting the fact that questions concerning
the moral or social acceptability of decisions are not answered just by
pointing out that they have been taken democratically, supports the claim
that more democracy does not mean a more social democracy. Democracy
may be necessary, but is not sufficient. My suggestion is that this is a
substantively important claim, not just an analytical claim which rests on the
argument that the morality of procedures does not determine the morality of
outcomes. It is substantively important because there are strong empirical
reasons to believe that more democracy will not necessarily mean more social
decisions. The upshot of this is that, in considering how to build a more social
democracy, we need to focus attention on the connections between the
'social' and the 'democratic'. Creating a social democracy is not just a
question of making things more democratic or even encouraging democratic
virtues among citizens. It is also a question of making things more social.
    Any theory of a social democracy must, therefore, contain a number of
distinct, but related, elements. The first would be an account of what sorts of
states of affairs would count as socially acceptable. The second would have to
be an explication of the relationship of democracy to the 'socially
acceptable'. The theory would have to explain, in other words, how and in
what ways democracy could contribute to the definition, and production of,
socially desirable outcomes. A theory of social democracy would have to pay
attention to both the 'social' and 'democracy' as independent elements
which, in principle, may be in conflict just as readily as in harmony. A focus
on this relationship may be properly thought of as a precondition for
confronting the problems blocking the path to a more social democracy.

The writings of the British socialist, R.H. Tawney, display an acute awareness of these problems.[3] Three distinct strands of argument emerge from his principal works. The first is a rich, if inchoate, vision of a good society characterized in terms of the realization of a moralized set of public purposes. The second is a commitment to democracy as a potential instrument through which public purposes could be realized. The third is an awareness of the uncertain relationship between the first two. Tawney is aware that decisions taken within a genuine democracy may be socially or morally objectionable. His theory, therefore, needs to give an account of the conditions under which democracy can be relied on to yield socially acceptable results. In more concrete terms, Tawney's account of a social democracy draws attention to what it is that we choose through democracy, asking the question, 'Have we chosen "correctly"?' (Perhaps more ac-curately, 'Have we not chosen "incorrectly"?') In drawing attention to this, it also draws attention to the related question, 'As what do we choose?' Tawney's objective is to show that a social democracy is possible only if we choose as members of a community and not if we continue to pursue a self-interest detached from social responsibility.

Tawney's analysis begins by considering how it is that socially desirable outcomes do not 'naturally' emerge within a society. He argues that they are inhibited by a combination of certain systemic features of advanced Western societies and by the character of individual motivation associated with them. To remove these systemic features is not alone sufficient to produce social outcomes. For this it is necessary also to encourage an active commitment by individuals to community purposes. The fact that something is in the public good needs to become a reason for individuals to support it, vote for it and work for it. Thus, the problem of achieving social outcomes from democratic procedures becomes a matter both of changing the context within which decisions are taken and of influencing or reorientating the motives of participants so that they become more socially conscious.

The systemic features which frustrate the emergence of social outcomes and attitudes are associated with capitalism. Capitalism, argues Tawney, is 'a system which stunts personality and corrupts human relations by permitting the use of man by man as an instrument of pecuniary gain'.[4] Market relations, in which the driving force is the motive to acquire wealth, encourage individuals to see their relationships, not as moral relationships between autonomous beings, but as instrumental non-moral relationships to be entered into and conducted for gain. In a society in which the successful acquisition of wealth is the foundation of public esteem, labour is degraded both by its inability to accumulate riches and because workers 'come to be regarded, not as ends for which alone it is worthwhile to produce wealth at all, but as instruments for its acquisition'.[5]

Capitalism is morally corrupt because it depends on motives which lead to a dehumanization of personal relationships. It leads to the adoption of attitudes of mind which encourage individuals to treat each other instrumentally. But the corruption of capitalism runs deeper than this. The moral basis of capitalism is interpreted as resting on a natural-rights philosophy from which issues a defence of private property rights which are unrelated to any common ends. Tawney argues that these rights became 'the ultimate political and social reality; and since they were the ultimate reality, they were not subordinate to other aspects of society, but other aspects of society were subordinate to them.'[6] The effect of this was that 'The currents of social activity did not converge upon common ends, but were dispersed through a multitude of channels, created by the private interests of the individuals who composed society.'[7] Tawney dismisses the standard argument that an 'invisible hand' mechanism transforms the pursuit of private self-interest into the attainment of the public good. He goes on to suggest that this conception of private property rights lies at the heart both of the dehumanization of relationships and the maintenance of grossly unequal power relations. The irony is that 'individualism begins by asserting the right of men to make of their own lives what they can, and ends by condoning the subjection of the majority of men to the few whom good fortune, or special opportunity, or privilege have enabled most successfully to use their rights.'[8] This inequality of power is particularly vicious in the way that it unfairly denies some individuals access to the conditions required to live a free, worthwhile and self-respecting life. It has at least two further consequences. First, it sustains circumstances in which labour is seen as a commodity to be manipulated. This is malicious 'because it classifies human beings as a part, and a subordinate part, of the mechanism of production, instead of treating that mechanism merely as an auxiliary of the labour of human beings.'[9] The interests of labour, as something more than a factor of production, are not protected within the authoritarian relationships of industry. Secondly, the democratic credentials of representative political institutions are damaged as capitalists are able to translate economic into political power. It follows, therefore, that, for Tawney, private property in capital constitutes a central obstacle to the development of a social society. This conclusion is only reinforced by the recognition that private property encourages a sense that individuals are owners of rights with no responsibility to the wider society for the way in which they behave, beyond respecting the rights of others.

Tawney puts forward an alternative conception of society, one which holds out the possibility of achieving a genuinely social democracy.

The socialist society . . . is not a herd of tame, well-nourished animals, with wise keepers in command. It is a community of responsible men and women working without fear in comradeship for common ends, all of whom can grow to their full nature, develop to the utmost limit the varying capabilities with which nature has endowed them, and – since virtue should not be too austere – have their fling when they feel like it.[10]

The development of this society depends critically on the eradication of a capitalism which is incompatible with a social and/or a democratic society. In its place needs to be established a society united in the pursuit of common ends.

The establishment of a set of public purposes or common ends is of central importance in Tawney's theory. It is these common ends which serve as the basis of co-operation. Individuals acting jointly to realize them are united behind a common objective, and this is the seed out of which fraternal sentiments can grow. They are important in another respect also. The legitimacy of individual claims or rights is to be defined relative to the function they have in contributing to the realization of these common objectives. One of the fundamental flaws of capitalism, Tawney argues, is that rights are claimed and acted on without thought of social purposes. Tawney might well have wanted to argue that talk of rights, where these are unrelated to any common purpose, is a kind of moral 'nonsense on stilts'. In removing rights of this kind and substituting, in their place, 'functional' rights, Tawney removes one barrier to the development of a social society.

Much depends, therefore, on the existence of a set of public purposes, relative to which rights may be defined, and behind which individuals may unite. Tawney seems to have taken it more or less for granted that such ends exist. It is assumed that once the absurdity and immorality of natural rights or capitalist ideology is revealed, its hold will be broken. All men of goodwill would naturally agree that certain ends were ends that they held in common. As a result the functions of particular institutions could be inferred without controversy. Thus, for example, Tawney asks, 'What is the function of industry?' And, in answering his own question, argues that its function is similar to that of the professions, namely providing a service. The rights, duties and responsibilities of the institution, and the individuals within it, follow inexorably from this statement of function. It does not appear to have occurred to Tawney to consider the possibility that the development of a consensus on this question might be prevented either by deep-seated conflict over the very nature of this function or by disagreement over the choice of ways to realise it. Tawney was far too optimistic in his assessment of the likelihood of a consensus on common ends existing. He may be justifiably criticized for underrating the importance and persistence of deep-seated moral conflict between people with sincerely and reflectively held views.

Tawney's account of the existence of common ends is imprecise and poorly defended. Nevertheless it is of central importance to the overall theory. Of equal importance is democracy. Democratic mechanisms stand in a significant relationship to the set of public purposes. Tawney seems to believe that democracy is the only method of engaging individual commitment to public purposes and of ensuring that power or authority is used for the public good. In part this seems to be just the employment of the most efficient mechanism (i.e., democracy,) through which active involvement can be encouraged. This argument is similar, in other words, to the argument that worker productivity can be increased by extending opportunities for participation to the shop-floor. The argument is more than just an instrumental one, however. It draws also on the arguments of J.S. Mill amongst others, who have suggested that opportunities for democratic participation can be morally creative. Participating in decision-making can lead to a reorientation of motivation as individuals are encouraged to accept responsibility for the decisions of the collectivity. Self-regarding may be replaced by other-regarding behaviour, and democracy may act as a form of political education capable of schooling people, through discussion and persuasion, into adopting socially responsible attitudes. Of course it will be successful in this respect only if the environment is conducive to it. And this means the eradication of those institutions and relationships which help sustain the selfish pursuit of private interests, namely natural rights, capitalism and inequality of power.

Democracy fulfils, therefore, two functions for Tawney. First, it provides a mechanism through which common ends may be articulated. It appears that democracy is a mechanism for discovering what the common ends of men in society are, rather than a device for creating them. (It is perhaps Tawney's belief that decent men, released from the moral and psychological fetters of capitalism, would be able to articulate statements of common purposes, that accounts for Tawney's own vagueness in their definition.) Secondly, it is an integral part of the process through which individuals develop the qualities (for example, public-spiritedness) which explain why they are willing to adopt those purposes, as if they were their own, and act in ways designed to realise them.

Tawney clearly believes that democracy is conducive to the fulfilment of these functions. He may even believe that it is necessary to them. Nevertheless, he does not abandon what remains an essentially procedural view of democracy, and his defence of it rests on his claims that it is instrumental to the realization of certain values. Tawney accepts that democratic mechanisms and the machinery involved in implementing decisions are neutral with respect to possible outcomes. For example, in his discussion of the state he points out that 'The State is an important instrument; hence the struggle to control it. But it is an instrument, and nothing more. Fools will use it, when they can, for foolish ends, criminals for criminal ends. Sensible and decent men will use it for ends which are sensible and decent'.[11] It follows that, if individuals are committed to social purposes, and if decisions are made democratically, then social purposes can and will be achieved.

As I have outlined it, Tawney's theory involves a number of important elements. The first is a critique of capitalism drawing attention to its effect on the character of human relationships. One strand of this critique involves the belief that capitalism is associated with a highly unequal set of power relationships which allow the few to dominate the many. These power relationships are thought of as an intrinsic part of a society in which individuals are subject to the arbitrary play of economic forces. A redistribution of power becomes, therefore, one part of a transformation of society into one in which individuals would dominate society rather than be dominated by it. 'The extension of democratic principles into spheres of life which previously escaped their influence'[12] is to be one part of that redistribution of power. In the absence of an 'invisible hand' mechanism to guarantee that individual interaction would produce socially acceptable outcomes, deliberate organization becomes necessary. This organization has to be democratic if only to prevent planners abusing their power. For Tawney the combination of a redistribution of power and democratic control is a precondition for establishing a socially desirable society.

As I have suggested, this is not sufficient, however, because democracy needs to be complemented by the existence of a set of public purposes, the co-operative pursuit of which acts as the foundation of the development of a sense of community. And it is this sense of community which, through its influence on individual motives and objectives, feeds back into the democratic process, in a way which protects the social acceptability of the decisions made.

Tawney's account of the problems confronting the establishment of a more social democracy was developed during the inter-war period and appeared well-suited to the circumstances of the time. By the 1950s, however, it began to appear to some writers, including C.A.R. Crosland,[13] that Tawney and other traditional socialists had been mistaken in their analysis of the circumstances inhibiting the development of a social democracy. In particular, it was alleged, they had overrated the importance of ownership as the key to the maintenance of an inequality of economic power, and underrated the importance of political democracy in undermining that inequality.

For Crosland, the establishment of the mass franchise had set in motion a process characterized by Evan Durbin as 'the democratic repudiation of capitalism',[14] the upshot of which was that representative political institutions had given 'the people enough power to ensure that private industry met public needs'.[15] The 'democratic repudiation of capitalism' worked in both direct and indirect ways. Direct repudiations include the establishment of social services to guarantee the satisfaction of certain basic needs and the attempt to establish the social control of business by direct interventions in the name of the public interest. Indirect repudiations included the granting of legal immunities to trade unions and the effect of an increased range of social services, both of which increased the bargaining power of trade unions. One other important change in the area of economic policy should be noted. This was that the Keynesian revolution held out the prospect of maintaining full employment through the manipulation of economic forces, thereby seemingly dissolving the stark choice between either uncoordinated capitalism or a centrally planned non-market command economy.

The importance of these changes to the revisionist social democrats should not be underestimated. Jointly they meant that many of the socially unacceptable consequences of inter-war capitalism could be overcome in a society which maintained private ownership in capital. Crosland believed that the availability of full employment, plus the capacity of a democratic electorate to hold governments responsible for their policies, constituted a major break with the circumstances of pre-war society. In 1956 Crosland wrote 'It is significant that the feature of post-war society which, for electoral reasons, is the least vulnerable to political reaction, namely full employment, is also one of the most decisive for the underlying balance of power . . . [I]t constitutes a basic cause of the shift of economic power away from the business class.'[16]

Crosland could argue, with some plausibility, that the problem of achieving a more social democracy was radically different than some traditional socialists, including Tawney, had believed. First, the power of capital had been eroded, and with it management's ability to exploit or subjugate labour. The combination of full employment, the welfare state and legal privileges gave trade unions sufficient power to defend the interests of their members. Under the conditions of the fifties it appeared that circumstances existed which ought to be sufficient to guarantee reasonably free and fair contracting between labour and capital. Secondly, economic growth, sustained by full employment, meant that resources were readily available to devote to social purposes, whether it be guaranteeing the satisfaction of certain basic needs or expanding the range of leisure opportunities. Thirdly, resources were available for redistributive purposes, in order to increase the effective range of alternatives facing individuals otherwise excluded from many of the benefits of modern society, and so on.

Crosland could claim to share many of the social concerns of a Tawney. He could claim that the most important differences of approach lay not in the ends to be produced, but in the assessment of the preconditions for realizing them. In these terms Crosland's theory represented a major change in the structure of social democratic theory. In particular, it rejected the claim that social outcomes needed to be deliberately sought through conscious democratic action. Instead socially acceptable outcomes would, for the most part, be generated automatically by individuals, each possessed of sufficient purchasing power to meet their needs, pursuing their self-interest in an economic environment influenced by government. Crosland's social democratic theory had returned to the assertion of what Tawney had characterized as the 'infallibility of the alchemy by which the pursuit of private ends is transmuted into the attainment of the public good'.[17] As a result he gave up the claim that a deliberate and intentional orientation to the public good was a prerequisite for its attainment, together with the argument that an extension of democratic methods of decision-making into new areas was a precondition of enlisting the requisite public-spiritedness. In its place he substituted the view that in the new social context of post-war Britain, characterized by highly developed welfare services, full employment and economic growth, self-interested motivation could be relied on to achieve social purposes.

In claiming to be concerned with the same ends as Tawney, Crosland could point to concerns with the damage to the self-respect of individuals produced by poverty or economic insecurity, with enhancing the freedom of individuals by providing or guaranteeing the material conditions which made the exercise of choice effective and realistic, and with the eradication of irresponsible concentrations of power. But these similarities should not obscure the importance of the differences between the two approaches. The new social democracy was simultaneously less 'social' and less 'democratic' than the older version. As I showed above, Tawney regarded the extension of democracy as a precondition of the achievement of social purposes, provided that individuals brought genuinely social attitudes to democracy. Social outcomes were to be achieved by their deliberate and conscious pursuit, and the fact that they were to be pursued deliberately underlay the rehumanization of personal relationships, as individuals were encouraged to see each other in non-instrumental terms. Democracy, for Tawney, was one essential prerequisite of this qualitative transformation of relationships, because he thought that the only way to consider and protect the dignity of individuals affected by decisions was through their participation in decision-making. Tawney believed that social outcomes required social motivation and these needed to be channelled through explicitly democratic modes of decision-making. A sense of commitment to community purposes was to be both the ground for and the object of the extension of democracy. Democracy was perceived as a necessary condition for making the facts of engagement in a co-operative enterprise a living reality.

At issue between these two approaches to the problem of achieving a more social democracy is a critical question. This concerns the extent to which the realization of valued outcomes requires deliberate, collective action. Some approaches, which stress the importance of 'invisible hand' mechanisms, suggest that acceptable outcomes can be produced by letting things work out on their own. For example, certain values may be achieved, protected, or exemplified by private action pursued for private reasons, constrained only by the prohibitions of certain universal rules. If outcomes fall short of what is desired, then some modification of the ground rules, or adjustment of actors' starting positions may nudge things in the right direction. Now, in part, the difference between Tawney and Crosland reflects different empirical judgements of the likelihood of acceptable 'invisible hands' existing and working. And this difference in turn reflects their differing judgements regarding the functioning of the economic and social system. But more than just this is at stake. With certain values, it is difficult to see, even in principle, how they could be realized through a concatenation of individual actions each pursued for private reasons. Some values cannot be protected by sleight of hand, but rather require a collective intention to bring them about. In these cases it makes no sense to think of things working out; one must think of them being brought about. In this context one may think of those values which express or are dependent on a sense of community, or those which seek to combine or relate a series of independent values into a set of public purposes. The difference between Tawney and Crosland appears to be that Crosland is more confident that valued states of affairs can be established through 'invisible hand' mechanisms and less prone to stress the importance of those values which can not.

In coming to a judgement about the possibilities of returning the social to democracy, it is important to decide whether the account of the social upon which one is relying is closer to Tawney's than Crosland's. At this point I assert, though I cannot argue it here, that, in some important respects, Tawney is more nearly right than Crosland. Crosland believed that, in the economic and social context of post-war Britain, it was possible to achieve social outcomes without having to appeal to the public-spirited commitment of citizens.[18] The decline in rates of economic growth and the return of mass unemployment suggest that, even on its own terms, Crosland's account no longer has application. Tawney may well have been right that public-spiritedness, a commitment to public purposes rooted in a sense of community membership, is a precondition of achieving a wider range of socially acceptable outcomes than Crosland admits. Perhaps a wide range of social outcomes needs to be actively, intentionally and collectively pursued.

Underlying these remarks is the suggestion that purely self-interested motivation, however constrained by a system of universal rules, is corrosive of a socially acceptable society. By the same token, a commitment to the community revealed in action is necessary to a social society. What this involves is a recognition of one's responsibility as a member of the community, based on a recognition of mutual interdependence. What this means is that individuals should not be prepared to insist on practices which benefit them, or bargain for advantages, to the full extent of their bargaining power. They should be prepared to recognize the moral claims of others, including, for example, those who are weak and would be seriously disadvantaged by a generalized free-for-all. In other words, in coming to discuss the collective arrangements of a society, particularly those which affect the distribution of opportunities and conditions of life, it would be necessary that individuals recognize themselves to be, first and foremost, members of the community. It is only if they are prepared to negotiate with each other, starting from this premise, that a prospect for establishing a genuinely social society exists.

What is being suggested here is that claims inherent in being a member of a community need to become active considerations in deliberations concerning the collective arrangements of a society. We need to be able to use the facts and responsibilities of community membership as reasons explaining and justifying mutual obligations in a society. The role that democracy can play here is, indeed, an important one. It does seem possible that democracy could play an educative role, by providing a forum in which the implications of community membership can be considered. It may play a further role, however. Tawney may well have over-simplified the problem by assuming that a set of common purposes existed and were waiting to be discovered through democratic mechanisms. There may be no set of public purposes waiting to be discovered. If they exist at all they may have to be actively created. It may be nearer the truth to say that, if there is no publicly endorsed set of common purposes, then the values the society realizes and the trade-offs between them will be determined more by power and luck than moral reasoning. If a society wishes to avoid this it needs to create a statement of a set of public purposes, adopted by this community because it is this kind of community (and not another kind).There seems no alternative to creating what amounts to a collective act of self-definition, through democratic processes. But note, this process could work only if individuals approach this kind of 'constitutional convention' with an awareness that they do so with a commitment to their status as a community member or if they are led to adopt this attitude through their engagement in democracy.

My remarks, in this final section, have been necessarily elliptical and a full defence of them would require considerable elaboration, which I can not offer here. What I have tried to suggest, however, is that the establishment of a genuinely social democracy requires an active sense of community member-ship. Part of this sense involves the deliberate adoption of community purposes and public-spirited action to bring them about. Democracy is a potential mechanism through which they may be created, and a device capable of generating among citizens an active commitment to them. But as the first part of this essay argued, the relationship between democratic procedures and socially acceptable outcomes is not clear-cut. As a result the problem of establishing a more social democracy involves not just making society more democratic, it involves also making democracy more social. Any optimism about the future prospects of achieving these goals must be guarded, because it is not obvious that we know enough about the springs of anti-social behaviour to know under what conditions adequately social behaviour would be freely forthcoming. Equally, however, it may be a mistake, and even self-defeating, to be too pessimistic about the future. After all the history of the world does display some moral progress, and why should this not continue in the future?

15

Bureaucracy and democracy

DENNIS F. THOMPSON

Democracy does not suffer bureaucracy gladly. Many of the values we associate with democracy – equality, participation and individuality – stand sharply opposed to the hierarchy, specialization and impersonality we ascribe to modern bureaucracy. Yet for a long time political theorists did not see bureaucracy as a threat to democracy, and, I shall argue, democratic theorists still have not formulated a satisfactory response to the challenge bureaucratic power poses to democratic government.

One response to this challenge denies bureaucracy any place at all in a genuine democracy. Theorists who take this approach usually realize that they must show that bureaucracy does not inevitably appear in every modern society, but only in those societies they consider nondemocratic. Thus, nineteenth-century writers often referred to bureaucracy as the 'Continental nuisance,' from which English democracy was immune.[1] Marx and other socialist writers agreed that France and Germany had the most highly developed bureaucracies, but they insisted that, as merely one manifestation of the bourgeois state, bureaucracy would disappear with the capitalism that gave rise to that state.[2] Yet socialist societies (admittedly not yet the democracies Marx had in mind) turned out to be more bureaucratic than the governments they replaced. Similarly, the belief that bureaucracy inheres in only socialist government could hardly be sustained once capitalist societies created the administrative structures necessary to maintain their large welfare states.

Still, from time to time, voices on both the left and the right revive the hope that bureaucracy might be abolished. Many have called for decentralization to eradicate bureaucracy. But smaller political jurisdictions develop petty bureaucracies of their own that usually are no more responsive than those of larger states. Other writers (and many politicians) insist that bureaucracy could be reduced if government simply did less. But even if government could do less, administrative power would simply shift to private bureaucracies, which may be more efficient but are hardly any more accessible to citizens.

No one has yet shown that the quality of life that citizens in modern democracies demand can be sustained without bureaucracy, or a form of organization very much like it. Weber's prognosis – that the further advance of bureaucracy is inevitable – has stood the test of time.³ Rather than confining itself to certain kinds of societies, bureaucracy has become ubiquitous. Our century has witnessed 'the bureaucratization of the world'.⁴

The other response to the conflict between democracy and bureaucracy – and the one on which I concentrate in this essay – assumes, with Weber, that bureaucracy is here to stay. The 'great question,' Weber wrote, is 'what we can set against this mechanization to preserve a section of humanity from . . . this complete ascendancy of the bureaucratic ideal of life?'⁵ Those who take this approach seek in various ways to tame bureaucracy through democratic controls. That these controls have proved insufficient has often been noticed.⁶ But that this failure in the practice of democratic control might indicate the inadequacy of its theory has not been so often considered. I shall examine four models according to which theorists suppose that bureaucrats may be held responsible in a democracy. None of these models of administrative responsibility provides a proper place for bureaucracy in a democracy, I shall argue, because each misconceives or misapplies the idea of democratic responsibility. I shall also suggest that one of the models – one that stresses citizen participation – is less deficient than the others.

Democratic responsibility refers both to a process of deliberation (giving reasons for policies of government) and to a process of accountability (identifying the agents of those policies, and punishing or rewarding them). An adequate concept of democratic responsibility must include a wide range of reasons that officials may give for their decisions. It should not, for example, limit deliberation to only technical issues, but should promote discussion of the values underlying the policies officials pursue. An adequate concept must also provide a basis for identifying which officials actually make specific policies. The model should not, for example, confine accountability to formal lines of authority, but should call for identification of officials who actually influence particular decisions. The problem of responsibility is of course only one of the many problems that bureaucracy poses for democracy, but, as I hope will become clear, it is a fundamental one.

The first and still most influential idea of administrative responsibility – what I shall call the hierarchical model – arose at a time when the power of bureaucracy seemed negligible. Even as the scope of government grew and bureaucracies burgeoned, theorists could presume that administrators posed no threat to political leaders. They understood the role of bureaucrats much as Hobbes had explained the role of public ministers: they resemble 'the nerves and tendons that move the several limbs of a body natural'.⁷ Because nerves and tendons of the body politic do not initiate anything on their own, political theory could safely ignore them. 'Of the ministerial and subordinate powers,' Locke comments, 'we need not speak' because they are all accountable to some other power in the commonwealth.[8] While the nerves and tendons might from time to time twitch on their own, none would show political will of its own. When democratic theorists later began to speak seriously of administration, they worried that politicians might constrain bureaucrats too much, not that bureaucrats would ever challenge their 'political masters'.[9]

It was Max Weber who turned the Hobbesian metaphor into a systematic theory of bureaucracy.[10] The hierarchical model that appears in his theory states, first, that administration follows 'fixed jurisdictional areas' and 'office hierarchy' in which there is 'a supervision of lower offices by the higher ones'. Secondly, it sharply distinguishes between administration and politics: administrators merely execute the policies set by politicians. Finally, the administrator and politician are subject to exactly the opposite principle of responsibility. The 'honor of the civil servant' consists in his executing the orders of his superiors, unlike the politician who must take 'personal responsibility' for his decisions. Although the model originally referred to a parliamentary form of government, it is compatible with a presidential form (and also with proposals for more presidential control or for more congressional control).

Empirical studies of modern bureaucracies present a picture of policymaking that departs drastically from the hierarchical model. In place of well defined jurisdictions and settled lines of authority, we find overlapping 'issue networks', with decisionmakers drawn from various agencies and various levels of government (and often also from outside government).[11] Instead of a clear distinction between politics and administration, we see bureaucrats exercising great discretion in defining the goals of policies, and bargaining with one another, politicians and citizens to win acceptance of these goals.[12] This discretion goes well beyond the traditional role of filling in the 'details' or the 'gaps' in legislation. It often involves mobilizing public support for or opposition to programs, determining priorities, choosing among possible beneficiaries, and evaluating the success or failure of programs.[13] Instead of standing at the end of the hierarchical chain, bureaucrats initiate a process in which they encourage citizens to ask their elected representatives to make certain policies, which bureaucrats then implement and finally assess.

Elected officials can, and do, review some of this political activity, especially controversial issues, but much of the public policy of the modern state results from the cumulative effect of many small, barely noticable decisions that middle- and low-level officials make.[14] It is true that bureaucratic decisions frequently anticipate what legislators want, but this is a distortion of the hierarchical model. Bureaucrats are responding neither to instructions of their superiors nor to the will of the legislature, but to the political clout of certain influential legislators, or members of their staffs.[15]

The discrepancies between the hierarchical model and actual bureaucratic behavior have been most clearly documented in American government but they appear in other industrial democracies too.[16] This is so even in Britain, where in the form of the doctrine of ministerial responsibility the model has probably come closer to realization than anywhere else.[17] As the size and complexity of administration have grown, so have the influence and the independence of British civil servants; it is estimated, for example, that only about two percent of all delegated rules are ever examined.[18] Few ministers hold a particular portfolio long enough to learn enough to master their departments. Neither are the lines of jurisdiction as clear as they once were. Civil servants formulate many policies and settle disputes as much in consultation with groups outside government as with other officials inside government.

That modern bureaucracies do not follow the hierarchical model as many democratic theorists hope, need not entail that we abandon the model as a normative standard or ideal. Weber himself recognized that bureaucrats could very well act independently, and were already beginning to dominate elected officials.[19] But this development discouraged neither him, nor a succession of other theorists, from insisting on the hierarchical model as the standard for judging the place of bureaucracy in a democracy.[20] In the most recent case for a return to the hierarchical model, Theodore Lowi proposes a package of reforms that would move American government toward what he calls juridical democracy – no delegation of legislative power without clear standards, more formal and explicit administrative rules, legal codification, and sunset laws.[21] Juridical democracy could promote democratic deliberation by discouraging the cosy clientelism that develops when bureaucrats deal mainly with the businessmen they are assigned to regulate, or even with the beneficiaries of the programs they are supposed to administer. It could also enhance democratic accountability, Lowi implies, by pushing political disputes to the highest levels of responsibility and thus subjecting them to greater public scrutiny.

Should the hierarchical model ever be realized, it may offer democracy these and other benefits. It may also create problems of its own. Even in the best circumstances in a complex society, the whole legislature or even its committees and subcommittees can hardly be expected to formulate all the specific provisions of law and oversee their execution. Much of this business would almost certainly fall to the staffs of legislative committees, those usually anonymous but already influential actors in legislative politics (particularly in the American Congress). The hierarchical model in this way could very well abolish administrative independence in the executive only to see it rise again in a legislative bureaucracy. As the experience of the growing power of legislative staffs suggests, the creation of a legislative bureaucracy would not represent an advance in democratic deliberation or accountability.

But the most pressing objection against the model turns not on the desirability of the system it proposes, but on the desirability of the process of change it encourages in present systems. That current practice departs from the model casts doubt on the use of the model, even as an ideal, to direct change in modern democracies. We should distinguish between the use of a model to recommend a state of affairs in the future, and its use to advocate criticism and reform under current conditions. A model that defines a perfectly acceptable ideal may not be the best guide to political practice under nonideal conditions. It may cause criticisms to miss their target, and it may urge reforms that though they approximate the ideal make the present system worse. Such consequences follow for democratic responsibility, I suggest, when we use the hierarchical model in conditions where it falls so far short of being realized.

Although the hierarchical model does not adequately represent bureaucratic practice in most democracies, it does shape political deliberation about administration. Its most general effect is to turn moral and political issues into technical and procedural ones. If bureaucrats simply implement the policies set by elected officials, the only serious criticism we can make of bureaucrats is that they fail to carry out their duties efficiently. The most common complaints about bureaucracies in fact center on the consequences of their inefficiency, such as the 'red tape' citizens encounter when they deal with government agencies.[22] Official inquiries also stress questions of efficiency. All of the major studies of the civil service that the British government has conducted since 1850 have concentrated almost wholly on matters of effective management and personnel policy.[23] As governments have turned over more and more economic planning and control to administrators, criticism and reform of this process have increasingly focused on technical questions of budgeting and forecasting. These techniques of course embody moral and political choices, but since bureaucrats are not supposed to make such choices, critics do not challenge the choices; they merely question the techniques.[24]

The hierarchical model also directs attention more to whether bureaucrats follow prescribed procedures than to whether they make proper substantive judgments. When the Special Counsel to the U.S. Energy Department in 1981 gave $4 million of government funds to four national charities, critics focused on the procedural propriety of his action, charging for example that he failed to clear his action with his superiors. The money had come from a government settlement with oil companies that had allegedly overcharged consumers for fuel. The specific consumers could not be identified, and the charities agreed to distribute the money to poor people for their fuel bills. Almost no one addressed the question of the criteria the government should apply in distributing funds of this kind, let alone the larger question of the role of government in the regulation of energy.

Similarly in Britain, the concern for procedure often predominates. Only great reverence for the hierarchical model could account for the preoccupation with the protocol of civil servants that often marks British political deliberation. The Select Committee on Parliamentary Questions in England in 1971 exhaustively examined the question, 'Should Ministers be permitted to ask civil servants to prepare questions for tabling by friendly MPs?' The Committee scarcely discussed the content of the questions, or how such a practice might affect the policies that civil servants formulated.[25]

The hierarchical model, applied under present conditions, also tends to weaken democratic accountability. By locating responsibility at the highest levels of government, the model neglects accountability not only for the many decisions made by lower- and middle-level officials, but also for some of the decisions made by higher-level officials as well. In general, the higher the level of government, the less significant is any particular decision in our overall appraisal of the performance of an official. We may, for example, ignore a President's deplorable position on health policy if we approve of his stand on other issues. But we would be less tolerant of the official whose principal job was to formulate and advocate this policy.

Because the hierarchical model directs our criticism upward and away from many of the actual decisionmakers in government, it encourages a ritualistic taking of responsibility: high officials regularly accept 'full responsibility' for decisions of their subordinates, whether or not the superiors had anything to do with the decisions.[26] This ritual depreciates the democratic value of ascriptions of responsibility since the persons who actually made the decisions escape scrutiny, and the officials who 'take responsibility' often suffer no political punishment (and sometimes may reap political rewards for seeming to be courageous leaders who do not pass the buck). When formal responsibility diverges radically from actual responsibility, even this ritualistic responsibility begins to disappear, but genuine accountability of lower-level officials rarely takes its place. In the Canadian system, for example, the principle that ministers are strictly responsible for the conduct of civil servants is increasingly ignored. But the other part of the doctrine of ministerial responsibility – the principle that ministers should not publicly blame individual civil servants – remains very much in force.[27]

The hierarchical model also discourages – and may even prevent – reforms that would strengthen the influence of citizens over the bureaucrats who actually make decisions and policies. In the absence of an effective hierarchical system, such reforms may be the only hope of establishing any accountability in the administrative process. If we assume, with the hierarchical model, that citizens through their elected representatives hold bureaucrats accountable, then we will discount changes that would bring citizens directly into the administrative process. Indeed, many reforms, such as requiring bureaucrats to consult with citizens or even to publicize their proceedings more extensively, would on the hierarchical model distort the democratic process by permitting particular groups to try to influence policy after the general public interest had already been determined by the legislators and elected executives.

But if we recognize that in any current system, this process is flawed in various ways at almost every stage, we are less likely to rely exclusively on the hierarchical model to ensure the accountability of administrators. The inequalities in the electoral process, the distortions in the legislative process, the diffusion of executive authority – all give ample reason to seek alternatives to the hierarchical model. Other models cannot completely dispense with hierarchy since it is an essential feature of bureaucracy, but they may moderate hierarchy by emphasizing other foundations for responsibility.

A second approach to reconciling bureaucracy and democracy relies on the professionalism of a civil service. This professionalist model first appears in systematic form in Hegel's theory of the state. Detached from the personal ties of family and friendship and educated in 'ethical conduct,' Hegel's civil servants express the universal interest of the state.[28] Although embracing very different conceptions of the general good, many democratic theorists adopt some form of the professionalist model to locate the proper place of administrators in a democracy.[29] Proponents of the model hold, first, that a substantial amount of administrative discretion is inevitable in the modern state; secondly, that this discretion is also desirable if bureaucrats exercise it according to the principles of their profession; and thirdly, that in order to enforce these principles, administrators should have professional education and be responsive to the professional opinion of their colleagues. This model may be compatible with the hierarchical model – some theorists explicitly combine them – but those who stress professionalism must grant administrators considerable independence from their political superiors. The professionalist model therefore must find its democratic legitimacy not only or mainly in the hierarchical chain leading back to the electorate, but in the content of the norms establishing the claims to expertise of the profession.

Whether professionalism encourages democratic deliberation, then, depends in part on what kind of expertise or special competence we attribute to the profession of public administration. If, as in some interpretations of the model, the expertise consists in a kind of technical knowledge, such as policy analysis, the model tends to insulate bureaucrats from substantive moral and political criticism in the same way that the hierarchical model does. The techniques of policy analysis, like the methods of utilitarianism and welfare economics from which they originate, are hardly morally and politically neutral.[30] In so far as policy analysts persuade politicians and citizens to accept their conclusions as completely objective, they use their professional standing to conceal the moral and political choices inherent in their methods of analysis. They thereby stifle the process of deliberation about these choices in a wider public forum.

More recently, however, administrators and politicians have begun to dispute about the use of the technique itself. Analysts who oppose much government regulation of occupational health and safety in the United States insist that every rule be justified by cost–benefit analysis. Their critics argue that such analysis tends to ignore the long-term benefits of regulation.[31] In so far as the method of analysis becomes a point of political contention in this way, administrators and their academic consultants cannot stand aloof from the political fray. A dispute, even among professionals, about the basis of professional expertise may contribute to democratic deliberation. But if it does so, it also exposes the weakness of any interpretation of the professionalist model that rests on technical competence. Such disputes transcend disagreement about technique. They turn on differences about the content of policy, and in resolving these differences technical experts can claim no special authority.

Other versions of the model locate the expertise of the profession in a more general competence – a cultivated ability to apply to public policy the fundamental values of a society. On its face, these interpretations of the model seem more democratic: bureaucrats appeal to values that all citizens share, and therefore engage in deliberation in which all citizens may take part. But we must ask what gives bureaucrats any special standing in this deliberation, as the claim of professionalism would require?

One answer cites the institutional position of bureaucrats: because they hold permanent appointments and are not subject to direct political pressures, they are less likely to act on their political biases and therefore are more likely to formulate and implement policy in an impartial manner. That institutional position overcomes biases of class and ideology – particularly the anti-socialism ascribed to top civil servants in some governments – has often been doubted, most recently in Australian political debates. But even if civil servants do not succumb to such biases, they may use their institutional position to pursue the interests of the profession itself in maintaining and enlarging its influence within government. Many policies in the modern state now affect the employment and compensation of civil servants, and public employee unions increasingly have pressed for pay increases and job protections that the politicians and other citizens deem contrary to the public interest. Also, civil servants may resist governmental reforms that appear to threaten their own influence, particularly on economic policy. Such resistance evidently played a part in Britain in the dispute about the Expenditure Committee's recommendation to return the management functions of the Civil Service Department to the Treasury.[32]

The other response to the question of the special competence of civil servants appeals to professional education. Through a broadened curriculum in schools of public policy, persons destined for careers in government would acquire the sensitivity and skills to shape public policy according to democratic values. This response offers a more promising basis for a professionalism that could be compatible with democracy, but advocates of this approach have barely begun to think about what would constitute the content of such a professional education in social values.[33] It cannot be sufficient for future bureaucrats even to learn how to translate the fundamental values of a society into public policy, since they will often have to choose among values about which citizens fundamentally disagree.

The distinctive form of accountability in the professions is collegial. Individual professionals (in principle) answer to their colleagues through the licensing and disciplinary procedures of professional associations or through the less formal peer review as in the scientific community. This kind of professional accountability is not without problems. Even when effective, it perpetuates a kind of paternalism in the professions that ill serves democracy.[34] Public administration may escape such problems, but only because it is not fully a profession. If public administrators have not agreed upon the standards and established the organizations that would call errant members to account, the professionalist model, applied to bureaucrats, lacks any adequate basis for accountability.

Neither has the search for other forms of accountability been notably successful. Some theorists have urged 'representative bureaucracy', which would recruit and promote public employees so that the ethnic, class and sexual composition of the civil service would approximate that of society as a whole.[35] While a representative bureaucracy might contribute to a more just policy of employment, it is not likely to reconcile professionalism and democracy. The social and ethnic origins of bureaucrats evidently affect very little the decisions and policies they make. Whatever their background, most civil servants quickly adapt to the expectations of their office and the prevailing culture of the bureaucracy.

More recently, other theorists have attempted to democratize the profession of public administration more directly. This 'new public administration' bids bureaucrats to serve the interests of the disadvantaged members of society.[36] This role will usually put administrators in confrontation with elected officials, who speak for majorities and privileged minorities in society.

The new public administrators are to be 'strong on personal commitment to justice for the poor, rather than on hierarchical obedience and professional neutralism.'[37] This new breed of bureaucrat may (or may not) strike us as a more virtuous public servant, but the new public administration offers no reason to suppose that its practitioners would be any more democratic than the old-style administrators. In face of the inevitable and legitimate disagreements about what justice requires in any policy, the new bureaucrats can look only to their own moral sense and that of their like-minded colleagues. Without abandoning their professionalism, they cannot permit other citizens – not even the poor themselves – to dictate the moral content of their decisions.

Despite its radical tone, the new public administration solves the problem of democratic accountability no better than the other versions of the professionalist model. The idea of a profession – whatever particular content we give it – implies exclusion and self-regulation that do not comport well with control by those who are not members of the profession. We may soften this tension in various ways, as proponents of the professionalist model do, but in so far as we do so, we supplant the model with other forms of democratic responsibility.

The remaining models I examine prescribe that citizens take part in the administrative process, but they conceive this participation in quite different ways. What I shall call the pluralist model would provide opportunities ('multiple points of access') for individuals and groups to petition, advise and in other ways influence administrative agencies.[38] Bureaucrats would then aggregate the claims of the individuals and groups who happen to take advantage of these opportunities. The other model – which may more justly claim the title of participatory – would expand the opportunities for participation by citizens whose voices the political process otherwise neglects.[39] On this view, bureaucrats would not simply adjudicate among contending groups who appear before them, but would encourage other groups and individuals to come forward. Bureaucrats themselves would bear some responsibility for making participation more egalitarian.

Traditional democratic theorists – even those who favor greater participation in other spheres of political life – have generally opposed any active involvement of citizens in the administration of government. Rousseau forbids citizens to take part in the making of executive decisions, which require judgments about particular individuals and would therefore corrupt the universality of the general will.[40] Similarly, Mill fears that partiality and incompetence result if private citizens have much to do with administration; he also cautions that responsibility becomes diffused when many people are charged with making executive decisions.[41] These warnings anticipate in a general way the major problems that both the pluralist and the participatory models have encountered in recent times (though the pluralist approach, I shall suggest, seems less capable of overcoming them).

The pluralist model comes closer to describing the pattern of administrative politics that prevails in modern democracies. By far the most active participants in national administration in recent years are interest groups, chiefly composed not of ordinary citizens but of highly-organized elites who represent various (predominantly economic) sectors of society.[42] These groups influence administrators in a variety of ways – ranging from informal personal contacts and exchanges of information to legally required consultation as in the *remiss* system in the Scandinavian governments or the group representation on official advisory boards of ministries in Germany. In some countries (for example, the Netherlands) interest groups actually administer much of the complex system of economic regulation of industry. Because the interactions between administrators and these groups are so intimate, and their joint decisions so independent of electoral and legislative control, administrators – ensconced in 'captive agencies' – often serve only the interests of the dominant groups in the society.

This kind of politics, it has often been observed, creates many problems for democracy; my concern is with the less noticed difficulties it presents for a democratic concept of administrative responsibility. The pluralist model, applied in current systems, focuses political deliberation on how well bureaucrats manage to aggregate the various demands that interest groups put forward. It permits bureaucrats to justify their decisions by claiming that they are merely arbitrating among groups, not making policy. When bureaucrats cannot maintain the pose of neutral arbiter, they may claim that they can take account of only those interests expressed by groups that actually participate in administrative proceedings. In either case, we do not ask them to justify why they choose to listen to only those groups, or why they do not attempt to bring other groups into the process. The model does not necessarily assume that all interests in society are represented in this process, but if they are not, administrators are not responsible for compensating for the misrepresentation. Yet, as we have seen, administrators can, and often do, use their discretion to influence what groups come forward and can also contribute to changing the structure of opportunities and incentives for participation. The pluralist model exempts bureaucrats from any praise or blame for using, or failing to use, their discretion in these ways.

The pluralist model also confounds the process of accountability. When bureaucrats and interest groups interact so closely, we may not be able to discover who actually contributed to a particular policy or decision, and to what extent, even when the participants make no effort to conceal their contributions. Moreover, the sheer number and variety of organizations that have a hand in the administrative process frustrate tracing their role in the making of policies. It is doubtful that anyone can accurately identify all of the enormous number of quasi-non-governmental organizations ('quangos') that carry on much governmental business in Britain.[43] Even if we can identify these and other organizations as agents of certain policies, we usually have no way to punish (or reward) them, except in the most flagrant cases. They stand outside government, yet they govern.

More recently, some governments have sought to expand the number and kind of groups that take part in the administrative process.[44] In the United States, some public interest groups now have legal standing before administrative agencies, and may initiate challenges rather than merely respond to decisions. Some agencies pay the expenses of groups that wish to participate in rule-making proceedings. These reforms no doubt mitigate the unfairness in the administrative process, and are for this reason to be welcomed. They also encourage more groups to take part in the process and in this respect tilt the pluralist politics in the direction of the participatory model.

But these reforms remain well within the bounds of the pluralist model, and do not overcome the deficiencies of that model. Bureaucrats still pose as mere adjudicators of the claims of contending groups. They need not take any responsibility for bringing more citizens into the administrative process as the participatory model urges, or even for maintaining a fair balance of representation in the process. Moreover, by multiplying the number and kinds of groups in the process, the reforms may actually further erode accountability. Faced with so many competing groups, bureaucrats can easily play them off one against another, blaming all or any of them for whatever policies are adopted, or – what is more likely – for the stalemates that produce no policy at all.

Proponents of the participatory model go beyond pluralist reforms by seeking to make participation more egalitarian. To pursue this aim, they usually turn their attention to local government because there the structures of power seem more accessible and the patterns of decisionmaking more comprehensible to ordinary citizens. Local bureaucracies that act on behalf of the central government have been the chief targets of reform. Early efforts proceeded fitfully in isolated localities in various countries, but a sustained nation-wide movement began with the passage of the Economic Opportunity Act of 1964 in the United States. The Act called for 'maximum feasible participation' of the poor in the planning and conduct of programs designed to reduce poverty.[45]

The ill-fated War on Poverty has been exhaustively examined by social scientists, who generally agree that the programs the Act created did not have much effect on poverty. But it is by no means certain that the participation mandated by the Act contributed to this failure, as some analysts suggest.

Nor is it clear that the participation itself had little value for citizens, as others charge. The kind and extent of participation varied greatly from city to city, and often when a community action agency threatened to become effective in mobilizing the poor, the established local authorities cut off their funds or reorganized the agencies. In any event, the Act spawned demands for increased citizen participation in many other areas of public life. Since 1964, Congress has required citizen participation in the administration of policies for urban renewal, community development, revenue sharing, flood control and health care, among others.

Even after nearly two decades, the evidence remains inconclusive, and both those who oppose and those who favor the participatory model can find support for their views. Its critics contend that these reforms brought into the political process not the poor and alienated but the mostly middle-class and politically sophisticated. Although representation of minorities (especially blacks) increased, the reforms simply added another group to the competition among elites. The participatory model would thus revert to the pluralist model, giving administrators yet another reason to conceive of their role as neutral arbiters: how can administrators dare speak for the poor when the poor now have their own spokesmen? Furthermore, since the jurisdiction of the representative bodies strictly follows the boundaries of policy areas, political deliberation disregards such important questions as the priorities among policies in the various areas.

Proponents of the participatory model could reply that the addition of new elites, especially from groups that previously did not take part, has at the least increased the attention that administrators and citizens give to the question of who participates. The issue of racial representation has won a more prominent place on the agenda of administrative politics, and administrative structures are now more often examined for their effects on the political power of various other disadvantaged groups. It is true that most of the new participatory boards, councils and the like tend to specialize in particular policy areas. But the participatory model itself does not require such specialization. It is possible to imagine a system of participatory bodies, structured so that at each higher level the body would take a more general perspective, progressively integrating more policy areas. The recommendations of the board that oversees the administration of health care, for example, might be reviewed by a board that examines health care in the context of mass transit plans, community development and welfare policy. Such a system could be extended to provide geographical as well as functional coordination, and in principle could be applied at the national as well as the local level. In such elaborate form, this system would put hierarchy back into the participatory model, but it would be a hierarchy of citizens instead of bureaucrats and politicians.

Critics of the participatory model also worry about its effects on accountability. As more citizens take part in administration, they are less likely to be informed and skillful in politics, and more likely to be vulnerable to the blandishments of bureaucrats. In place of the captive agencies of pluralist administration, we find captive citizens, coopted to legitimize decisions that bureaucrats want made. Cooptative participation obscures the identity of the agents of policy, making accountability more difficult. When citizens do manage to control the bureaucrats through the institutions proposed by the participatory model, they usually act on their own, free from any further requirement to answer to other citizens. The Health Systems Agencies in the United States, and the Health Council System in Scotland, for example, both lack adequate procedures for communicating with constituents, let alone for giving constituents power to influence their representatives on the board.[46]

To avoid cooptative participation, defenders of the participatory model urge that governments provide programs to educate citizens who assume positions on the various boards and councils that control administrators. Some 'participatory experiments' in Sweden, Austria, and the Netherlands suggest that even in science policy, citizen advisory councils can be effective (though controversial) if their members have the benefit of educational programs.[47]

The problem of the accountability of the citizens who serve as representatives could be partly overcome by increasing the publicity about the proceedings in which they take part. The Swedish practice of maintaining written records of administrative deliberations and permitting citizens (including the press) to inspect them at any time could encourage not only bureaucrats but also citizen representatives to be more responsible.[48] The flaws in accountability would not be so troublesome if the citizens who participate in administration did not come disproportionately from certain classes and groups. Most recent reforms favor those citizens who already have the time and interest to participate; for example, in the community action agencies in the poverty program the routine clerical positions were salaried but the more influential policymaking positions were not. While proponents of the participatory model would not, like an Aristotelian democrat, replace administrators with citizens chosen by lot, they would select by lot at least some of the citizens who serve on boards or in other ways participate in administration. Like citizens who take their turn on juries, these citizens would be paid.

The movement toward greater participation in administration has fallen far short of the goals of the participatory model. But the difficulties we have noticed in the participatory reforms are not so much failures of the model as failures to apply the model consistently and comprehensively. Unlike the effects of incompletely applying the hierarchical model, those of the participatory model do not typically worsen the condition of democratic responsibility. The changes the participatory model prescribes usually improve deliberation and accountability, and, when they do not, the model itself provides the basis for criticism and further reform. Unlike the professionalist model, the participatory model does not contain any principles, such as claims to special competence, that may inherently constrain democratic responsibility. And unlike the pluralist model, the participatory model does not relieve bureaucrats of the responsibility to consider the views and encourage the involvement of citizens beyond those who happen to take part in the administrative process at any particular time.

If the participatory model is in these respects superior to the others, it may be the best starting-point from which to continue a search for the place of bureaucracy in a democracy. But the model bristles with problems of its own, and though some may be overcome through further exploration of the ideas and institutions mentioned earlier, others seem more intractable. Perhaps the most troublesome is the accountability of the citizens who participate in the administrative process to the citizens who do not participate.

Even if we were to accept the participatory model, we would need to find a way to combine with it the indispensable features of the other models. We cannot completely do without hierarchy in administration: when the legislative will is clear and proper, bureaucrats should not obstruct it. Moreover, legislators (and elected officials more generally) should have the authority to tell bureaucrats how to organize administrative processes. On a participatory model, legislators would still be the principal architects even of structures that encourage citizens to take part in administration. They would devote more time to making the administrative process more democratic than to eliminating administrative discretion.

Professionalism, too, must have a place in any effective bureaucracy. The participatory model may encourage us to take a more favorable view of rotation of office, and perhaps even political patronage. But we can hardly neglect the need for expertise and political independence in modern government – a need that a professional civil service may not always fulfill but for which it seems essential. The various boards of citizen representatives that the model recommends would not preclude the exercise of considerable discretion by professionals in administration. Many of these boards would stand ready to intervene, but only if administrators consistently reached decisions that citizens deemed wrong. Finally, we should wish to preserve some of the procedures that the pluralist model prescribes, such as representation of public interest groups before administrative agencies. If the participatory model provides a promising approach to the problem of the place of bureaucracy in a democracy, it is at best an incomplete approach.

Apart from its inherent difficulties, the model has so far failed to accommodate adequately the legitimate claims of the other models.

Neither democratic theory nor democratic practice has yet discovered a form of administrative responsibility that would let democrats comfortably consort with bureaucrats in the governing of society. To appreciate the extent of the failure of democracy to come to terms with the problem of bureaucracy is not to show where success might lie. But it is to take a necessary step in the pursuit of democratic ways to subdue bureaucratic power in the modern state.

16

Beginning at the end of democratic theory

HENRY S. KARIEL

. . . curves and arabesques flourishing around a centre of complete emptiness.

Virginia Woolf (1927)

The preceding set of essays – the context of this one – holds a promise for democratic practice at a time when there is good reason for despair. The company of theorists, philosophers, and scholars here assembled shows itself so fully implicated in recapitulating classical positions, in bringing history to bear on analyses, and in taking sober account of the critiques of democracy that the very spirit of their enterprise can serve to dispel our fashionable malaise. Their vitality, their sheer obstinate resolve to keep communicating, certainly deprives of its finality my view that we are at the end of democracy. Clearly some kind of participatory action remains alive, however much its academic end-product, now bound between covers, may be still-born, buried in libraries or remainder warehouses of publishers. In the end, there is still endless talk among contributing authors who have written at least for one another, exchanged their views, and flirted with deadlines, who have been engaged in small-scale maneuvering and politicking in plain view of their equals, all connoisseurs of maneuvers and politics. Surely they demonstrate the possibility of staying on this side of despair, of continuing to give practical expression to the theory of democracy even while they may share Pericles' inarticulate conviction that it has no future. In fact, Pericles' posture would seem to be precisely relevant: his radiant affirmation of the promise of democracy when he knew it ceased to be promising offers a model for persisting in the face of inconsequence. Though dead, Athens' democracy remains alive. In our memory and in our publications we continue to participate in it. Pericles knew, as Eric Voegelin has noted, that 'nothing will remain but the memory of ephemeral brilliance and power . . . [T]here is a wintry anachronism about this consolation with remembrance of actions both glorious and corrupt. And, indeed, if Athens is remembered today it is not because she once ruled the sea.'[1]

It is becoming easier to acknowledge that discussions about sovereign individuals engaged in democratic participation are increasingly unrelated to the underlying forces governing public life in technologically sophisticated parts of the world. Talk about politics – politics itself – emerges as an idle exercise in view of the consensus on the agenda of problems to which government is expected to respond. And here it matters little whether agreement is generated by impersonal forces, imposed by elites attuned to technology and in control of the media, or expressed by reasonably free electorates. What is critical is the pervasiveness of the prevailing settlement, the virtually global consensus on the need to reverse population growth, narrow the gap between the developed and the underdeveloped world, stop the pollution of the environment, arrest the depletion of energy sources, reduce the poverty and unemployment of vast sectors of the population, halt the arms race, and, in so far as there is resistance to these objectives, suppress those who dissent. The only question about these fundamental objectives has become one of techniques, and these are for the specialists – the authorities – in problem-solving. In the United States, as Sheldon Wolin has recently observed, the Reagan administration merely gives explicit expression to the dominance of apolitical processes which are becoming characteristic of modern government generally:

Stated briefly, there has been an evolution . . . to something like a state system. A state exists when power and authority are centralized; when their scope and application are, in principle and for the most part, unlimited except for procedural requirements; and when the basic tendency is toward the integration of the various branches of government . . .

If we bear these tendencies in mind . . . the apathetic electorate ceases to be an anomaly and appears, instead, as a necessary condition for the legitimation of the state whose effectiveness would be impaired if the electorate were to be seized by an extended fit of participatory zeal. The state needs taxpayers and soldiers, not active citizens. It requires occasional citizens in order to lend plausibility to the fiction that the state is based upon democratic consent and that its actions are therefore legitimate. But in a world of nuclear weapons, a rapidly changing international economy, and uncertain power relations throughout the world, the state must be free in order to act quickly and rationally. The unspoken assumption of its leaders is that it neither needs nor can it function with the uncertainties and divisions inherent in a democratic politics . . .

The modern state is operated by technicians according to the hierarchical model of administrative management, rather than by equal participants according to a model of deliberation and persuasion . . .[2]

The situations to be transformed without recourse to democratic politics are of course but the surface manifestations of the awesome growth of technology, and it is the emergence of technology as autonomous governor which allows us to witness the erosion of politics and which leads me to reflect on the pathos of those who stay to praise democracy by affectionately analyzing it even while their vague uneasiness teaches them that they are powerless to participate in its rehabilitation. They have no viable prescriptions for moving from the dismal present to the ideal future. They know that the dying patient, too, consents to the technician's ministrations: no ritual, no deliberation, no language is left to mediate between himself and his utterly private end. At most there are those marvelously elaborate formalities which medical technology currently ordains for terminal cases. Perhaps my postulate that technology is pushing activities that are widely regarded as political toward the end of politics may seem less eccentric when reinforced by Robert Heilbroner's relentlessly grim account of the human prospect, Heidegger's stunning if unassimilated exposé of the technological society, Henry Adams' calculation that the exponential growth of explosive would bring the world to an end when he would reach his own, and, going back further, Mary Shelley's myth of Dr Frankenstein's ungovernable creation.

'Politics,' Mircéa Eliade remarked in his journal in 1961,

doesn't interest me because all the problems discussed day after day seem to me to be already resolved. Naturally there are still men who don't know or who don't want to know that the problems of freedom, social justice, economic planning, etc., have been resolved and that their solutions are irreversible. But what sense would it make to devote your energy and your intelligence to convincing them? It's as though, in the eighteenth century, you had struggled for the triumph of heliocentricism because in the seminaries certain priests continued to support geocentricism.[3]

If Eliade's detachment fails to give further plausibility to my sense of fatality, perhaps it can nevertheless serve to provoke a counter-argument, an opposition I should finally like to enlist not because of its merits but because of its vigor, for it is precisely its vigor which testifies to the irrepressible human tendency to defy necessity, to make public appearances however perverse or futile, to participate in public life even when action is devoid of substance.

Participation which fails to issue in end-products, monuments, or great deeds – all those terminal finalities that are associated with heroism in the Western world – seems incoherent and pointless to us. It seems incomprehensible because it lacks all boundaries. Yet however difficult it may be to make it comprehensible, we can begin to identify its character by reflecting on projects which keep incorporating elements external to them in their varying operations, which, sustained by a commitment to a transcendent whole, put all conclusions into doubt. Positing no final purposes, such projects are open to repressed, underprivileged, and taboo subjects, to seeming asides, digressions, and irrelevancies. They display a mode of interpretation – of *action* – which assumes that particular elements of experience become increasingly comprehensible as one keeps enlarging the context in which they can be perceived. In this approach the boundaries drawn around 'individual' or 'state' or around *any* concept cease to be determined by some fixed external standard. Reality having no inherent limits, there can be no real determination of inside and outside, of cause and effect. As new interests continuously participate and jeopardize the claims of old ones, causality fades along with the conventional sense of circumscribed time, orderly sequence, and structured plot. Nietzsche, James, Bergson, Whitehead, Bentley, Dewey – theorists of process – replace Descartes, Bentham, Skinner, and others who have searched for real limits, boundaries, closure, and certainty, for systems which will really secure the line between pleasure and pain as well as good and evil, the line that will maintain established political conventions no less than the vacation home at the edge of the sea.

In a holistic perspective structures of knowledge are seen as a function of a continuous process of participation. What is known empirically or morally emerges as but a changeable side-effect of human transactions. Being a mere by-product of communication, knowledge is an always precarious, un-finished, ever-variable body of the meanings of whatever individuals claim to be going through at the moment. Expressing themselves in the process of living they are creating meanings. Sharing their impressions, they draw the attention of others to experience previously unexpressed because perceived as meaningless, as insignificant, trivial, irrational, or unclean. For them, things cease to be merely alive, merely dead, merely what they have been said to be. Whatever is encountered is always full of further meaning: it intends to be more fully alive, strains to affirm something, and is thereby implicated in the process of communicating within a more com-prehensive context than the reality presumed to exist at any given moment.

Expressing himself – using public space to *give* shape to elements that had not emerged publicly before – an individual is *de facto* a practitioner of social science. As such he creates contexts that necessarily deprive well secured segments of reality of their distinctiveness, of their purported boundaries, discreteness, and specificity. He redefines, de-idealizes, and demystifies established structures, and he allows their content to spill into those contiguous fields he had postulated. Looking at allegedly discrete elements of society from the outside where life remains unsettled and unknown, he gives point to previously uncomprehended realities. Legitimating new, unfamiliar aspects of being, he salvages patterns of behavior which the established culture dismisses as wild, deformed, dirty, ungrammatical, frivolous, brutal, or mystical. That is, he acts precisely like the artist who treats as meaningful those parts of life which dominant intellectual frameworks and dominant political systems exclude from participation. In doing so, he himself emerges as a self-activating agent who always sees himself and others within a context larger than any familiar one. He treats all behavior, including his own, as an expression of the need to break out of identified fields into unidentified ones, and he discloses himself and his world to the extent that he openly remains in an interminable process of deliberate, symbolized interaction. Because he claims knowledge of his world only to the extent that he succeeds in interacting with it, his knowledge – his science – is inherent not in a static body but in a social activity. Moreover, it is one in which everything is implicated, the social scientist no less than his so-called subject-matter. Under his influence, authorities lose control, footnotes become untrustworthy, authors become suspect. Exposed to him, we begin to think of appearance without reality, openness without closure, falsehood without truth, form without content, and finally hope without hope. We take pains to affirm nothing but our disavowals, and keep disavowing this very affirmation. We try to accept not only Kant's proposition that nothing can be shown to connect specific human ideals with some morality 'in the starry heavens above' but also Nietzsche's that the only heaven is the one we have the strength to project.

This commitment is not only a manifestation of the modern temper. Just as artists have again and again subverted inherited perspectives, political theorists have recurrently been ready to deprive conventional concepts of their definitive qualities, of the alleged 'naturalness' of the boundaries which the powerful and their servants have attributed not only to 'consciousness', 'knowledge', or 'environment' but also to such institutions as the school, the hospital, the market, or the single-family dwelling. There is nothing new in enterprises that seek to de-create and de-sublimate, somehow to put prevailing ideals in jeopardy and to clear ground for action. Yet today this ground, as Hannah Arendt noted shortly after the Second World War, possesses an unprecedented quality. It is so radically insecure that the very term 'ground' is misleading. It seems no longer to contribute a reliable basis and source of authority – *any* authority.

Our new difficulty is that we start from a fundamental distrust of everything merely given, a distrust of all laws and prescriptions, moral or social, that are deduced from a given comprehensive universal whole. This difficulty involves the sources of authority of law and questions the ultimate goals of political organizations and communities; it forces us not only to find and devise new laws, but to find and devise their very measure, the yardstick of good and evil, the principle of their source. For man, in the sense of the nature of man, is no longer the measure, despite what the new humanists would have us believe. Politically, this means that before drawing up the constitution of a new body politic, we shall have to create – not merely discover – a new foundation for human community as such.

In historical terms this would mean not the end of history, but its first consciously planned beginning.[4]

Arendt defined the ground which has now been cleared for action as that public arena that Aristotle has reserved for politics. Quoting Aristotle, Arendt identified it as

the space of appearance in the widest sense of the word, the space where I appear to others as others appear to me, where men exist not merely like other living or inanimate things but make their appearance explicitly . . . To be deprived of it means to be deprived of reality, which, humanly and politically speaking, is the same as appearance. To men the reality of the world is guaranteed by the presence of others, by its appearing to all; 'for what appears to all, this we call Being' and whatever lacks this appearance comes and passes away like a dream, intimately and exclusively our own but without reality.[5]

In this formulation, the distinction between Appearance and Being is obliterated. The reality behind appearances only appears to be real for human beings: appearances alone are real. The point of our aspirations is nothing definitive – merely the participation in a process of appearances, expressions, performances, actions.

If our most basic need is to capture ever more ample ground for participation in some common agony, Aristotelian politics, confined as it was to 'citizens', cannot be seen as indubitably fixed by nature. No unchanging category or principle can be assumed to command the exclusion of mystics, fools, jesters, poets, children, barbarians, women, or madmen. Everyone is here to act in time and space cleared of every pre-established social order of niceties, equal justice under the law, or wholesome heterosexual living. Ours is a clearing for the realization of undreamt dreams, there being no God-given rhyme or reason for the lines we draw between good and evil, means and ends, private and public, physician and patient.

To remind ourselves that the institutions which exist in this clearing are human constructions and not ordained by Nature or History or Common Sense, we can put them in quotes, thereby implying that they are only so called. Thus a Justice Department becomes a so-called 'justice department', a Living Room a so-called 'living room', and a Doctor a so-called 'doctor'. More broadly, by putting such terms as 'center' and 'margin' in quotes we can allow that things are only defined as central or marginal. Nothing will remain self-evidently inside or outside. Thus when we redraw lines so as to increase the participation of outside interests, the term 'environment' loses its current meaning. The environment cannot be regarded as something fixed *surrounding* human activities. Instead:

It is their *medium* or *milieu*, in the sense in which a *medium* is *inter*mediate in the execution or carrying *out* of human activities, as well as being the channel *through* which they move and the vehicle *by* which they go on. Narrowing of the medium is the direct source of all unnecessary impoverishment in human living; the only sense in which 'social' is an honorific term is that in which the medium in which human living goes on is one by which human life is enriched.[6]

Adhering to this redefinition of environment by Dewey and Bentley we are kept from assuming that some indubitably real order of things exists and that scrupulously objective observation will surely reveal its real design, laws, causes, decisions. Converting these inert nouns into active verbs – speaking of designing, lawmaking, causing, deciding, designating, informing, and valuing – we enlarge our sphere of action.[7] We become aware of currently prevailing fixtures and fixations – the immense amount of equipment we have for protecting ourselves against the possibility that our lives are meaningless. We can begin to see that structures which at one time effectively worked to enhance our energies have turned into dead truths, dead rituals, dead forms. We can recognize how the flux of experience has been fragmented and how the fragments have become so fixed that we believe in the objectivity and concreteness of conventional dichotomies, whether those of individual and society, man and nature, means and ends, cause and effect, departure and arrival, private and public, or real and unreal. We come to believe each of these fragments is some autonomous whole – fenced in and locked up, secure, privileged, and sacrosanct.

To transform these hardened entities into processes is to allow new forces to emerge in our midst and to begin moving toward the realization of a community which George Kateb, relying on an all too unobtrusive sense of irony, has rightly identified as the aim of a new egalitarian movement:

> The aim is to rehabilitate the idea of citizenship and to extend the practice of citizenship into as many areas of life as possible; from the original locus of citizenship, i.e., public affairs, to private institutions and associations and activities of almost every sort. What is in play is a positive concept of politics, and a corresponding desire to make as many kinds of human relations as possible into political relations. Put negatively, there is a disdain for passivity. There is a repugnance toward being administered, commanded, or manipulated; and not only that, but a repugnance toward being represented. The perversions of 'usual politics' are not the only object of attack: usual politics itself stands under indictment. The spokesmen for participation want, insist on, politics; want it for themselves and for others; seek to extend it as far as it can be extended, until tiredness sets in. But it is politics without hierarchy, procedures, delimited purpose, legalism, practiced compromise, and permanent roles, as well as politics without *frozen* postures, fakery, cheating, arrogance, self-imposition, and rivalry. It is politics as conversation, not speeches, transaction, not battle. Politics at its best defines experience at its best, whether the form of experience be political (strictly speaking) or not.[8]

To sustain such politics – to keep our interest in increased participation from turning once again into an objective that demands a closing of ranks and a limitation of participation – it is imperative to embrace what Kant called 'Zweckmässigkeit ohne Zweck' – purposiveness without purpose.[9] Not only must the forms assumed by participation be kept from fully representing any ideal end but the energy conventionally invested in the pursuit of ideals must continue to flow through one's current activities.

The grip of specific ideals can only be loosened in forums that allow for the elaboration and integration of competing ideals. Within such forums, polar opposites of experience – whether manifestly present or idealized types – can be integrated by a discipline which holds them in a state of suspense. Each of such opposites as male and female may claim to exist fully but, while the claim may be recognized, it can never be fully met, for to meet it would resolve all tension and leave no opposition to integrate. We keep asking what this state of irresolution and tension really is; we search for a theory that will specify its essential nature; we want to idealize. But as Gregory Bateson, William Irvin Thompson, and others have been pointing out, there can be no theory defining such a state, simply because it is forever in process of transformation. Its character always depends on the varying potency of the claims of terminal opposites such as individual versus society, big versus little, clean versus dirty, or intellectual versus emotional. Although there can be no fixed theoretical formulation of an ever-varying state, it is possible to become explicit about the discipline and posture required to sustain it – whether it is a theological system, a mythology, a work of art, a piece of science or scholarship, a person, or a community. It is a discipline manifest in a certain readiness – a readiness to evoke and arouse new interests, to strengthen weak ones and deflect strong ones, to remain an empathic and yet detached participant-observer, to maintain a state of tense irresolution, to refuse to deny or affirm anything conclusively, to give no assent to anything but a posture of irony and whatever forums can be shown to support such a posture.

Yet today the forums in which we feel encouraged to play one set of ideals against another seem scarce or inaccessible. Reality, Nature, and Necessity – all capitalized – are believed to be so overpowering that open space for politics is categorized as a luxury available only to duly 'developed' individuals and communities. It is claimed that the business of getting a living is so demanding that only the few can be permitted to take time out for activities which are inherently rewarding. Moreover, it is generally advertised that the freedom for politics is a kind of residual value: first the necessities of life must be met and then, if time and resources remain, man's need to express and give of himself can be satisfied. Thus men and women are subjected to repressive, demeaning disciplines until the time might be ripe, in Marx's metaphor, for the appearance of the realm of freedom in which man will at last be involved in intrinsically rewarding activities. We commit ourselves to a distant Kingdom of Ends and are led (temporarily, it is always said) to accept the exclusion of interests. We are led to esteem achievements rather than processes. And we accordingly legitimate not only experts in violence trained to move us toward utopia but also licensing agencies, accreditation boards, and professionals skilled in telling us how far we can go.

When we de-authorize agencies empowered to judge potentially participating interests in relation to predefined standards – that is, when we leave open to redefinition what is defined as incompetent, disfigured, irrational, illiterate, or weak – we begin to open the way to increased participation. For some time now, it is true, we have approached the weak at least with compassion and opened the way to their integration. The difficulty is to muster the same openness toward the manifestly competent, privileged, and strong elements in society and in ourselves. We find it difficult to face up to the meanness and hardness of commanding interests, to see and develop their soft shadows, their idle, playful aspects. Yet to increase participation there is no choice but to confront whatever dreadful façades we encounter, to give expression to the death-dealing forces in power, affectionately opening them up, drawing them out, elaborating on them, playing with them. 'Petrified social conditions,' Marx argued, 'must be made to dance by singing their own melody to them.'[10]

The procedure is the one revealed in the judgment-suspending flirtation implicit in the strategy of phenomenological or hermeneutic interaction with a text. It is seen in the nondirective therapy which treats people labelled 'hyperactive' or 'autistic' or 'suicidal', treating them as engaged in symbolic action. It is seen in the anthropology practiced by Jean Duvignaud who reported in *Change at Shebika* (1970) how thoroughly he and a group of his students interacted with Tunisian villagers. It is embodied in Jack Nicholson's act in *One Flew over the Cuckoo's Nest* (1975) – Nicholson seductively engaging an inflexibly benign doctor and a ward of catatonic patients, even if failing to engage a frigid head nurse. It is displayed by the organizers of the Smithsonian Institution's 'Signs of Life: Symbols in the American City,' a memorable exhibit of signs, billboards, and home furnishings that provide a full view of the interiors of three American houses as well as of the artifacts lining 'Route 66', the whole exhibit an exercise in generosity which makes the *most* of suburban sprawl and its plastic artifacts, which embraces these uncritically as expressive of a messy vitality, an unanticipated order.[11]

However attenuated these procedures and however meager these stages, they show possibilities for retrieving and incorporating unnoticed elements of our lives, for animating inert nonparticipants. They include what little happens to be left and celebrate it. Surely such possibilities for inclusion exist in embryonic form in virtually all educational arrangements, families, sports, psychotherapy, literary works, classrooms, artistic ventures, scientific enterprises, and books such as this one – in fact in all practices designed to help individuals disarm and thus enable them to interact with interest in matters which the dominant culture regards as properly excluded, as lost causes, or as untouchable mysteries.

Once we treat familiar settings as ground for enriching the life we live, we gain confidence for expanding them. In the end we may even wonder why we should *ever* settle for anything less than the world at large as self-expressive spectacle, a universal play signifying nothing, an undirected performance open to forms of action which allow us to confront the knowledge of our insignificance. We would then be content to do nothing more abusive than design and exhibit our various masks. We would then treat all forms of behavior as play and recognize what we now call theater to be human life in a concentrated, stylized, self-conscious form – in a form easier to disown than the compulsive routines of undramatized existence. We would then surrender our deadly emblems of authenticity and merely pretend to be authentic, truthful, sincere, honest, scholarly, and truly in touch with ourselves. We would then not mind knowing that nature defined no center for society and no self for us.

Such a posture would surely make it easier to move into those silent spaces where accredited civilization ends. It would allow us to realize that an impending period of incoherence offers opportunities not only for annihilation but also for enlarging the realm of action. A manifestly incoherent future, as Alvin Gouldner has speculated, can provide the ground for precisely that existence which Plato created by choosing the role of playwright for himself. Writing nothing but drama and turning the world into a stage, Plato resolved to ignore the line between theater and life outside. He adopted the kind of dramaturgic perspective which becomes attractive whenever men feel they must somehow bear up without secure foundations. At such times, Gouldner has noted, men gain the freedom to assume responsibility for creating scenes and appearing in public:

As they lose a sense of their place in history, they come to feel themselves moving through a mere succession of situations, each linked to the other by sheer propinquity or by a surface symbolic consistency, rather than inwardly as cause and effect.
   The dramaturgic view of life arises when experience is losing its continuity and is dissolving into episodic shreds, when the larger architecture of experience is crumbling, when the rhythm and movement of life sprawls and lacks organizing centers or familiar punctuations and accents. The dramaturgic view arises when living leaves no sense of residual accomplishment, where each moment is much like the other (for there are no culminations in prospect), and when men are becoming dangerously bored. It is when social theorists do not believe that 'the best is yet to come,' when they lose a sustaining sense of the upward trend, that they devise dramaturgic perspectives on human life and groups. A Plato enters, then, when social theorists come to feel that history has no exit.
   Such dramaturgy has its inner dialectic. On the one side, it insists on the importance of appearances, for it says that appearances are normally all we have and may therefore constrain us to take them seriously. On the other side, the dramaturgic view devalues realms of life that men ordinarily imbue with special value, for it tells us that, like the others, they, too, are no more than appearances. In saying that appearances count and that how things look is important, the dramaturgic view says that life is

serious. Yet it is appearance – a flickering shadow on the wall of the cave – and should not be taken too seriously. This ambivalence about the seriousness with which life may be viewed is expressed quite clearly in Plato: '[H]uman affairs are hardly worth considering in earnest and yet we must be in earnest about them – a sad necessity constrains us.'[12]

A view of life that establishes the whole of reality as aspects of play may well appear to leave us precisely where we are – quite implicated in forms of behavior which, for the life of us, look anything but playful. To the adjusted citizen of developed countries or to the social scientist sustained by the prevalent positivism, Sisyphus no doubt looks as if he is wholly exhausted by his enterprise. To recognize his behavior as also playful would be to rely on an unverifiable act of empathy. What sort of demonstration would suffice to persuade us that people engaged in mundane labor or in making conventional distinctions actually draw on reserves which enable them to go *deliberately* through the normal curves of their days? How can we tell the deliberate, self-conscious participant apart from the mindless individual who has become powerless to direct his will, whose movements are conditioned, who has annihilated his consciousness, who has surrendered to the flow of things? All we appear to have is the naked, wholly unaccredited claim that people who undergo a certain discipline – a complex testing of self that remains unfamiliar to the Western world generally and to the social sciences specifically – are likely to move beyond the currently established nihilism and, once on the other side, able to do and say what they have always done and said, but in a way that continuously reveals their knowledge of the transitoriness of their acts. To believe this, we have only the assurance of stories such as the one told about Ch'ing Yaun who, after thirty years of Zen study, arrived in the undifferentiated continuum of nihilism in which nothing is required and everything is permitted. Prior to his study, he had made conventional distinctions. Evil had been evil and goodness had been goodness. He had seen mountains as mountains and waters as waters. After his course of study, however, he saw that mountains were not mountains and waters not waters. He seems to have passed an intensive introductory course: things were no longer what they seemed to be, if indeed they were anything at all. But instead of remaining caught up in this hard-won nihilism, Ch'ing Yaun studied thirty more years and finally reached the incommunicable heart of Zen where it was all right for anything to be anything. He now had no trouble seeing mountains as mountains and waters as waters. Yet he had not simply returned to the beginning, for he was now attached neither to the labels men give to things in nature nor to an unlabelled nature – only to the poetry and dance that mediates between them.

Homilies such as this one do not, of course, teach us how we can manage to embrace a state of tension. Nor is there much in industrialized societies or respectable academic settings which allows us to appreciate action engaged in for its own sake. We should still like to do some *good*, to change more than the spirit in which we conduct ourselves. Yet if more is impossible – if the major tendencies of the age conspire, as I believe, to block us from transforming reality – we can still commit ourselves to Plato's dramaturgical perspective and the discipline necessary to sustain it. We can rely on a residue of individual and social energy for integrating whatever lies at the edge of known experience. If we have but communication without significant substance, we still do have that: a welter of life-sustaining diversions, of ways of deflecting despair. We can keep journals recording the cries and whispers indicative of the disease of the body politic, ghetto logs that make us attentive until the end. Although we may know that the city is dying and have no cause for assuming that we can manage to come to terms with the deadly forces of technology, it does remain possible to avoid hysteria or paralysis. We can still use what wit we have to engage in enterprises like the one engaging me at this very moment, to keep contributing to a volume which is itself a demonstration of democratic practice, to keep *enacting* the theory of democracy during times that deny this possibility.

Notes

BACKGROUNDS TO THE ARGUMENTS

1 Introduction

I wish to thank the Netherlands Institute for Advanced Study in the Humanities and Social Sciences for awarding me a fellowship which gave me the time to put this collection together.

1 See James O'Connor, *The Fiscal Crisis of the State* (New York, 1973) and *The Corporations and the State* (New York, 1974), and Jürgen Habermas, *Legitimation Crisis* (London, 1976). One problem, from the perspective of these authors, is that the crisis may lie dormant as far as the attitudes of the people are concerned.

2 W. Connolly, *Appearance and Reality in Politics* (Cambridge, 1981), p. 18.

3 As is the case with Connolly. For concrete analysis see especially Ch. 6, 'Personal Identity, Citizenship and the State', and for a more theoretical or abstract discussion, Ch. 1, 'The Politics of Political Explanation'.

4 There were some bold moments, encouraging exaggeration, when the champions of 'classical democratic theory' took on the descriptivists. Some elements of retraction or concession will be found in certain of these essays.

5 G. Sartori, 'Anti-Elitism Revisited', *Government and Opposition*, 13: 1 (Winter 1978), p. 74. There is little point in raking over dead coals, but it might be observed that Duncan and Lukes (two of the very few identified anti-elitists) were arguing essentially that certain (named) empirical theorists had a very loose conception of classical democratic theory, and that in simply substituting a definition of a functioning or real-world democracy for a classical one, they were ignoring the critical and idealistic character of that classical theory (See G. Duncan and S. Lukes, 'The New Democracy', *Political Studies*, 11 (1963)). I should add that our own conceptions of classical theory have become more sophisticated with the years.

6 M. Vajda, *The State and Socialism* (London, 1981), p. 9.

7 *Ibid.*, p. 14.

8 C.B. Macpherson, *The Real World of Democracy* (Oxford, 1966), p. 29.

9 See Paul Corcoran's essay (Ch. 2).

10 Aspects of this argument are taken up in my essay (Ch. 12).

11 For a related discussion, see Q. Skinner, 'The Empirical Theorists of Democracy and their Critics', *Political Theory*, 1: 3 (August 1973), pp. 298–9.

12 See Michael Margolis's essay (Ch. 8).
13 For an account of the strengths and weakness of two influential models of democracy – those of Schumpeter and Downs – see David Miller's essay (Ch. 9).
14 See Alan Cawson's essay (Ch. 11).
15 See Carole Pateman's essay (Ch. 13).
16 C.B. Macpherson, *The Life and Times of Liberal Democracy* (Oxford, 1977).
17 S. Bowles and H. Gintis, 'The Invisible Fist: Have Capitalism and Democracy Reached a Parting of the Ways?', *American Economic Review* (Papers and Proceedings), 68 (1978) pp. 358–63. See also A. Wolfe, *The Limits of Legitimacy* (New York, 1977).
18 Bowles and Gintis, *op. cit.*, p. 363.
19 C.B. Macpherson, *The Political Theory of Possessive Individualism*. Marx himself, and many later Marxists, strongly criticized the morality appropriate to capitalist, market or liberal society.
20 Traditional Marxist criticism along these lines is considered in Michael Levin's essay (Ch. 6).
21 See Henry Kariel's essay (Ch. 16).
22 See Alan Cawson's essay (Ch. 11).
23 See Carole Pateman's essay (Ch. 13).
24 See David Harris's essay (Ch. 14).
25 See Dennis Thompson's essay (Ch. 15).

2 The limits of democratic theory

1 Plato's critique is given in its most elaborate form in Bk VIII of *The Republic*, ed. F.M. Cornford (Oxford, 1949), esp. at pp. 282–6 and 290–2. Aristotle's critique of democracy is pervasive in *The Politics*, trans. E. Barker (Oxford, 1948), esp. in Bk III, Chs VII–XI, and Bk IV, Ch. IV. Also see pp. 207, 240–1, 265, 275, 288 and 302.
2 This is the dilemma to which John Dunn turns our attention in *Western Political Theory in the Face of the Future* (Cambridge, 1979), Ch. 1.
3 Aristotle, *op. cit.*, p. 265.
4 This critique amounts to a rejection of the moral and psychological benefits Rousseau and other 'participation' theorists expected to redound to the individual and his community from active self-government.
5 Plato gives the profile of the democratic character in *The Republic*, Bk VIII, Ch. XXXI.
6 G. Almond and S. Verba, *The Civic Culture* (Princeton, 1963) provided a five-nation comparative study, and served as the model for a number of larger, more sophisticated studies.
7 Carole Pateman, *Participation and Democratic Theory* (Cambridge, 1970) is unduly enthusiastic about this correlation.
8 Karl Marx, 'Private Property and Communism' (1844), in *The Marx–Engels Reader*, ed. R.C. Tucker (New York, Norton, 1972), pp. 68–70.
9 Marx, 'The German ideology' in Tucker (ed.), *op. cit.*, pp. 124–5.
10 The influence here was decidedly that of Montesquieu and Locke, rather than Rousseau. Madison's arguments are set forth in *The Federalist* (Cleveland, Meridian, 1961), Nos. 10, 38, 41, 49 and 51. In No. 47, Madison supports the idea of divided powers by stating 'The oracle who is always consulted and cited on this subject is the celebrated Montesquieu.'
11 J.-J. Rousseau, *The Social Contract*, in *The Social Contract and Discourses* trans. and ed. G.D.H. Cole (London, Dent, 1973), Bk IV, Ch. 8, esp. pp. 275–6.

12 This is the pervasive theme of Michels' *Political Parties, A Sociological Examination of the Oligarchical Tendencies of Modern Democracy* (Glencoe, Ill., The Free Press, 1958), esp. pp. 37, 40, 402–3, 417–25.

13 A recent survey of the various classificatory models in democratic theory is Roland Pennock, *Democratic Political Theory* (Princeton, Princeton University Press, 1979).

14 An example is Michael Margolis, *Viable Democracy* (Harmondsworth, Penguin, 1979), esp. at pp. 154–5 and Ch. 7.

15 C.B. Macpherson, *The Political Theory of Possessive Individualism* (Oxford, Oxford University Press, 1962).

16 Thucydides, *The History of the Peloponnesian War*, trans. R. Livingstone (Oxford, Oxford University Press, 1960), pp. 110–17, esp. 111–12.

3 The historical study of 'democracy'

1 A short bibliography of the protagonists can be found at the end of Quentin Skinner's article 'Empirical Theorists of Democracy and their Critics', *Political Theory*, 1: 3 (1973), pp. 304–6.

2 Robert Dahl in *Political Behavior*, ed. H. Eulau *et al.* (Glencoe, Ill., 1956), p. 87.

3 G. Duncan and S. Lukes, 'The New Democracy', *Political Studies*, 11 (1963).

4 Skinner, *op. cit.*, p. 298.

5 I have in mind the more extreme versions of Skinner's own methodological claims as to the importance of intentionality as a criterion of interpretation, although he has considerably revised his position. 'Meaning and Understanding in the History of Ideas', *History and Theory*, 8 (1969) represents a position from which much has been conceded.

6 In classical and Renaissance political thought election was considered an aristocratic device. In true democracies public positions were liable to be filled by lot. Aristotle, *The Politics* II, xi, 7. J.G.A. Pocock, *The Machiavellian Moment* (Princeton, 1975), Chs. v and vii, discusses the Renaissance views on the subject.

7 Explored originally by J.L. Austin, *How to do Things with Words* (Oxford, 1962) and subsequently by John R. Searle, *Speech Acts* (Cambridge, 1969), amongst others.

8 A. MacIntyre, *A Short History of Ethics* (London, 1967), p. 5.

9 As the would-be believer, George Moore II puts it in *Jumpers*, despondently reflecting on another equally imperceptible and irreversible shift in religious attitudes: 'Well the tide is running his (the atheist's) way, and it is a tide which has turned only once in human history . . . There is presumably a calendar date – a *moment* – when the onus of proof passed from the atheist to the believer, when, quite suddenly, secretly, the noes had it' (Tom Stoppard, *Jumpers* (London, 1975), p. 25).

10 Classical political theorists followed Aristotle in so classifying constitutions. Thus there were 'good' democracies and 'bad' democracies, depending on whether they ruled according to constitutional restraints or not. Polybius applied the term 'ochlocracy' (from the word *ochlos*, a crowd or mob) to 'bad' forms of democracy.

11 Karl Popper, *The Open Society and its Enemies* (revised edn, London, 1966) pp. 91–9.

12 Skinner, *op. cit.*, p. 298.

13 Sir Robert Filmer, *Patriarcha and other Political Works*, ed. P. Laslett (Oxford, 1949), p. 197. Filmer's interpretation of Aristotle does him no credit.

14 Bernard Mandeville, *The Fable of the Bees*, ed. F.B. Kaye (Oxford, 1949), Vol. 1, p. 17.

15 The infamous 'two Acts' (36 Geo. II c7 & 8) extended the definition of treason and prohibited the act of associating for political discussion in an attempt to suppress the agitation of the reform societies. For an evergreen history see G. Veitch, *The Genesis of Parliamentary Reform* (London, 1913).

16 Major John Cartwright, *The Commonwealth in Danger* (London, 1795), p. 90. Cartwright was a famous proponent of universal suffrage from the 1770s until the second decade of the nineteenth century.

17 John Thelwall, *The Natural and Constitutional Rights of Britons* (London, 1795), p. 47; Thelwall was an orator, radical democrat and activist member of the working-class London Corresponding Society.

18 Alan Ryan, 'Two Concepts of Politics and Democracy', in *Machiavelli and the Nature of Politics*, ed. M. Fleisher (New York, 1972), p. 76.

19 W. Godwin, *Enquiry Concerning Political Justice*, ed. F.E.L. Priestley (Toronto, 1946) Vol. 1, pp. 75–6.

20 Godwin, *op. cit.*, Vol. 2, pp. 16, 119.

21 Godwin, *op. cit.*, Vol. 1, p. 5; Vol. 3, p. 140; Vol. 1, p. 44; Vol. 2, p. 119. Godwin's attempt to establish the self-creating nature of human consciousness is pitched against Enlightenment attempts, such as that of Montesquieu to establish the influence of natural factors such as climate.

22 'The Need for a Philosophy of Democracy' in *Contemporary American Philosophy*, ed. J.E. Smith (London, 1970); S. Benn and R.S. Peters, *Social Principles and the Democratic State* (London, 1959), p. 352.

23 J.L. Walker, 'A critique of the Elitist Theory of Democracy', *American Political Science Review*, 60 (1966), p. 288.

24 Such a demonstration is of course beyond the scope of this paper but it is important to recognize the range of Godwin's influence at the time. 'Tom Paine was considered for the time as a Tom Fool to him, Paley an old woman, Edmund Burke a flashy sophist' (William Hazlitt, *The Spirit of the Age* (London, 1969), p. 36. The high price of *Political Justice*, did not, as Pitt had confidently predicted, render its influence on the lower classes negligible. Working men's clubs subscribed to buy the expensive volumes and organized readings were held.

25 R. Dahl, 'Further Reflections on "The Elitist Theory of Democracy"', *American Political Science Review*, 60 (June, 1966), p. 303.

26 R. Dahl, Address to the American Political Science Association: 'Power Pluralism and Democracy' (Chicago, 1964).

27 James Mill, *Essay on Government* (Bobbs-Merrill, Chicago, 1955), *passim*.

28 Brian Barry draws attention to this in his *Sociologists, Economists and Democracy* (Cambridge, 1970), pp. 9–11 and throughout.

29 As urged by C.B. Macpherson. I am grateful to David Miller for pointing out this aspect of my argument.

30 It is of course an unfortunate fact that Godwin's undoubtedly self-developmental view of democracy is based ultimately on utilitarian premises, although his is a highly idiosyncratic and, some would argue, inconsistent utilitarianism.

CLASSICAL THEORIES

4 Mill and Rousseau: utility and rights

1 G.C. Duncan and S.M. Lukes, 'The New Democracy', *Political Studies*, 11 (1963), pp. 156–77; Carole Pateman, *Participation and Democratic Theory* (Cambridge, 1970), pp. 1–35.
2 L. Davis, 'The Cost of Realism: Contemporary Restatements of Democracy', *Western Political Quarterly*, 17 (1964), pp. 37–46.
3 J.A. Schumpeter, *Capitalism, Socialism and Democracy* (London, 1943), p. 269.
4 Schumpeter, *op. cit.*, pp. 282–3, 295.
5 S.M. Lipset, *Political Man* (London, 1960), Chs. 4 and 5.
6 Davis, *op. cit.*, p. 39.
7 Pateman, *op. cit.*, Ch. 2.
8 *Ibid.*, p. 109; Dahl, *After the Revolution?* (New Haven, Conn., 1970), pp. 143–66.
9 Pateman, *op. cit.*, pp. 22ff.
10 J.-J. Rousseau, *Social Contract and Discourses* trans. G.D.H. Cole (revised edn, London, 1973), Bk III Ch. iv, p. 218.
11 *Ibid.*, III iv, p. 217.
12 *Ibid.*, III, v, p. 219.
13 J.S. Mill, *Utilitarianism, Liberty and Representative Government* (London, 1964), pp. 229–30.
14 Dahl, pp. 140ff.
15 Rousseau, *op. cit.*, III, xv, p. 240.
16 *Ibid.*
17 R. Dworkin, 'Liberalism' in *Public and Private Morality*, ed. S. Hampshire (Cambridge, 1978), pp. 133–4.
18 R.P. Wolff, *In Defense of Anarchism* (New York, 1970), p. 27.
19 Rousseau, *op. cit.*, I, iv, p. 169.
20 R.M. Hare, 'The Lawful Government', in *Philosophy, Politics and Society*, Series III, eds. P. Laslett and W.G. Runciman (Oxford, 1967), pp. 157–72.
21 It is also open to us to dilute the notion of consent as Locke does, and count as tacit consenters all those who derive benefits from the government; then the non-consenting will become a different group posing different problems. J. Locke, *Two Treatises of Government* (Cambridge, 1967), Vol. 2, §§ 119–22, pp. 365–7.
22 T. Hobbes, *Leviathan* (London, 1962), Ch. 19, p. 97.
23 *Ibid.*
24 Rousseau, *Social Contract*, IV, xviii, p. 245.
25 *Ibid.*, v, ii, pp. 249–51.
26 Wolff, *op. cit.*, p. 70.
27 Rousseau, *op. cit.*, IV, xv, p. 240.
28 *Ibid.*, II, vi, p. 193.
29 J. Lively, *Democracy* (Oxford, 1975), p. 17.
30 Rousseau, *op. cit.*, IV, ii, p. 250.
31 *Ibid.*
32 R.M. Hare, 'Political Obligation', in *Social Ends and Political Means*, ed. T. Honderich (London, 1976), pp. 1–12.
33 James Mill, *An Essay on Government* (Indianapolis, 1955), pp. 66–7.
34 *Ibid.*, p. 60.
35 *Ibid.*, pp. 75–7.

36 Alan Ryan, 'Utilitarianism and Bureaucracy', in *The Growth of Nineteenth Century Government*, ed. G. Sutherland (London, 1972), pp. 33–62.
37 James Mill, *op. cit.*, pp. 73–4.
38 Rousseau, *op. cit.*, III, xvi, pp. 242–3.
39 *Ibid.*, III, xvii, p. 244.
40 *Ibid.*
41 *Ibid.*
42 *Ibid.*, III, viii, pp. 227–30.
43 *Ibid.*, IV, iv, pp. 253ff.
44 *Ibid.*, II, iii, pp. 183–4.
45 *Ibid.*, III, xviii, p. 245.
46 *Ibid.*
47 *Ibid.*, IV, i, p. 247.
48 J.L. Talmon, *The Origins of Totalitarian Democracy* (London, 1952).
49 J.S. Mill, *op. cit.*, p. 202.
50 *Ibid.*, pp. 205–6.
51 *Ibid.*, p. 73.
52 Ryan, *op. cit.*, p. 45.
53 This, of course, does not entail that each man has only one vote; Mill defends plural votes as well as the equality of the sexes. J.S. Mill, *op. cit.*, pp. 290–1.
54 J.S. Mill, *Principles of Political Economy* (Toronto, 1965), IV, vii, 6, p. 793.
55 *Ibid.*, IV, vii, 1, pp. 763–4.
56 J.S. Mill, *Utilitarianism*, p. 247.
57 *Ibid.*, pp. 216–7.
58 Rousseau, *op. cit.*, II, vi, pp. 192–3.
59 Rousseau, *op. cit.*, II, i, p. 182.
60 Hans Reiss (ed.), *Kant's Political Writings* (Cambridge, 1970), p. 79.
61 J. Rawls, *A Theory of Justice* (Oxford, 1972).
62 J.-J. Rousseau, *The Government of Poland* (Indianapolis, 1972), pp. 5ff.
63 J.S. Mill, *Utilitarianism*, pp. 74, 132.
64 *Ibid.*, pp. 68–9.
65 C.L. Ten, *Mill on Liberty* (Oxford, 1980).

5 'Classical' images of democracy in America: Madison and Tocqueville

1 For studies of the genesis and evolution of the classical republican or civic humanist concept in early modern political thought, see Hans Baron, *The Crisis of the Early Italian Renaissance* (Princeton, 1966); J.G.A. Pocock, *The Machiavellian Moment* (Princeton, 1975); and Quentin Skinner, *The Foundations of Modern Political Thought* (2 vols., Cambridge, 1979).
2 Montesquieu, *L'Esprit des Lois* (hereafter E.L.; Roman numerals refer to book numbers, Arabic numerals to chapter numbers), in *Oeuvres Complètes*, ed. Roger Callois (2 vols, Paris, 1949–51; hereafter O.C.), E.L., I, 1–2 (O.C., II, 239–44). Montesquieu distinguishes between democratic republics (in which the body of people rule) and aristocratic republics (in which power is vested in a part). But democracy is more fully and perfectly republican than aristocracy for Montesquieu, and I shall follow him in focusing attention on the former type of regime.
3 On the principle and preconditions of republicanism, see E.L., IV, 4–8; V, 2–7; VII, *passim*. (O.C., II, 266–73; 274–81; 332–49).

4 See esp. *O.C.*, I, 1127 (Pensée 598). On the obsolescence of the virtuous republic, see R. Shackleton, *Montesquieu: A Critical Biography* (Oxford, 1961), p. 277; and Melvin Richter, 'Comparative Political Analysis in Montesquieu and Tocqueville,' *Comparative Politics*, 1 (1969), p. 157. For a contrary view see N. Keohane, 'Virtuous Republics and Glorious Monarchies: Two Models in Montesquieu's Political Thought,' *Political Studies*, 20 (1972), pp. 394–5.

5 On the nature and principle of monarchy see *E.L.*, II, 4; III, 5–7 (*O.C.*, II, 247–9; 255–7). On the nature and principle of despotism, see *E.L.*, II, 5; III, 8–9 (*O.C.*, II, 249–50; 258–9).

6 *E.L.*, III, 5 (*O.C.*, II, 255).

7 See esp. *E.L.*, IV, 7 (*O.C.*, II, 270); and XXIX, 3 (*O.C.*, II, 866–7).

8 On the relationship between the theory of the constitutional separation of powers and the theory of mixed government, see M.C. Vile, *Constitutionalism and the Separation of Powers (Oxford, 1969)*; and W.B. Gwyn, *The Meaning of the Separation of Powers* (New Orleans, 1965).

9 *E.L.*, XI, 6 (*O.C.*, II, 399–400); XIX, 27 (*O.C.*, II, 576).

10 *E.L.*, XIX, 27. Cf. David Lowenthal, 'Montesquieu', in *History of Political Philosophy*, ed. Leo Strauss and Joseph Cropsey (Chicago, 1963), pp. 481–2.

11 See esp. Thomas Pangle, *Montesquieu's Philosophy of Liberalism* (Chicago, 1973), pp. 48–106 and *passim*; also Lowenthal, 'Montesquieu and the Classics: Republican Government in the Spirit of the Laws' in *Ancients and Moderns*, ed. Joseph Cropsey (New York, 1964), pp. 280–4; and Henry J. Merry, *Montesquieu's System of Natural Government* (West Lafayette, Indiana, 1970), pp. 12, 195ff. But cf. Keohane, *op. cit.*, pp. 394–5.

12 See Paul Spurlin, *Montesquieu in America* (Louisiana, 1940).

13 'A number of citizens, whether amounting to a majority or minority of the whole, who are united and actuated by some common impulse, adverse to the rights of other citizens, or to the permanent and aggregated interests of the community', *Federalist* 10, in *The Federalist*, ed. Benjamin F. Wright (Cambridge, Mass., 1961), p. 130. (All references are to this edition, hereafter cited as *Fed.*; all further references to *Fed.* 10 incorporated in page references in the text.)

14 *The Writings of James Madison* (hereafter *Writings*), ed. Gaillard Hunt (9 vols., New York, 1900–1910), V, 29.

15 See, e.g., *Fed.* 55, pp. 378–9.

16 On the use of the terms democracy and republic in eighteenth-century European and American political discourse see R.R. Palmer, *The Age of the Democratic Revolution* (2 vols., Princeton, 1959–1964), I, 13–20; and 'Notes on the Use of the Word Democracy, 1789–99', *Political Science Quarterly*, 68 (1953), pp. 203–26; Roy N. Lokkin, 'The Concept of Democracy in Colonial Political Thought', *William and Mary Quarterly* 3rd Ser., 16 (1959), 570–80; Robert Shoemaker, 'Democracy and Republic as Understood in Late Eighteenth Century America', *American Speech*, 61 (1966), pp. 83–95; Bernard Bailyn, *Ideological Origins of the American Revolution* (Cambridge, Mass., 1967), pp. 162–4 and *passim*; and Gordon Wood, *The Creation of the American Republic* (New York, 1972), pp. 222–3 and *passim*.

17 Madison, *Writings*, V, p. 31.

18 *Ibid.*, II, 368. 'The true principles of Republican Government . . . prove, *in contradiction to the concurrent opinions of the theoretical writers*, that the form of Government . . . must operate not within a small but an extensive sphere' (V, 28). (My emphasis both times.) Madison's argument draws upon Hume's 'Idea of

a Perfect Commonwealth', *Essays: Moral, Political and Literary* (Oxford, 1963), pp. 514–15. On Madison's indebtedness to Hume, see Douglass Adair, 'That Politics May be Reduced to a Science: David Hume, James Madison and the Tenth Federalist'. *Huntington Library Quarterly*, 20 (1957), pp. 343–60.

19 *E.L.*, IX, I (O.C., II, 369).

20 *Ibid.*

21 For a sampling, see Cecelia Kenyon (ed.), *The Antifederalists* (New York, 1966), esp. pp. 10–11 ('Letters of Centinel') and p. 133 ('Letters of Agrippa'). On the republican ideology of the antifederalists, and for a somewhat conflicting assessment of the genuineness of their democratic commitments, see Kenyon, 'Introduction' and 'Men of Little Faith: The Anti-Federalists on Nature of Representative Government', *William and Mary Quarterly*, 3rd Ser., 12 (1955), pp. 3–46; and Jackson Turner Main, *The Antifederalists: Critics of the Constitution* (Chapel Hill, N.C., 1961).

22 *Fed.* 9, p. 127. For a critical assessment of Hamilton's use of Montesquieu, see Martin Diamond, 'The *Federalist's* View of Federalism' in George C. Benson (ed.), *Essays in Federalism* (Claremont, Calif., 1961), pp. 23–33.

23 *De la démocratie en Amérique* (2 vols., Paris, 1951), I, p. 12 (further page references incorporated in the text). I have largely followed the translation of George Lawrence, *Democracy in America* (New York, 1969).

24 *Ibid.*, II, 356 (Appendix: 'Rapport fait a l'Académie des Sciences Morales et Politiques, le 15 Janvier 1848, sur l'ouvrage de M. Cherbuliez, intitulé: "De la démocratie en Suisse"').

25 See Tocqueville's travel notes in *Journey to America*, trans. George Lawrence and ed. J.P. Mayer (New York, 1971), pp. 174–5, 269. Also, his advocacy of two-stage elections, *D.A.*, I, pp. 207–8.

26 *Journey to America*, p. 175.

27 *The European Revolution and Correspondence with Gobineau*, ed. and trans. John Lukacs (Gloucester, Mass., 1969), p. 192 (to Count Gobineau, 5 September 1843).

28 *Memoir, Letters and Remains of Alexis de Tocqueville* (2 vols., Boston, 1862), II, p. 333 (to Madame Swetchine, 20 October 1856).

29 *Ibid.*, I, pp. 312–13 (to M. de Kergorlay, 10 October 1836).

30 Cf. Steven Lukes, *Individualism* (New York, 1973), pp. 3–16. On Tocqueville's concept of individualism, see esp. Jean Claude Lamberti, *La Notion d'individualisme chez Tocqueville* (Paris, 1970).

31 *Journey to America*, pp. 217–18.

32 J.P. Mayer (ed.), 'De Tocqueville: Unpublished Fragments', *Encounter*, 12 (April, 1959), p. 21.

33 *Ibid.* Professor Melvin Richter has called attention to this and other uses of Montesquieu by Tocqueville: 'The Uses of Theory: Tocqueville's Adaptation of Montesquieu', in *Essays in History and Theory*, ed. M. Richter (Cambridge, Mass., 1970), pp. 74–102.

34 This theme is stressed in two excellent studies of Tocqueville: Jack Lively, *The Social and Political Thought of Tocqueville* (Oxford, 1963); and Marvin Zetterbaum, *Tocqueville and the Problem of Democracy* (Stanford, 1967).

35 For a discussion of the role played by these two competing concepts in two other classical democratic theorists see Alan Ryan, 'Two Concepts of Politics and Democracy: James and John Stuart Mill,' in *Machiavelli and The Nature of Political Thought*, ed. M. Fleisher (New York, 1972).

36 See Gaetano Mosca. *The Ruling Class* (New York, 1939); and James Meisel, *The Myth of the Ruling Class: Gaetano Mosca and the Elite* (Ann Arbor, 1958).

37 Cf. Quentin Skinner, 'The Empirical Theorists of Democracy and Their Critics: A Plague on Both Their Houses', *Political Theory*, 1 (August, 1973), pp. 287–306; also, Iain Hampsher-Monk, Ch. 3 above.

38 See, e.g., Peter Bachrach, *The Theory of Democratic Elitism* (Boston, 1967); and Carole Pateman, *Participation and Democratic Theory* (Cambridge, 1970).

39 See especially the essays contained in Chs. 11–15 below.

6 Marxism and democratic theory

I am very grateful to Neil Harding for comments on an earlier draft.

1 K. Marx, F. Engels, *Collected Works*, hereafter *MECW* (London, Lawrence and Wishart, 1976), Vol. 6, pp. 392, 391.

2 Engels to Bebel, in K. Marx and F. Engels, *Selected Correspondence* (Moscow, Foreign Languages Publishing House, 1965), p. 293.

3 *Ibid.*, p. 371.

4 *MECW* (London, Lawrence and Wishart, 1975), Vol. 3, p. 75.

5 G.W.F. Hegel, *Philosophy of Right* (Oxford, Oxford University Press, 1971), p. 199, para. 307.

6 *MECW*, Vol. 3, p. 114.

7 *Ibid.*, p. 162.

8 S. Hook, *From Hegel to Marx* (Ann Arbor, University of Michigan Press, 1962), p. 46.

9 *MECW* (London, Lawrence and Wishart, 1979), Vol. 11, pp. 114–15.

10 *MECW*, Vol. 3, p. 79.

11 Marx and Engels, *Selected Correspondence*, p. 35.

12 *MECW* (London, Lawrence and Wishart, 1978), Vol. 10, p. 626.

13 *Ibid.*, pp. 469, 470.

14 J.-J. Rousseau, *The Social Contract Discourses*, trans., with introd., G.D.H. Cole (London, Dent, 1961), p. 86.

15 *MECW* (London, Lawrence and Wishart, 1975), Vol. 4, p. 37.

16 *MECW*, Vol. 6, p. 497 (my emphasis).

17 Marx and Engels, *Selected Correspondence*, p. 269.

18 *MECW*, Vol. 4, p. 37.

19 K. Marx, *Capital* (Harmondsworth, Penguin, 1976), Vol. 1, p. 899.

20 *MECW*, Vol. 6, p. 519 (my emphasis).

21 *MECW*, Vol. 10, p. 122.

22 *MECW*, Vol. 11, p. 191.

23 *MECW* (London, Lawrence and Wishart, 1977), Vol. 7, p. 179.

24 *MECW*, Vol. 11, p. 180.

25 *Ibid.*, p. 146.

26 K. Marx, *The First International and After* (Harmondsworth, Penguin, 1974), p. 324.

27 K. Marx and F. Engels, *Selected Works in Two Volumes* (Moscow, Foreign Languages Publishing House, 1962), Vol. 1, p. 134.

28 *MECW*, Vol. 3, p. 119.

29 K. Marx and F. Engels, *Selected Works in Two Volumes*, Vol. 1, p. 522.

30 *Ibid.*, p. 520.

31 *Ibid.*, p. 519.
32 N. Harding, *Lenin's Political Thought* (2 vols., London, Macmillan, 1977 and 1981), Vol. 2, pp. 84–92.
33 V.I. Lenin, *State and Revolution* (Moscow, Foreign Languages Publishing House, n.d.), p. 159.
34 *Ibid.*
35 *Ibid.*, p. 76.
36 *Ibid.*, p. 160.
37 *Ibid.*, p. 161.
38 *Ibid.*, p. 192.
39 M. Liebman, *Leninism under Lenin* (London, Cape, 1975), p. 214.
40 See M. Djilas, *The New Class* (London, Allen and Unwin, 1966).
41 L. Trotsky, *Terrorism and Communism* (Michigan, University of Michigan Press, 1961), p. 43.
42 R. Luxemburg, *The Russian Revolution* (Michigan, University of Michigan Press, 1962), p. 59.
43 V.I. Lenin, *Collected Works* (45 vols., Moscow, Progress Publishers, 1974), Vol. 26, p. 437. Also see pp. 379, 439.
44 Quoted in K. Kautsky, *The Dictatorship of the Proletariat* (Michigan, University of Michigan Press, 1964), p. 84.
45 V.I. Lenin, *Collected Works*, Vol. 29, p. 183.
46 V.I. Lenin, *Collected Works*, Vol. 32, p. 48.
47 L. Trotsky, *Terrorism and Communism*, p. 97.
48 M. Liebman, *op. cit.*, p. 258.
49 Quoted in *The Guardian*, 15 June 1965.
50 Quoted in M. Liebman, *op. cit.*, p. 201.
51 V.I. Lenin, *Collected Works*, Vol. 31, p. 454.
52 E. Mandel, *From Stalinism to Eurocommunism* (London, New Left Books, 1978), p. 115.
53 T. Roszak, *Where the Wasteland Ends. Politics and Transcendence in Postindustrial Society* (London, Faber and Faber, 1973), pp. 50, 54–5.
54 J.-J. Rousseau, *The Social Contract*, p. 73.
55 *Daily Mirror*, 9 May 1980.

7 Consensus and community: the theory of African one-party democracy

1 C.B. Macpherson, *The Real World of Democracy* (Oxford, 1966), p. 26.
2 Aimé Césaire, *Return to my Native Land* (Harmondsworth, 1969) p. 75.
3 W.E. Abraham has used the Akan people to create a paradigm of such a community. See Abraham, *The Mind of Africa* (London, 1962), Ch. 2.
4 Ferdinand Tönnies, *Community and Society* (New York, 1963), p. 231. Gemeinschaft is defined in these terms (pp. 228–9): 'Family life is the general basis of life in the Gemeinschaft. It subsists in village and town life. The village community and the town themselves can be considered as large families, the various clans and houses representing the elementary organisms of its body . . . Here original kinship and inherited status remain an essential, or at least the most important, condition of participating fully in common property and other rights . . . in Gemeinschaften property is considered as participation in the common ownership and as a specific legal concept is entirely the consequence and result of freedom or ingenuity, either original or acquired.'

5 J. Reed and C. Wake (eds.), *Senghor: Prose and Poetry* (London, 1965), p. 44.
6 *Ibid.*, p. 45.
7 *Ibid.*, pp. 32 and 34 (Senghor's emphasis).
8 J.K. Nyerere, *Ujamaa: Essays on Socialism* (Dar-es-Salaam, 1968), p. 3–4.
9 J.K. Nyerere, *Freedom and Unity* (Dar-es-Salaam, 1967), p. 11.
10 Reed and Wake, *op. cit.*, p. 61.
11 Nyerere, *Ujamaa*.
12 Reed and Wake, *op. cit.*, p. 60.
13 *Transition*, 1: 3 (December 1961), p. 9.
14 Nyerere, *Freedom and Unity*.
15 *Transition*, 1: 3 (December 1961), p. 9.
16 Reed and Wake, *op. cit.*
17 K. Nkrumah, *I Speak of Freedom* (London, 1961), p. 107.
18 Ali A. Mazrui and G.F. Engholm, 'Rousseau and Intellectualised Populism in Africa', *The Review of Politics*, 30: 1 (January 1968), pp. 19–32.
19 Thomas Hodgkin, *Nationalism in Colonial Africa* (London, 1956), p. 144.
20 J.-J. Rousseau, *The Social Contract and Discourses*, trans. with introd. by G.D.H. Cole (London, 1958), p. 205.
21 Nyerere, *Ujamaa*, pp. 110–11.
22 'In fact, laws are always in use to those who possess and harmful to those who have nothing: from which it follows that the social state is advantageous to men only when all have something and none too much' (J.-J. Rousseau, *The Social Contract* (London, 1958), p. 19).
23 *Ibid.*, p. 13.
24 Nyerere, *Freedom and Unity*, p. 196.
25 *Ibid.*
26 *Ibid.*, p. 122.
27 A. Cobban, *Rousseau and the Modern State* (London, 1934), p. 170.
28 *Ujamaa* is a Swahili word meaning 'brotherhood' or 'familyhood'. The association between 'family' and 'socialism' is significant in the light of Tönnies' definition of Gemeinschaft. See note 4 above.
29 See, for example, Cranford E. Pratt, *The Critical Phase in Tanzania 1945–1968: Nyerere and the Emergence of a Socialist Strategy* (Cambridge, 1976).
30 See, for example, Issa Shivji, *Class Struggles in Tanzania* (New York, 1976). For a discussion of these criticisms see P. Nursey-Bray, 'Class Formation and the Post-Colonial State in Africa', *Africa Quarterly*, 20: 3–4, and 'Tanzania: The Development Debate', *African Affairs*, 79: 314 (January 1980).
31 Shivji, *op. cit.* See especially Pt 3, p. 63.
32 For example, see Joel Samoff, 'The Bureaucracy and the Bourgeoisie: Decentralization and Class Structure in Tanzania', *Comparative Studies in Society and History*, 21: 1 (January 1979), pp. 30–62.
33 See, for example, J. Saul, 'Tanzania's Transition to Socialism', in his *The State in Eastern Africa* (New York, 1979).
34 Karl Marx, *Early Texts*, ed. D. McLellan (Oxford, 1971), p. 94.
35 *Ibid.*
36 *Ibid.*, p. 104.
37 As L. Colletti has discussed at length in *From Rousseau to Lenin* (London, 1972).
38 *Ibid.*, p. 108.

REVISIONS AND CRITIQUES

8 Democracy: American style

1 John Stuart Mill, *Considerations on Representative Government* (Chicago, Henry Regnery Co., 1962), pp. 6–7.
2 Cf. Angus Campbell *et al.*, *The American Voter* (New York, John Wiley, 1960), Ch. 8.
3 Cf. Louis Hartz, 'Democracy: Image and Reality', in *Democracy Today: Problems and Prospects*, eds. William N. Chambers and Robert H. Salisbury (New York, Collier Books, 1962), pp. 25–8.
4 Lord (James) Bryce, *Modern Democracies* (New York, Macmillan, 1921), p. 149.
5 Andrew Hacker, 'Power to do What?' in *The Bias of Pluralism*, ed. William Connolly (Chicago, Atherton, 1967), p. 68. Hacker of course goes on to mock the fact that the people's power extends to driver education courses in high schools and low-brow comedies on television, while it fails to control important things, such as conditions in the workplace.
6 Alfred E. Smith, speech 27 July, 1933, quoted in Bergen Evans, *Dictionary of Quotations* (New York, Avenel, 1978), p. 163.
7 Alexis de Tocqueville, *Democracy in America* (1935), Pt I, Ch. 15–16. John Stuart Mill, *On Liberty*, (1859) *passim*; H.L. Mencken, *Notes on Democracy* (1926), *passim*; Walter Lippmann, *Essays in the Public Philosophy* (1955) Chs. 2, 3, 8.
8 Cf. Paul F. Lazarsfeld *et al.*, *The People's Choice* (New York, Duell, Sloan and Pearce, 1944), Ch. 3, and Appendix; Campbell *et al.*, *op. cit.*, Ch. 6.
9 Arthur Bentley, *The Process of Government: A Study of Social Pressures* (Chicago, University of Chicago Press, 1908).
10 *Ibid.*, p. 201.
11 David B. Truman, *The Governmental Process* (New York, A.A. Knopf, 1951).
12 Gabriel Almond, *The American People and Foreign Policy* (New York, Praeger, 1960); Robert A. Dahl, *A Preface to Democratic Theory* (Chicago, University of Chicago Press, 1956); Robert A. Dahl and Charles Lindblom, *Politics, Economics and Welfare* (New York, Harper and Row, 1953); Earl Latham, *The Group Basis of Politics: A Study in Basing Point Legislation* (Ithaca, Cornell University Press, 1952); William Kornhauser, *The Politics of Mass Society* (Glencoe, Ill., Free Press, 1959); Seymour M. Lipset, *Political Man* (New York, Doubleday, 1960); Nelson Polsby, *Community Power and Political Theory* (New Haven, Conn., Yale University Press, 1963); Aaron Wildavsky, *Dixon-Yates: A Study in Power Politics* (New Haven, Conn., Yale University Press, 1962).
13 Dahl, *Preface*, p. 132.
14 Cf. Samuel Stouffer, *Communism, Conformity and Civil Liberties* (Garden City, Doubleday, 1955).
15 Truman, *op. cit.*, Ch. 16.
16 Cf. Gabriel Almond and Sidney Verba, *The Civic Culture* (Boston, Little, Brown, 1965), Ch. 10; E.E. Schattschneider, *The Semi-Sovereign People; A Realist's View of Democracy in America* (Hinsdale, Ill, Dryden Press, 1960), Ch. 2; Herbert Simon *et al.*, *Public Administration* (New York, A. Knopf, 1961), Ch. 14.
17 Cf. Harold Lasswell and Abraham Kaplan, *Power and Society* (New Haven, Conn., Yale University Press, 1950), pp. 60–75, 111ff.
18 Samuel Beer, 'New Structures of Democracy; Britain and America', in Chambers and Salisbury, *op. cit.*, p. 46.

19 Committee on Political Parties of the American Political Science Association, *Toward a More Responsible Two-Party System, American Political Science Review,* 44: 3, Pt 2 (1950).

20 E.E. Schattschneider, *Party Government* (New York, Rinehart, 1942).

21 E. Pendleton Herring, *The Politics of American Democracy: American Parties in Action* (New York, Norton, 1940), Pt I.

22 Cf. Anthony Downs, *An Economic Theory of Democracy* (New York, Harper, 1957), Chs. 7–9.

23 Joseph A. Schumpeter, *Capitalism, Socialism and Democracy* (3rd edn, New York, Harper Torchbooks, 1962), p. 269.

24 Cf. Fred I. Greenstein, *Children and Politics* (New Haven, Conn., Yale University Press, 1965); Robert D. Hess and Judith V. Torney, *The Development of Political Attitudes in Children* (Chicago, Aldine, 1967).

25 Cf. Paul A. Beck, 'The Role of Agents in Political Socialization', in *Handbook of Political Socialization: Theory and Research,* ed. Stanley Renshon (New York, Free Press, 1976); Robert E. Lane and David O. Sears, *Public Opinion* (Englewood Cliffs, N.J., Prentice-Hall, 1964), Chs. 3–4.

26 Almond and Verba, *op. cit.,* p. 30.

27 *Ibid.,* Ch. 13; Lester Milbrath, *Political Participation* (Chicago, Rand McNally, 1965), Ch. 6.

28 Bernard Berelson *et al., Voting* (Chicago, University of Chicago Press, 1954), Ch. 14.

29 Herbert McClosky, 'Consensus and Ideology in American Politics', *American Political Science Review,* 58 (1964), pp. 361–82.

30 V.O. Key, *Public Opinion and American Democracy* (New York, A.A. Knopf, 1961), p. 537.

31 See, especially, *Essays on the Scientific Study of Politics,* ed. Herbert Storing (New York, Holt, Rinehart, Winston, 1962); also Michael Margolis, 'The New Language of Political Science', *Polity,* 3 (Spring 1971), pp. 416–26.

32 Cf. Russell Kirk, 'Segments of Political Science not Amenable to Behavioristic Treatment', in *The Limits of Behavioralism in Political Science,* ed. J.C. Charlesworth (Philadelphia, American Academy of Political and Social Science, 1962), pp. 49–67.

33 Robert Horowitz, 'Scientific Propaganda: Harold D. Lasswell', and Leo Weinstein, 'The Group Approach: Arthur F. Bentley', in Storing (ed.), *op. cit.,* pp. 225–304 and 151–224.

34 Cf. Heinz Eulau, 'Segments of Political Science Susceptible to Behavioristic Treatment', in Charlesworth (ed.) *op. cit.,* pp. 68ff. and John Schaar and Sheldon Wolin, 'Essays on the Scientific Study of Politics: A Critique', *American Political Science Review,* 57 (1963), pp. 125–50.

35 Cf. *Contemporary Political Analysis,* ed. J.C. Charlesworth (New York, Free Press, 1967).

36 Michael Margolis, 'The New American Government Textbooks', *American Journal of Political Science,* 17 (1973) pp. 457–63.

37 Cf. Jack L. Walker, 'A Critique of the Elitist Theory of Democracy', *American Political Science Review,* 60 (1966), pp. 285–95; Arthur Miller, 'Political Issues and Trust in Government', *American Political Science Review,* 68 (1974), pp. 951–72.

38 C. Wright Mills, *The Power Elite* (Oxford, Oxford University Press, 1957).

39 Cf. Henry S. Kariel (ed.), *Frontiers of Democratic Theory* (New York, Random House, 1970), Pt 3.

40 Mills, *op. cit.*, p. 300.

41 Cf. Arnold Brecht, *Political Theory* (Princeton, Princeton University Press, 1959), Introduction and Chs. 3, 9, and 10; Peter Bachrach, *The Theory of Democratic Elitism* (Boston, Little, Brown, 1967); *Kariel (ed.), op. cit.*; William A. Gamson, 'Stable Unrepresentation in American Society', *American Behavioral Scientist*, 12 (1968), pp. 15–21.

42 Cf. Kariel (ed.), *op. cit.*, Pt 4; Charles McCoy and John Playford (eds.), *Apolitical Politics: A Critique of Behavioralism* (New York, Crowell, 1967). Theodore Lowi, *The End of Liberalism* (New York, Norton, 1969).

43 Cf. Lewis Lipsitz, 'On Political Belief: The Grievances of the Poor', and Michael Parenti, 'Assimilation and Counter Assimilation: From Civil Rights to Black Radicalism', in *Power and Community: Dissenting Essays in Political Science*, eds. Philip Green and Sanford Levinson (New York, Vintage Books, 1970), pp. 142–72 and 173–94.

44 Michael Margolis, 'From Confusion to Confusion: Issues and the American Electorate 1952–1972', *American Political Science Review*, 71 (1977), Table 4, p. 38.

45 Cf. David Hill and Norman R. Luttbeg, *Trends in American Electoral Behavior* (Itasca, Ill., F.E. Peacock Publishers, 1980), Chs. 2–4. W.D. Burnham, 'American Politics in the 70s: Beyond Party?', in (2nd edn, Oxford, Oxford University Press, 1975) *The American Party System*, eds. William N. Chambers and W.D. Burnham, pp. 308–57.

46 Cf. Carl Bernstein and Bob Woodward, *All the Presidents' Men* (New York, Warner Books, 1976); Louis Harris and associates, *Confidence and Concern: Citizens View American Government* (a Report to the Senate Subcommittee on Intergovernmental Relations) (Cleveland, Regal Books, 1974); Miller, *op. cit.*

47 Cf. Bachrach, *op. cit.*; Connolly (ed.), *op. cit.*; Kariel (ed.), *op. cit.*; Lipsitz, *op. cit.*; Grant McConnell, *Private Power and American Democracy* (New York, Vintage Books, 1970); McCoy and Playford (eds.), *op. cit.*; Walker, *op. cit.*

48 The Caucus fostered a new journal, *Politics and Society* (inaugural issue November 1970), with a policy which 'encourages a variety of methodological approaches, . . . promotes undersupported areas of research, emphasizes the use of lucid English in articles, and examines what Robert Lynd called "some outrageous hypotheses"'. *American Political Science Review*, 65 (March 1971), p. 287.

49 Margolis, *op. cit.* in note 36.

50 Cf. Robert A. Goldwin (ed.), *How Democratic is America? Responses to the New Left Challenge* (Chicago, Rand McNally, 1971).

51 Cf. William Ophuls, *Ecology and the Politics of Scarcity: Prologue to the Political Theory of the Steady State* (San Francisco, Freeman, 1977); Lester C. Thurow, *The Zero-Sum Society: Distribution and the Possibilities for Economic Change* (New York, Penguin, 1981).

52 See also Gabriel A. Almond, 'The Intellectual History of the Civic Culture Concept', in *The Civic Culture Revisited*, eds. Gabriel Almond and Sidney Verba (Boston, Little, Brown, 1980), pp. 1–37.

53 Robert A. Dahl, 'Liberal Democracy in the United States', in *A Prospect of Liberal Democracy*, ed. William S. Livingstone (Austin, University of Texas Press, 1979), pp. 57–72; Wilson Carey McWilliams, 'Democracy and the Citizen: Community, Dignity and the Crisis of Contemporary Politics in America', in *How Democratic is the Constitution?*, eds. Robert A. Goldwin and William A. Schambra

(Washington, D.C., American Enterprises Institute, 1980), pp. 79–101; Frederick Thayer, *An End to Hierarchy: An End to Competition! Organizing the Politics and Economics of Survival* (New York, New Viewpoints, 1973); Robert Paul Wolff, *In Defense of Anarchism* (New York, Harper Torchbooks, 1970); Michael Margolis, *Viable Democracy* (New York, Penguin, 1979), Ch. 7.

54 Theodore Lowi, *The End of Liberalism* (2nd edn, New York, Norton, 1979), Ch. 11.

55 Samuel Beer, 'In Search of a New Public Philosophy', and Hugh Heclo, 'Issue Networks and the Executive Establishment,' in *The New American System*, ed. Anthony King (Washington, D.C., American Enterprise Institute, 1978), pp. 5–44, 87–124.

56 Michael Best and William Connolly, *The Politicized Economy* (Lexington, Mass., 1976), Ch. 6; Robert Dahl, 'On Removing Certain Impediments to Democracy in the United States', *Political Science Quarterly*, 92 (1977), pp. 1–20; Ralph Nader *et al.*, *Taming the Giant Corporation* (New York, Norton, 1976), pp. 118–31; Margolis, *op. cit.*, Ch. 7.

57 Ithiel de Sola Pool (ed.), *Talking Back: Citizen Feedback and Cable Technology* (Cambridge, Mass., M.I.T. Press, 1973); Margolis, *op. cit.*, pp. 158–70.

58 Thayer, *op. cit.*; Henry S. Kariel, *Beyond Liberalism: Where Relationships Grow* (San Francisco, Chandler and Sharp, 1977); McWilliams, *op. cit.*

59 Cf. Nathan Glazer and Irving Kristol (eds.), *The American Commonwealth* (New York, Basic Books, 1976) (this is the 10th Anniversary Issue of the quarterly journal, *The Public Interest*), especially essays by Samuel Huntington, Aaron Wildavsky, and Irving Kristol.

60 Cf. Glazer and Kristol (eds.) *op. cit.*; also Austin Ranney, 'The Political Parties; Reform and Decline,' in King (ed.) *op. cit.*, pp. 213–48; Jeane J. Kirkpatrick, *Dismantling the Parties* (Washington, D.C., American Enterprise Institute, 1978).

9 The competitive model of democracy

1 J. Mill, *An Essay on Government*, ed. C.V. Shields (New York, Bobbs-Merrill, 1955); J.-J. Rousseau, *The Social Contract*, ed. C. Frankel (New York, Hafner, 1947).

2 J.S. Mill, *Considerations on Representative Government* in J.S. Mill, *Utilitarianism; On Liberty; Representative Government*, ed. A.D. Lindsay (London, Dent, 1964). An illuminating comparison of the two Mills, bringing out the conflict in underlying values to which I refer, is contained in A. Ryan, 'Two Concepts of Politics and Democracy: James and John Stuart Mill' in *Machiavelli and the Nature of Political Thought*, ed. M. Fleisher (London, Croom Helm, 1972).

3 This error is close to the surface in the most celebrated critique of 'modern' democratic theory, G. Duncan and S. Lukes, 'The New Democracy', *Political Studies*, 11 (1963), pp. 156–77, but the authors' sensitivity to the interweaving of normative and empirical claims in both 'classical' and 'modern' theories prevents them from committing it grossly; their less sophisticated disciples have not been so careful.

4 A. Downs, *An Economic Theory of Democracy* (New York, Harper, 1957), p. 29.

5 J.A. Schumpeter, *Capitalism, Socialism and Democracy* (5th edn, London, Allen and Unwin, 1976), p. 282.

6 The close connection between explanation and justification in utilitarian theories

in particular has been noted by Plamenatz. See J.P. Plamenatz, *Democracy and Illusion* (London, Longmans, 1973), Ch. 1. For a more general argument to the same effect see C. Taylor, 'Neutrality in Political Science' in *Philosophy, Politics and Society*, 3rd Ser., ed. P. Laslett and W.G. Runciman (Oxford, Blackwell, 1967), pp. 25–57.

7 See Schumpeter, *op. cit.*, Ch. 21.

8 *Ibid.*, p. 263.

9 *Ibid.*, p. 262.

10 *Ibid.*, p. 269.

11 *Ibid.*, p. 295.

12 *Ibid.*

13 I have explored the historical tensions between liberalism and democracy in 'Democracy and Social Justice', *British Journal of Political Science*, 8 (1978), pp. 1–19, reprinted in *Democracy, Consensus and Social Contract*, eds. P. Birnbaum, J. Lively and G. Parry (London, Sage, 1978), pp. 75–100.

14 Downs, *op. cit.*, Chs. 2–3.

15 For an incisive critique, see B. Barry, *Sociologists, Economists and Democracy* (London, Macmillan, 1970), Ch. 2.

16 Downs, *op. cit.*, p. 64.

17 *Ibid.*, pp. 114–22.

18 For an analysis, see Barry, *op. cit.*, Ch. 5.

19 See W.H. Riker and P.C. Ordeshook, *An Introduction to Positive Political Theory* (Englewood Cliffs, N.J., Prentice-Hall, 1973), pp. 371–5; H. van den Doel, *Democracy and Welfare Economics* (Cambridge, Cambridge University Press, 1979), pp. 113–16.

20 For a forceful critique of this presupposition, see P. Dunleavy and H. Ward, 'Autonomous Voter Preferences and Parties with State Power: Some Internal Problems of Economic Theories of Party Competition', *British Journal of Political Science*, 11 (1981), pp. 351–80.

21 See, for example, P.E. Converse, 'The Nature of Belief Systems in Mass Publics' in *Ideology and Discontent*, ed. D.E. Apter (New York, The Free Press, 1964), and the discussion in Barry, *op. cit.*, Ch. 6.

22 For discussion, see D.E. Butler and D. Stokes, *Political Change in Britain* (2nd edn, London, Macmillan, 1974), Ch. 14.

23 See *Ibid.*, Ch. 2.

24 For a fuller discussion, see D. Robertson, 'Surrogates for Party Identification in the Rational Choice Framework', in *Party Identification and Beyond*, eds. I. Budge, I. Crewe and D. Fairlie (London, Wiley, 1976), pp. 365–81.

25 J.P. Plamenatz, 'Electoral Studies and Democratic Theory', *Political Studies*, 6 (1958), 1–9, esp. p.8.

26 See I. Crewe, 'Party Identification Theory and Political Change in Britain' in Budge, Crewe and Fairlie (eds.), *op. cit.*, pp. 33–61.

27 See D. Robertson, *A Theory of Party Competition* (London, Wiley, 1976), which is the most thorough attempt to date to test the Downsian model empirically. Interestingly enough, Robertson found (in the context of British politics) that the Conservative Party tended to move to the right when in a strong electoral position, whereas the Labour Party tended to move to the centre when *it* was strong.

28 See further Robertson, *op. cit.*, Ch. 2.

29 See above, pp. 142–3.

30 Rousseau's *Social Contract* is the most celebrated endorsement of this variant.

31 J.S. Mill distinguishes the two kinds of justification, and gives weight to each, in Ch. 2 of *Considerations on Representative Government*. Notice, however, that a full vindication of democracy may need to invoke other values as well; see the final section of my 'Democracy and Social Justice'.

32 See, for example, R.A. Dahl, *A Preface to Democratic Theory* (Chicago, University of Chicago Press, 1956), esp. Ch. 4.

33 Both logrolling and point voting are analysed more fully in D.C. Mueller, *Public Choice* (Cambridge, Cambridge University Press, 1979), Ch. 3.

34 See p. 143.

35 See further van den Doel, *op. cit.*, esp. pp. 115–16.

36 A point that is stressed to good effect in R.A. Dahl, *After the Revolution?* (New Haven, Conn., Yale University Press, 1970).

10 Marcuse and autonomy

I would like to acknowledge the help of the following: Graeme Duncan and Michael Levin; my colleagues at Queen's University, Belfast – Bob Eccleshall, Richard Jay and Mick Cox; Phil Lawrence and Steve Gill of Wolverhampton Polytechnic who kindly invited me to present an earlier version of this essay; and my friend John Le Juen. The errors are of course my own.

1 C.B. Macpherson, *The Life and Times of Liberal Democracy* (Oxford, Oxford University Press, 1977), pp. 9–10.

2 W. Bagehot, *The English Constitution* (London, Collins/Fontana, 1971), p. 277; quoted in D.J. Manning, *Liberalism* (London, Dent, 1976), p. 107.

3 Quoted in E. Fromm, *The Sane Society* (London, Routledge and Kegan Paul, 1976), p. 185.

4 *Ibid.*

5 *Ibid.*

6 M. Seliger, *The Marxist Conception of Ideology* (Cambridge, Cambridge University Press, 1979), pp. 30–1.

7 H. Marcuse, 'Thoughts on the defense of Gracchus Babeuf', in *The Defense of Gracchus Babeuf*, ed. J.A. Scott (Amherst, University of Massachusetts Press, 1967), p. 96.

8 H. Marcuse, *Five Lectures* (London, Allen Lane, 1970), p. 60.

9 H. Marcuse, *One Dimensional Man* (London, Sphere Books, 1972), p. 46.

10 H. Marcuse, 'Some Social Implications of Modern Technology' in *The Essential Frankfurt School Reader*, ed. A. Arato and E. Gebhardt (Oxford, Blackwell, 1978), p. 142.

11 *Ibid.*, pp. 143–4.

12 Marcuse, *Five Lectures*, p. 14.

13 *Ibid.*, p. 49. In *Eros and Civilization* Marcuse assessed the significance of the decline of the family somewhat differently. See V. Geoghegan, *Reason and Eros* (London, Pluto, 1981), pp. 59–60.

14 H. Marcuse, *One Dimensional Man*, pp. 23–4.

15 *Ibid.*, p. 20.

16 M. Cranston, 'Herbert Marcuse' in *The New Left*, ed. M. Cranston (London, The Bodley Head, 1970), p. 87.

17 A. MacIntyre, *Marcuse* (London, Collins, 1970), p. 90.

18 E. Vivas, *Contra Marcuse* (New York, Dell, 1972), p. 172.

19 H. Marcuse, 'Repressive Tolerance' in *A Critique of Pure Tolerance*, ed. R.P. Wolff, B. Moore Jnr and H. Marcuse (Boston, Beacon Press, 1969), p. 81.
20 *Ibid.*, p. 82
21 *Ibid.*, pp. 95–6.
22 *Ibid.*, p. 87
23 *Ibid.*, p. 105.
24 Marcuse, *One Dimensional Man*, p. 10.
25 Marcuse, 'Repressive Tolerance', p. 87.
26 Marcuse, *One Dimensional Man*, p. 45.
27 H. Marcuse, 'Postscript 1968', in Wolff, Moore Jnr and Marcuse (eds.), *op. cit.*, p. 122.
28 H. Marcuse, *Negations* (Harmondsworth, Penguin, 1972), pp. 120–1.
29 H. Marcuse, 'Remarks on a Redefinition of Culture', *Daedalus*, 94:1 (1965), p. 196.
30 Marcuse, *Five Lectures*, p. 57.
31 Marcuse, *One Dimensional Man*, p. 16.
32 *Ibid.*, pp. 199–200.
33 Marcuse, *Five Lectures*, p. 97.
34 *Ibid.*, pp. 92–3.
35 H. Marcuse, *An Essay on Liberation* (Harmondsworth, Penguin, 1972), p. 52.
36 Marcuse, 'Repressive Tolerance', pp. 103–4. The translation is from F. Fanon, *The Wretched of the Earth*, trans. C. Farrington (Harmondsworth, Penguin, 1967), p. 21.
37 H. Marcuse, 'The Paris Rebellion', *Peace News* (28 June 1968), p. 7.
38 *Ibid.*, p. 6.
39 *Ibid.*
40 Marcuse, *An Essay on Liberation*, p. 30.
41 *Ibid.*
42 H. Marcuse, 'Interview with Marcel Rioux', *Forces*, 22 (1973), p. 76.
43 H. Marcuse, discussion in *La Liberté et l'ordre social* (Neuchâtel, Rencontres Internationales de Genève, 1969), p. 270 (extract translated by Y.J. Le Juen).
44 Marcuse, *An Essay on Liberation*, pp. 73–4 and 'Ethics and Revolution', in *Ethics and Society*, ed. R.T. de George (London, Macmillan, 1968), pp. 418–19.

11 Functional representation and democratic politics: towards a corporatist democracy?

1 C.B. Macpherson, *Democratic Theory: Essays in Retrieval* (Oxford, Clarendon Press, 1973), p. 172.
2 J.A. Schumpeter, *Capitalism, Socialism and Democracy* (1942). The references in this essay are to the 4th edition (London, Allen and Unwin, 1954).
3 *Ibid.*, p. 143.
4 The application of pure logical models to politics should be distinguished from the economic analogy described here. The former has become firmly associated, at least in Britain, with the neo-Conservative (or radical right) position. See Institute of Economic Affairs, *The Economics of Politics* (London, I.E.A., 1978).
5 C.B. Macpherson, *The Life and Times of Liberal Democracy* (Oxford, Oxford University Press, 1977), pp. 83–4.
6 *Ibid.*, pp. 91–2.
7 Schumpeter (*op. cit.*, pp. 78–9) traces the model to the work of Augustine Cournot, but refers the reader to E.S. Chamberlin's *Theory of Monopolistic*

Competition (Cambridge, Mass., Harvard University Press, 1933), and Joan Robinson's *The Economics of Imperfect Competition* (London, Macmillan, 1933).

8 Schumpeter, *op. cit.*, p. 82.

9 Joan Robinson, 'Solving the stagflation puzzle', *Challenge*, 22: 5 (November–December 1979), p. 41.

10 *Ibid.*

11 *Ibid.*, p. 42.

12 Joan Robinson, 'Foreword', to *A Guide to Post-Keynesian Economics*, ed. A.S. Eichner (London, Macmillan, 1979), p. xvii.

13 A. Downs, *An Economic Theory of Democracy* (New York, Harper, 1957).

14 S. Rousseas, *Capitalism and Catastrophe: A Critical Appraisal of the Limits to Capitalism* (Cambridge, Cambridge University Press, 1979), p. x.

15 J.K. Galbraith, *The New Industrial State* (2nd edn, London, Andre Deutsch, 1972) and *Economics and the Public Purpose* (London, Andre Deutsch, 1974); J. O'Connor, *The Fiscal Crisis of the State* (New York, St Martin's Press, 1973); S. Holland, *The Socialist Challenge* (London, Quartet, 1975); Eichner, *op. cit.*; J.A. Kregel, *The Reconstruction of Political Economy: An Introduction to Post-Keynesian Economics* (London, Macmillan, 1973); and, of course, Keynes himself but not the neo-classical authors who called themselves 'Keynesians'.

16 Macpherson, *Life and Times*, Ch. 3.

17 Schumpeter, *op. cit.*, p. 269.

18 *Ibid.*, pp. 270–1.

19 R.A. Dahl, *A Preface to Democratic Theory* (Chicago, Chicago University Press, 1956), pp. 150–1.

20 Schumpeter, *op. cit.*, pp. 79–80.

21 *Ibid.*, p. 291.

22 *Ibid.*, p. 292; emphasis in original.

23 *Ibid.*, pp. 415–25.

24 C. Offe, 'The Theory of the Capitalist State and the Problem of Policy Formation', in *Stress and Contradiction in Modern Capitalism: Public Policy and the Theory of the State*, eds. L. Lindberg, C. Crouch, C. Offe and R. Alford (Lexington, D.C., Heath, 1975), pp. 125–44.

25 See A. Cawson, *Corporatism and Welfare: Social Policy and State Intervention in Britain* (London, Heinemann, 1982).

26 See, in particular, B. Jessop, 'Corporatism, Parliamentarism and Social Democracy' in *Trends Toward Corporatist Intermediation*, eds. P.C. Schmitter and G. Lehmbruch (London and Beverly Hills, Sage, 1979), and other contributions in the same volume; A. Cawson, 'Pluralism, Corporatism and the Role of the State', *Government and Opposition*, 13: 2 (1978), pp. 178–98; and for a historical view R.K. Middlemas, *Politics in Industrial Society: The Experience of the British System since 1911* (London, Andre Deutsch, 1979).

27 S.H. Beer, *Modern British Politics* (London, Faber, 1965), p. 319.

28 *Ibid.*, p. 71.

29 P. Dunleavy, 'The Political Implications of Sectoral Cleavages and the Growth of State Employment', *Political Studies*, 28: 3 and 4 (1980), pp. 364–83, 527–49.

30 Beer, *op. cit.* (2nd edn, 1969), p. 428.

31 *The Times*, 17 May 1976.

32 A. Gamble, 'The Free Economy and the Strong State', in *The Socialist Register 1979*, eds. R. Miliband and J. Saville (London, Merlin Press, 1979).

33 See, for example, Michael Margolis' essay, Ch. 8.

POSSIBLE FUTURES

12 Human nature and radical democratic theory

My thanks are due to Bob Alford, Paul Corcoran, Henry Kariel and John Keane for critical comments on an earlier draft.

1 It is a commonplace – and also true – that there is no democratic theory, only democratic theories. But, more than that, such 'classical democratic' thinkers as Rousseau and Mill, whose central views differ at many points, are each presented by their own interpreters in a variety of ways. Alan Ryan's essay in this volume (Ch. 4) indicates some of the shortcomings of certain simple distinctions between Mill and Rousseau, and of some established views of their democratic credentials.

2 For a different but related criticism of empirical democratic theory (for a false ideological move) see Q. Skinner, 'The Empirical Theorists of Democracy and Their Critics', *Political Theory*, 1: 3 (August 1973).

3 For example, a justification of democracy may link the growth of democratic virtue with better education, more significant decentralization, an end to poverty, or the achievement of economic equality. Of course, whether these conditions are possible rather than hypothetical is a matter for further analysis.

4 It may seem misleading to write in these terms, as political theory and political science alike are characterized by anarchy, incoherence, and drifting in many directions. But in hard times 'realism' comes into its own, and the optimistic side of the democratic tradition is likely to seem peculiarly unconvincing. My comment falls short of asserting an ideological hegemony or a single paradigm in contemporary Western political theory and political science.

5 Talmon, J.L., *The Origins of Totalitarian Democracy* (London, 1961), p. 232.

6 That would be a task in itself. Some of the diverse strands of democratic theory are filled out in the second section of this book. Radical democratic theory finds some expression in Mill, more in Rousseau, Marx and Marcuse. The articles collected in Playford and McCoy, *Apolitical Politics: a Critique of Behavioralism* (New York, 1967) and in the latter part of Henry Kariel, *The Frontiers of Democratic Theory* (New York, 1970), lie also within that broad tradition.

7 As by John Plamenatz in 'Electoral Studies and Democratic Theory', *Political Studies*, 6 (1958) pp. 1–9.

8 N. Chomsky, *American Power and the New Mandarins* (New York, 1969).

9 Gabriel Jackson, *The Spanish Republic and the Civil War: 1931–1939* (Princeton, 1965).

10 Chomsky, *op. cit.*, pp. 124, 99.

11 *Ibid.*, p. 87.

12 E.P. Thompson, *The Making of the English Working Class* (London, 1968), p. 603.

13 H. Marcuse, *One Dimensional Man* (London, 1970), p. 153.

14 R.D. Laing, *The Politics of Experience* (Harmondsworth, 1967), p. 53.

15 R.D. Laing, *Self and Others* (Harmondsworth, 1969), p. 69.

16 R.D. Laing, *The Divided Self* (Harmondsworth, 1961), p. 18.

17 Whether it is right to treat man on principle as a self-acting agent is a moot point.

18 H. Marcuse, *The Dialectics of Liberation*, ed. D. Cooper (Harmondsworth, 1968), p. 182.

19 Clearly the systematic broadening of the causal framework must stop at some point. Problems include the facts that the larger units at which explanation stops,

e.g. capitalism or even the total cosmos, tend to be slippery or all-embracing, as well as difficult to manipulate, and that in a complex social universe neat and universal causal connections are hard to establish.

20 Sydney Hook, *Towards the Understanding of Karl Marx* (London, 1933), p. 261.

21 Sigmund Freud, *Civilisation and its Discontents* (London, 1975), pp. 50–1.

22 This point is ignored by Laing, especially in *The Politics of Experience*. It underlies the claim that energies or potentialities may need redirection or sublimation.

23 It may be that without radical change, in some cases, claims may be forced outside the system, or deformed and distorted, with the result that existing interests and desires are blocked by established practice.

24 Karl Popper, 'Utopia and Violence', in *Conjectures and Refutations* (London, 1972), pp. 355–63.

25 Consider, in this light, the pursuit of nuclear parity rather than nuclear disarmament.

26 Marcuse, *One Dimensional Man*, p. 22.

27 Paul Goodman somewhere described the progressive English school, Summerhill, as 'an affectionate family of autonomous persons'.

28 J.S. Mill, 'On Liberty', in *On Liberty, Utilitarianism and Representative Government* (London, 1960), p. 161.

29 Cf. Murray Bookchin's discovery of the seeds of a utopian life-style in the new sub-cultures. '"Dropping out" becomes a mode of dropping in, into the tentative, experimental, and as yet highly ambiguous, social relations of utopia' *Post-Scarcity Anarchism* (London, 1974), p. 16.

30 See their contributions to *The Dialectics of Liberation*.

31 Carole Pateman, *Participation and Democratic Theory* (Cambridge, 1970).

32 These comments are in part a dialogue with Sartori, 'Anti-Elitism Revisited', *Government and Opposition*, 13: 1 (Winter 1978), pp. 58–80. I agree with Sartori that a face-to-face democracy and a nationwide democratic forum are not strictly comparable and are not on the same continuum (p. 70), and that 'large-scale democracy is not a static blow-up or a sheer adding up of many little democracies' (p. 72). But while there is clearly some fudginess in participatory theory, Sartori, who is not especially good at identifying his opponents, misstates the dividing line between elitists and anti-elitists. He writes that the divide comes over 'whether participatory democracy can replace, at the polity level, representative democracy' (p. 75). Few participatory theorists go so far.

33 Eckstein, 'A Theory of Stable Democracy' in Eckstein, *Division and Cohesion in Democracy* (Princeton, 1966), p. 237.

34 That is only one possibility, of course. The strength of entrenched interests, along with harsh circumstances of recession, high inflation and high unemployment, may kill or end possibilities.

35 In *Viable Democracy* (Harmondsworth, 1979), Michael Margolis tries to show how liberal democracy might be adapted to the political and technological facts of the later twentieth century.

36 Sartori, *op. cit.*, p. 60.

13 Feminism and democracy

1 B.R. Barber, *The Death of Communal Liberty* (Princeton, Princeton University Press, 1974), p. 273. The comment on citizen-soldiers is very revealing. There is no reason why women should not be armed citizens and help defend the *patrie* (as

guerrilla fighters and armies have shown). However, one of the major arguments of the anti-suffragists in Britain and the U.S.A. was that the enfranchisement of women would fatally weaken the state because women by nature were incapable of bearing arms. I have commented on these issues in C. Pateman, 'Women, Nature and the Suffrage', *Ethics*, 90: 4 (1980), pp. 564–75. Some other aspects of the patriarchal argument from nature are discussed below.

2 S. Verba, N. Nie and J.-O. Kim, *Participation and Political Equality* (Cambridge, Cambridge University Press, 1978), p. 8.

3 M. Margolis, *Viable Democracy* (Harmondsworth, Penguin, 1979), p. 9.

4 J.G. Fichte, *The Science of Rights*, trans. A.E. Kroeger (London, Trubner, 1889), 'Appendix', §3.1, p. 439 (my emphasis).

5 J. Locke, *Two Treatises of Government*, 2nd edn, ed. P. Laslett (Cambridge, Cambridge University Press, 1967), I, §47, 48; II, §82.

6 For amplification of these necessarily brief comments see T. Brennan and C. Pateman, '"Mere Auxiliaries to the Commonwealth": Women and the Origins of Liberalism', *Political Studies*, 27 (1979), pp. 183–200: R. Hamilton, *The Liberation of Women: A Study of Patriarchy and Capitalism* (London, Allen and Unwin, 1978); H. Hartmann, 'Capitalism, Patriarchy and Job Segregation by Sex', *Signs*, 1: 3, Pt 2 (1976), pp. 137–70: A. Oakley, *Housewife* (Harmondsworth, Penguin, 1976), Chs. 2 and 3.

7 Page references in the text are to J.S. Mill, 'The Subjection of Women', in J.S. Mill and H. Taylor, *Essays on Sex Equality*, ed. A. Rossi (Chicago, Chicago University Press, 1970).

8 It is worth noting that Mill implicitly distinguishes between the actions and beliefs of individual husbands and the power given to 'husbands' over 'wives' within the structure of the institution of marriage. He notes that marriage is not designed for the benevolent few to whom the defenders of marital slavery point, but for every man, even those who use their power physically to ill-treat their wives. This important distinction is still frequently overlooked today when critics of feminism offer examples of individual 'good' husbands personally known to them.

9 Mill, and many other feminists, see the lack of a sense of justice (a consequence of confinement to domestic life) as the major defect in women's characters. The assertion that the defect is natural to women is central to the belief – ignored by writers on democracy – that women are inherently subversive of political order and a threat to the state; on this question see C. Pateman, '"The Disorder of Women"; Women, Love and the Sense of Justice', *Ethics*, 91: 1 (1980), pp. 20–34.

10 It need not be granted. *The Subjection* owes a good deal to William Thompson's (much neglected) *Appeal of One Half the Human Race, Women, Against the Pretensions of the Other Half, Men, to Retain them in Political, and Hence in Civil and Domestic, Slavery* (New York, Source Book Press, 1970), originally published in 1825. Thompson was very willing to question these matters in his vision of a co-operative–socialist and sexually egalitarian future.

11 For an early critique see, for example, M. Goot and E. Reid, 'Women and Voting Studies: Mindless Matrons or Sexist Scientism', *Sage Professional Papers in Contemporary Sociology*, 1 (1975); more recently, for example, J. Evans, 'Attitudes to Women in American Political Science', *Government and Opposition*, 15: 1, (1980), pp. 101–14.

12 M.M. Lee, 'Why Few Women Hold Public Office: Democracy and Sexual Roles', *Political Science Quarterly*, 91 (1976), pp. 297–314.

13 A detailed discussion of the paradoxical manner in which political theorists have

treated women's consent, and references to the empirical evidence on which these comments are based, can be found in C. Pateman, 'Women and Consent', *Political Theory*, 8: 2, (1980), pp. 149–68. In some legal jurisdictions, for example the States of New South Wales, South Australia and Victoria in Australia, rape within marriage is now a criminal offence. Legal reform is extremely welcome, but the wider social problem remains; one of the saddest conclusions I reached during my research was that rather than rape being 'a unique act that stands in complete opposition to the consensual relations that ordinarily obtain between the sexes . . . rape is revealed as the extreme expression of, or an extension of, the accepted and "natural" relation between men and women' (p. 161).

14 On the other hand, the experience of women in the 'participatory democratic' New Left was a major impetus to the revival of the feminist movement. The New Left provided an arena for political action, the development of skills, and was ideologically egalitarian – but it remained male supremacist in its organization and, especially, its personal relations: see S. Evans, *Personal Politics* (New York, Knopf, 1979).

15 For some comments on the ambiguous place of the family, see my '"The Disorder of Women"': on the wider question of public and private, see C. Pateman, 'Feminist Critiques of the Public–Private Dichotomy', in *Conceptions of the Public and Private in Social Life*, ed. S. Benn and G. Gaus (London, Croom Helm, forthcoming).

16 A steady increase in the employment of married women has been one of the most striking features of the post-war development of capitalism. However, it is worth re-emphasizing that (working-class) wives have always been in the paid workforce. In Britian in 1851 about a quarter of married women were employed (Oakley, *op. cit.*, p. 44). Moreover, domestic service, until the late 1930s, was a major occupation for (usually single) women. One reason that Mill is able to overlook the fundamental importance of wives' (private) childrearing duties for their public status is that middle-class mothers had other women to look after their children; similarly, upper- and middle-class suffragettes could go to prison secure in the knowledge that domestic servants were caring for their homes and children (on this point see J. Liddington and J. Norris, *One Hand Tied Behind Us: The Rise of the Women's Suffrage Movement* (London, Virago, 1978)).

17 Z.R. Eisenstein, *The Radical Future of Liberal Feminism* (New York, Longman, 1980), pp. 207–8.

18 On sexual harassment see, for example, C.A. Mackinnon, *Sexual Harassment of Working Women* (New Haven, Conn., Yale University Press, 1979).

19 J.-J. Rousseau, *Emile*, trans. B. Foxley (London, Dent, 1911), p. 328.

20 See, for example, the discussion by R.P. Petchesky, 'Reproductive Freedom: Beyond "A Woman's Right to Choose"', *Signs*, 5: 4 (1980), pp. 661–85.

14 Returning the social to democracy

1 C.A.R. Crosland, *The Future of Socialism* (1st edn, London, Jonathan Cape, 1956), p. 110.

2 J.S. Mill, *On Liberty* (New York, Library of Liberal Arts, 1956), p. 6.

3 This essay is based on a reading of: *Equality* (4th edn, London, Allen and Unwin, 1964); *The Acquisitive Society* (1st edn, London, Bell, 1921); *The Radical Tradition* (Harmondsworth, Penguin, 1966).

4 Tawney, 'British Socialism Today', in *The Radical Tradition*, p. 176.

5 Tawney, *Acquisitive Society*, p. 38.
6 *Ibid.*, p. 14.
7 *Ibid.*, p. 15.
8 *Ibid.*, p. 51.
9 Tawney, 'The Conditions of Economic Liberty', in *The Radical Tradition*, p. 114.
10 Tawney, 'British Socialism Today', p. 176.
11 Tawney, 'Social Democracy in Britain', in *The Radical Tradition*, p. 172.
12 *Ibid.*, p. 147.
13 See, for example, J. Strachey, *Contemporary Capitalism* (New York, Random House, 1956) and the publications of the Socialist Union.
14 This process is outlined in E. Durbin, *The Politics of Democratic Socialism* (London, Routledge 1940).
15 C.A.R. Crosland, *Social Democracy in Europe*, Fabian Tract 483 (London, Fabian Publications, 1975), p. 5.
16 Crosland, *Future of Socialism*, p. 61.
17 Tawney, *Acquisitive Society*, p. 16.
18 For a discussion of this and its implications see Fred Hirsch, *The Social Limits to Growth* (Cambridge, Mass., Harvard University Press, 1976).

15 Bureaucracy and democracy

1 Thomas Carlyle, 'The New Downing Street', in *Works of Thomas Carlyle* (30 vols., New York, Scribner, 1898), Vol. XX, p. 143.
2 Karl Marx and Friedrich Engels, *The Marx–Engels Reader*, 2nd edn, ed. R. Tucker (New York, Norton, 1978), pp. 23–5, 607, 614.
3 Max Weber, *Gesammelte Aufsätze zur Soziologie und Sozialpolitik* (Tübingen, Mohr, 1942), p. 413; also see Weber, 'Bureaucracy', in *From Max Weber* eds. H.H. Gerth and C.W. Mills (Oxford, Oxford University Press, 1958), pp. 196–244.
4 Henry Jacoby, *The Bureaucratization of the World* (Berkeley, University of California Press, 1973).
5 Weber, *Gesammelte*, p. 414. *Pace* Weber, democrats seek to preserve more than a 'section' of humanity from bureaucracy.
6 B. Guy Peters, *The Politics of Bureaucracy* (London, Longman, 1978), pp. 229–36.
7 Thomas Hobbes, *Leviathan*, ed. M. Oakeshott (London, Macmillan, 1962), pp. 180–1.
8 John Locke, *Two Treatises of Government*, ed. P. Laslett (New York, New American Library, 1965), p. 415.
9 *The Federalist Papers*, ed. C. Rossiter (New York, New American Library, 1961), pp. 423–5, 435–6, 447; and John Stuart Mill, *Considerations on Representative Government*, in *Collected Works*, ed. J.M. Robson (Toronto, 1977), Vol. XIX, pp. 435–47, 520–33. For a recent 'Madisonian' defense of administrative agencies, see James O. Freedman, *Crisis and Legitimacy* (Cambridge, Cambridge University Press, 1978), pp. 260–1.
10 Weber, 'Bureaucracy', pp. 196–7, 214–16; and 'Politics as a vocation', in *From Max Weber*, p. 95.
11 Hugh Heclo, 'Issue networks and the executive establishment', in *The New American Political System*, ed. A. King (Washington, American Enterprise Institute, 1978), pp. 87–124.
12 Graham Allison, *Essence of Decision* (Boston, Little, Brown, 1971), pp. 144–84.

13 Donald P. Warwick, 'The ethics of administrative discretion', in *Public Duties*, eds. J. Fleishman *et al.* (Cambridge, Mass., Harvard University Press, 1981), pp. 93–127.

14 Michael Lipsky, *Street-Level Bureaucracy* (New York, Russell Sage, 1980), pp. 81–156.

15 R. Douglas Arnold, *Congress and the Bureaucracy* (New Haven, Conn., Yale University Press, 1979), pp. 207–16.

16 Arnold Heidenheimer and Donald P. Kommers, *The Governments of Germany* (New York, Crowell, 1975), pp. 238–51; Ezra Suleiman, *Politics, Power and Bureaucracy in France* (Princeton, Princeton University Press, 1974), pp. 155–80; H. Bakkerode *et al.*, 'The responsibility of the civil servant in the Netherlands', *Administration*, 23 (1975), pp. 400, 408–9; and Kenneth Kernaghan, 'Politics, policy and public servants', *Canadian Public Administration*, 19 (1976), pp. 432–56.

17 Maurice Wright, 'The responsibility of the civil servant', *Administration*, 23 (1975), pp. 374–9; F.F. Ridley, 'Responsibility and the official', *Government and Opposition*, 10 (1975), pp. 444–72; Douglas E. Ashford, *Policy and Politics in Britain* (Philadelphia, Temple University Press, 1981), pp. 31–43.

18 H.W.R. Wade, *Administrative Law* (4th edn, Oxford, Clarendon Press, 1977), p. 735.

19 Weber, 'Bureaucracy', pp. 232–42.

20 Woodrow Wilson, 'The study of administration', *Political Science Quarterly*, 2 (1887), pp. 197–222; Herman Finer, 'Administrative responsibility in democratic government', *Public Administration Review*, 1 (1941), pp. 335–50; Herbert Simon, *Administrative Behavior* (3rd edn, New York, Macmillan, 1976), pp. 57–8; and R.J.S. Baker, *Administrative Theory and Public Administration* (London, Hutchinson, 1972), pp. 94, 130–6.

21 Theodore J. Lowi, *The End of Liberalism* (2nd edn, New York, Norton, 1979), pp. 107–8, 291–311.

22 Herbert Kaufman, *Red Tape* (Washington, Brookings, 1977).

23 Ashford, *op. cit.*, pp. 69, 73.

24 Peters, *op. cit.*, 178–89.

25 *Report from the Select Committee on Parliamentary Questions*, 1971–72, H.C. 393 (London, HMSO, 1972).

26 Dennis F. Thompson, 'Moral responsibility of public officials', *American Political Science Review*, 74 (1980), pp. 905–16.

27 Kernaghan, *op. cit.*, pp. 451–4.

28 G.W.F. Hegel, *Philosophy of Right*, trans. T.M. Knox (Oxford, Oxford University Press, 1967), pp. 192–3, 291.

29 Jeremy Bentham, *Works*, ed. J. Bowring (11 vols., New York, Russell and Russell, 1962), Vol. II, p. 195, V, p. 448, X, p. 337; J.S. Mill, *op. cit.*, pp. 520–33; Carl J. Friedrich, 'Public policy and the nature of administrative responsibility', *Public Policy*, 1 (1940), pp. 3–24; Joseph Schumpeter, *Capitalism, Socialism and Democracy* (4th edn, London, Allen and Unwin, 1961), pp. 293–4; and Frederick Mosher, *Democracy and the Public Service* (Oxford, Oxford University Press, 1968), pp. 99–133.

30 Peter Self, *Econocrats and the Policy Process* (London, Macmillan, 1975); and Robert A. Goldwin (ed.), *Bureaucrats, Policy Analysts, Statesmen* (Washington, American Enterprise Institute, 1980).

31 Martin J. Bailey, *Reducing Risks to Life* (Washington, American Enterprise

Institute, 1980); and U.S. Senate, Committee on Governmental Affairs, 96th Congress, 2nd session, *Benefits of Environmental, Health and Safety Regulation* (Washington, D.C., Government Printing Office, 1980).

32 Ashford, *op. cit.*, pp. 84–5.

33 Joel L. Fleishman and Bruce L. Payne, *Ethical Dilemmas and the Education of Policymakers* (Hastings-on-Hudson, N.Y., Hastings Center, 1980).

34 Dennis F. Thompson, 'Paternalism in medicine, law and public policy', in *Ethics Teaching in Higher Education*, eds. D. Callahan and S. Bok (Hastings-on-Hudson, Hastings Center, 1980), pp. 256–61.

35 Samuel Krislov, *Representative Bureaucracy* (Englewood Cliffs, N.J., Prentice-Hall, 1974). The best general critique is: Kenneth John Meier, 'Representative bureaucracy' *American Political Science Review*, 69 (1975), pp. 526–42.

36 H. George Frederickson, 'Toward a new public administration', in *Toward a New Public Administration*, ed. F. Marini (Scranton, Pa., Chandler, 1971), pp. 309–31.

37 Lewis C. Mainzer, *Political Bureaucracy* (Glenview, Ill., Scott Foresman, 1973), p. 135.

38 Emmette S. Redford, *Democracy in the Administrative State* (Oxford, Oxford University Press, 1969), p. 106. Cf. Paul H. Appleby, *Morality and Administration in Democratic Government* (Baton Rouge, Louisiana State University Press, 1952), p. 251; Norton Long, *The Polity* (Chicago, Rand McNally, 1962), pp. 50ff.; and Victor A. Thompson, 'Bureaucracy in a democratic society', in *Public Administration and Democracy*, ed. R. Martin (Syracuse, N.Y., Syracuse University Press, 1965), pp. 210–12.

39 For a brief discussion and a bibliography, see Mainzer, *op. cit.*, pp. 135–48, 181–2.

40 Jean-Jacques Rousseau, *The Social Contract*, trans. M. Cranston (Harmondsworth, Penguin, 1968), pp. 101–7, 112–16.

41 Mill, *op. cit.*, pp. 528–33.

42 Peters, *op. cit.*, pp. 141–59; Suleiman, *op. cit.*, pp. 316–51; Wright, *op. cit.*, p. 382; and Lowi, *op. cit.*, pp. 50–63, 295–8, 311–12.

43 Outer Circle Policy Group, *What's Wrong with Quangos?* (London, Outer Circle Policy Unit, 1979).

44 Richard B. Stewart, 'The reformation of American administrative law', *Harvard Law Review*, 88 (1975), pp. 1709–90.

45 John H. Strange, 'Citizen participation in Community Action and Model Cities Programs', *Public Administration Review*, 32 (1972), pp. 655–9; J. David Greenstone and Paul E. Peterson, *Race and Authority in Urban Politics* (New York, Russell Sage, 1973); Lowi, *op. cit.*, pp. 223–6; and Howard I. Kalodner, 'Citizen participation in emerging social institutions', in *Participation in Politics* eds. J.R. Pennock and J.W. Chapman (New York, Lieber-Atherton, 1975), pp. 161–85.

46 James A. Morone and Theodore R. Marmor, 'Representing consumer interests', *Ethics*, 91 (1981), pp. 440–2; and Dorothy Bochel and Morag MacLaran, 'Representing the interest of the public', *Journal of Social Policy*, 8 (1979), pp. 449–72.

47 Dorothy Nelkin, *Technological Decisions and Democracy* (Beverly Hills, Calif., Sage, 1977).

48 Roger Choate, 'The public's right to know', *Current Sweden*, No. 93 (Stockholm, Swedish Institute, 1975), p. 4.

16 Beginning at the end of democratic theory

1 Eric Voegelin, *Order and History* (Baton Rouge, Louisiana State University Press, 1957), Vol. II, pp. 371–2.

2 Sheldon Wolin, 'Reagan Country', *New York Review of Books* (December 18 1980), p. 9. Wolin's remedy – 'a long revolution' aimed at 'deconstituting the present structure of power' and creating 'new forms, new scales, new beings' – becomes poignant in view of the obstacles to which he is fully sensitive (see his 'The People's Two Bodies', *Democracy: A Journal of Political Renewal and Radical Change*, 1 (January, 1981), pp. 9–24).

3 Mircèa Eliade, *No Souvenirs* (New York, Harper and Row, 1977), p. 140.

4 Hannah Arendt *The Origins of Totalitarianism* (New York, Harcourt, Brace, 1951), pp. 434–6.

5 Hannah Arendt, *The Human Condition* (Chicago, University of Chicago Press, 1958), pp. 198–9 (emphasis supplied).

6 John Dewey and Arthur F. Bentley, *Knowing and the Known* (Boston, Beacon Press, 1949), p. 272.

7 Dewey and Bentley noted that 'we have no "something known" and no "something identified" apart from it know*ing* and identify*ing*, and . . . we have no know*ing* and identify*ing* apart from somewhats and somethings that are being known and identified' (*op. cit.*, p. 54). Leaning on Gilbert Ryle, Roy Schafer has argued for a new language for psychoanalysis – a language that would express all actions in verbs and the mode in which they are performed in adverbs. (*A New Language for Psychoanalysis* (New Haven, Conn., Yale University Press, 1976).)

8 George Kateb in *Participation in Politics* eds J. Roland Pennock and J.W. Chapman (New York, Lieber-Atherton, 1975), p. 91 (emphasis supplied).

9 '*Beauty*', Kant wrote, himself supplying the emphasis, 'is the form of the *purposiveness* of an object, so far as this is perceived in it *without any representation of a purpose*' (*Critique of Judgement*, trans. by J.H. Bernard (New York, Hafner, 1951), pt 17, p. 73).

10 Karl Marx, 'The Critique of Hegel's *Philosophy of Right*', in *Early Writings* (London, C.A. Watts, 1963), p.47.

11 Renwick Gallery, *Signs and Symbols* (Washington, D.C., National Collection of Fine Arts, Smithsonian Institution, 1976). The exhibit was designed by the architectural firm of Venturi and Rauch. Robert Venturi is the author of *Learning from Las Vegas* (1972), a celebration of pop architecture that finds a fictional counterpart in Stanley Elkins' *The Franchiser* (1976), an ode to franchises, in particular Radio Shack and Dairy Queen.

12 Alvin W. Gouldner, *Enter Plato* (New York, Basic Books, 1965), pp. 386–7; the quotation is from *The Laws*, 803A. An appreciation for nothing more than appearance can be seen to inform the physical sciences and virtually all the arts today.

Index